WALLACE STEVENS

◇　*The Poems of Our Climate*

WALLACE STEVENS
◇ *The Poems of Our Climate*

by HAROLD BLOOM

Cornell University Press   ITHACA AND LONDON

26708

First published 1977 by Cornell University Press.
Published in the United Kingdom by Cornell University Press Ltd., 2-4 Brook Street, London W1Y 1AA.

Quotations from Stevens' works are taken from *The Necessary Angel*, copyright 1951 by Wallace Stevens; *The Collected Poems of Wallace Stevens*, copyright 1954 by Wallace Stevens; *Opus Posthumous*, copyright © 1957 by Elsie Stevens and Holly Stevens; *The Letters of Wallace Stevens*, copyright © 1966 by Holly Stevens; and *The Palm at the End of the Mind*, copyright © 1967, 1969, 1971, by Holly Stevens. They are used with the permission of Holly Stevens and the publishers, Alfred A. Knopf, Inc., and Faber and Faber, Ltd.

International Standard Book Number 0-8014-0840-7
Library of Congress Catalog Card Number 76-55482
Printed in the United States of America by Vail-Ballou Press, Inc.
Librarians: Library of Congress cataloging information appears on the last page of the book.

In the punctual centre of all circles white
Stands truly. The circles nearest to it share

Its color, but less as they recede, impinged
By difference and then by definition
As a tone defines itself and separates

And the circles quicken and crystal colors come
And flare and Bloom with his vast accumulation
Stands and regards and repeats the primitive lines.

—Stevens, *From the Packet of Anacharsis*

For Holly Stevens

◇ Preface

This book attempts a full commentary upon nearly all of what I judge to be Stevens' poetic canon. I have emphasized the long poems and sequences, and their complex relations both to one another and to the work of Stevens' unacknowledged precursors: Wordsworth, Shelley, Keats, Emerson, and, most crucially, Whitman.

Inasmuch as my commentary follows the ordering and dating by Holly Stevens in *The Palm at the End of the Mind*, I give no page references to that volume, which I trust my own readers will employ as their text of the poet. I do give page references for all citations from other volumes of Stevens: *Collected Poems* (*CP*), *Opus Posthumous* (*OP*), *The Necessary Angel* (*NA*), and Holly Stevens' edition of the *Letters* (*L*).

Though my readings follow on from my essays on Stevens in *A Map of Misreading*, *Poetry and Repression*, and *Figures of Capable Imagination*, I have tried to make the book independent of my earlier work. The first chapter, on American poetic stances from Emerson to Stevens, explains the dialectic of Fate, Freedom, and Power which I invoke throughout. But my contribution to a theory of lyric poetry, the idea I call poetic crossing, is not fully developed until the concluding chapter. Since I map many of Stevens' poems in terms of their crossings, or "negative moments," some readers may prefer to start with this chapter, or to read it in conjunction with my analyses of specific poems. The deferment of theory is due to the dialectical relation that exists in the book between practical criticism and the use of paradigms: chapters 2–13 illustrate chapters 1 and 14, but are themselves illustrated by the two theoretical chapters.

I began writing what finally turned out to be this book in the first year I taught Stevens (or any other poet), the year of the poet's death, 1955. Since then the published criticism concerning Stevens has been copious. I have read most of it and been much influenced by it. Where I am conscious of indebtedness, including the stimulation of disagreement, I have noted such influx, but I cannot hope to map my own misprision. The book's dedication expresses my largest debt, which is to the most devoted of all Stevens' readers.

HAROLD BLOOM

New Haven, Connecticut
August 24, 1976

◇ Contents

WALLACE STEVENS

◇ *The Poems of Our Climate*

1 American Poetic Stances: Emerson to Stevens

I begin by proposing an antithetical formula as the motto for post-Emersonian American poetry: *Everything that can be broken should be broken*. American poetry since Emerson follows a triple rhythm: *It must be broken; It must not bear having been broken; It must seem to have been mended*. In Stevens, this rhythm will mature into the titles of the three parts of *Notes toward a Supreme Fiction: It Must Be Abstract* ("abstract" as *abstractus*, withdrawn from or taken out of), *It Must Change, It Must Give Pleasure*. Or, in the dialectic of all Stevens' poetry, this reads: One must have a mind of winter, or reduce to the First Idea; one must discover that to live with the First Idea alone is not to be human; one must reimagine the First Idea.

I return to my Gnostic apothegm, *Everything that can be broken should be broken*, which I think is nearly the only formula that can ally Emerson and such visionary opponents of his affirmative force as Poe and Melville. Emerson had an immense "poverty" or imaginative need for what he called "Self-Reliance," and necessarily he directed his passion for self-dependence against his authentic precursors, Coleridge and Wordsworth. Coleridge had done for him what he was to do for Whitman—found him simmering and brought him to a boil. Wordsworth—whom initially he had resisted—redefined poetry for him, and I think induced a repressive anxiety that prevented him from centering his literary ambitions upon verse, which is the same effect that Wordsworth was to have upon the later Coleridge, and on Ruskin and then Pater. Wordsworth made Shelley and Keats into poets, and even more dialectically he made Emerson and Thoreau, Ruskin and Pater, into masters of the alternative eloquence of prose. But Emerson and the Americans after him differed from British Wordsworthians in the extremism with which they defended against the Wordsworthian stance.

Emerson, according to Stephen Whicher, experienced two major intellectual crises, the first culminating in 1832, when he was twenty-nine, and the second a decade later, culminating in his fortieth year. Whitman also can be said to have had two major spiritual and poetic crises, the first ensuing in the 1855 *Leaves of Grass*, when the poet was thirty-six; the second in the winter of 1859–60, when he was forty, and resulting in the great poems added to the third edition of *Leaves of Grass* in 1860, *Out of the Cradle Endlessly Rocking* and *As I Ebb'd with the Ocean of Life* (to use their later titles). I do not find that Wallace Stevens ever underwent an intense crisis of an intellectual variety, but his work is most certainly in the Romantic traditions—British and American—of the crisis-poem. To explain such a judgment, I resort to the theory of poetic crossing.

A crossing within a crisis-poem, like a poetic crisis, is a process of disjunction, a leaping of the gap between one kind of figurative thinking and another. As with poetic crossings, so is it with crises of vision. They can be of three kinds: from ironic to synecdochal thinking; from metonymic to hyperbolic thinking; and from metaphoric to transumptive thinking. When a poetic career goes on long enough, I suspect all three of these liminal crises occur. Stevens like Yeats can be said to have experienced three poetic crises, though there is no evidence—as there is with Wordsworth, Emerson, Whitman, Yeats, and most strong poets—that Stevens suffered spiritually in these transitions. But then, Stevens had a stoic temperament as well as a massively repressed psychic life, and he was capable of such suffering without telling it to anyone, whether in a letter or through a poem.

For Stevens, what I will call the crisis or Crossing of Election took place in 1915, when his first strong poems were written. The Crossing of Solipsism lasted a long time in him, but its crux was in 1921–22, and it was not resolved until 1934–36.

The final crossing, that of Identification, took place in 1942, and gave him *Notes Toward a Supreme Fiction*. But it would be absurd to say that his remaining years were without poetic crises, since *The Auroras of Autumn* in 1947 and *The Rock* in 1950 are High Romantic, Wordsworthian–Whitmanian crisis-poems again. Still, they rely upon *Notes* at every point and are resolved upon the basis of imaginative formulations already in *Notes*. But these formulations, in turn, are traceable back to Whitman and, through Whitman, to Emerson. So I would urge that any analysis of Stevens' poetic stances must rely upon some account of the way in which the Romantic dialectic of *ethos*, *logos*, and *pathos* in Wordsworth, Shelley, Keats, and Tennyson was modulated by Emerson into an American dialectic that he called Fate, Freedom, and Power. This introductory chapter will examine the Emersonian dialectic, sketch some of its appearances in Whitman and Dickinson, and then conclude by considering briefly its first appearances in Stevens.

We can begin with Freedom, which for Emerson is the *logos*, his test for the conversion of mere signification into meaning. True Freedom for Emerson was initially the Newness or Influx, "the God within," but faced by inspiration's rhythm of ebb and flow he fell back upon substitution or the second chance. Here is Whicher's summary:

> His later thought is characteristically an affirmation of a *second best*. If a perfect freedom was clearly out of reach, man's fate as he found it still turned out to allow him adequate means to free himself. The two chief second-best means of freedom that Emerson found were "obedience to his genius" and "the habit of the observer"—Vocation and Intellect.

If we are to apply Whicher's comment to Freedom-as-meaning, or the *logos* of poetry, then we need to consider the Emersonian synonyms for "Vocation" and "Intellect." Vocation is also "Temperament" and "Exaggeration," while Intellect is also "Thought" or the Coleridgean "Reason" or "Truth" as opposed to the mere Understanding. Emerson's original synonym for Freedom had been "Wildness," and we can say that rhetorical substitution or the second-best gave him Reason and Temperament as tropes for Wildness. Freedom, in Emerson's dialectic, therefore has to be translated as a mode of vision conditioned by vagary, or most simply as the whim that Emerson exalted as Self-Reliance and finally as Solitude. This multiplication of terms is more than a little maddening, though it is crucial to Emerson, and in its place I will cite some passages where the *aporia,* or mental dilemma, of Freedom is most clearly set before us, before I return to the multiplicity. Here is one of the most famous affirmations from the rhapsodic essay *The Poet:*

> The poets are thus liberating gods. The ancient British bards had for the title of their order, "Those who are free throughout the world." They are free, and they make free. An imaginative book renders us much more service at first, by stimulating us through its tropes, than afterward when we arrive at the precise sense of its author. I think nothing is of any value in books excepting the transcendental and extraordinary.

What does Emerson mean by "free" here? This looks like wildness, rather than a second-best, and "the transcendental" is of course Emerson's most famous trope for Reason or the *logos.* But *The Poet* is a very curious essay, more in love with an idea of poetry than with any poetry actually written. As Emerson says, later in the essay: "But when we adhere to the ideal of the poet, we have our difficulties even with Milton and Homer. Milton is too literary, and Homer too literal and historical."

To see fully Emerson's ambivalence we must read another text, less famous than *The Poet* yet more insightful and direct. *The Poet* was printed in *Essays, Second Series* (1844), but there is an earlier lecture, on *The Poet,* delivered in 1841, only a few bits of which were used in the essay. Here Emerson says of the poet that "he is not free, but freedom" and then adds wistfully, of all poets, that "Nature . . . wished them to stand for the Intellect and not for the Will." This translates as poets themselves being tropes of *pathos* rather than embodiments of the *logos,* and gives us a clue as to why Emerson and all his poetic descendants in our central tradition—Whitman, Dickinson, Frost, Stevens, Hart Crane—use so bewilderingly multiform a series of substi-

4

tute words for the meaning they long to embody. Let me venture a full list now for Emerson, the father of us all. *Ethos:* Fate, Destiny, Necessity, Fortune, Race, Powerlessness, Experience, Limitation, and Nature, but Nature only in its most alienated or estranged aspect. *Logos:* Freedom, Wildness, Nature (in its humanized or redeemed aspect), Vocation, Temperament, Self-Reliance, Solitude, Reason, Transcendentalism, Thought, Subjectiveness, Wholeness. *Pathos:* Power, Potential, Will, Vitality, God, Greatness, Salvation, Vital Force, Victory, Inspiration, Surprise, Mastery, Ecstasy. Emerson's most frequent triad was the famous Fate, Freedom, and Power, but I think we can render his dialectic most effective for the understanding of his descendants' poems if we adopt the triad Necessity, Solitude, and Surprise. As I will show later, such a triad is a version of the three governing deities of American Orphism, the natural religion of our poetry, where Necessity takes the place of the goddess Ananke or the Muse, while Solitude stands for Dionysus or Bacchus, the god of meaning-through-*sparagmos*, and Surprise substitutes for Eros, the ultimate form of *pathos* or representational power.

I return to Emerson's lecture on *The Poet*, where he says of Pegasus, "Surprise and wonder always fly beside him. There is no poetry where they are not." The same emphasis upon surprise is at the center of the late, rambling essay, *Poetry and Imagination*, where after rightly observing that "conversation is not permitted without tropes," Emerson more daringly makes of natural change only a series of tropes: "The poet accounts all productions and changes of Nature as the nouns of language, uses them representatively, too well pleased with their ulterior to value much their primary meaning. Every new object so seen gives a shock of agreeable surprise."

"Surprise," as Emerson uses it, does not seem to mean to encounter suddenly or unexpectedly, or to take or be taken unaware. It means for him the *pathos* of Power, the sudden manifestation of the vital will. It means Victory and ecstasy, a seizure, as in the etymology of the word. Is it not the most American of tropes for poetic power? Here is Emerson in the most aggressive of all his essays, *History*, which he chose to lead off *Essays, First Series*, praising Goethe's second part of *Faust* because it has the sound of surprise:

> And although that poem be as vague and fantastic as a dream, yet is it much more attractive than the more regular dramatic pieces of the same author, for the reason that it operates a wonderful relief to the mind from the routine of customary images—awakens the reader's invention and fancy by the wild freedom of the design, and by the unceasing succession of brisk shocks of surprise.

I think we are at the heart of Emersonianism, and of the American poetic, and also of the poetry of Wallace Stevens. For *surprise* is the American poetic stance, in the peculiar sense of surprise as the poet's Will-to-Power over anteriority and over the interpretation of his own poem. As Emerson says, in his very oddly named essay, *Compensation:* "The law of nature is, Do the thing, and you shall have the power; but they who do not the thing have not the power." Yet this power is so dialectical as to be self-deconstructing, on the basis of what Emerson keeps saying, as here in the essay *The Over-Soul*, where the very title prophesies Nietzsche's Over-Man and where Emerson calls for an Over-Poet: "The great poet makes us feel our own wealth, and then we think less of his compositions. His best communication to our mind is to teach us to despise all he has done."

I think that Emerson takes so unappreciative a view of even the greatest poetry because of his pragmatically de-idealizing view of the imagination. As in so many other respects, Emerson anticipated (and influenced) Nietzsche in quite simply identifying the imagination with figurative speech. Emerson also saw that figuration was not wholly free, but was governed partly by the limitation of *ethos* that he called Fate. Thus, in *Poetry and Imagination*, he says, "The selection of the image is no more arbitrary than the power and significance of the image. The selection must follow fate." The same essay appears to deny that the poet's personality is any more fixed than the trope he employs, which implies that personality is simply a collection of tropes of *pathos*. Yet Emerson dialectically hedges, antic-

6

ipating Stevens' conditional moods, when he adds, "All writings must be in a degree exoteric, written to a human *should* or *would*, instead of to the fatal *is*." That is why Emerson, again leaping ahead of Nietzsche, continues the same discourse by saying that poetry is the *gai science* and by uttering a great prayer to the Orphic god of meaning: "O celestial Bacchus! drive them mad,—this multitude of vagabonds, hungry for eloquence, hungry for poetry, starving for symbols." This extraordinary neglected rhapsody attains its climax in a brilliant final troping of "surprise" for the *potentia* or power of American making:

> The nature of things is flowing, a metamorphosis. The free spirit sympathizes not only with the actual form, but with the power or possible forms; but for obvious municipal or parietal uses God has given us a bias or a rest on today's forms. Hence the shudder of joy with which in each clear moment we recognize the metamorphosis; because it is always a conquest, a surprise from the heart of things.

Emerson rightly sees that form, in nature or in poems, is itself only one trope or another. The metamorphosis or interplay of forms is victory, surprise, joy, when seen from the perspective of Power rather than that of Fate. Freedom or "the free spirit" makes form into *potentia*, into the strength that Emerson defines as eloquence. So, in the late essay *Eloquence*, he gives this as his final word on that most desired of gifts: "It is a triumph of pure power, and it has a beautiful and prodigious surprise in it." Power, in Emerson as in his American descendants, means to be of *capable* imagination, not so much to have the lordship as to have the ability. Fate, as a word, comes from a root meaning "speech," but by one of Emerson's characteristic dialectical reversals Power takes on the meaning of eloquent speech while Fate is a script or writing opposed to speech. Freedom, as a word, actually goes back to a root meaning "love," but again Emerson prefigures a subsequent American Romantic reversal by associating freedom with the *logos* of Dionysiac meaning and by identifying love with the *pathos* of eloquence.

I have been describing Emerson, yet any deep reader of Ste-

7

vens will be aware that I am describing Stevens also, just as most of the description, with a few adjustments, applies to Whitman, Dickinson, and Frost. Since common literary and scholarly opinion automatically would disbelieve my association of the great Transcendentalist with more "naturalistic" or "realistic" poets who came after him, I will turn now to the description of the major aspects of Emerson's rhetorical stance, which has not yet been read with the strength that it requires.

Emerson wanted Freedom, reconciled himself to Fate, but loved only Power, from first to last, and I believe this to be true also of the central line of American poets coming after him. What kind of a stance is it to have (or quest after) a power of voicing? In his early manifesto, *Nature*, Emerson equated "the exercise of the Will" with "the lesson of power" and found both to be the consequence of Influx or the Newness, that is, of the flowing in of an absolute inspiration: "examples of Reason's momentary grasp of the sceptre; the exertions of a power which exists not in time or space, but an instantaneous in-streaming causing power."

This is the prophetic Emerson, inventor for American poetry of the Optative Mood, who in *The American Scholar* could say of nature that, to the scholar, it is "always circular power returning into itself"; or who, in *Self-Reliance*, could say, "Power is, in nature, the essential measure of right"; and even proclaimed, in *Circles*, "The only sin is limitation." That early Emerson is matched in Stevens by the poet of *Harmonium*, even as the harmonious skeptic Emerson who wrote the essay *Experience* is matched by the poet of *Ideas of Order*, and finally as the later Emerson of *The Conduct of Life*, with his worship of Fate as the Beautiful Necessity, is matched by the Stevens who confronts Ananke in *The Auroras of Autumn* and in *The Rock*. I cite what I take to be the last stand of the early Emerson, in a famous Journal entry of April 1842:

There ought to be no such thing as Fate. As long as we use this word, it is a sign of our impotence and that we are not yet ourselves. . . . Moreover, whilst this Deity glows at the heart, and by his unlimited presentiments gives me all Power, I know that tomorrow will be as this day, I am a dwarf, and I remain a dwarf. That is to say, I believe in Fate. As long as I am weak, I shall talk of Fate; whenever the God fills me with his fulness, I shall see the disappearance of Fate.

Three years later, this vision had abandoned Emerson, and Surprise or the trope of Power, as well as two tropes of Freedom, Temperament and Subjectiveness, show up in the essay *Experience* in a list of seven "lords of life," thus being outnumbered together by four rather Stevensian tropes of *ethos* or Fate: Illusion, Succession, Surface, and Reality. Unlisted, but present in the essay, is what became in both Dickinson and Stevens one of the most dialectical of tropes, which Emerson strikingly called "poverty":

And we cannot say too little of our constitutional necessity of seeing things under private aspects, or saturated with our humors. And yet is the God the native of these bleak rocks. That need makes in morals the capital virtue of self-trust. We must hold hard to this poverty, however scandalous, and by more vigorous self-recoveries, after the sallies of action, possess our axis more firmly.

This "poverty" is imaginative need, the result of Emerson's version of a reduction to a First Idea. It was only another step to the essay *Fate*, strongest rhapsody in *The Conduct of Life*, where Freedom and Power have all but yielded to the ultimate *ethos*, to what Stevens at the close of *The Auroras* was to call "the full of fortune and the full of fate." Yet, at his most necessitarian and reductive, Emerson did not cease being dazzlingly dialectical. Rather than trace this in the late prose, I turn to the chant *Merlin* of 1846, where Emerson again states his dialectic of Freedom, Fate, and Power. The poem begins by demanding "free" chords to start the "wild blood," but this freedom and wildness have been assimilated already to Ananke:

> The kingly bard
> Must smite the chords rudely and hard,
> As with hammer or with mace;
> That they may render back
> Artful thunder, which conveys
> Secrets of the solar track,
> Sparks of the supersolar blaze.

9

Emerson is never more American than he is here or in the essay *Fate*, since his solution for having failed to assert his power over natural process is to join himself to that process. His peculiar refusal to be defeated is the true explanation of what Emerson means when, in *Fate*, he says, "We are as law-givers; we speak for Nature; we prophesy and divine," and then adds, "This insight throws us on the party and interest of the Universe, against all and sundry; against ourselves as much as others." Unfortunately, the result is again a poetry of *ethos* or limitation, as in *Merlin*, which first tells us that "Merlin's blows are strokes of fate" but inevitably leads to a Snow Man's vision:

> Chiming with the forest tone,
> When boughs buffet boughs in the wood;
> Chiming with the gasp and moan
> Of the ice-imprisoned flood.

This vision rather chills the ensuing trope of Power, when the angels urge the ascending bard to evade the celestial ennui of apartments: "But mount to paradise / By the stairway of surprise." What can "surprise" mean finally in a poem dominated at its close by Nemesis, particularly after we are told that "trade and counting use / The self-same tuneful muse"? Emerson is not joking, any more than Stevens is when he assures us that money is a sort of poetry. The American Will-to-Power, in poetry, has a tendency to end in a worship of force, of Nemesis:

> Who with even matches odd,
> Who athwart space redresses
> The partial wrong,
> Fills the just period,
> And finishes the song.

Though Stevens read Emerson early and fully, and remembered much more than he realized, his Emersonianism was filtered mostly through Whitman, a pervasive and of course wholly unacknowledged influence upon all of Stevens' major poetry. I am using "influence" in my rather controversial but I think quite useful sense of "misprision" or revisionist interpretation of tradition, an interpretation manifest in the later poet's own work. But before I begin the very complex account of the interpoetic relation between Whitman and Stevens that will run all through these chapters, I want first to examine Whitman's own modification of Emersonian theory, by way of looking at crossings or rhetorical disjunctions in one of Whitman's strongest and most influential poems. This is another way of asking, what was Whitman's own poetic stance? The question must seem needless, since no poet was ever more overt or more frequent in proclaiming his supposed stance than Whitman was, as profusely in verse as in prose. But by stance I mean something very precise and indeed traditional; I mean rhetorical stance as formulated first about 150 B.C. by Hermagoras. Stance is the major *heuristic* device for a poet; it is his way of path-breaking into his own inventiveness.

Whitman's stance is very much the fourth and final stance recommended by Hermagoras: metalepsis, which translates the orator's own belatedness into a perpetual earliness. In the patterns of Romantic imagery, Wordsworthian or Emersonian, this is the ultimate version of a stance of *pathos*, of potential power, of Emersonian surprise or the vital will achieving a victory over every limitation and particularly over the final antagonist, which is not death but time and time's "it was," to use Nietzsche's formulation. We found that in Emerson the original meaning of meaning was freedom or wildness but that Emerson learned to substitute for this with solitude or "poverty," the combination of vocation and temperament that ensued in Transcendentalist Self-Reliance. This substitution Whitman declined to make, though by the winter of 1859–60 it caught up with him anyway.

Whitman's was always a poetry of passion and suffering rather than of act and incident, of personality and *pathos* rather than character and *ethos*. But the revisionary patterns of misprision worked to make Whitman, in his strongest and most famous poems, a kind of American Wordsworth, in that these poems do follow the paradigm of the High Romantic crisis-ode. As such they invest their meaning, their freedom and wildness, in the *logoi* of their crossings, quite as much as the *Intimations* ode does. Fate, necessity, experience, limitation—these Emersonian tropes for *ethos* do not greatly engage the powerful Walt, who is a kind of American will incarnate, but their place is taken by the other major Emersonian trope of *ethos*, nature in its alien side or aspect. This alien aspect, in Whitman, mostly does *not* include night, death, the mother, and the sea, which for Whitman are images of vital force and imagination, Sublime or even metaleptic tropes for power or surprise. But nature's alien side, in Whitman, does include what he calls the soul, as opposed to the self, and with this difficult and wavering distinction we enter into the true problematic of Whitman's poetic stance.

The quite Emersonian dialectic of Whitman's strongest poetry is an *ethos-logos-pathos* or Fate–Freedom–Power triad, but its characteristic terms are not the rather abstract Emersonian necessity-solitude-surprise, but *my soul–my self–the real me*, or *me myself*. My soul, in Whitman, is the dark side or alienated, estranged element in nature. My self is Walt Whitman, one of the roughs, an American, malest of males. The real me or me myself is night, death, the mother, and the sea. The crossings in Whitman's poetry therefore take place in the realm of my self, the world of anxiety, negativity, meaning. But the crossings move from the realm of my soul, unknown nature, to the known world of the real me or me myself, where what night, death, the mother, and the sea have in common is restitution, the function of compensating Whitman for what an estranged nature keeps taking from him. The persona of my self, as in the title *Song of Myself*, is only a perpetual breaking of forms or shattering of vessels, a dance of roles constantly substituting for one another, an interplay of re-cognitions that leads Whitman from the haunts of his soul to the recognitions of the real me.

The theoreticians of deconstruction in effect say, "In the beginning was the trope," rather than "In the beginning was the troper." This follows Nietzsche, but Whitman follows Emerson, who as usual said both. Deconstructing Emerson is of course impossible, since no discourse ever has been so overtly aware of its own status as rhetoricity. Deconstructing Whitman is possible but uninteresting, because Whitman at his strongest is a breathing and yawping trope, a giant metalepsis that repeals all of the poet's own metonymic catalogings or emptyings out of "myself." More interesting is the application to Whitman's prime tropes of their equivalents in Anna Freud's pattern of defenses, not because Whitman ought to be reduced to any paradigm whatsoever but because all his poetry is an enormous act of psychic defense, of what his master Emerson called Self-Reliance, or freedom troped as solitude and "poverty."

On this view, Whitman's "my soul" goes from reaction formation through regression to sublimation, a sequence that is not unilluminating. Similarly, the hidden, sensitive "me myself" goes from a reversal-into-the-opposite through repression to end in an act of introjection. Most interesting is the realization that the crossings from "soul" to "the real me" pass *through* the self-reliant Walt Whitman, one of the roughs, an American, which is a passage to the Sublime and to greater repression. But I will turn to a text for those crossings, and I choose *Out of the Cradle Endlessly Rocking*, primarily because it is the single poem by Whitman that most pervades Stevens' work, though *The Sleepers* and *When Lilacs Last in the Dooryard Bloom'd* are almost always close behind.

Out of the Cradle falls almost too neatly into a pattern of three crossings or crises. The first radical disjunction in the poem comes at the end of the first verse-paragraph where Whitman, "a man, yet by these tears a little boy again," throws himself upon the sand, confronting the ocean, and suffers a reminiscence. Before the reminiscence is developed, the Crossing of Election is enacted, for the hidden grief of the opening stanza is the ebbing of Whitman's poethood. The Crossing of Solipsism comes after the love aria of the mockingbirds ends, and intervenes just before line 130, where the aria sinks, the winds blow, and the fierce old maternal ocean moans incessantly for Walt, her castaway. Here Whitman disjunctively confronts the loss of eros, reflecting the mysterious and presumably erotic crisis he weathered in the winter of 1859–60. The Crossing of Identification, troping ambivalently for and against death, comes where we would expect it, after the fivefold repetition of "death," the word out of the sea, just before the last verse paragraph.

What is gained by this location and naming of crossings? How does it aid the interpretation of *Out of the Cradle* to know its negative moments in this way, and what difference will any interpretation of the poem make to a reading of Wallace Stevens? The answer to both questions is, again, "stance." Whitman makes of his rhetorical disjunctiveness a metaleptic stance, and Stevens, though with Sublime repressiveness, inherits Whitman's stance. Though he insisted he did not read Whitman, and resented Whitman's persona as the tramp-poet, Stevens is hardly to be believed in his insistences. In 1947 he wrote two of his most Whitmanian poems, *The Auroras of Autumn* and *The Owl in the Sarcophagus*, and soon afterward, in a lecture at Yale called *Effects of Analogy*, he quoted the little poem *A Clear Midnight* as an instance of Whitman's strength in the context of a poet's stance, that is, "the relation of the poet to his subject" and "his sense of the world" (*NA*, 119, 121). *A Clear Midnight* is very late and little-known Whitman:

> This is thy hour O Soul, thy free flight into the wordless,
> Away from books, away from art, the day erased, the lesson done,
> Thee fully forth emerging, silent, gazing, pondering the themes thou lovest best,
> Night, sleep, death and the stars.

Night, sleep, death, the ocean, the mother; this Whitmanian composite trope of Power or *pathos* became the strongest of Stevens' reimaginings of that characteristic reduction he learned to call the First Idea, or image of Fate, trope of *ethos*, or simply the condition of his own soul, in the Whitmanian sense of "soul" as unalterable character. *Out of the Cradle*, Whitman's demonic romance of poetic incarnation, haunted Stevens because of its vision of solitude as the scene of instruction, its sense of lovelessness redressed by the coming of poetry, by its identification of the muse with a maternal night and the ocean of reality. But most of all because Stevens was as attracted by something in Whitman as he was repelled by him, in ways ambivalently similar to the reactions of Pound, Eliot, and Williams to Whitman, and quite unlike Hart Crane's more overt and moving sense of identity with Whitman. A rather bad poem in *Harmonium*, *Jasmine's Beautiful Thoughts underneath the Willow* (*CP*, 79), mocks Whitman by speaking of "the love that will not be transported" but rather

> Is like a vivid apprehension
> Of bliss beyond the mutes of plaster,
> Or paper souvenirs of rapture,
>
> Of bliss submerged beneath appearance,
> In an interior ocean's rocking
> Of long, capricious fugues and chorals.

This uneasy animadversion on *Out of the Cradle* kept going on in Stevens. In *The Comedian as the Letter C*, Crispin is spoken of as a poet

>   too destitute to find
> In any commonplace the sought-for aid.
> He was a man made vivid by the sea
> A man come out of luminous traversing,
> Much trumpeted, made desperately clear,
> Fresh from discoveries of tidal skies,
> To whom oracular rockings gave no rest.
> Into a savage color he went on.

Another *Harmonium* poem, *Stars at Tallapoosa*, again repudiates (or attempts to repudiate) Whitman's curious warble:

> The lines are straight and swift between the stars.
> The night is not the cradle that they cry,
> The criers, undulating the deep-oceaned phrase.
> The lines are much too dark and much too sharp.

These are all overt allusions and so conceal as much as they reveal of Whitman's deepest and most anxiety-inducing influences upon Stevens. More interesting, even on the relatively trivial level of verbal echoes, is the Stevensian defense against the "endlessly" of Whitman's hypnotically suggestive opening line. It is still Whitman who lurks in the "endless pursuit or endlessly pursued" of *The Greenest Continent* (*OP*, 52–60) in *Owl's Clover;* still Whitman rocking on "among the endlessly emerging accords" of the late *Things of August,* and still Whitman who haunts Stevens on an ordinary evening in that notoriously ordinary city, New Haven:

> This endlessly elaborating poem
> Displays the theory of poetry,
> As the life of poetry. A more severe,
>
> More harassing master would extemporize
> Subtler, more urgent proof that the theory
> Of poetry is the theory of life,
>
> As it is, in the intricate evasions of as,
> In things seen and unseen, created from nothingness,
> The heavens, the hells, the worlds, the longed-for lands.

We can identify the endlessly elaborating Whitman as that more severe and harassing master of extemporization, though a severe and harassing mastery over "things seen and unseen" belongs more to Dickinson, another unacknowledged precursor. Here is Dickinson's version of demonic romance, her *Childe Roland to the Dark Tower Came:*

> Our journey had advanced –
> Our feet were almost come
> To that odd Fork in Being's Road –
> Eternity – by Term –
>
> Our pace took sudden awe –
> Our feet – reluctant – led –
> Before – were Cities – but Between –
> The Forest of the Dead –
>
> Retreat – was out of Hope –
> Behind – a Sealed Route –
> Eternity's White Flag – Before –
> And God – at every Gate –

I would locate the crossings here, as always, in the breaks between one mode of figurative thinking and a mode sharply an-

tithetical to that one. The Crossing of Election intervenes between the irony of "Being's Road" and the synecdoche
"Eternity – by Term –." The Crossing of Solipsism comes between the metonymy of "Our feet – reluctant – led –" and the
hyperbolical vision of the Cities of salvation and destruction,
and the Forest of the Dead. Between the metaphor of "a Sealed
Route –" and the transumption of "Eternity's White Flag –
Before –" Dickinson traverses the Crossing of Identification.
The critical question must be: how can my apparently arbitrary
locations and namings of these rhetorical disjunctions aid in an
interpretation of this poem? A further question, dictated by the
context of this chapter, is: what do Dickinson's poem and a
Kabbalistic method for interpreting it have to do with the poetry of Wallace Stevens?

The connection with Stevens is that he and Dickinson, more
than any other Americans, more than any other moderns, labor
successfully to make the visible a little hard to see. Here I have
Geoffrey Hartman as precursor, and perhaps all my crossings
can do is to systematize his insights in his problematic essay on
language from the point of view of literature in *Beyond For-
malism*. Indeed, Hartman even applies to the poem a tag from
Stevens that I will employ: "a seeing and unseeing in the eye."
Dickinson's stance, Hartman remarks, is *profanus*, "on the
threshold of vision." There is something of Stevens in such a
stance, I would observe, and the Emersonian dialectic of Fate,
Freedom, and Power is again highly relevant in calibrating the
stance. Fate is a reseeing series of tropes, but Power is a reaiming. Fate is taboo, but Power is transcendence. In between, in
the realm of Freedom or meaning, revision is neither a reseeing
nor a reaiming but only a re-estimating, and such freedom to es-
teem again is neither taboo nor transcendence but transgression, or the threshold-state proper. Let us see how this may
be applicable to Dickinson's lyric.

A reader, truly confronting the text of "Our journey had advanced," learns to ask "*how* does it mean?" I think that *how*
might begin with a further question: what is the place and the
temporal condition out of which the voice of this lyric rises?
Where and when does Dickinson stand, as dramatic speaker, in

relation to the negative moments or crossings described in the poem? Is she not stalled precisely where and when she sets herself in her anecdote? "Our" may mean "you, the reader," as well as Dickinson. We *had* advanced in our journey, but we saw it in a curiously passive perspective; "Our feet were almost come," the "almost" introducing the liminal element that governs the poem. Almost come where? The ironic answer is: to an absence rather than a presence, to a crossing or fork not between two roads but in a road that is no road, Being rather than Consciousness, in which any fork is odd, since Being compels a conjunctive rhetoric just as Consciousness (where your journey *can* advance) demands a disjunctive rhetoric. At that odd Fork, a hopeless crisis of poetic Election waits, but Dickinson subtly saves herself from it by her "almost" and then names the Fork with the equivocal synecdoche "Eternity – by Term –." "Term" echoes, jarringly, the "tern" of "Eternity," and raises a number of conflicting significations that Dickinson declines to translate into definite meaning. Eternity ought to be time without term. "Term" as a word goes back through the Latin *terminus* (boundary, limit) to a root meaning "to get over, break through," as in the Sanskrit *tirati*, which means "crossing over." Etymologically, a term is thus a crossing or transgression, and I think this is one of the many instances of Dickinson's romancing of the etymon. But all the meanings of "term" are in play in "Eternity – by Term –," including: 1) a limited period of time; 2) a space of time assigned a person to serve, whether in office or in prison; 3) a point in time, at the start or end of a period, or a deadline; 4) a word with a precise meaning; 5) the logical or mathematical meaning, as in propositions or equations; 6) the pillar that marks a boundary, or emblem of Terminus, Roman god of limits. As synecdoche, "Eternity – by Term –" stands for all this and more, but essentially the Crossing of Election just before it teaches us that as a trope of power it is oxymoronic, for the synecdoche of Eternity is qualified by "Term" as a term of *ethos*, as Limitation, putting into question the powers of poetry more than the power of Dickinson as specific power.

The next two lines metonymize, with our pace troping for

our consciousness and our feet for our being. "Awe" is one of Dickinson's prime tropes for Fate or *ethos* raised to apocalyptic pitch. After the strong limitation of our passivity ("– reluctant – led –"), the Crossing of Solipsism or crisis of eros comes, just before a "Before" and a "Between." Again, we can observe that Dickinson takes up her stance on Term, or as Hartman says, *profanus*, before judgment and death, but going no further toward the last sublimities.

The third stanza begins in a bewildering perspectivism of metaphor, where the trope is the "Sealed Route" of "Retreat," which carries quite contrary significations. It can mean that Dickinson has no hope of turning back, because the Road is sealed off. Or it can mean that a meditative retreat is available because of hope, in that the Route back to life could be unsealed by Apocalypse. Either way, meaning in the sense of thought or wholeness is invested in the Crossing of Identification that follows, which is, however, as ambiguous or as much an *aporia* as the rest of the poem. It is not possible to decide whether "Eternity's White Flag" is a surrender to belatedness or a banner of transumptive victory, which means that the "Before" would then take on a temporal as well as a spatial sense. Nor can we know whether the God "at every Gate" is there as welcomer or as Covering Cherub, the blocking angel. Whether death is being projected or introjected depends upon our reading of the crisis, and at least our notion of crossings helps us to see how acute the mental dilemma is that Dickinson finally requires us to confront.

I come back to "a seeing and unseeing in the eye" so as at last to advance our journey to reach Stevens. We cannot *see* crossings in the text of a poem; precisely we need to unsee them as we encounter rhetorical disjunctiveness, the transgression from one figuration to another. Dickinson is part of the prelude to Stevens because she thinks powerfully but not discursively and in *antithetical* images that disrupt the realm of the bodily eye.

If the study of poetic crossing, in its American variant, leads inevitably to the study of Stevens, then some glimpses at early texts should be useful at this point in my progress toward major Stevens. The first poem in which Stevens shows something of what is to be his strength is *Blanche McCarthy*, written in 1915, which he thought unworthy of *Harmonium* but which should have found a place there anyway:

> Look in the terrible mirror of the sky
> And not in this dead glass, which can reflect
> Only the surfaces—the bending arm,
> The leaning shoulder and the searching eye.
>
> Look in the terrible mirror of the sky.
> Oh, bend against the invisible; and lean
> To symbols of descending night; and search
> The glare of revelations going by!
>
> Look in the terrible mirror of the sky.
> See how the absent moon waits in a glade
> Of your dark self, and how the wings of stars,
> Upward, from unimagined coverts, fly.

I have commented on this lyric already, in the opening chapter of *A Map of Misreading*, but there my stress was thematic: upon the poem's involuntary and desperate Transcendentalism. Here I want to examine it as a problem in rhetorical disjunctiveness. Robert Buttel, in his useful book *The Making of "Harmonium,"* sees in this poem the effect of Baudelaire, and doubtless he is right, but I apply here another principle of antithetical criticism: an "influence" across languages is, in our time, almost invariably a cunning mask for an influence relation within a language. Blanche is a daughter, not of Mallarmé and of Baudelaire, but of Emerson, Whitman, Dickinson. Stevens speaks to her as he will speak to all his other interior paramours, admonishing her to behold her true form in the terrible mirror presented by the imagination's antagonist, the unfriendly sky of *Sunday Morning*, whose very blue is dividing and indifferent. Blanche's narcissistic self-regard blinds her to the truth that she also is a soldier in the war of the mind against the sky. The sky is a live glass, reflecting the depths of a woman, and the glare of its revelations concerns Blanche's own self. Her dark or undiscovered self contains both the moon and the stars, waiting to fly upward. She is a kind of older sister to Stevens' Hoon, though she cannot be expected to know that yet.

Rhetorically, the thrice-repeated "Look in the terrible mirror of the sky" serves as three different tropes, changing with each altered context. Initially a simple irony, it says Blanche must look at the sky but means she must look within her own dark self. In its next appearance it is a metonymic undoing of the sky itself; the sky empties itself out into invisibility, the mirror being terrible because it is no longer even a functioning mirror. The third time around, the sky is a metaphor for Blanche herself, outside to her inside, waiting for the moon and the stars that she must cease to conceal. These tropes are three degrees of Emersonian Fate, three indications of Blanche's own character, her acceptance of limitation, powerlessness, and fear, particularly her fear of time's ravages, as she surveys arm, shoulder, and her own searching eye in the dead glass of her narcissistic reverie.

The tropes of Power answering these contractions begin with the synecdoches or symbols of descending night—her own arm, shoulder, and eye as parts of which her death will be the whole—and continue with the hyperbolical "glare of revelations going by," the first appearance in Stevens of an American Sublime that will culminate in the glare of revelations in the great sweep of autumn's auroras. The *potentia* of a transumptive Will is represented by the covert and begladed self, out of which celestial lights may fly upward, if Blanche will open herself to influx. But now I will cease mapping poor Blanche, and instead will attend to her disjunctions, to those crossings in her text that intimate *how* she means what she yet may mean. The first crossing is located at the Dickinsonian dash in line 3 after "surfaces"; the second after "descending night" in line 7; the third after "dark self" in line 11. Can we not say that the Crossing of Election here concerns Stevens' admonition to himself to forsake the mimetic "terrible mirror" for his own "searching eye"? Is it Stevens then who must make the Crossing of Solipsism as he leaves inherited Whitmanian or Baudelairean symbols of descending night and searches what flares upon the frame of everything he is? And finally, who is it but Stevens the poet who must internalize even further, so as to make the Crossing of Identification, and find himself more truly and more strange in "unimagined coverts"? Yet in thus reading, we are like Blake's Los, reading not the tropes or stars of Albion but the *topoi* or voids between the stars. Freedom or the second chance, the saving blend of Vocation and Temperament, has been discovered in the dance of substitutions, not in the substitutions themselves.

Blanche may be too ever-early a candor; let us try the whiteness of a year later. In 1916, about a year after finding himself as a poet with *Sunday Morning*, Stevens tried to write a long poem in terza rima, *For an Old Woman in a Wig*. Though we have only an incomplete manuscript of the poem, there is enough to show that it, rather than *Sunday Morning*, prophesied the mode of his major poetry to come.

The reader who knows *Notes toward a Supreme Fiction* and *The Auroras of Autumn* will be fascinated by *For an Old Woman in a Wig*, though the poem or fragment has only a mixed intrinsic value. In it, Stevens, one of the slowest developers among the major poets, tried to write a poem he was not ready to write. He made few such mistakes again, after 1916, and his canon has astonishing completeness, a sense of ripeness unique in American poetry. Premature poems can be very revealing, and Stevens was always on guard against involuntary self-revelations. A patient reading of *For an Old Woman in a Wig* yields little in personal revelation but deep insight into Stevens' first finding of himself as a poet.

When Moneta, the chastising muse of *The Fall of Hyperion*, condemns Keats (falsely) as "a dreaming thing; / A fever of thyself" she bids him to "think of the Earth" instead of himself. The profound implication is that thus, and only thus, can Keats find what will suffice. This was always to be Stevens' burden, from *Sunday Morning* until, forty years later, *A Mythology Reflects Its Region*:

> The image must be of the nature of its creator.
> It is the nature of its creator increased,
> Heightened. It is he, anew, in a freshened youth

And it is he in the substance of his region,
Wood of his forests and stone out of his fields
Or from under his mountains.

This is Stevens at seventy-five, master of a simplification through intensity that approximates clairvoyance. *Sunday Morning*, for all its justly renowned eloquence, contains nothing of this clairvoyance. *For an Old Woman in a Wig* has a certain monotony of movement and much mere filling in its language, but it begins the visionary side of Stevens' argument, without which his curious late radiance would not have been possible. The alliance in Stevens between naturalism and a visionary faculty is not an easy one to understand (many of his critics will not even acknowledge it), but it is not unique to him, as readers of Wordsworth or Whitman know.

The old woman in her wig seeks to approximate "a freshened youth." The poem is addressed to her because she is one of the "pitiful lovers of earth . . . keeping . . . count of beauty," rather than a seeker-out of "the unknown new in your surrounding." The woman of *Sunday Morning* is another of these "pitiful lovers of earth," a retrospective brooder upon the splendors of natural experience. In *Sunday Morning* the voice of the poet, responding to her doubts and reservations, has no visionary argument with which to assuage her but relies instead upon the pungency of earth in contrast with the unknown darkness of surrounding space. The poetic voice that rises up in *For an Old Woman in a Wig* is able to utter a more imaginative argument against the woman's implied lament of mutability. The argument, as in the late poem *An Ordinary Evening in New Haven*, is founded on "a moment's flitter," here at dawn. Metric and the reference to Virgil establish a Dantesque Inferno, but "Hell is not desolate Italy." Hell is ironically here and now, lit by the rising sun, and depends upon the *ethos* of our study of the nostalgias, our "too poignant grieving" for all the yesterdays, by which we would make each fresh morning only into "the things we knew." To live thus is to live for Fate's sake, as though the cocks of morning crowed for Fate and not for us. The *pathos* of our imagination, "cut by sorrow," will not apprehend new moods, and we are reduced to "the mumble / Of sounds returning." This first part of *For an Old Woman in a Wig* is prologue to *It Must Change* in *Notes toward a Supreme Fiction*.

The second part takes *Sunday Morning* as its given and makes a fresh beginning for the imagination. Heaven too is a death, like the "sweet golden clime" of Blake's Sunflower lyric. As with Blake's lovers, who arise from their graves only to aspire again after a more imaginative heaven, so Stevens' spirits are "riven / From out contentment by too conscious yearning" and go on quest again "to those old landscapes, endlessly regiven," from which the hells, the heavens, and more vitally the longed-for lands first were begotten. These spirits are poets, fellows "of those whom hell's illusions harry," and who thus demonstrate that death cannot complete their imaginations.

Neither of these sections, except for attitude, is particularly promising as poetry. But the third rises to a vision, of perhaps Stevens' most characteristic kind, prophetic of the great "privileged moments" or "times of inherent excellence," the "spots of time" that are to inform his greatest poems of the nineteen forties and fifties. The Arabian moon of *Notes toward a Supreme Fiction* glances over the dreamers, creating poetry by satisfying our desire for metaphor, for resemblances, and "The dreamers wake and watch the moonlight streaming." But this is too easy a satisfaction for resemblances too ready, and Stevens makes a powerfully implicit attack upon his own conception of the decadence of the Wordsworthian mode of poetry, upon the quest for afterimages and the study of nostalgias. Though feeling may come in aid of feeling and diversity of strength attend us, if but once we have been strong, the consequence is still only "a deeper dreaming." For "the sweeping / Poetry of sky and sea" has been written, and to rewrite it is only "keeping / Such count of beauty." These poetic dreamers are "pitiful lovers of earth" who can see only remembered landscapes and so live within the circumference of a codified vision. They lack will, and abundance, and are not among those few who will find themselves more truly and more strange, as the first major Romantics did when they began. Stevens is rejecting his own easy naturalism, but only for a more heroic, strenuous naturalism, a "wish for revelation" that will at last bring him into the transumptive company of those who "sought out the unknown new" in their surrounding.

Stevens' place in the company of Romantic visionaries is denied or slighted in almost all criticism that has been devoted to him. He had, we are told repeatedly, a very different sense of being than the Romantics had, but we are never given much cause for confidence that his critics have as accurate a sense of the Romantics as even he did. I shall conclude this chapter by considering one of *Harmonium*'s most insouciant and apparently anti-Romantic poems, so as to see the American Romantic stance of Stevens where his critics are least inclined to place it. In one of the last flashes of Stevens' essential gaudiness and exuberance in his first major phase, which can be said to have lasted from 1915 to 1919, he wrote his paean to an American Aphrodite, in *The Paltry Nude Starts on a Spring Voyage.*

A. Walton Litz usefully relates *The Paltry Nude* to the first stanza of *Le Monocle de Mon Oncle*, written the year before, where the speaker has an ironic vision of the beloved as the Botticelli "Birth of Venus": "The sea of spuming thought foists up again / The radiant bubble that she was." Robert Buttel demonstrates the parodistic relation of Stevens' *Paltry Nude* to imagistic poems on the same subject by Amy Lowell and H.D. They may indeed have been Stevens' starting point, but his fierce lyric confronts a true precursor in Pater's great prose poem *Sandro Botticelli* in *The Renaissance.* I suspect that Pater's account of the painting "The Birth of Venus" is one of the hidden sources of Stevens' notion of the First Idea, called by Pater "the first impression." We know more about the Greeks than Botticelli did, Pater says, yet familiarity has dulled the lesson for us:

But in pictures like this of Botticelli's you have a record of the first impression made by it on minds turned back towards it. . . . Men go forth to their labours until the evening; but she is awake before them, and you might think that the sorrow in her face was at the thought of the whole long day of love yet to come. . . . What is unmistakable is the sadness with which he has conceived the goddess of pleasure, as the depositary of a great power over the lives of men.

"She too is discontent," Stevens raffishly remarks of his paltry nude, as if to say that Pater's Venus must be undercut in her High Decadent sadness. The American Venus starts out, not on the half shell but "on the first-found weed," impatient for the Hoonian purple "of the high interiors of the sea." The American Venus is an Emersonian (what else?) and attains the American Sublime even as she finds herself the compass of that sea:

> The wind speeds her,
> Blowing upon her hands
> And watery back.
> She touches the clouds, where she goes
> In the circle of her traverse of the sea.

But even this is "meagre play" for an American goddess, and Stevens transcends his own ironic diction in a metaleptic conclusion. Just as there will be an American god of the sun, "not as a god but as a god might be," so there will be in some visionary and now introjected future a greater American Venus than this paltry beauty, whose movement is "not as when the goldener nude / Of a later day / Will go." Pater's goddess is a touch sado-masochistic, because she suffers a sense of her own belatedness. Stevens' goddess-to-be will manifest "an intenser calm" because she will have emulated Emerson's program of joining yourself to Fate after discovering that you can't beat Fate, and as an American she will demand Victory, "the centre of sea-green pomp." The price is that she will be Fate's kitchen-wench, but nothing is got for nothing, and at least she will go

> Across the spick torrent, ceaselessly,
> Upon her irretrievable way.

"Spick," as Stevens, the Pennsylvania Dutchman, would have known, means "spotless, neat, clean, fresh, new," from the Dutch for "spike-splinter-new." What better emblem for Stevens' own poetic stance than the prospective voyage of an American nude beauty, goldener than tradition had yet prophesied?

2 *Harmonium:*
The Poetry of Earth

There is a primary Stevens, and he is a Lucretian poet, like Whitman or an aspect of Shelley. I have traced Emerson's American modification of the Coleridge–Wordsworth dialectic of *ethos*, *logos*, *pathos* into a necessitarian triad of Fate, Freedom, and Power. In Stevens, we will see Emersonian Fate turning into a metonymic reduction that Stevens will learn to call the First Idea. Transcendental Freedom in Stevens becomes the refusal to bear so dehumanizing a reduction. Power or Will in Stevens' mature poetry is the reimagining of a First Idea. This may seem to be getting ahead of the story, but the story begins in *Harmonium*, long before Stevens had a vocabulary perfected in which the story might be told.

Sunday Morning remains Stevens' most famous single poem, an eminence achieved at the expense of even stronger poems in *Harmonium*. But *Sunday Morning* is a wonderful poem by any standards. I venture a full interpretation here, partly out of dissatisfaction with all of the readings available and partly because Stevens will rewrite *Sunday Morning* so often in his later poetry.

We can say that the first stanza of *Sunday Morning* is the true *clinamen* for Stevens, his grand, initial swerve away from origins. There is something curiously embowered about the dreaming woman, who is the first instance of Stevens' muse, his interior paramour. The poet has something of the same subtle relationship to her that Tennyson had to his Mariana, and I think it not accidental that *Sunday Morning*, with all its Wordsworthian, Keatsian, and even repressedly Whitmanian touches, should be Stevens' most Tennysonian poem, with a clear debt to the elegiac intensities of *Tears, Idle Tears* and perhaps also to *Tithonus*. Of course, the reverie-laden woman of *Sunday Morning* suffers from repressed religiosity rather than from Mariana's more luscious repressed sexuality, but both ladies are waiting for fulfillments they by no means are prepared to accept.

I don't believe it has been often realized that Stevens is decisively a muse-poet, indeed much more an erotic poet (severely repressed) than an ironist. What is the dreaming woman there for in *Sunday Morning* anyway? Like all muses she is invoked, as Eric Havelock says of Hesiod's muses, to be the voice of instruction and also the voice of pleasure. Her presence has the purposes of relieving anxiety, of assuaging grief, but above all else, of helping the poet to remember much that once he knew but has repressed. Or, as Vico intimated, she is there to help the poet divinate; she is an apotropaic sibyl whose function is to help Stevens survive, as poet and as man. How does she aid him in this poem?

Certainly the overt relation of poet and woman here seems quite unlike a muse-attachment. Stevens keeps editorializing about his Sunday morning brooder, about as constantly as Milton maintains a moralizing commentary upon poor Eve. But Eve is quite external to Milton; Stevens addresses an aspect of himself as surely and intimately as Tennyson confronts his own early poetic psyche in Mariana. I marvel continuously at the critical attempts to find a Christian sensibility in Stevens. Like all involuntary Emersonians, he has a gorgeous capacity for solipsistic transport, that is, for becoming a Gnostic Godhead when he feels most exuberant. When he has apparent nostalgia for religion, it is truly for such influxes of Power. In *Sunday Morning*, he starts where Keats started: God and the gods are dead, quite dead, but the Sublime survives anyway, and one of its survivals is in sympathy, and indeed in self-sympathy.

Let us return to stanza I and examine it as an instance of the American *ethos* that Emerson called "Fate," noting first the necessitarian irony that says the opposite of what it means, since the odor of the oranges and the color of the uncaged cockatoo, far from dissipating the holy hush of the Lord's day, provoke instead a phantasmagoria, in which the dreaming woman walks the wide water, emulating Christ, until she reaches his Palestinian grave. That wide water without sound returns in the poem's final stanza, when a third voice, neither the poet's nor the woman's, cries upon it the truth of Christ's mortality. The inescapable and soundless water is scarcely distinguishable from the procession of the dead winding across it, and ironically it becomes a trope for our chaotic and divinely unsponsored freedom.

All through the poem Stevens speaks as though he were instructing his interior paramour, yet she instructs him as well, particularly when she speaks, in stanzas IV and V. Her teaching is the need for an *ethos*, a permanent sense of Eden, an undying joy. His counter-tuition is in praise of the American *pathos* of "Power": passions, pleasures, and pains, remembrance, undying desire. Like all her later manifestations in Stevens, she is a reductionist, a seeker after the First Idea, and so she is uneasy even in her "complacencies" or happinesses, her contentment that she knows depends upon a wavering and so illusory present.

How well does Stevens teach her, which is to say, how persuasively does he argue here with himself? Rather clearly, he moves himself, as he does us, yet he cannot persuade himself. His affirmations in this poem, though eloquent and even Sublime, are quite derivative; they are the exultations and obsessions of the tradition, of Wordsworth, Keats, Tennyson, Whitman, more than they are the hard-earned misprisions of Stevens himself. We can locate Keats throughout stanzas II and III, Wordsworth and Tennyson in stanzas IV and V, Whitman in stanzas VI and VII, with Wordsworth returning toward the end of VII and Keats toward the end of VIII. This is predictable enough, since *Sunday Morning*, like *Le Monocle de Mon Oncle* and so many subsequent poems by Stevens, joins one of the major strains in British and American poetry, which is the continual revision of Wordsworth's *Intimations* ode. As I am proposing in these chapters that Stevens' poetry follows rather faithfully the Wordsworthian crisis-poem model, in its Emersonian–Whitmanian modification, I need to show something of the workings of the model in *Sunday Morning*.

As a dialectical alternation between Fate and Power, or

American *ethos* and American *pathos*, the poem maps roughly in the following divisions:

> Stanzas, I, *ethos* or Fate; Contraries and Contradictories of secular and sacred, leading to imagery of presence and absence of the religious vision.
>
> II, *pathos* or Power; Definition and Division of and between human or natural, and divinity, leading to imagery of "all pleasures and all pains," of summer and winter visions as synecdoches of the divine made human.
>
> III *ethos*, or Fate's spatial Cause and Effect of our earthly desires and paradisal fulfillments, leading to metonymic images of the emptiness both of the sky and of our desires.
>
> IV *pathos*, or Power; Comparison of images of paradise with images of earth, leading to Sublime vision of natural experience.
>
> V and VI, final *ethos* or Fate; topics of Resemblance and Dissimilarity between natural change and eternal stasis, leading to metaphors of horizons and shores, imagery of insides seeking to coincide with outsides.
>
> VII and VIII, final *pathos* or Power; Antecedents and Consequents, or temporal effects reversing causes, between mortality and immortality, leading to metaleptic imagery of dancers introjecting an earliness of origins, and birds sinking into darkness, projecting the belatedness of our ends.

This is all merely schematic and tells us only that *Sunday Morning* indeed does follow the sombre figurations of the post-Wordsworthian crisis-poem. Criticism, or the quest for meaning, must take place in the *logos* or Freedom, the wildness of substitution, *between* these topics and tropes of Fate and Power. To that *between* I now address myself, with Stevens' first crossing in the poem, his rhetorical question "Why should she give her bounty to the dead?"

Her "bounty" is her consciousness, and the "dead" is Jesus. How close Stevens is, in stanza II, to the Emerson of the 1842 Notebooks, in granting the supreme *ethos*, the character and exemplary Fate of Christ, while demanding Power, an even more exemplary American *pathos*, a greater than Christ who shall come:

The history of Christ is the best document of the power of Character which we have. A youth who owed nothing to fortune and who was "hanged at Tyburn,"—by the pure quality of his nature has shed this epic splendor around the facts of his death which has transfigured every particular into a grand universal symbol for the eyes of all mankind ever since.

He did well. This great Defeat is hitherto the highest fact we have. But he that shall come shall do better. The mind requires a far higher exhibition of character, one which shall make itself good to the senses as well as to the soul; a success to the senses as well as to the soul. This was a great Defeat; we demand Victory.

Stevens in his second stanza also asks a larger synecdoche than Christ, "a success to the senses," a Victory of *pathos*. There is an *aporia* between this stanza and stanza I, the breaking or blinding movement that is a negative or deconstructive moment, a crossing or path-breaking between two kinds of image-thinking, ironic or allegorical and synecdochal or symbolic. From the *ethos* of Christ as an absence, though a longed-for presence, we pass to the *pathos* of an internalized divinity, whose representatives are passions, moods, grievings, elations, emotions, pleasures, pains, remembrances, all of them measures, parts of a greater music. But this synecdochal stanza, though it opens with three rhetorical questions, addresses its largest question implicitly to itself. What is a divinity that is this discontinuous, this reliant upon seasonal cycle? The ominous word in the stanza is "destined" in its last line, which reintroduces the limitations of character and incident. There is no wholeness to this divinity, but only an aggregate of passions, and where there is an aggregate there is no closure, not even an illusion of closure.

Hence we are given the transition to the reductive and undoing stanza III, with its self-mocking, outrageously alliterative diction, the myth-maker as the letter M: "mother . . . large-mannered motions . . . mythy mind . . . moved among . . . muttering . . . magnificent . . . move among . . . commingling." In this metonymic muttering, the maker mangles his manner to mock his own meaning. Yet the meaning, which is the breaking of a definition into its contiguous aspects, survives the mockery, and gives us a superbly Keatsian *ethos:*

> Shall our blood fail? Or shall it come to be
> The blood of paradise? And shall the earth
> Seem all of paradise that we shall know?
> The sky will be much friendlier then than now,
> A part of labor and a part of pain,
> And next in glory to enduring love,
> Not this dividing and indifferent blue.

This is what we think of as Keats's notion of sympathetic imagination, in which he followed Hazlitt. The sky will be friendlier by an act of identification or mutual introjection between it and our own future desires. Again, meaning intervenes *between* this quest for a larger or merged identity and the heroic *pathos* of stanza IV, a stanza intricately weaving together images of voice out of *Tears, Idle Tears,* the *Ode on Melancholy,* and the *Recluse* fragment. That this is an involuntary intertextuality only strengthens its deconstructive force, for the traditional texts all center thematically on versions of an earthly paradise:

> Ah, sad and strange as in dark summer dawns
> The earliest pipe of half-awakened birds
> To dying ears, when unto dying eyes
> The casement slowly grows a glimmering square;
> So sad, so strange, the days that are no more.

◇　◇　◇

> Paradise, and groves
> Elysian, Fortunate Fields—like those of old
> Sought in the Atlantic Main—why should they be
> A history only of departed things,
> Or a mere fiction of what never was?

◇　◇　◇

> But when the melancholy fit shall fall
> 　Sudden from heaven like a weeping cloud,
> That fosters the droop-headed flowers all,
> 　And hides the green hill in an April shroud;
> Then glut thy sorrow on a morning rose

Stevens' birds are Tennyson's, his April's green is Keats's, his denials of the mythological earthly paradises is Wordsworth's. Stanza IV proclaims the endurance of a hyperbole of *pathos*, of a natural desire doomed to evanescence despite its Sublime troping. What is the *logos* or meaning that breaks and blinds between a figuration of identity and a desire made transcendent through hyperbole? In the critical language of Paul de Man, Jacques Derrida, J. Hillis Miller, we would have to say that meaning is produced by the ways in which the tropes of stanzas III and IV deconstruct one another, so as to give us a large figuration of doubt. But I return to my insistence that post-Enlightenment tropes are figures of will and not of doubtful knowledge or knowing doubt. Both stanzas III and IV lie against time, but the meaning engendered between them (in my view) depends upon a single and I think answerable question: which stanza lies more persuasively against time, which stanza holds better the will's revulsion and the will's revenge?

It is not very simple to define the philosophical anteriority of the will in Stevens, since William James, Nietzsche, Bergson, and probably Schopenhauer are all part of the notion. More obscurely, so is Emerson, both directly (when Stevens was young) and indirectly through James and Nietzsche. The Stevens of *Sunday Morning* is rather close to the James of *Pragmatism*, as several commentators have noted. Yet the will in *Sunday Morning* is not so much a will to believe as it is an Emersonian Will-to-Power, where "power" means "vitality" or even a Laurentian kind of vitalism. The woman of Stevens' reverie desires "June and evening" as part of the impulse that has led her to give the cockatoo its "green freedom," and we can remember again Emerson's solipsizing definition of "freedom," in an American context, as meaning "wildness."

With the movement to stanzas VI and VII, we return for the last time in the poem to the sublimations of *ethos*, "the need of some imperishable bliss." For two stanzas Stevens rather massively overanswers his muse, in a curious amalgam of Keatsian diction and Whitmanian blendings of death and the mother. The overanswering betrays Stevens' inability to accept his own wisdom, particularly in its unfortunate formula, "Death is the mother of beauty." Marie Borroff usefully interprets the formula as meaning essentially what "It Must Change" means in *Notes toward a Supreme Fiction*, since change is in Stevens a requirement for beauty, and death is the final form of change. Keats says of his muse in the *Ode on Melancholy* that "she dwells with Beauty—Beauty that must die," a formula more precise but not erotically as comprehensive as Stevens'. Both stanzas, v and vi, are a little unnerving in their repetitive self-curtailments. They satisfy our desire for resemblances too well and our desire for dissimilarities too poorly. Not enough meaning breaks or blinds itself in the transition from the hyperbolical thinking of stanza iv to the metaphorical musings of v and vi.

Yet the poem recovers greatly with the passage to its final movement, commencing with the famous chant of stanza vii, with its metaleptic reversals of the poem's prior figurations:

> Supple and turbulent, a ring of men
> Shall chant in orgy on a summer morn
> Their boisterous devotion to the sun,
> Not as a god, but as a god might be,
> Naked among them, like a savage source.
> Their chant shall be a chant of paradise,
> Out of their blood, returning to the sky;
> And in their chant shall enter, voice by voice,
> The windy lake wherein their lord delights,
> The trees, like serafin, and echoing hills,
> That choir among themselves long afterward.
> They shall know well the heavenly fellowship
> Of men that perish and of summer morn.
> And whence they came and whither they shall go
> The dew upon their feet shall manifest.

The "comforts of the sun" earlier in the poem were fruits and birds, pungencies of odor and of color. The sun-worship of stanza vii represents a different idea of order, one that is yet to be and that relates itself to the image of Zarathustra's solar trajectory in Nietzsche, whose spirit dominates here. The god among men, "like a savage source," is Zarathustra as prophet of the Over-Man, and his followers manifest origin and purpose alike as the "dew," synecdoche throughout Stevens for the fecundity of earth. Meaning emerges most vitally in *Sunday Morn-*

ing just here, as Stevens reverses temporal order in his imagery, for these chanters are not "men of sun" but attendants upon the sun-as-man, a true First Idea of the sun and a true First Idea of man. Yet the trope itself knows and says that these are "men that perish" in fellowship with a "summer morn" that must perish also, so that the thinkers of a First Idea must perish with the thought of it.

The final stanza gives three possibilities only for the place we live, which already in Stevens is neither our own nor ourselves, a hard home in spite of blazoned days. As "an old chaos of the sun," earth remains uncreated by the sun as it was and is rather than the sun as it might be. As an "old dependency of day and night," earth is at best a colony ruled by antithetical masters. But most likely, earth is an "island solitude" in space, free and so wild, yet dangerously free, because unsponsored, in that wide water which now becomes an ocean of atmosphere. Are not the meanings of the eloquent final seven lines dependent upon their transumptive breaking of the inside / outside metaphors of man-against-the-sky earlier in the poem?

> Deer walk upon our mountains, and the quail
> Whistle about us their spontaneous cries;
> Sweet berries ripen in the wilderness;
> And, in the isolation of the sky,
> At evening, casual flocks of pigeons make
> Ambiguous undulations as they sink,
> Downward to darkness, on extended wings.

If we are isolated, so is the sky, in a cosmos where all power is "spontaneous" and "casual." There are no causes, only temporal effects, in this concluding topos, where the ripening is all and where the extended wings of the evening birds have ambiguous significances but no actual meanings. Resemblances have receded here, because these tropes turn only from previous tropes. There is just a premonitory, introjective gesture, downward and outward, into the darkness, appropriate to a world where no spirits linger.

The other popular success in *Harmonium* is *Peter Quince at the Clavier,* written almost simultaneously with *Sunday Morning* and best read now as an erotic grace note to the greater poem, perhaps even as an epilogue exposing the repressed eroticism of Stevens' meditation upon his muse, death, and the death of God and the gods. As in Stevens' other "music-poems," most notably *The Man with the Blue Guitar*, there is a curious, partly buried relation to Browning here, particularly to the erotic masterpiece *A Toccata of Galuppi's*. Shakespeare's Peter Quince is no Galuppi, but Stevens has a touch of Browning's monologist who performs Galuppi, and it is Stevens who speaks directly of his own desire in the opening section of his own touchpiece. The title, outrageous in itself, may allude to the stage-managing carpenter's remark that "there is two hard things: that is, to bring the moonlight into a chamber," the other hard thing being the personification of a wall. Stevens, at the clavier, also confronts problems in representation, though in a rather finer tone. Music *is* pathos, Stevens asserts, and is identical with desire or the will-to-possession. But in Stevens, the desire deprecates itself, by an identification with the desire of the elders for Susanna rather than with the more refined and repressed desire of Susanna herself, in section II of the poem. Susanna studies the nostalgias with a superbly narcissistic self-absorption, and so persuasively that we too are startled by the breath of the elders' lust.

It is section IV, ending the poem, that matters most, and here the doctrine and something of the voice of Walter Pater first enter fully into the world of *Harmonium*. Pater, Emerson, and Nietzsche had strange affinities, despite the authentic differences between Epicurean aestheticism, skeptical idealism, and "philological" perspectivism. These were rightly blended, overtly and knowingly by Yeats, hiddenly and probably unknowingly by Stevens. The text that hovers near in *Peter Quince*, IV, is the "Conclusion" to *The Renaissance:* "Every moment some form grows perfect in hand or face; some tone on the hills or the sea is choicer than the rest; some mood of passion or insight or intellectual excitement is irresistibly real and attractive for us,—for that moment only."

One sees that, for Pater, "Beauty is momentary in the mind," yet he extends the fitful tracing to the flesh also, as Stevens professes not to do. But Stevens tropes upon "dies" and "lives":

The body dies; the body's beauty lives.
So evenings die, in their green going,
A wave, interminably flowing.

"Green" as a catachresis here takes us back to *Sunday Morning*'s "As April's green endures." April dies; April's green lives, yet only as remembrance and desire. Beauty is immortal in the flesh because it provokes memory, that other mode of thought in poetry, or the only rival to rhetorical substitution, which thrusts or defends against memory. Memory in turn provokes desire, activating the will. The immortality of "the body's beauty" reduces thus to the persistence of the will, if only the will-to-representation. Like Pater, Stevens has a precursor in Rossetti, who represented "body's beauty" in the phantasmagoria of his sonnets and poems and who would have endorsed the paradoxes of *Sunday Morning* and *Peter Quince at the Clavier.*

Three years later, aged thirty-nine, Stevens wrote *Le Monocle de Mon Oncle,* a poem transcending *Sunday Morning* and *Peter Quince* and yet completing their mode, which is the bringing up to date of the crisis-poem of the *Intimations* ode or *Tintern Abbey* kind. Such "modernization" in *Le Monocle* makes of its bravura first stanza one of the most ferocious ironies in our poetry, where the imagery of presence and absence refers less to the muse (now bedraggled) or the beloved (now somewhat faded) than to the language of passion; the tropes of her hyperbolical anteriority now become the catachreses of her inadequate presence:

"Mother of heaven, regina of the clouds,
O sceptre of the sun, crown of the moon,
There is not nothing, no, no, never nothing,
Like the clashed edges of two words that kill."
And so I mocked her in magnificent measure.
Or was it that I mocked myself alone?
I wish that I might be a thinking stone.
The sea of spuming thought foists up again
The radiant bubble that she was. And then
A deep up-pouring from some saltier well
Within me, bursts its watery syllable.

The poem's title fools no one; "Mon Oncle" is Stevens himself, and "Le Monocle" is his erotic outlook in his fortieth year. The "two words that kill" may be "no, no" as a sexual refusal, or they may be only any or all of the grand pairings in the opening tropes of extravagance, in which case the killing effect is based upon the absence/presence contrast. Either way, the opening measure *is* magnificent and prophesies the somewhat less ironic address to the muse in *To the One of Fictive Music* three years later. But the hyperbole catachresized into irony mocks the poet as well as his dream of female beauty; hence his wish that he might retain consciousness and yet be stone rather than sexual flesh. R. P. Blackmur usefully noted that the words "foist" and "bubble" are purged of their residue of vulgarity by "the sea of spuming thought" and the idea of radiance, so that "they gain force while they lend their own lightness to the context." I would add to this only the notion of *ethos*, for the sea of thought always up-pouring *is* the poet's *ethos*, or as Stevens will say later, the mind can never be satisfied, and the motive for troping always will remain. Again, the radiant bubble of the lost beauty rises, but as rhetoric, only to have its watery syllable burst by an ironic language that had been repressed. What follows, in stanza ii, is a series of tropes of *pathos*, synecdoches for a lost vision of erotic fulfillment:

> A red bird flies across the golden floor.
> It is a red bird that seeks out his choir
> Among the choirs of wind and wet and wing.
> A torrent will fall from him when he finds.
> Shall I uncrumple this much-crumpled thing?
> I am a man of fortune greeting heirs;
> For it has come that thus I greet the spring.
> These choirs of welcome choir for me farewell.
> No spring can follow past meridian.
> Yet you persist with anecdotal bliss
> To make believe a starry *connaissance*.

In *Out of the Cradle Endlessly Rocking*, once entitled *A Word Out of the Sea*, the boy Whitman contrasts his lovelessness and songlessness to the passionate hymns of "two together," two migrant mockingbirds. Stevens' red bird against a golden background is more heraldic, yet the torrent of song that will fall from the red bird when he finds his choir is reminiscent of Whitman's "dusky demon and brother." But Stevens greets no choir. "Shall I uncrumple this much-crumpled thing" may presage the closing passages of *An Ordinary Evening in New Haven:* "A woman writing a note and tearing it up," in which case the reference is to the abortive first four lines of *Le Monocle,* as though Stevens kept crumpling and recrumpling his attempt at starting the poem. But more likely the question refers to Stevens' own sexual organ, with about as bitter a humor as Stevens ever attempts. The man of fortune has accumulated too many years, and his inheritors are presumably the years to come. Nearly forty, and the advent of spring anything but a reimagining, the poet reproves himself for anecdotal bliss, for studying the nostalgias of a once-starred sexual knowledge, or more cruelly he may be reproving his muse.

As tropes of *pathos,* the wounding synecdoches of stanza II are all self-mutilations, or defensively they are all turnings against the self. The extraordinary four stanzas following are this poem's *kenosis,* as Stevens empties out his own poethood. Each of the four is dominated by a reductive image that reifies or deidealizes the poet's earlier error; successively these are the hair of the beloved, the apple of the Fall, the evening star of Venus, and finally and most pungently "the basic slate, the universal hue," which is a belated version of Wordsworth's "sober coloring" (from the *Intimations* ode). Yet this fourfold *kenosis,* or humbling of the erotic self, is performed with a gusto at least as admirable and vitalistic as Stevens devotes to any of his self-celebrations.

Stanza III, having hymned the tittivations of three traditions, ends in a rhetorical question and then an open question, each capable of at least two competing interpretations:

> Alas! Have all the barbers lived in vain
> That not one curl in nature has survived?
> Why, without pity on these studious ghosts,
> Do you come dripping in your hair from sleep?

For "barbers" read "poets," and for "curl" read whatever the imagination has contrived to add to nature. The question is certainly rhetorical, and yet it could take the Paterian or Wildean answer that nature does imitate the barbers. But if it is to be answered thus, by a "no," then the open question, addressed to muse or aging beloved, becomes nearly barbarous in its cruelty. Either way, the "studious ghosts" are also the poets, and the woman coming from sleep is no beauty of Utamaro's and no beldame of Bath.

Hamlet, meditating upon the skull of Yorick, is the ultimate model in stanza IV, where the sexual bitterness begins to be a little acrid but the verve intensifies:

> An apple serves as well as any skull
> To be the book in which to read a round,
> And is as excellent, in that it is composed
> Of what, like skulls, comes rotting back to ground.

Reading a round means tracing a cycle, from sexuality to death. A more complex round is read in the next stanza, as the metonymy of cause and effect undergoes a catachresis, through irony, to become a more temporal and so more mortal image:

> The measure of the intensity of love
> Is measure, also, of the verve of earth.
> For me, the firefly's quick, electric stroke
> Ticks tediously the time of one more year.
> And you? Remember how the crickets came
> Out of their mother grass, like little kin,
> In the pale nights, when your first imagery
> Found inklings of your bond to all that dust.

The verve of earth reduces to its movement through passional time, as opposed to the clock time when eros is ended, even if the clock is composed of fireflies. When the beloved is addressed, in this context, she is reduced to poetic theme, since "your first imagery" must mean "the first imagery you provoked in me," an imagery discovering also the link between love and death.

The movement of undoing attains a climax in stanza VI, where "painting lakes" is a curious trope for sexual passion, though premonitory of a later contrast in Stevens between lakes and oceans, the larger entity hinting again at death. "The basic slate, the universal hue" can be called a reality principle, a reduction leading to a minimal vitalism: "There is a substance in us that prevails." That is as much affirmation as the poem presently affords, and an elegant bitterness comes on to complete this aspect of love's overthrow:

> But in our amours amorists discern
> Such fluctuations that their scrivening
> Is breathless to attend each quirky turn.
> When amorists grow bald, then amours shrink
> Into the compass and curriculum
> Of introspective exiles, lecturing.
> It is a theme for Hyacinth alone.

Hyacinth, as a thematic center, suggests the death of love through love, slain by the discus of the enamored Apollo. As critics of love's tropings, we become exiles from love, scholarly Ovids panting to keep up with the quirky turns of rhetoric. As a trope of *ethos* or Fate, this is intolerable though delicious, and Stevens recoils from it by a hyperbolical pathos concentrated in a formula of the Whitmanian flow and ebb of sexual power:

> The honey of heaven may or may not come,
> But that of earth both comes and goes at once.

Yet the culminating pathos of "a damsel heightened by eternal bloom" is too weakly transcendental a hyperbole, and necessarily but eloquently Stevens collapses his Sublime into the grotesque, in an absurdly grand litotes:

> Like a dull scholar, I behold, in love,
> An ancient aspect touching a new mind.
> It comes, it blooms, it bears its fruit and dies.
> This trivial trope reveals a way of truth.
> Our bloom is gone. We are the fruit thereof.
> Two golden gourds distended on our vines,
> Into the autumn weather, splashed with frost,
> Distorted by hale fatness, turned grotesque.
> We hang like warty squashes, streaked and rayed,
> The laughing sky will see the two of us
> Washed into rinds by rotting winter rains.

Passion could go no further as a passion for self-destruction, of poet and beloved alike. Stevens tropes and simultaneously tells us both that he is troping and how he is turning from golden to grotesque. With a rhetoricity grown so overt, there remains only the last *daemonization* in which the verse declares its own status as verse and denounces its own bare pretenses to closure. Who could hope to deconstruct any further a stanza as self-deconstructing as this?

> In verses wild with motion, full of din,
> Loudened by cries, by clashes, quick and sure
> As the deadly thought of men accomplishing
> Their curious fates in war, come, celebrate
> The faith of forty, ward of Cupido.
> Most venerable heart, the lustiest conceit
> Is not too lusty for your broadening.
> I quiz all sounds, all thoughts, all everything
> For the music and manner of the paladins
> To make oblation fit. Where shall I find
> Bravura adequate to this great hymn?

"Nowhere" is the evident answer, in this power too blustery, this *pathos* too self-realizing. In 1918, Stevens was uneasy with the Sublime, or uneasily aware that he had too natural a talent for the mode. *Le Monocle* makes its last movement back into limitation, into tropes of *ethos*, in stanzas X and XI, the poem's *askesis* or self-curtailment. With this limitation, Fate and character enter again together and lead to a contrast of the peculiarly perspectivizing metaphors that dominate a brief vision of resemblance:

> But, after all, I know a tree that bears
> A semblance to the thing I have in mind.
> It stands gigantic, with a certain tip
> To which all birds come sometime in their time.
> But when they go that tip still tips the tree. . . .

> ◇

> Anguishing hour!
> Last night, we sat beside a pool of pink,
> Clippered with lilies scudding the bright chromes,
> Keen to the point of starlight, while a frog
> Boomed from his very belly odious chords.

There is no sexual Eden, no timeless realm of magic trees and balmy boughs, with Miltonic enameled fruits. Resemblance is found first in the gigantic tree that provides a resting place for birds and has still its own dignity when standing alone. This hardly satisfies the desire for resemblances, giving only another emblem of solipsistic self-sufficiency, and one that borders on the grotesque by its phallic innuendo. Much finer is the pragmatic valorization of the affective reactions to sex rather than of sex itself. *Ethos* has become "the unconscionable treachery of fate," or the rhetoric of love, always in excess of or substituting for the *pathos* of love. Stevens' final attack, in this poem, upon his own rhetoricity is in the chromatic vision of last night's "anguishing hour," when the erotic dissolved not into the semblance of starlight but into pink pool, clippered lilies, and the boom of a frog's love song, passing upon all amorous diction the judgment of "odious chords."

So elegant a disgust is itself perspectivized by the poem's last stanza and best, perhaps the first of Stevens' really masterly transumptions. The now remote past is thrown out into the world of the dark rabbi, the present is resigned to the absences of fluttering, and the ongoing and what is to be are introjected as the vision of the rose rabbi:

> A blue pigeon it is, that circles the blue sky,
> On sidelong wing, around and round and round.
> A white pigeon it is, that flutters to the ground,
> Grown tired of flight. Like a dark rabbi, I
> Observed, when young, the nature of mankind,
> In lordly study. Every day, I found
> Man proved a gobbet in my mincing world.
> Like a rose rabbi, later, I pursued,
> And still pursue, the origin and course
> Of love, but until now I never knew
> That fluttering things have so distinct a shade.

The final accent is again a Lucretian or Paterian one, as the final accent always will be in Stevens. How ought we to define the noble *pathos* of this stanza? What Will-to-Power does Stevens intend over his own text? The blue and white pigeons are the same bird, the dark and rose rabbis the same poet, with the rose rabbi grown tired of flight. "Mincing" here means "affectedly refined." When the idea of man is no longer a chunk of raw meat, no longer a gobbet inedible for a dainty sensibility, it must be because an ordinary aesthete has become a truly Paterian aesthete, a poet perceiving clearly his own mortality. The end of love is beyond this quester's pursuit; its purpose is closed to his enquiry. As rose rabbi, or wounded scholar of love, he studies origin and course, and vows to go on with his study. What then is the opportune knowledge, the illusive "now" of his poem? Fluttering things, pigeons or passions, cast fluttering shadows yet possess distinct shades. A "shade" is only comparatively a darkness; something has come between oneself and the sun, but light still shines through. The color is obscure or darkened as the poem ends, and the trope is knowingly uncertain. Stevens has ended the best poem he has written up to his fortieth year with an *aporia*, or "uncertain notice," yet he *interprets* his own mental dilemma as being a distinctness and thus a kind of gain amidst the erotic loss.

I close this chapter by going ahead four years to consider *Harmonium*'s final invocation of the muse, *To the One of Fictive Music*. Stevens once allowed himself to say, of this invocation, that "after writing a poem, it is a good thing to walk round the block; after too much midnight, it is pleasant to hear the milkman, and yet, and this is the point of the poem, the imaginative world is the only real world, after all" (*L*, 251–52). As a comment, this is rather less ambivalent than the poem, which oddly though beautifully mixes a pre-Raphaelite phantasmagoria with a specifically American distrust of the hyperbole that European and British tradition had called the Imagination. The tone is the problematic here. Nothing else in *Harmonium*, or indeed elsewhere in Stevens, seems so dangerously sentimental or even cloying as does part of this diction. It is a sensible temptation that some of Stevens' commentators yield to when they wonder whether the poem is more ironic than it sounds. So, Joseph Riddel says that "it almost mocks the old tradition from which it derives," and Robert Pack reads it as mocking itself. Yet is this a rhetoric of mockery, however subtle?

Sister and mother and diviner love,
And of the sisterhood of the living dead
Most near, most clear, and of the clearest bloom,
And of the fragrant mothers the most dear
And queen, and of diviner love the day
And flame and summer and sweet fire, no thread
Of cloudy silver sprinkles in your gown
Its venom of renown, and on your head
No crown is simpler than the simple hair.

I think that the ancient distinction between ironies applies here; this is irony as a figure of thought and not as figure of speech. The muses are named strangely as "the sisterhood of the living dead," and the one of fictive music is named most strangely of all. What is it to be "of fictive music"? A. Walton Litz has made the fullest attempt at an answer:

The title has the form of an invocation, an address to the deity, and the phrase "fictive music" may recall the term *musica ficta* which was used by medieval theorists to describe accidentals that lie outside a harmonic system. The muse-goddess addressed in *To the One of Fictive Music* reigns over a universe of natural harmonies and artificial "accidentals," and the gist of the poem is that poetry must tremble between semblance and resemblance.

I think one can add to Litz that this muse-goddess is a kind of patroness of error and so is herself a kind of *clinamen* away from more traditional muses. She is nearest, clearest, and in flower, and is uncrowned and free of the venom of fame. But the internal rhyming of "gown," "venom of renown," and "crown" calls attention to what she is not, a daughter of memory. If she is of "the living dead," then she is indeed "of the fragrant mothers," as she was for Whitman. She is a *familial muse* and prophesies the startling epiphany, a quarter of a century later, of the imago of the poet's own mother in *The Auroras of Autumn:*

Farewell to an idea . . . The mother's face,
The purpose of the poem, fills the room.

Poets have domesticated the muse in their wives as in their mistresses; Stevens takes the Oedipal risk, as Keats and Whitman did, and invokes the muse as his actual mother and as the other women of his family. Am I overliteralizing his figurations? I think not, for the irony of thought somewhat concealed by his evasions is very much like the Whitmanian vision of Fate as the mother in *The Sleepers*. Stevens' poem is a speculation upon the transgressive origin of poetry and upon the transcendent purpose of the poem, which appears to be not separate from the origin:

> Now, of the music summoned by the birth
> That separates us from the wind and sea,
> Yet leaves us in them, until earth becomes,
> By being so much of the things we are,
> Gross effigy and simulacrum, none
> Gives motion to perfection more serene
> Than yours, out of our imperfections wrought,
> Must rare, or ever of more kindred air
> In the laborious weaving that you wear.

The birth itself here takes proper meaning rather than figurative, as birth our birth into consciousness, separating us from nature. Yet in this account, a residue of the human remains in nature. Nature, as "gross effigy and simulacrum," is an inadequate image of us, an unlike likeness or unreal semblance. The music summoned by birth is music in its etymological sense, an "art of the muses," and here it is wholly figurative, being the mother's "laborious weaving" of our mature selves "out of" (meaning "away from") our imperfections. These maternal "laborious weavings" contrast favorably to the fantasia of "the silken weavings of our afternoons" in *Sunday Morning*.

For Stevens, the art of the muses is his poetry and, however evasively, he is naming his own mother as the origin and purpose of his poetry. When Whitman gives us the fourfold of night, death, the sea, and the mother, we are not startled, but that is because Whitman's evasiveness lies elsewhere. Yet Stevens' evasiveness is somewhat less overt in the next stanza:

> For so retentive of themselves are men
> That music is intensest which proclaims
> The near, the clear, and vaunts the clearest bloom,

And of all vigils musing the obscure,
That apprehends the most which sees and names,
As in your name, an image that is sure,
Among the arrant spices of the sun,
O bough and bush and scented vine, in whom
We give ourselves our likest issuance.

Your name is the mother's name, the surest of images, and certainly "our likest issuance." To muse thus is anything but "musing the obscure," and it is inevitable that the poem's final stanza moves away from the maternal to a pre-Raphaelite other woman, a Paterian Mona Lisa–like image of otherness:

Yet not too like, yet not so like to be
Too near, too clear, saving a little to endow
Our feigning with the strange unlike, whence springs
The difference that heavenly pity brings.
For this, musician, in your girdle fixed
Bear other perfumes. On your pale head wear
A band entwining, set with fatal stones.
Unreal, give back to us what once you gave:
The imagination that we spurned and crave.

"Difference" is the crucial word, related to "strange, unlike," "other perfumes," "fatal stones," and, above all, "unreal." To "spurn" the imagination here paradoxically is to return to the mother; to "crave" the imagination is to substitute for the imago of the mother. "Imagination" has narrowed its meaning to the desperate belatedness it carries in the Rossetti–Pater context. Between the two images of the muse, mother and fatal woman, there is an *aporia*, a dilemma that cannot be resolved by the Stevens of *Harmonium.* The poetry of earth, in *Harmonium*, is a permanent achievement, but for Stevens himself it was an impasse.

3 *Harmonium*: Reduction
to the First Idea

Early in 1918, Stevens wrote his version of a "war poem,"
The Death of a Soldier:

> Life contracts and death is expected,
> As in a season of autumn.
> The soldier falls.
>
> He does not become a three-days personage,
> Imposing his separation,
> Calling for pomp.
>
> Death is absolute and without memorial,
> As in a season of autumn,
> When the wind stops,
>
> When the wind stops and, over the heavens,
> The clouds go, nevertheless,
> In their direction.

I think that readers deeply versed in Stevens recognize in this
poem, as in *The Snow Man*, written three years later, the
emergence of the poet's most characteristic voice. *The Death of a
Soldier* introduces Stevens the reductionist, though it does not
show us the goal of his reductiveness, the First Idea, which
enters his poetry with *The Snow Man*. Stevens later found a
term in Simone Weil for his process of reduction, the rather in-
appropriate term "decreation." His own *Mrs. Alfred Uruguay*, of
1940, a far more exuberant being than Simone Weil, splendidly
defines reductiveness as having "said no / To everything, in

order to get at myself. / I have wiped away moonlight like mud." When Stevens, in a letter, attempted an explanation of the First Idea, in regard to *Notes toward a Supreme Fiction*, he gave a wholly positive tone to his most reductive thinking: "If you take the varnish and dirt of generations off a picture, you see it in its first idea. If you think about the world without its varnish and dirt, you are a thinker of the first idea" (*L*, 426–27).

The only relevant philosophical notion would seem to be C. S. Peirce's Idea of Firstness. In a letter of 1944, Stevens said he long had been curious about Peirce but implied that other interests had kept him from reading the philosopher. Yet he may have seen some summary of Peirce, or quotation from Peirce, since the First Idea and the Idea of Firstness are so close. Stevens emphasizes a stripped-down idea of the sun, while Peirce cites a heliotrope as one instance of Firstness. Firstness is the chance variation or *clinamen* of any one felt quality in relation to any other, that is, an Idea of Firstness is a mere appearance, an "unanalyzed total impression made by any manifold not thought of as actual fact, but simply as a quality."

Whether or not Peirce contributed to Stevens' notion, the need to get down to a First Idea seems always to have inhered in Stevens' consciousness. He does not name the First Idea as such until he writes *Notes toward a Supreme Fiction* in 1942, but *Harmonium* contains the notion and process without the name. The root meaning of "first" is "forward" or "early," and the root meaning of "idea" is "to see." We might say that a First Idea always involves priority, "to see earliest," which makes it a necessity for a poet like Stevens, who could not tolerate any sensation of belatedness and who refused to acknowledge the influence of any precursors.

But what has the First Idea, or an idea of Firstness, to do with the poem *The Death of a Soldier?* Stevens seeks what is not possible, in a tradition that goes back to Homer yet never has gone beyond Homer. He seeks to see earliest what the death of a soldier is. His reduction is fourfold:

1) The soldier falls expectedly, in and by seasonal contraction; this is the primal *ethos*, the soldier's character as it is autumn's, and so a limitation of meaning.

2) The soldier is not and has no part in Christ; he will not rise, after three days, separated from the common fate and requiring celebration.

3) Any death, by synecdoche, is as final in itself and beyond language as is an autumnal moment of stasis.

4) That is, any death is also without consequence, in the context of natural sublimity; for us, below the heavens, there is stasis, but the movement of a larger intentionality always goes on above the heavens.

As paraphrase, this omits what matters about the poem, which is rhetorical gesture, tonal *askesis*, dignity of a minimal *pathos*, excluding lament. Yet what it most omits is the poem's undersong, which is its *logos* or crossing. Rhetorically, the poem intimates that any such earliest seeing of a soldier's death is dehumanizing, intolerable, not to be sustained. This brief poem is almost all *ethos*, all contraction; the human in us demands more of a poem, for us, and where *pathos* is so excluded a death-in-life comes which is more that of the poem's shaper, speaker, reader than it could have been of the fictive soldier before he fell.

This self-chastisement of the First Idea, by the First Idea itself, is worked out with startling dialectical skill in a triad of poems written in 1921, which seem to me to possess among them all the elements that were to emerge, in triumphant integration, two decades later in *Notes toward a Supreme Fiction*. The reader who masters the interrelationships of these three brief texts, *The Man Whose Pharynx Was Bad*, *The Snow Man*, and *Tea at the Palaz of Hoon*, has reached the center of Stevens' poetic and human anxieties and of his resources for meeting those anxieties. I will read the three poems as though they formed one larger, dialectical lyric when run together, akin to Coleridge's *Dejection: An Ode* and Wordsworth's *Intimations* ode. The *Pharynx* poem states the crisis of poetic vision; *The Snow Man* meets the crisis by a reduction to the First Idea; exuberantly, the great hymn of Hoon, so invariably misread as irony, reimagines the First Idea and restitutes, momentarily yet transumptively, the contraction of meaning provoked by the crisis. We can say, in the terms I have been developing, that the *Pharynx* poem is answered first by a poem of Fate and then

own capacity for solipsistic transport, and we can be grateful
that the lines have been restored to us:

> Perhaps, if summer ever came to rest
> And lengthened, deepened, comforted, caressed
> Through days like oceans in obsidian
>
> Horizons full of night's midsummer blaze.

Horizons like volcanic glass would be both black and shiny,
and the horizons epitomize the baffling attractions of this passage, with its Edenic days that are gorgeous nights, the oceanic
sense all but infinitely extended. From this Sublime of *pathos,*
Stevens characteristically recoils, in lines he felt no hazard in
retaining:

> Perhaps, if winter once could penetrate
> Through all its purples to the final slate,
> Persisting bleakly in an icy haze;
>
> One might in turn become less diffident.

Certainly he recalls the trope of *ethos* in stanza VI of *Le Monocle:* "The basic slate, the universal hue." As certainly, he thus
suggested to himself the very ecstasy of reduction, *The Snow
Man,* on which the critics of Stevens too frequently follow
Stevens by seeing the poem as a *celebration* of the Freudian reality principle. But here I want to urge a very comprehensive
reading indeed.

I've said that there may be a link between Peirce's Idea of
Firstness and Stevens' First Idea, but Peirce himself was in one
sense in Emerson's tradition, in his view of Fate. More profoundly, Stevens in this notion is the direct heir of several
traditions. One passes from Montaigne through Pascal to Descartes and ultimately leads to Valéry in our time. Another
embraces Emerson, Pater, and Nietzsche in the nineteenth century, as well as certain related figures, including Whitman and
Ruskin. A third, more specifically American, includes William
James, Santayana, and such Emersonian poets as E. A. Robinson and Frost. The fourth is not so much a tradition as it is one
titan without true precursors, Freud. All these strains have in

common the quest for a reality principle, a moral, aesthetic, and psychological reductiveness willing to risk the ruin brought about by the destruction of illusions, in oneself and in others, by knowing the worst truths about our condition. None of these strains falls into the reductive fallacy, which is to assume that the ultimate truth about us is, by definition, the very worst that can be said about us. Stevens frequently was tempted to that fallacy, and he fought against the temptation. To use the Emersonian terms, Fate in Stevens is the First Idea, Freedom is the realization that the First Idea cannot suffice, and Power or Will is a finding of what may suffice, a revision of the First Idea.

That is, of course, rather too much tradition to apply to *The Snow Man*, complex as this brief poem is. I will confine my account of the poem's anteriority to some inescapable precursors: Ruskin on what he called the pathetic fallacy; Emerson in *Nature* experiencing his notorious metamorphosis into a transparent eyeball; Whitman, at the close of *Song of Myself*, diffusing himself in air; Nietzsche, propounding the will; and lastly, but I think most crucially, Shelley, reinventing the Homeric–Miltonic figuration of the leaves in a form that was to haunt Stevens till the very end.

The voice speaking *The Snow Man*, which by the end of the poem has become the voice of the Snow Man, urgently seeks to avoid any indulgence of the pathetic fallacy. There is no evidence that Stevens knew Ruskin well, but he is rather likely to have known the most famous passage in *Modern Painters*. Here is a cento of Ruskin on the pathetic fallacy, from *Modern Painters*, III (1856), where he begins by saying the point in question is

the difference between the ordinary, proper, and true appearances of things to us; and the extraordinary, or false appearances, when we are under the influence of emotion, or contemplative fancy; false appearances, I say, as being entirely unconnected with any real power or character in the object, and only imputed to it by us. . . .

When Dante describes the spirits falling from the bank of Acheron "as dead leaves flutter from a bough," he gives the most perfect image possible of their utter lightness, feebleness, passiveness, and scattering agony of despair, without, however, for an instant losing his own clear perception that *these* are souls, and *those* are leaves; he makes no confusion of one with the other. But when Coleridge speaks of

> The one red leaf, the last of its clan,
> That dances as often as dance it can,

he has a morbid, that is to say, a so far false, idea about the leaf; he fancies a life in it, and will, which there are not; confuses its powerlessness with choice, its fading death with merriment, and the wind that shakes it with music.

The temperament which admits the pathetic fallacy, is . . . that of a mind and body in some sort too weak to deal fully with what is before them or upon them; borne away, or over-clouded, or over-dazzled by emotion; and it is a more or less noble state, according to the force of the emotion which has induced it. For it is no credit to a man that he is not morbid or inaccurate in his perceptions, when he has no strength of feeling to warp them; and it is in general a sign of higher capacity and stand in the ranks of being, that the emotions should be strong enough to vanquish, partly, the intellect, and make it believe what they choose. But it is still a grander condition when the intellect also rises, till it is strong enough to assert its rule against, or together with, the utmost efforts of the passions; and the whole man stands in an iron glow, white hot, perhaps, but still strong, and in no wise evaporating; even if he melts, losing none of his weight.

If one were to print just these Ruskinian extracts as a critique of *The Snow Man*, one would be rather closer to the poem than many of its exegetes have been, even though Ruskin's Snow Man is "the whole man" glowing with his own heat. Pragmatically, this difference makes little difference; both fictive "men" will melt, though only one will evaporate. But though the problematic is shared, Ruskin and Stevens do differ, complexly and subtly. Where is the emphasis in Ruskin? Is it on the *pathos*, or the untruth, in Romantic trope?

I recall having written, in another context, that Ruskin's analysis of the pathetic fallacy is an attack against Wordsworthian imagistic homogeneities, an attack implying that such homogeneities were the product of a Romantic further estrange-

ment of the object-world, and so of a dualism more extreme
even than the Cartesian vision that Romanticism supposedly
wished to overturn. I am more inclined to this judgment than
before. When Wordsworth and Coleridge speak of a joy in
seeing the beauty of nature, they rejoice in their own reductions to a First Idea, their own initial substitutions of the tropes
and topics of *ethos* for those of *pathos*. When they go on to further substitutions and arrive at figurations of *pathos*, then they
arouse in their ephebe, Ruskin, an acutely ambivalent response.
He distrusts both their mode of limitation and their mode of
representation, yet he knows that such modes are inevitable for
"reflective" poetry, his word for a consciously belated poetry,
for a heightened rhetoricity.

Though he was to lose this balance later, the Ruskin of *Modern Painters*, III, is persuasively and sanely judicious in his view
of the Romantic trope or pathetic fallacy as a necessary lie
against nature and so also against time. Whereas the classical
and medieval poets and painters, according to Ruskin, expressed the actual qualities of the thing itself, the Renaissance
and modern artists first made the thing itself into an imagined
thing and then reimagined that already altered object. Stevens,
in *The Snow Man*, is less judicious than Ruskin, or perhaps
ironically he is willing to *appear* less judicious. He knows, as
Ruskin does, that no modern can write a poem without tropes
of *pathos* dominating, yet he writes a poem that *seems* to exclude
pathos or at least announces as its manifesto the intention of
such an exclusion:

> One must have a mind of winter
> To regard the frost and the boughs
> Of the pine-trees crusted with snow;
>
> And have been cold a long time
> To behold the junipers shagged with ice,
> The spruces rough in the distant glitter
>
> Of the January sun; and not to think
> Of any misery in the sound of the wind,
> In the sound of a few leaves,

Which is the sound of the land
Full of the same wind
That is blowing in the same bare place

For the listener, who listens in the snow,
And, nothing himself, beholds
Nothing that is not there and the nothing that is.

Is there a difference, for Stevens, between regarding and beholding, or is this merely an elegant variation? How would the poem change if it ended saying that "the listener . . . nothing himself, regards / Nothing that is not there and the nothing that is"? In the immensely moving *Nomad Exquisite,* my personal favorite in *Harmonium,* the hymn-maker is a beholder beholding rather than a regarder regarding. I think that the difference is very much there, in Stevens, and that, as almost always, he is an orator with accurate speech. To "behold" is to gaze at or look upon, but with a touch of expressed amazement. The beholder *possesses* the object; his scrutiny is active, going back to the root *kel,* meaning to drive or to set in swift motion. To "regard" is a warier and more passive verb. It is to look at something attentively or closely, but with a touch of looking back at, a retrospect, stemming ultimately from the root *wer,* meaning to watch out for something. *The Snow Man* starts with a wary "regard" that is replete with negative intentionality, prophesying such characteristic later Stevensian instances as those in *Dry Loaf,* in *Credences of Summer,* IX, most memorably in the *Auroras* where the father sits in space "of bleak regard," and in *The Rock* where the poet must "regard the freedom of seventy years ago" and finds, "It is no longer air." When *The Snow Man* closes, with the hint of an amazement of possession in "beholds," we encounter one of Stevens' most persistent, even obsessive verbs. From a wealth of instances, we might choose Crispin the Comedian who, when he beheld, "was made new," or the vision of the singing girl at Key West, "as we beheld her striding there alone," or the beholding of the Sublime in *The American Sublime,* or most movingly the grand *pathos* of the final lines of *Extracts from Addresses to the Academy of Fine Ideas:*

> Behold the men in helmets borne on steel,
> Discolored, how they are going to defeat.

I venture the formula that, in Stevens, "regard" tends to introduce a trope of *ethos* or of Fate, or of a reduction to the First Idea, while "behold" tends to commence a trope of *pathos* or of Power, a revision or reimagining of the First Idea. When Stevens "regards," he indeed guards again and guards against, and here at the opening of *The Snow Man* it is against the major Romantic fiction of the leaves, which is not the Coleridgean passage from *Christabel* quoted by Ruskin but is of course this:

> Thou, from whose unseen presence the leaves dead
> Are driven, like ghosts from an enchanter fleeing,
>
> Yellow, and black, and pale, and hectic red,
> Pestilence-stricken multitudes.

Nothing could be more unlike Stevens, in tone, burden, and spirit, and yet no poem haunts his poetry more. I will return to Shelley's poem often again, in discussing the conclusion of *Like Decorations in a Nigger Cemetery*, section xxviii of *The Man with the Blue Guitar*, *The Motive for Metaphor*, *Notes toward a Supreme Fiction*, *The Auroras of Autumn*, *An Ordinary Evening in New Haven*, *The Rock*, and *The Course of a Particular*—in short, major Stevens. *Sombre Figuration* (*OP*, 66–71), a section of *Owl's Clover*, sums up this central fiction in Stevens, both by its title and by some highly revelatory lines:

> The man below beholds the portent poised,
> An image of his making, beyond the eye,
> Poised, but poised as a mind through which a storm
> Of other images blows, images of time
> Like the time of the portent, images like leaves,
> Except that this is an image of black spring
> And those the leaves of autumn-afterwards,
> Leaves of the autumns in which the man below
> Lived as the man lives now, and hated, loved,
> As the man hates now, loves now, the self-same things.
> The year's dim elongations stretch below
> To rumpled rock, its bright projections lie

The shallowest iris on the emptiest eye.
The future must bear within it every past,
Not least the pasts destroyed, magniloquent
Syllables.

Certainly *The Snow Man* would destroy all the poet's fictions
of the leaves, fictions which culminate in Shelley's *Ode to the
West Wind,* and yet Stevens' poem bears within it Shelley's
transumption of the past. The fiction of the leaves begins with
Homer, in Book Six of the *Iliad,* when Diomedes and Glaukos
come together bent on battle in the space between the two ar-
mies. Diomedes asks Glaukos his ancestry, lest he make the
mistake of fighting a god. Glaukos begins his reply with the
magnificent simile that compares the generation of leaves with
that of humanity: "The wind scatters the leaves on the ground,
but the live timber / burgeons with leaves again in the season of
spring returning. / So one generation of men will grow while
another / dies." In the *Aeneid,* Virgil recalls this simile, trans-
posing it to the crowds of the newly dead, waiting for Charon
to take them across the river. Dante, developing Virgil, relates
the image to the Fall of Man. Milton, gathering all these
together, and overgoing them, applies the image to the fallen
host of Satan, before they are rallied by their leader. All four of
these poets are in Ruskin's "creative" grouping, rather than in
the post-Wordsworthian "reflective" order (including Shelley)
who rely upon the pathetic fallacy or, as I would say now,
upon the substitution of a trope of *pathos* for one of *ethos,* so as
to internalize the fiction of the leaves. For Shelley, there is an
apocalyptic misery in the sound of the wind and in the fall of
the leaves, and in his trope life is being imputed to the stricken
object-world.

I am ready at last to attempt a close reading of *The Snow Man,*
reserving the poem's relation to Emerson, Whitman, and
Nietzsche for its closing trope, where that relation is most illuminating. *The Snow Man* begins with the impersonal "one," but
before the single sentence that constitutes the poem has finished
bending back upon itself that "one" will have become "the listener," who is also the man of the title. I have remarked already
on the Stevensian use of "regard," which is the poem's opening

mode of perception, where I suggest "regard" can be translated as a retrospective *aftering* or a finding of retroactive meaningfulness, on Freud's model of belatedness in his *Nachträglichkeit*. Protectively impersonal, as though holding oneself at arm's length, one appeals to the *ethos* of Fate, to the necessity of having a mind of winter, in order to avoid indulgence in the fallacy of imputing human "misery" to the wind and the leaves. What does it mean, though, to "have a mind of winter," and how does such a having differ from having "been cold a long time"? The mind of winter *regards* pine-trees *crusted* with snow; one who has been cold a long time *beholds* junipers *shagged* with ice. There is a slight touch of figuration in the crusting, and a rather larger figuration in the shagging. "Crusted" need not refer to bread-making, having a proper meaning as any hard, crisp covering, but "shagged" means to be tangled as with rough hair or perhaps rough cloth. "Regarding" as a retrospective, negating Stevensian term for perception leads to at most an ironic figuration, and so is appropriate for the *mind* of winter rather than the emotions of winter. But "beholding" with its more positive edge of astonishment or discovery leads to an image bordering on a *pathos*, and so is more appropriate for the affective, indeed almost temperamental, condition of having been cold a long time. The trope is faint but there, just as a figuration is hinted again by "The spruces *rough* in the distant glitter / Of the January sun."

It is not simple to locate the rhetorical disjunctions I have been calling "crossings" in a poem that knots itself into one intricate sentence. But I think the crucial crossing in *The Snow Man* comes between lines 9 and 10, where "the sound of a few leaves" acquires the deeper tonality of being identified with "the sound of the land," since each is equal to the same thing, the wind's sound. We are not hearing a Shelleyan or Ruskinian plenitude of music in the wind; more New Englandly, we are hearing a few dead leaves being blown about as we stand in the snow, in a bare place.

I suggest now that we can identify that "bare place" as precisely as we have identified the wind and the leaves. Here is what can be called, without hyperbole, the central passage in

American literature, since it is the crucial epiphany of our literature's Central Man, Emerson. The text is the Sublime and grotesque triumph, uneasily melded into one, from *Nature*, I:

> Crossing a bare common, in snow puddles, at twilight, under a clouded sky, without having in my thoughts any occurrence of special good fortune, I have enjoyed a perfect exhilaration. I am glad to the brink of fear. . . . There I feel that nothing can befall me in life,—no disgrace, no calamity (leaving me my eyes), which nature cannot repair. Standing on the bare ground,—my head bathed by the blithe air, and uplifted into infinite space,—all mean egotism vanishes. I become a transparent eyeball; I am nothing; I see all.

Emerson will go on to say that "nature always wears the colors of the spirit," so that for him the pathetic fallacy is no fallacy but is *potentia*, or *pathos* as Power, the Will rampant. Stevens is a very involuntary Emersonian here or later, but the intertextual crossing between his poem and Emerson's rhapsody is unmistakable. Emerson's "bare common, in snow puddles" is Stevens' "bare place." The Snow Man is "nothing himself"; Emerson says, "I am nothing." The Snow Man "beholds / Nothing that is not there and the nothing that is"; Emerson says, "I see all" and earlier had said that nothing could happen to him that nature could not repair, with the single proviso of his eyes. Stevens would have protested that as Snow Man he was stripped of delusions ("nothing that is not there") and of illusions ("the nothing that is") whereas Emerson was obsessed with Transcendental delusions and illusions. To which Emerson might reply by falling back into that Sublime emptiness or great American repression, the "transparent eyeball" which certainly qualifies as a "nothing that is not there and the nothing that is." Nietzsche, in the most celebrated aphorism of *On the Genealogy of Morals*, had judged that man would prefer the void as purpose or "the nothing that is" rather than be void of purpose. His remark is closer to Emerson's supposed idealism than to Stevens' only apparent surrender to the reality principle.

How are we to interpret *The Snow Man?* I want to juxtapose to the poem Whitman, at the close of *Song of Myself*, and

Nietzsche in *The Birth of Tragedy*. Whitman, in section 52, the concluding passage in *Song of Myself*, reduces not to a Snow Man but to a man of air and of grass. Effusing his flesh in eddies, drifting it in lacy jags, he bequeaths himself to the dirt. He too could say he is nothing himself, but he prefers to be more enigmatic: "You will hardly know who I am or what I mean." Is he still celebrating himself when he diffuses into the atmosphere and into the earth? "Yes," ought to be our wary response, because his reduction is, as he said in section 51, a concentration: "I concentrate toward them that are nigh, I wait on the door-slab." Whitman may have reduced to a First Idea, but he remains Whitman: "I stop somewhere waiting for you." Is the Snow Man, in any sense, waiting for his reader?

I return to the distinction between "regard" and "behold." As the Snow Man listens to the wind, a wind in which he hears no fictions, of misery or of music, he beholds as a nihilist beholds. Only those who do not know Emerson well, in his last phase, would be surprised at how close this is to the Emerson of 1866: "For every seeing soul there are two absorbing facts,—*I and the Abyss.*" What, we can ask about Stevens' seeing soul, can one behold in the "nothing that is"? How can the beholder possess "nothing," in a positive sense of seeing-with-amazement? Or, most simply, how can a "nothing that is" be a trope of *pathos*, a fiction of Power, a variation upon or reimagining, however slight, of the First Idea?

J. Hillis Miller appears to read "nothing that is" more as a trope of *ethos*, by equating this "nothing" with "being," in the sense that "being is a pervasive power, visible nowhere in itself and yet present and visible in all things. It is what things share through the fact that they are. Being is not a thing like other things and therefore can only appear to man as nothing, but it is what all things must participate in if they are to exist at all." This reading seems to me persuasive for elsewhere in Stevens, particularly later Stevens, but not quite so much for *The Snow Man*, where I read the final "nothing" as a passion for transumption, as a trope-undoing trope, rather than as a trope for "being." To behold the "nothing that is" is also "to behold the junipers *shagged* with ice," so that "nothing" is rather a tangled and mangled nothing. "Being" in Stevens can live with the First Idea, but at the price of ceasing to be a "human" being. The listener, reduced to nothing, remains human because he beholds something shagged and rough, barely figurative, yet still a figuration rather than a bareness. This "nothing" is the most minimal or abstracted of fictions, and yet still it is a fiction.

I juxtapose, at the last, Nietzsche, in *The Birth of Tragedy,* saying that the self must be made divine because the human being stands now empty in the wreck of all past times. But, before this god-making takes place in the self, the last mythologies must be stripped from the human. This appears to be the purpose of the reduction in *The Snow Man.* The poem does not go on to intimate the return of the divinity to man; that takes place in its gorgeous counterpoem, *Tea at the Palaz of Hoon.* The Snow Man is not yet Hoon, but he is going to be, and that *potentia* is felt in the *pathos* of his poem's closing trope. The worst reading possible then of this poem, I suggest, is the canonical one we received from Stevens himself, when he said in a letter: "I shall explain *The Snow Man* as an example of the necessity of identifying oneself with reality in order to understand it and enjoy it" (*L,* 464). That takes care of less than half the poem, the part in which "reality" is "regarded," and not the larger part in which "reality" is "beheld" and so begins to become a passion.

Replying to the apt suggestion of Norman Holmes Pearson that Hoon was Hoon, Stevens made one of his most stimulating remarks about a poem of his own: "You are right in saying that Hoon is Hoon although it could be that he is the son of old man Hoon. He sounds like a Dutchman. I think the word is probably an automatic cipher for 'the loneliest air,' that is to say, the expanse of sky and space" (*L,* 871). I think that Hoon is a composite of Stevens and Whitman, with an edge of Pater, all three of them "Dutchmen" in their ancestry and all of them Epicurean–Lucretian in their ultimate metaphysics. The poem should be regarded as the synthesis or third term of the triad, of which *The Man Whose Pharynx Was Bad* and *The Snow Man* are thesis and antithesis. Let us call *Pharynx* a large, composite trope of *ethos,* *The Snow Man* such a trope of *logos* or "crossing,"

and *Hoon* the most beautiful, so far, of Stevens' exaltations of
the will or of *pathos* conceived as Emersonian Power.

As with the two antecedent poems, *Hoon* is spoken as a little
dramatic monologue, or rather as an apostrophe, which is what
most dramatic monologues after Browning and Tennyson are
anyway. An apostrophe originally was directed to the dead but
swerved into an address to the absent. *Tea at the Palaz of Hoon* is
directed against what is absent in the reader, which is the imagination or a felt potential of the reader's own power of representation. The reader is all but present, in the crossing between
The Snow Man and this poem, for in that intervenient space the
reader, or the skeptic-in-Stevens, has said something like this to
Hoon: "Descending into the ocean, through the loneliest air, as
a purple sunset, you have ceased to be yourself."

To this, the expanse of sky and space, the spirit that we seek,
grandly replies:

> Not less because in purple I descended
> The western day through what you called
> The loneliest air, not less was I myself.
>
> What was the ointment sprinkled on my beard?
> What were the hymns that buzzed beside my ears?
> What was the sea whose tide swept through me there?
>
> Out of my mind the golden ointment rained,
> And my ears made the blowing hymns they heard.
> I was myself the compass of that sea:
>
> I was the world in which I walked, and what I saw
> Or heard or felt came not but from myself;
> And there I found myself more truly and more strange.

Let us commence with the Sublime title. The palaz of Hoon
is sky and space seen as a gaudy and ornate dwelling; to have
tea at the palaz is to watch the twilight while conversing with
the setting sun, who is hardly lonely since all the air is his and
since all directions are at home in him. He is himself when
most imperial, in purple and gold, and his setting is a corona-

tion. To the Idiot Questioner who grants the coronation but stints on the ceremonial, he makes a doubly crushing reply. The ointment, hymns, and sea are not external to him; and because he, Hoon, is the center and origin, he is unstinting in his own investiture. The golden ointment rained, not sprinkled, on his beard, as it came out of his mind. The hymns blew like trumpets, not buzzed, for his ears both made and heard such music. If the tide swept through Hoon, it did not encompass him. Seeing, hearing, and feeling find objects only from his own self, and nothing through which he moves is outside him. And yet, as his triumphant final line makes clear, he is *not* a solipsist, because the "there" of his world is an arena in which he is at work finding himself, more truly the more he expands, and more strange, probably because Pater, one of his high priests, had defined the Romantic imagination as adding strangeness to beauty. The formula "I was the world in which I walked" thirteen years later would become the germ of *The Idea of Order at Key West.* But Hoon was to have other progeny, since I would judge that he appears again in 1935 as the Walt Whitman in section 1 of *Like Decorations,* and in his own name and right again, later in 1935, in *Sad Strains of a Gay Waltz,* and finally as the insouciant *Well Dressed Man with a Beard* in 1941. Why link him to Whitman? Compare to Hoon's appearances, and to Whitman's in Stevens, the start of section 25 in *Song of Myself.* Whitman has challenged nature, it taunts him, and he rises triumphantly to the challenge:

> Dazzling and tremendous how quick the sun-rise would kill
> me,
> If I could not now and always send sun-rise out of me.

> We also ascend dazzling and tremendous as the sun,
> We found our own O my soul in the calm and cool of the day-
> break.

> My voice goes after what my eyes cannot reach,
> With the twirl of my tongue I encompass worlds and volumes
> of worlds.

Speech is the twin of my vision, it is unequal to measure itself,
It provokes me forever, it says sarcastically,
Walt you contain enough, why don't you let it out then?

Come now I will not be tantalized, you conceive too much of
  articulation,
Do you not know O speech how the buds beneath you are
  folded?
Waiting in gloom, protected by frost,
The dirt receding before my prophetical screams,
I underlying causes to balance them at last,
My knowledge my live parts, it keeping tally with the meaning
  of all things.

We can compare Whitman and his vision with Hoon, and
speech or the skeptic with Hoon's Idiot Questioner. Whitman,
like Hoon, both contains everything else and is an idea of the
sun, not as a god but as a god might be. Hoon is himself the
compass of the sea whose tides sweep through him; Walt en-
compasses worlds but himself is not to be encompassed. The
line in which the two are closest is "My knowledge my live
parts, it keeping tally with the meaning of all things." It ought
not to surprise us then that Whitman is both the sun and the
world in which he walks, in the sublime opening of *Like Decorations:*

In the far South the sun of autumn is passing
Like Walt Whitman walking along a ruddy shore.
He is singing and chanting the things that are part of him,
The worlds that were and will be, death and day.
Nothing is final, he chants. No man shall see the end.
His beard is of fire and his staff is a leaping flame.

Walt, Hoon, and the girl at Key West stride against a sea-
scape, singing and chanting the things that are part of them,
their knowledge their live parts, and what they know keeping
tally with the meaning of all things. But this glory, constant in
Emerson, wavered in Stevens even as it did in Whitman. After
fourteen years, the Hoon of *Sad Strains of a Gay Waltz* was more
than a little chastened:

And then
There's that mountain-minded Hoon,
For whom desire was never that of the waltz,

Who found all form and order in solitude,
For whom the shapes were never the figures of men.
Now, for him, his forms have vanished.

There is order in neither sea nor sun.
The shapes have lost their glistening.

It is Stevens' own illumination of *Tea at the Palaz of Hoon,* reminding us that Hoon's solitude was not solipsism but also that the spirit withers, however gloriously, in the air of solitude. Hoon was too large a reimagining of the First Idea, and Stevens could not sustain, in *Harmonium* or in *Ideas of Order,* so belatedly High Romantic a vision. But it is important to see what criticism has mostly evaded seeing. Of the two contrary answers to *The Man Whose Pharynx Was Bad,* Stevens' later poetry finally relies more upon Hoon's chant than upon the Snow Man's reductive regardings and somewhat less reductive beholdings.

4 *Harmonium:* Crisis and the *Comedian*

When Stevens first became a strong poet, with *Sunday Morning* in 1915, he was thirty-six years old. We might regard this as an astonishingly late entrance, were it not that Whitman was also thirty-six when in 1855 he wrote the first versions of *Song of Myself* and *The Sleepers*. Emerson was thirty-three when he wrote *Nature*. Dickinson's great years begin with 1859–60, when she was turning thirty. Frost, who seems to me Stevens' true twentieth-century rival, rather than Eliot, Pound, or Williams, was thirty-nine when he wrote most of the strong poems in *North of Boston* (1914), his first important book. The Native Strain or Emersonian tradition is not an affair of adolescent genius or even of youth, and so too much cannot be surmised from the nearly fifteen years that separate Stevens' undergraduate poems from *Sunday Morning*. It is rather the silence that came upon Stevens from 1924 to 1930 that is significant and almost unique and that demands the surmise it scarcely has received. The poet of *Harmonium* came to an end with the very fatigued and, to me, very poor though popular poem, *Sea Surface Full of Clouds*, in 1924. The poet of *Ideas of Order*, though he had written *Academic Discourse at Havana* in 1923, got started again with *The Sun This March* in 1930. What ended the poetry of a man of forty-five, who had done magnificent work, and what began it again with a new glory when he was fifty-one?

Only the first question is my concern in this chapter, since the second belongs to a consideration of *Ideas of Order*. But the juxtaposition of the lines that trail off in 1924, and that inaugurate Stevens again in 1930, is a revealing one:

The sovereign clouds came clustering. The conch
Of loyal conjuration trumped. The wind
Of green blooms turning crisped the motley hue

To clearing opalescence. Then the sea
And heaven rolled as one and from the two
Came fresh transfigurings of freshest blue.

⋄   ⋄   ⋄

The exceeding brightness of this early sun
Makes me conceive how dark I have become,

And re-illumines things that used to turn
To gold in broadest blue, and be a part

Of a turning spirit in an earlier self.

The finicky language of *Sea Surface Full of Clouds* recalls the
self-satirizing diction of *The Comedian as the Letter C,* while *The
Sun This March* prophesies the metaphysical pathos of *The Idea of
Order at Key West.* But the first passage in the juxtaposition also
satirizes the Shelley of *Ode to the West Wind,* and the Whitman
of *As I Ebb'd with the Ocean of Life,* and as always in Stevens such
grand victims make the later poet very uneasy. The verbs carry
the contrast between 1924 and 1930; from "trumped" and
"crisped" to "conceive" and "re-illumines" is a transition from a
mockery that knowingly mocks also the mocker to a painful
searching out of the grounds for a reimagining. Even the difference between the two uses of "turning" is directly instructive. The first leads to a clearing that is an opalescence, the
milky iridescence of a gem, and so this troping merely colors.
The second is a troping of the spirit, a nostalgia for an earlier,
fresher, and presumably better self. The first passage heightens
rhetoricity for its own sake; the second seeks to heighten consciousness while maintaining a more controlled rhetoric that insists less upon its own status as rhetoric. Here, in little, is a
portrayal of the crisis that led to Stevens' silence and a hint of
the resolution of the crisis.

The poetic crisis dramatized in 1921 by the triad of bad
pharynx, Snow Man, and Hoon becomes an allegorical narra-

tive in 1922, in Stevens' first long poem, *The Comedian as the Letter C*, which can be read either as the crown or as the exasperation of *Harmonium*. The *Comedian*, by no accident, is in its form the least original and the least American major poem in *Harmonium*, though it is in every other respect a very American poem. Its place in literary history is, in one sense, very clear, because it is the satyr-poem or parody that culminates and almost undoes the tradition of the High Romantic quest-poem. Its precursor poem, most nearly, is Shelley's *Alastor*, and not, as so many critics have said, Wordsworth's *Prelude*. Wordsworth, as always, was Shelley's precursor for *Alastor*, but in *The Excursion*, particularly with the Solitary as he is presented in the opening books of that giant catastrophe of a poem. Behind the Solitary is the *Penseroso* of Milton, but Wordsworth alters the tradition permanently, making the quest a voyage through self-consciousness in search of a capable imagination, purged of the despair of self. Stevens speaks in the summer of 1899 of reading Keats's *Endymion*, which is a rival poem to *Alastor* as a corrective of Wordsworth's Solitary, but *Endymion*'s more humane and gregarious notion of quest is less the starting point for Stevens than the remorseless Poet of *Alastor*, who can tolerate neither nature nor other selves and who voyages until he dies, a victim of his own visionary intensity.

The tradition from Shelley on passes through the whole course of nineteenth-century verse, and has its last strong descendants in Yeats's *Wanderings of Oisin* and *Shadowy Waters*. A juxtaposition of *Oisin* and the *Comedian* can be unnerving, the more so because I agree with Helen Vendler, as against most Stevens critics, that the *Comedian* is by no means primarily a comic poem. It is funny in places, it is bitter almost everywhere, frequently to the point of rancidity, and yet it shares fully in the obsessive quest that it only ostensibly mocks. That so outrageous a poem, the most outrageous in modern poetry, should be an authentic crisis-poem is surprising, but Stevens seems to have intended it as his farewell to poetry. It almost did end him as a poet, and though he went on writing throughout the next year, 1923, he went on with a self-inflicted wound, which effectively silenced him from 1924 to 1930.

No one can discuss the *Comedian* without an opening wonderment at its language, which carries rhetoricity or word-consciousness to a pitch where many readers cannot tolerate it and where no reader can be comfortable for long. There is a perceptive general comment by Frank Kermode: "This is in every sense a fantastic performance: it is a narrative of obscurely allegorical intent, harsh and dream-like; and its manner is a sustained nightmare of unexpected diction, so that one sometimes thinks of it less as a poem than as a remarkable physical feat."

Kermode here can remind one of a review of Whitman by the young Henry James, where our national Bard's *Drum-Taps* is dismissed as "the effort of an essentially prosaic mind to lift itself, by a prolonged muscular strain, into poetry." James later repented of this early judgment, but Kermode's jest doesn't call for revision. The *Comedian* is a kind of remarkable physical accomplishment, and no brief description of it could surpass "a sustained nightmare of unexpected diction." Another excellent description, Helen Vendler's, follows Blackmur in emphasizing "that no matter how slyly and briskly the poem moves, its subject is serious and skirts the tragic, and that in spite of its mock-heroic mode the poem conveys some sort of heroism." Stevens himself was unhelpful on the *Comedian*; his own comments on the poem play obsessively on the sounds of the letter C, which he says we are to hear in the background all through the poem. Even less helpful was Stevens' act of canonizing the interpretation of the poem by Hi Simons, which is essentially an idealizing of the modern at the expense of Romanticism and which the poem cannot sustain.

Stevens' Comedian, as scholarship has shown, is an amalgam of the Crispin of seventeenth- and eighteenth-century French burlesque drama with Candide, and also with the Crispinus of Ben Jonson's *Poetaster*. This is Stevens' starting joke; to cast the mocking valet of tradition as the hero of the symbolic Shelleyan–Yeatsian voyage and to turn the joke against himself, with considerable bitterness, by seeing this voyage as the odyssey of his own soul. Since the figure of Crispinus goes back to the legendary butt who dared to challenge Horace to a fast-writing contest, a self-identification with the figure courts, quite deliberately, a poetic suicide. And Stevens' Comedian, as we ought not to forget, is a dead man, for whom the entire poem serves as a frankly dubious elegy.

What the reader encounters in this poem might be described as a wilderness of differences. There are not many texts as overtly heterogeneous as this. What Stevens called an "anti-mythological poem" (L, 778) is so obsessed by myths that its incessant allusiveness becomes a burden. Yet Stevens so tropes against tradition that there are very few demonstrable allusions, as A. Walton Litz observes. What I myself have attempted to show as being a covert element in all strong post-Enlightenment poems is in the *Comedian* the overt and central problem. This is a poem "about" the anxiety of influence, which means that it is a poem about those writers who induced such anxiety, however repressed, in Stevens. These writers are the central figures in the British and American Romantic tradition; they are not the French Symbolists or the fashionable modernists contemporary with Stevens. The crucial one among them is Whitman, who remains, on the surface, an apparent antithesis to Stevens.

The *Comedian* is, conveniently, a poem in six parts, and it maps rather closely to the post-Wordsworthian crisis-poem model, which need surprise no one. Part I, *The World without Imagination*, is aptly titled, as its topics and tropes fall under *ethos* or Fate. The central irony is an epitome of the poem, which is that the Romantic Imagination cannot voyage unchanged to America, since any poet-quester is dwarfed by the Atlantic. Shelley and Keats are not possible in the New World, and so what will be the fate of their ephebe, Crispin? The starting point is the Cartesian dualism of any Romantic origin: man is the ghost in the world's machine but this eminence makes him only a Socrates of snails. A cruel rhetorical question sets the topic of contraries for Part I: "is this same wig / Of things, this nincompated pedagogue, / Preceptor to the sea?" Crispin is hardly the intelligence of his ocean, and we need to ask, whose ocean is this anyway? As always, in Stevens, the ocean, like death, night, and the mother, belongs to Whitman, the Whitman of *The Sleepers* and the *Sea-Drift* pieces, just as the reference to the nineteenth century as "that century of wind in a single puff" acknowledges Shelley and looks forward to *The Course of a Particular* nearly thirty years later, where the cry of the leaves is said to be not "the smoke-drift of puffed-out heroes." The Romantic mythology of self still counts, though irreparably blemished, "blotched out beyond unblotching." As poor Crispin peers into the mirror of the sea, a word rises up out of the sea, as it did for Whitman, and it appears to be the same word, death:

> What word split up in clickering syllables
> And storming under multitudinous tones
> Was name for this short-shanks in all that brunt?
> Crispin was washed away by magnitude.
> The whole of life that still remained in him
> Dwindled to one sound strumming in his ear,
> Ubiquitous concussion, slap and sigh,
> Polyphony beyond his baton's thrust.

The sea sings beyond Crispin's genius, and yet the genius of the sea, Triton, suffers now from belatedness, "the old age of a watery realist." Triton is a verbose remnant,

> nothing left of him
> Except in faint, memorial gesturings,
> That were like arms and shoulders in the waves.

One remembers Whitman's *Out of the Cradle Endlessly Rocking,* once called *A Word Out of the Sea,* with its similar vision of "the white arms out in the breakers tirelessly tossing." Confronted by the sea, which Whitman said made him a poet, Crispin accepts a reduction to a First Idea, the cost of being an American poet, or the Fate of a Snow Man:

> The salt hung on his spirit like a frost,
> The dead brine melted in him like a dew
> Of winter, until nothing of himself
> Remained, except some starker, barer self
> In a starker, barer world, in which the sun
> Was not the sun because it never shone
> With bland complaisance on pale parasols,
> Beetled, in chapels, on the chaste bouquets.
> Against his pipping sounds a trumpet cried

> Celestial sneering boisterously. Crispin
> Became an introspective voyager.

This is the sun of the American Sublime, beating down directly against the self, and the celestial trumpet sneering boisterously in outcry against Crispin's pippings is probably Whitman's transformation of Shelley's "trumpet of a prophecy." "Just as much whence we come that blare of the cloud-trumpets," Whitman cries out close to the end of *As I Ebb'd with the Ocean of Life*. Against so powerful a nature, Emersonian rather than Wordsworthian, Crispin takes the path of Emerson, introspective voyaging to those "ever-satisfying and ever-unsurveyable seas and shores," the shores of America that Whitman credited Emerson with having found. Crispin becomes the veritable Emersonian self confronting the Not-Me:

>   free
> From the unavoidable shadow of himself
> That lay elsewhere around him. Severance
> Was clear. The last distortion of romance
> Forsook the insatiable egotist. The sea
> Severs not only lands but also selves.
> Here was no help before reality.
> Crispin beheld and Crispin was made new.

The poet-quester of *Alastor* could not get free of his *daimon*, "the unavoidable shadow of himself" or his *Alastor*. But severance is clear. The Atlantic severs the American Romantic Selfhood from its British precursor, and internalized romance becomes only internalization or insatiable egotism. The estranging sea here again is less Arnold's than it is the sea between birth and death in *As I Ebb'd*. The American reality is sea and sky, the immensity of space, and like Emerson and Whitman, Crispin beheld and became that new man, the American. Something of Stevens' defensive irony breaks down as Part 1 ends with at least a semi-exaltation of the strange fate of being an American poet:

> The imagination, here, could not evade,
> In poems of plums, the strict austerity
> Of one vast, subjugating, final tone.

> The drenching of stale lives no more fell down.
> What was this gaudy, gusty panoply?
> Out of what swift destruction did it spring?
> It was caparison of wind and cloud
> And something given to make whole among
> The ruses that were shattered by the large.

"Here" is America, the land of the First Idea, "the World without Imagination." The "final tone" goes beyond Shelley's "deep, autumnal tone," the *Ode to the West Wind* alluded to throughout these lines. The American theatre of the Sublime features not only nature as creator and destroyer but also a saving difference, "something given to make whole" among the tropes or ruses that are shattered by reality, the sea or "the large." That "something given," a fresh part that can become the whole, is the crossing that takes us to the American *pathos* or Power of Part II, *Concerning the Thunderstorms of Yucatan.* Can we surmise this "something given" as the word out of the sea, "the low and delicious word death"?

We find Crispin, at the start of Part II, in Yucatan, which is not yet a place but a state of mind, an American pre-Raphaelitism or the poetic mode dominant when Stevens was a Harvard undergraduate. "The Maya sonneteers" may include such Harvard poets as Trumbull Stickney, George Cabot Lodge, and even Santayana, who despite the exotic American reality "still to the night-bird made their plea," following Milton and Keats while evading barbarous raspberry tanagers in Stevens' favorite trees. But Crispin–Stevens was more in the Emersonian–Whitmanian Native Strain, "too destitute to find / In any commonplace the sought-for aid." As Emerson said in *Experience,* inventing the characteristic Stevensian usage of "poverty": "We must hold hard to this poverty, however scandalous, and by more vigorous self-recoveries, after the sallies of action, possess our axis more firmly." So Crispin goes on, not so destitute as he might wish, since he is being shadowed by the oracular rocking of *Out of the Cradle.*

> He was a man made vivid by the sea,
> A man come out of luminous traversing,
> Much trumpeted, made desperately clear,

> Fresh from discoveries of tidal skies,
> To whom oracular rockings gave no rest.
> Into a savage color he went on.

The "savage color" is the Floridian world of *Harmonium*, a world whose topics are definition and division, and whose thinking is synecdochal (like Freud's). Mapping the poem, we would expect to find in this movement a defensive turning against the self, and it is not lacking. The *pathos*, or failed Will-to-Power, of finding the self to be only a mutilated part of a desired wholeness dominates Part II, as it dominates most of the volume *Harmonium*. Vendler, in her most telling indictment of Stevens, says of him that

in his earlier years he seems to have been mistaken about what parts of the earth he had an instinct for. He felt obliged to pretend an instinct for the fertility of earth, when his true instinct was for its austerities and its dilapidations. Pursuing the *ignis fatuus* of luxuriance, he came to grief. . . .

Crispin's dilemma is not a universal one, as some readers of Stevens assume; it is only a dilemma for Stevens' very special vantage point in the person of Crispin, the vantage point of the man for whom the senses do not provide transcendent moments, who is repelled as the provocations of the senses reach excess. . . .

Stevens' self seems to have presented him with a world excessively interior, in which the senses, with the exception of the eye, are atrophied or impoverished, and he writes about the world he has, putting in active terms, as a voyage, what is in fact involuntary.

Though the critic here is mostly accurate, her description by no means applies to Stevens alone. Granted that he is not Wordsworth or Keats, his dilemma remains Emersonian, and is central to the Native Strain in our literature. Who came to more grief than Whitman, in pretending an instinct for the fertility of earth or in pursuing the luxuriance of the senses? A world overinternalized is the product not of Stevens' self but of a broad movement of post-Enlightenment consciousness, in which Wordsworth and Keats participated and which Emerson and Americans after him advanced considerably. Few critics have excelled Vendler at indicting Romanticism, rather than just Stevens, for is it not as true of Shelley, Tennyson, and

Yeats, as it is of Stevens, that they wrote about the world they had, while putting in active terms, as visionary voyages, what in fact was largely involuntary? The critic has diagnosed a malady, yet the affliction does not belong to an individual temperament or sensibility but to a large family of strong poets, and not to poets alone.

The price of *pathos*, or the American tropes of Power, begins to be paid for by a defensive movement turned against the self, and this is the Romantic affliction of Crispin when he moves on to what Freud called the vicissitudes of instinct and to what Stevens also calls "vicissitudes" or the "violence . . . for aggrandizement":

> That wrote his couplet yearly to the spring,
> As dissertation of profound delight,
> Stopping, on voyage, in a land of snakes,
> Found his vicissitudes had much enlarged
> His apprehension,˙ made him intricate
> In moody rucks, and difficult and strange
> In all desires, his destitution's mark.

"Destitution" again is imaginative need, felt lack, and prompts the heroism of Crispin, as it did of Stevens. This heroism is necessarily in the pattern of Emerson and Whitman, and is accomplished by a yielding to the dialectic of Fate, Power, and Freedom, which come together in one crucial passage:

> Crispin foresaw a curious promenade
> Or, nobler, sensed an elemental fate,
> And elemental potencies and pangs,
> And beautiful barenesses as yet unseen.

Here the *ethos* is "an elemental fate," the *pathos* "elemental potencies and pangs" and the *logos* or freedom of crossing the "barenesses as yet unseen." Vendler's analysis is most apt in the "jostling festival" of earth that follows, which indeed is "too juicily opulent," but not so much in itself as because mutilated Crispin as synecdoche for the American poet lacks the strength to confront all this life. The Comedian goes on making notes, until nature or the Not-Me asserts itself through a thunderstorm, akin to the oncoming storm of Shelley's *Ode* or the stinging sea-wind of Whitman. As "tempestuous clarion" the storm-wind proclaims that Crispin's synecdochal vision is incomplete. He must expand in force and freedom if he is to represent the transcendental selfhood not present in his European origins and awaiting him in America:

> And while the torrent on the roof still droned
> He felt the Andean breath. His mind was free
> And more than free, elate, intent, profound
> And studious of a self possessing him,
> That was not in him in the crusty town
> From which he sailed. Beyond him, westward, lay
> The mountainous ridges, purple balustrades,
> In which the thunder, lapsing in its clap,
> Let down gigantic quavers of its voice,
> For Crispin to vociferate again.

The "self possessing him" is abroad in the storm, and the voice of the storm needs to be vociferated again through his lips, to the unawakened American earth. Part II has ended rather less ironically than we could have expected, but clearly the enterprise will be hopelessly large for Crispin, as it proved to be for Whitman before him.

What follows in Part III, *Approaching Carolina*, is the *kenosis* or self-emptying of the poem, Crispin's knowing loss of his poetic heroism, or his metonymic reduction of imagination to "realism." R. P. Blackmur's summary is apt and economical: "Crispin conceives that if the experience of the senses is but well enough known, the knowledge takes the form of imagination after all." Simons, with Stevens' sanction, defends Crispin's "simpler realism" as necessary for a style as ornate as *Harmonium*'s. But both Blackmur and Simons idealize Crispin here more than the poem does. What *Approaching Carolina* shows is that the metonymic style is a defensive isolation of the self, and even a regression, in the confrontation of poet with his huge enterprise, as the catalog techniques of Whitman prophesied. Against Crispin, we can recall the complaint attributed to Emerson about Whitman: "I expect—him—to make—the songs of the Nation—but he seems—to be contented to—make the inventories." Crispin-as-cataloger is considerably more belated and finicky than the exuberant Walt:

> He savored rankness like a sensualist.
> He marked the marshy ground around the dock,
> The crawling railroad spur, the rotten fence,
> Curriculum for the marvelous sophomore.
> It purified. It made him see how much
> Of what he saw he never saw at all.
> He gripped more closely the essential prose
> As being, in a world so falsified,
> The one integrity for him, the one
> Discovery still possible to make,
> To which all poems were incident, unless
> That prose should wear a poem's guise at last.

Crispin has acquired a fierce case of the anxiety of influence, but is self-deceived in believing that "the essential prose" is for him "the one / Discovery still possible to make." For "a world so falsified" is simply a world that has been troped to death, and "the essential prose" is simply metonymy. "It is the use of life to learn metonymy," Emerson shrewdly observed, but hardly is the use of poetry, as Crispin learns by going on to his own version of the Sublime, to the learning of hyperbole in Part IV, *The Idea of a Colony.*

Blackmur said of Part IV that it is comprised of "images of freedom and the satisfaction of instinct" and that it is "a long series of synonymous tropes stating instances of the new intelligence." If we turn Blackmur upside down, we are much closer to Stevens' hyperboles and litotes. Images of repression and of instinctual satisfaction denied inform a series of repetitive tropes that show we cannot be released from the stale intelligence of our shadowy precursors. Crispin's idea is that each man should write the poems of his climate, but the climate has prevailed for a long time. Stevens both knows this and represses the knowledge, for his anxiety is authentic and intense:

> What was the purpose of his pilgrimage,
> Whatever shape it took in Crispin's mind,
> If not, when all is said, to drive away

> The shadow of his fellows from the skies,
> And, from their stale intelligence released,
> To make a new intelligence prevail?

Crispin's brash aspiration is belied further on in *The Idea of a Colony*:

> These bland excursions into time to come,
> Related in romance to backward flights,
> However prodigal, however proud,
> Contained in their afflatus the reproach
> That first drove Crispin to his wandering.
> He could not be content with counterfeit.

These lines deny the Sublime yet leave Crispin nothing except the pathos of being "a clown, perhaps, but an aspiring clown." Part IV had begun with the adage "his soil is man's intelligence," which forecloses poetry unless misapplied, and Crispin certainly misapplies it as he romances his commonplaces and threatens to end just where he began. The crux of the section, and its only distinction, is in four lines that reject the value of poetic repression and, at the same time, by their Sublime pathos evidence such repression grandly at work:

> There is a monotonous babbling in our dreams
> That makes them our dependent heirs, the heirs
> Of dreamers buried in our sleep, and not
> The oncoming fantasies of better birth.

This admits repression, and deprecates it, yet hints at a nostalgia for prophetic dreams. Crispin has reached statement, that is, he has gotten as far as Stevens had by 1922. What remains in the poem is prophecy, but it is the prophecy of defeat, or the end of Stevens' poetry in 1924. Indeed, the *Comedian* as poem deteriorates very rapidly after this, and the conspicuous failure of most of the two remaining sections is a disconcerting instance of self-fulfilling prophecy.

Part v, grimly entitled *A Nice Shady Home*, centers on the metaphor of Crispin's cabin, which is a greatly reduced version of what Emerson meant at the close of *Nature* when he chanted, "Every spirit builds itself a house, and beyond its house a world, and beyond its world a heaven." Crispin's cabin is the plum that substitutes for a continent, but it is also the death of a poem:

> He first, as realist, admitted that
> Whoever hunts a matinal continent
> May, after all, stop short before a plum
> And be content and still be realist.
> The words of things entangle and confuse.
> The plum survives its poems.

We are in a world of sublimation, but one in which the poem has been sublimated. Why go on as a poet? Confronted by the question, Stevens responds with a wild series of rhetorical questions of his own that destroy the poetic *ethos* beyond retrieval:

> Was he to bray this in profoundest brass
> Arointing his dreams with fugal requiems?
> Was he to company vastest things defunct
> With a blubber of tom-toms harrowing the sky?
> Scrawl a tragedian's testament? Prolong
> His active force in an inactive dirge,
> Which, let the tall musicians call and call,
> Should merely call him dead? Pronounce amen
> Through choirs infolded to the outmost clouds?
> Because he built a cabin who once planned
> Loquacious columns by the ructive sea?

Emerson, in his essay on Montaigne, said of Americans and American poets: "We are golden averages, volitant stabilities, compensated or periodic errors, houses founded on the sea." Crispin, following Whitman, had "planned / Loquacious columns by the ructive sea," but the sea having proved too ructive or noisy, he settled for a cabin. In yielding to fate, Crispin follows the later Emersonian pattern, and Stevens has the torment, in the rest of Part v, of showing us Crispin's marital sex life as a sublimation of poetry, in a passage rancid enough but otherwise not much of a poetic accomplishment.

It would be pleasing to see Part vi, *And Daughters with Curls,* as a poetic recovery, but all one can say for it is that it is better than Part v. One can even wonder if Stevens is attempting to write badly, though the sourness of human and poetic failure is so evident that any critic must hesitate before ascribing intentionality to some manifest poetic blots. These blots most palpably include Crispin's four grotesque daughters, whom Vendler definitively characterizes as "overwhelming." These ladies appear to be the poetry of Stevens' seasonal cycle, possibly based ironically upon Keats's *Human Seasons*. But Stevens, who until this point had followed the tropological structure of the Romantic crisis-poem, appears in this final section to despair of his model as of himself. It is the poetic future that is projected and so cast away, and Crispin, by implication, has died in "proving what he proves / Is nothing." There is a revealingly bitter passage directed against Whitman's great *Lilacs* elegy, as if to tell us how far short of Whitman poor Crispin had ended:

> All this with many multings of the man,
> Effective colonizer sharply stopped
> In the door-yard by his own capacious bloom.
> But that this bloom grown riper, showing nibs
> Of its eventual roundness, puerile tints
> Of spiced and weathery rouges, should complex
> The stopper to indulgent fatalist
> Was unforeseen.

That is to say, the malady indeed was belatedness. Whitman came early, or early enough; but Crispin–Stevens came later. The reader looks in vain for the transumption of this lateness into an ever-earliness, but that will not take place until *Ideas of Order* and afterward. It is because Stevens is blocked out from such a figurative reversal here that he ends in the bitterness of "So may the relation of each man be clipped." This line is capable of many interpretations, one of which is certainly, "Let each man's story or poem be cut off in just this way."

That leaves us with the question, what is the blocking agent? After the *Comedian*, Stevens' poems from 1922 to 1924 do not renew their exuberance. Barely beneath the colors of such gaudy verses as *Bantams in Pine-Woods, The Ordinary Women, The Emperor of Ice-Cream,* and even in *To the One of Fictive Music,* there is felt a kind of desperation not present in the *Harmonium* poems of 1915–19. We have seen the Whitmanian vision of the muse as the mother emerge from *To the One of Fictive Music,* with a hint of regressive intensity that is surprising in the Stevens of *Harmonium.* The debt to Whitman, and the overt anxiety at the debt, come out more clearly in *Stars at Tallapoosa,* which has a dark relation to *Out of the Cradle Endlessly Rocking:*

> The lines are straight and swift between the stars.
> The night is not the cradle that they cry,
> The criers, undulating the deep-oceaned phrase.
> The lines are much too dark and much too sharp. . . .

◇

> Let these be your delight, secretive hunter,
> Wading the sea-lines, moist and ever-mingling,
> Mounting the earth-lines, long and lax, lethargic.
> These lines are swift and fall without diverging.

The double meaning of "lines" is itself Whitmanian, but comes from *As I Ebb'd* rather than from *Out of the Cradle.* Whitman, walking the beach, "was seiz'd by the spirit that trails in the lines underfoot," the "lines" belonging both to his poetry and to the beach. Stevens, beholding the stars at Tallapoosa, speaks at once of the lines of his own poem and of the lines above, "between the stars." Emerson had observed that in nature there were no straight lines, and what Stevens beholds is therefore very much his own deliberate vision, surely in contrast to lines of verse that Whitman himself might have written: "Wading the sea-lines, moist and ever-mingling, / Mounting the earth-lines, long and lax, lethargic." Out of the cradle of the sea-as-origin come all natural lines, all arcs inside and out, but Stevens asserts an antithetical origin for his lines: "The night is not the cradle that they cry." Yet his reduction, he admits at last, is only another study of the nostalgias, another monocle de mon oncle, another hymn to "lost vehemence." We are left with lines that "are much too dark and much too sharp." Compare this to the stronger poem, written a few months later, *Anecdote of the Prince of Peacocks,* where Stevens, or the Prince, meets Berserk in the moonlight: "Oh, sharp he was / As the sleepless!," befitting the spirit of the antithetical. Berserk is the reductive element or First Idea lurking in the imagination, and his warning was precisely what Stevens, in 1923, did not need to hear: "But I set my traps / In the midst of dreams." Yet few final stanzas in either edition of *Harmonium* match the inevitable strains of the Prince's self-realization:

> I knew from this
> That the blue ground
> Was full of blocks
> And blocking steel.
> I knew the dread
> Of the bushy plain,
> And the beauty
> Of the moonlight
> Falling there,
> Falling
> As sleep falls
> In the innocent air.

One could wish for a knowledge like that in the last two parts of the *Comedian*. But Stevens was ebbing rapidly in 1923. The waning is evident in *Academic Discourse at Havana*, written then but not included in a book until *Ideas of Order* (1935), where in tone and temper it is badly out of place, though it prophesies some of the turnings in that volume. Section IV of the poem begins with an open question that was to go on tormenting Stevens:

> Is the function of the poet here mere sound,
> Subtler than the ornatest prophecy,
> To stuff the ear?

Fifteen years later, in *The Man on the Dump*, Stevens was to extend the same question in a darker social context:

> One sits and beats an old tin can, lard pail.
> One beats and beats for that which one believes.
> That's what one wants to get near. Could it after all
> Be merely oneself, as superior as the ear
> To a crow's voice? Did the nightingale torture the ear,

Pack the heart and scratch the mind? And does the ear
Solace itself in peevish birds?

These questions are open also, yet by then Stevens could
bear them better. A final text for Stevens' crisis of poetic ebbing is the famous and overrated set-piece of 1924, *Sea Surface
Full of Clouds.* Joseph Riddel, in the best reading yet made of
this poem, rightly calls it "an epistemological exercise" and convincingly sees it as "somewhat of an impasse, a drama in isolation, the experience of the effete rather than the common self."
I would put this even more negatively. A. Walton Litz is jus-
tified in calling the poem "an artificial and somewhat preten-
tious effort to revive the exhausted imagination, a use of language as if it were a stimulant." The poem is the *Comedian* a
step further on, over into the abyss. By the time Stevens
reaches section v, the Whitmanian ocean has been evaporated,
and what remains is a beholding that is replete with signification yet quite devoid of meaning, as nothing here could aid in
the survival of any reader's mode of discourse:

> And a motley green
> Followed the drift of the obese machine
>
> Of ocean, perfected in indolence.
> What pistache one, ingenious and droll,
> Beheld the sovereign clouds as jugglery
>
> And the sea as turquoise-turbaned Sambo, neat
> As tossing saucers—cloudy-conjuring sea?

No series of chapters on *Harmonium,* the best "first book" of
poems in our literature since the 1855 *Leaves of Grass,* ought to
be allowed to end with the quoting of such lines. I conclude
therefore by going back to 1919, to my favorite poem in *Harmonium,* the superbly exuberant *Nomad Exquisite:*

> As the immense dew of Florida
> Brings forth
> The big-finned palm
> And green vine angering for life,

As the immense dew of Florida
Brings forth hymn and hymn
From the beholder,
Beholding all these green sides
And gold sides of green sides,

And blessed mornings,
Meet for the eye of the young alligator,
And lightning colors
So, in me, come flinging
Forms, flames, and the flakes of flames.

Stevens-as-tourist mocks himself in the title, but only because he is so far from mocking himself in this Keatsian and Paterian poem. On the model of Huxley's vision of Wordsworth
in the tropics, so we might think of Walter Pater rewriting the
"Conclusion" to *The Renaissance* not on "this short day of frost
and sun," in an Oxford winter, but on a summer morning,
confronted by "the immense dew of Florida." I cannot be persuaded that Stevens is deceiving himself here as to his instinct
for the fecundities of earth rather than its austerities and dilapidations. Keats once said that unless poetry came as naturally as
leaves to a tree, it had better not come at all, which is a beautiful, untrue remark. So, alas, it is beautifully untrue that "the
immense dew of Florida / brings forth hymn and hymn" from
the beholding Stevens, but the poet knows this and knows his
reader knows this also. Mornings so blessed are meet, not for
the eye of the human beholder, but "for the eye of the young
alligator." For the human beholder, "lightning colors" are rapidly substituting tropes, and in Stevens the tropes come fighting. Marvelous as the last line is, I wish Stevens had kept its
earlier version: "So, in me come flinging / Fruits, forms,
flowers, flakes, and fountains." The fruits, flowers, and fountains were deleted, not because Stevens lacked an instinct for
them but to place the poem finally out of nature and into the
Paterian Condition of Fire: "So, in me, come flinging / Forms,
flames, and the flakes of flames." Not perhaps a gem-like flame,
this is still a hard or antithetical one, flaking off into the compo-
nent tropes of the poem. What confronts a heightened reality

here is a visionary capacity for response, but just such a capacity cannot prevail indefinitely, a melancholy lesson learned successively by Wordsworth, Coleridge, Emerson, and Whitman. The crisis of 1922–24 in Stevens had been the crisis of Wordsworth in 1802 and of Whitman in 1860. What Stevens had was persistence, as he was to discover again, but six years of poetic silence had to intervene before the sun of March 1930 reillumined things for this master of evasions and prompted a prayer that subsequent poems strongly answered:

> Oh! Rabbi, rabbi, fend my soul for me
> And true savant of this dark nature be.

5 *Ideas of Order*

Most of Stevens' ideas of order, and not just in the nineteen thirties, are ideas of limitation, or tropes of *ethos*, images of character or of Fate-revealing incident. In Freudian terms, they tend to begin as reaction formations, pass through the defense of isolation, and climax as sublimations. We can surmise that there is a direct line in Stevens that goes from the reductiveness of *The Snow Man* through various ideas of order to culminate in the First Idea of *Notes toward a Supreme Fiction*. Fortunately, Stevens rarely made the error of reducing any of his own poems to ideas of order alone, which is one reason why his poetry revived so vigorously from 1934 to 1936, after the almost total silence of 1924 to 1930. *The Sun This March* poignantly broke that silence in 1930, but then Stevens suffered nearly four more years of his unresolved dilemmas as a creator before he truly recovered himself with *The Idea of Order at Key West* in 1934. There are literally only a handful of memorable poems written after *The Sun This March* and before the Wordsworthian meditation at Key West. Even these are uniformly elegiac, as though hymning a dead poetic self: *Anatomy of Monotony, Autumn Refrain, The Brave Man, A Fading of the Sun.*

When, in 1934, Stevens wrote his *Key West* poem, he renewed a self-confidence and a poetic exuberance that he had last shown in Hoon's chant, thirteen years before. It is no accident that the singing girl at Key West is spoken of in the precise phrases that Hoon had used of himself. After Stevens had written again of a walker making a world by singing it, he was free for the great year of his work that carried from *Evening without Angels* through to *Farewell to Florida*, the high chant that presaged *The Man with the Blue Guitar* about a year later. From then on Stevens was never headed. Not a year out of the last twenty of his life is undistinguished by the writing of a great poem, and here I would locate his lasting eminence, in that persistence and diversity of strength that attended him between the ages of fifty-five and seventy-five, a glory almost unique in the poetry of the last several centuries.

The glory, so long repressed, returns from out the winter's air in *The Sun This March*, but its return scarcely can be borne in that poem, where the self protests that cold is its element, and Stevens prays to the rabbi to fend his soul, as if he could not do it for himself. "Fend" means both to ward off and to shift or venture, and both meanings work here. Stevens said that for him the rabbi was "the figure of a man devoted in the extreme to scholarship and at the same time to making some use of it for human purposes" (*L*, 786), which means that Stevens' "rabbi" is the same as Emerson's "scholar." Stevens uses the two words interchangeably, and like Emerson he uses "scholar" to mean "poet." In *The Sun This March* the rabbi, like the poet, is always in the sun, and his function is both to defend and to shift Stevens, to reilluminate the poet's dark nature so that he can write poems again.

But how slow and painful this recovery was, the poems of 1930 to 1934 reveal in every line. *Anatomy of Monotony* was included in the second edition of *Harmonium* (1931), but in date and spirit it belongs to this dark, painful phase of Stevens' poetic reawakening. The first stanza brings together the crucial emblems of the first *Harmonium*—the earth, the mother, autumn, wind, the cold, the sky—in a panorama of reduction:

> If from the earth we came, it was an earth
> That bore us as a part of all the things
> It breeds and that was lewder than it is.
> Our nature is her nature. Hence it comes,
> Since by our nature we grow old, earth grows
> The same. We parallel the mother's death.
> She walks an autumn ampler than the wind
> Cries up for us and colder than the frost

> Pricks in our spirits at the summer's end,
> And over the bare spaces of our skies
> She sees a barer sky that does not bend.

The singularity of our origin is denied, even as our purpose, aim, or end is seen to be also that of earth. Earth was lewder, as we were; now earth and we grow old together. The mother is not only dead but, as in Whitman, she *is* death. Perhaps we might remember Nietzsche's smack at Hegel: "What if the *Aufhebung* were a Christian mother?" It is true enough that in Whitman and in Stevens the *imago* of the mother works as the three degrees or meanings of the Hegelian *aufgehoben*. As a metonymy, it means to cancel, annul, or undo; as a metaphor, to maintain or preserve through sublimation; and as a hyperbole, to exalt to a higher degree or idea of order. In *Anatomy of Monotony*, I, the mother ends as muse of the American Sublime, seeing the ultimate *ethos* of Fate as " a barer sky that does not bend," a vision beyond pathetic fallacy. The *pathos* of the second stanza is, by design, only a partial restitution:

> The body walks forth naked in the sun
> And, out of tenderness or grief, the sun
> Gives comfort, so that other bodies come,
> Twinning our phantasy and our device,
> And apt in versatile motion, touch and sound
> To make the body covetous in desire
> Of the still finer, more implacable chords.
> So be it. Yet the spaciousness and light
> In which the body walks and is deceived,
> Falls from that fatal and that barer sky,
> And this the spirit sees and is aggrieved.

The pathetic fallacy or trope of Power here knows and shows its own rhetoricity, "Twinning our phantasy and our device." Stevens proclaims his inability to reimagine the mother's First Idea. He can dally with a false surmise, "the spaciousness and light / In which the body walks and is deceived," but this is not the trope of representation it appears to be. It falls from the limitation of Fate, "from that fatal and that barer sky," and so the poem willfully truncates itself. "Falls" is the crucial trope, returning to the mother's walking "an autumn ampler than the wind / Cries up for us." Stevens ends the poem with the spirit (his own) seeing what the mother sees, Fate, or the power-lessness of poetry, which is the "anatomy of monotony" of the title.

Autumn Refrain, in 1931, is an even more poignant poem, yet also reduces itself to the irony of *ethos* or Fate. I cannot agree with A. Walton Litz, who says that in it "Stevens recovers his full poetic power," though one sympathizes with the critical temptation to yield to a poem as nobly stoic as this:

> The skreak and skritter of evening gone
> And grackles gone and sorrows of the sun,
> The sorrows of sun, too, gone . . . the moon and moon,
> The yellow moon of words about the nightingale
> In measureless measures, not a bird for me
> But the name of a bird and the name of a nameless air
> I have never—shall never hear. And yet beneath
> The stillness that comes to me out of this, beneath
> The stillness of everything gone, and being still,
> Being and sitting still, something resides,
> Some skreaking and skrittering residuum,
> And grates these evasions of the nightingale
> Though I have never—shall never hear that bird.
> And the stillness is in the key, all of it is,
> The stillness is all in the key of that desolate sound.

We might call this poem a debate between the grackles and Keats, and remember that "the grackles crack their throats of bone in the smooth air" in *Banal Sojourn*. There is also a pro-lepsis of "the blatter of grackles" in *The Man on the Dump*. A poorish poem of 1932, *Snow and Stars* (*CP*, 133), had tried to sing along with the grackles, but in rather ill humor, excusably so, since crow blackbirds are hardly a provocation to joy. *Autumn Refrain* is a most minimal celebration, yet it seeks and finds a "residuum" in the "desolate sound" of the grackles. "Residuum" is a eulogistic word for Stevens; it means rather more than something that remains after a part has been removed. A de-cade after *Autumn Refrain*, it becomes a noble synecdoche in several crucial lines of Stevens' most underrated long poem, *Ex-*

tracts from Addresses to the Academy of Fine Ideas: "Stanzas of final peace / Lie in the heart's residuum"; "The chants of final peace / Lie in the heart's residuum"; "the acutest end / Of speech: to pierce the heart's residuum / And there to find music." Or, closer to the end, there is the vision of New Haven in *An Ordinary Evening,* xx, where "The town was a residuum, / A neuter," yet remained alive in its imaginative and emotional transcripts. Even in *Autumn Refrain,* when "something resides, / Some skreaking and skrittering residuum," that residuum is more a synecdoche for the psychic defense of reversal than for a turning against the self. As a trope of the spirit, the residuum is what has survived the most reductive decade of Stevens' creative life; it is that part of the First Idea which demands to be reimagined. The interplay of *Autumn Refrain* with the world of Keats's odes manifests a rising near to the surface of one of Stevens' deepest influence-repressions. But, in this poem, he lacks the daemonic force for the even greater repression that would lift him, against Keats, into his own Counter-Sublime.

Whitman, rather than Keats, is the barely repressed anxiety of the two companion poems of 1933, *The Brave Man* and *A Fading of the Sun,* both of which glance back sadly at stanza VII of *Sunday Morning* with its Nietzschean prophecy of an Over-Sun fitted to Over-Men: "Not as a god, but as a god might be." Both of the 1933 sun pieces are effective and wishful, and both remain firmly in the *aporia* of the Stevensian impasse. As brave man, the sun "walks without meditation," meditation here being equated with Stevens' weakness: "Fears of my bed, / Fears of life and fears of death." Hoon, the Whitman of *Like Decorations,* and the girl at Key West walk without meditation, walk singing and chanting the things that are part of them. *A Fading of the Sun* equates "the sun costuming clouds" with "night endazzled," again in Whitman's manner of celebrating origins, and then reduces both to a filial cry for help: "Within as pillars of the sun, / Supports of night." By 1934, Stevens badly needed to demonstrate, to others but most of all to himself, that he was still a strong poet. The demonstration came in *The Idea of Order at Key West,* not only the most powerful poem in what was to be the *Ideas of Order* volume but also surpassing any single poem in either edition of *Harmonium*. Yet the *Key West* poem has its desperate equivocations and its unresolvable difficulties, more perhaps than even so strong a poem can sustain. In some respects, it is an impossible text to interpret, and its rhetoric may be at variance with its deepest intentionalities.

Our difficulties start with the title. Is the emphasis upon the idea of order, an idea perhaps momentarily vacationing at Key West? Or are we encountering a *genius loci*, with Key West as the *locus?* And why is the poem not called *The Rage for Order at Key West* or even *The Rage to Order at Key West?* Just as, finally, we can identify the precise intimations of immortality in Wordsworth's ode, can we identify precisely what the idea of order at Key West is?

In these chapters I have been taking up and then letting fall again, free-style, the reading techniques of the antithetical criticism that I have been attempting to develop, particularly in *A Map of Misreading* and *Poetry and Repression*. I choose to map *The Idea of Order at Key West* rather rigorously, so as to reveal how faithfully it follows the model of the Wordsworthian crisis-poem, in its American Romantic modification, as traced in Chapter 1.

Stevens himself tried to define the "order" of his poem and volume in some letters of 1935:

> If poetry introduces order, and every competent poem introduces order, and if order means peace, even though that particular peace is an illusion, is it any less an illusion than a good many other things that everyone high and low now-a-days concedes to be no longer of any account? Isn't a freshening of life a thing of consequence? . . .

> In *The Idea of Order at Key West* life has ceased to be a matter of chance. It may be that every man introduces his own order into the life about him and that the idea of order in general is simply what Bishop Berkeley might have called a fortuitous concourse of personal orders. But still there is order. [L, 293]

I think it fair to say that this doesn't help at all. "A freshening of life" is a moving phrase but not an idea of order, and all

Stevens has committed himself to saying is that order may be an illusion, but so is everything else.

To define Stevensian "order," I return to *Tea at the Palaz of Hoon*, twelve years earlier, because that is clearly the last poem before *The Idea of Order at Key West* in which Stevens knew and showed that he was a strong poet. *Sad Strains of a Gay Waltz*, in the volume *Ideas of Order*, identified Hoon with a finding of order in solitude, which recalls Stevens himself proposing solitude to his future wife in letters of 1904–05: "I long for Solitude—not the solitude of a few rooms, but the solitude of self. I want to know about myself, about my world, about my future when the world is ended" (*L*, 80). The capitalized "Solitudes" in Stevens' letters, like all the instances of "solitude" in his verse, are Emersonian, as I think even Stevens would have realized if he could have borne to think about his indebtedness. The title essay of Emerson's *Society and Solitude* gave Stevens his image of the poet as "the scholar of one candle" through a reduction of Emerson's "A scholar is a candle which the love and desire of all men will light." But it gave Stevens also an early defense of solitude, in a fine passage on the unsociability of Dante, Michelangelo, and Columbus: "Yet each of these potentates saw well the reason of his exclusion. Solitary was he? Why, yes; but his society was limited only by the amount of brain nature appropriated in that age to carry on the government of the world."

But that is late Emerson, of 1857 or so. Twenty years before, in his Notebooks, he had stated the necessity of Solitude with a more Stevensian pungency: "No, the Sea, vocation, poverty, are seeming fences, but man is insular and cannot be touched. Every man is an infinitely repellent orb, and holds his individual being on that condition." Can we not surmise that Stevens could recover his full strength as a poet only when he ceased to fear his own solipsism? His true idea of order is the Emersonian–Whitmanian Self-Reliance, in which the Self accepts an expansiveness with all attendant dangers. Form and order are found in solitude as early as *Sunday Morning*, in the image of our "island solitude, unsponsored, free." The girl at Key West makes an idea of order by measuring "to the hour its solitude," prophesying the late poem *Things of August* of 1949, where Stevens chants

> The solemn sentences,
> Like interior intonations,
> The speech of truth in its true solitude,
> A nature that is created in what it says,
> The peace of the last intelligence.

In what sense does Hoon exemplify "the speech of truth in its true solitude," or how does his poem justify the judgment that he "found all form and order in solitude"? Any answers should explain how and why *Tea at the Palaz of Hoon* became the nucleus of *The Idea of Order at Key West*. One answer is: Schopenhauer, an answer in which I have been preceded by Frank Doggett. Schopenhauer begins *The World as Will and Idea* by saying that the philosopher learns that "the world which surrounds him is there only as idea, i.e., only in relation to something else, the consciousness, which is himself." In his discussion of lyric poetry, Schopenhauer presents it as an art never completely realized, a view that Nietzsche protested in *The Birth of Tragedy*. In a lyric poem, according to Schopenhauer, a consciousness is manifested as being divided between desire or will and a purer contemplation. Nietzsche idealized the poet in *The Birth of Tragedy*, though with his usual irony, by saying *contra* Schopenhauer that an authentic poet has freed himself of individual will "and has become a medium through which the True Subject celebrates the True Subject's own redemption in illusion." But Schopenhauer, with his profound insight that equated repression and the Sublime, was truer to the realities of the modern lyric in seeing that for the poet "the subjective disposition, the affection of the will, imparts its own hue to the perceived surrounding, and conversely, the surroundings communicate the reflex of their color to the will." Schopenhauer's will is close to Stevens' solitude, even as Schopenhauer's pure contemplation is close to Stevens' idea of order. Hoon is the precursor of the girl at Key West because, like her, he is a Whitmanian finder of himself "more truly and more strange," and where there is a further finding of the self solipsism moves toward its apotheosis in a final realism, as it does in Schopenhauer (or in his descendant Wittgenstein).

Stevens is not quite in solitude as he listens to the girl at Key West, though we don't know that until rather late in the poem, just as we are startled to find late in *Tintern Abbey* that Wordsworth is accompanied by Dorothy. Ramon Fernandez, of course, is no Dorothy, and in spite of some grumpy protestations in Stevens' letters he was a modern French critic whom Stevens certainly had read. As a formalist, Fernandez had much in common with Stevens, but *The Idea of Order at Key West* is a High Romantic poem, and Fernandez was anti-Romantic, being in this a Gallic equivalent of Eliot or Tate. Kermode usefully remarked that the poem exemplifies the constant theme of Coleridge and Wordsworth, which is the power of the mind over what Milton had called a universe of death. But I would add, before attempting a very close, antithetical analysis of the poem, that this Romantic *topos* appears in its drastic American version, the Emersonian–Whitmanian dialectic of Fate, Power, and Freedom.

I take it that the title refers us to the genius or spirit of place *at* Key West, which is why the first line emphasizes that the girl's singing transcends the *genius loci*. Did Whitman sing *beyond* the genius of the sea, and did Emerson prophesy such a transcendence? The American crisis-poem, from Emerson to A. R. Ammons, is a shore-lyric, as I emphasized in Chapter 1. Here is Emerson, in his splendid and neglected poem of 1856, *Seashore*, taking his later, necessitarian view, in which no one can sing beyond the genius of the sea:

> I heard or seemed to hear the chiding Sea
> Say, Pilgrim, why so late and slow to come?
> Am I not always here, thy summer home?
> Is not my voice thy music, morn and eve? . . .

◇

> Behold the Sea
> The opaline, the plentiful and strong, . . .

◇

Washing out harms and griefs from memory,
And, in my mathematic ebb and flow,
Giving a hint of that which changes not.
Rich are the sea-gods:—who gives gifts but they?
They grope the sea for pearls, but more than pearls:
They pluck Force thence, and give it to the wise. . . .

◇

I too have arts and sorceries;
Illusion dwells forever with the wave.
I know what spells are laid. Leave me to deal
With credulous and imaginative man.

If we want an opponent for *The Idea of Order at Key West*, certainly Emerson's *Seashore* would do. But in taking up such an antithetical stance, Stevens merely opposes the earlier Emerson, prophet of Power and seer of Influx, to this later Emerson, sage of Fate and high priest of Ananke. How large is the difference in argument between Stevens' poem and this characteristic passage of the earlier Emerson? "The poet is the Namer or Language-maker, naming things sometimes after their appearance, sometimes after their essence, and giving to every one its own name and not another's, thereby rejoicing the intellect, which delights in detachment or boundary. The poets made all the words. . . . Language is fossil poetry."

At Key West, the idea of order is incarnated by one singing woman "striding there alone," because her solitude, like Hoon's, is itself the compass of the sea. She is a language-maker, rejoicing Stevens' intellect, which delights in detachment or boundary. Is there a better first line, or a better first stanza, in all of Stevens?

She sang beyond the genius of the sea.
The water never formed to mind or voice,
Like a body wholly body, fluttering
Its empty sleeves; and yet its mimic motion
Made constant cry, caused constantly a cry,
That was not ours although we understood,
Inhuman, of the veritable ocean.

Emerson once quoted a lady of his acquaintance as saying that, for her, Transcendentalism always meant "a little beyond." "Beyond" is a peculiarly haunting word throughout Stevens' poetry. His aim always is to play "a tune beyond us, yet ourselves," and to teach us, somehow, to "bear brightly the little beyond." But there are so many "beyonds" in this supposedly stubborn naturalist of the imagination that a reader can chart the whole progress of a lifetime's poetry in those persistent "beyonds." Such charting could begin with "the blazing passes, from beyond the sun" in *Le Monocle*, and with all the "beyonds" of Crispin's voyagings, and then pass through the metaphysical "beyonds" of *Extracts* and the aspiring "beyonds" of the Angelic canon of *Notes*, to attain a climax in the visionary "beyonds" of *The Owl in the Sarcophagus*, with its "diamond jubilance beyond the fire" and "sad splendor, beyond artifice." The Transcendental epilogue, in Stevens, comes also with its "beyonds," with the "cure beyond forgetfulness" of *The Rock*, the "life beyond this present knowing" of *The Sail of Ulysses* and the final rising "beyond the last thought" in the death-poem *Of Mere Being*. With so many more instances that might be adduced, we have an almost obsessive pattern of a poet constantly willing more than a little beyond, endlessly striving to transcend the given, the "reality" that he asserts so often yet so self-deceivingly. We can summarize by saying that "beyond" in Stevens is where the self must go to find itself more truly and more strange, and we can venture the formula "beyond" means "beyond the First Idea." There can be no idea of order in Stevens without reducing to a First Idea and then imagining beyond that idea to a new and heightened solitude of power and will.

To sing beyond the genius of the sea is to defy the poetics of Whitman, who found the muse his mother to be his oceanic sense and who identified his father with the shore. The *ethos* or American Fate of the first stanza of Stevens' poem marks a withdrawal from meaning, conveyed figuratively by a curious irony. For the ocean is at once an enormous presence, a body wholly body making constant cry, and also a total absence, fluttering the empty sleeves of a scarecrow, with no motion but a mimic one. What is this water but a substitute for the fiction of the leaves, here divested of the *pathos* of its outcry? The divestiture is accomplished both by "mimic" and by the movement from "made" to "caused." Can we not judge the peculiar mark of limitation here to be what the stanza says is our understanding, our freedom from the pathetic fallacy? All that we understand of the cry is that it is not our own, not human, that it is of the veritable ocean, free from our imaginings.

I recur now to the notion of "crossings." The *topos* of the first stanza is that of Contraries, opposing the woman's song to the cry of the sea and opposing to each other the sea's palpable presence and its truer limiting absence. The second stanza locates itself, through figurations of *pathos* or Power, in the *topoi* of Definition and Division. Here the song is a part of which the human self, or the concept of a self, is the whole:

> The sea was not a mask. No more was she.
> The song and water were not medleyed sound
> Even if what she sang was what she heard,
> Since what she sang was uttered word by word.
> It may be that in all her phrases stirred
> The grinding water and the gasping wind;
> But it was she and not the sea we heard.

This stanza denies mimesis in favor of an expressive theory of poetry. The sense emphasized is hearing, as in the first stanza but now intensified and more precise, able to distinguish clearly word from word in the song and song from water. Again, there is a movement of externalization, from first to second stanza, as all masking falls out of the mimic motion. As our theoretical description earlier had prophesied, we have the three marks of a crossing or disjunctiveness between the first two stanzas, which I have called a Crossing of Election, where the *aporia* or mental dilemma addresses the self with a crucial question: Am I still a poet? A dark shadow of mimesis brushes by Stevens as he reluctantly concedes the grinding and gasping that stir in his own language, yet the stanza concludes strongly, affirming power and will as it tells us that it is Stevens and not the sea that we hear. The disjunctiveness is most radically felt between "the veritable ocean" and "it was she," so that the Crossing of Election takes place between an inhuman cry and the affirmation of the human, an affirmation made only through the "word by word" of a veritable poem.

The second movement of *The Idea of Order at Key West* centers on the Crossing of Solipsism, to resort again to my schema, a crossing that is made between the third and fourth stanzas, or between the *topos* of Cause and Effect in the third stanza and of Comparison in the fourth. Here is the third stanza, where the crucial question "Whose spirit is this?" works as the *kenosis* or ratio of emptying out in the poem:

> For she was the maker of the song she sang.
> The ever-hooded, tragic-gestured sea
> Was merely a place by which she walked to sing.
> Whose spirit is this? we said, because we knew
> It was the spirit that we sought and knew
> That we should ask this often as she sang.

Why did Stevens feel compelled not only to ask the question but to go on asking it, even as she sang? The effect here is the metonymizing or undoing of the sea, despite its tragic trappings, into one of its aspects, that of being "merely a place by which she walked to sing." The cause ought to be the spirit, yet the question "Whose spirit is this?" undoes the cause. Whose spirit can it be, if not the singer's own spirit, since it is not the spirit of the sea? Does Stevens seek *the* spirit, or the *spirit?* The first presumably, which suggests a longing for another "beyond" here, a spirit beyond the singing woman's spirit. And just here the crossing or disjunction is crucial, since it intervenes between these ambiguities and the Sublime stanza that follows, to mark the poem's glory of repressive strength, its daemonic intensity of heaping up the imagery of height, the hyperboles of vision:

> If it was only the dark voice of the sea
> That rose, or even colored by many waves;
> If it was only the outer voice of the sky
> And cloud, of the sunken coral water-walled,
> However clear, it would have been deep air,

> The heaving speech of air, a summer sound
> Repeated in a summer without end
> And sound alone. But it was more than that,
> More even than her voice, and ours, among
> The meaningless plungings of water and the wind,
> Theatrical distances, bronze shadows heaped
> On high horizons, mountainous atmospheres
> Of sky and sea.

The crossing to this *topos* of Comparison, from the place of Cause and Effect, is an *aporia* or *logos* of Solipsism. Of this extraordinary restitution of Power, we can say that it restitutes too much, despite its palpable attempts to deprecate the Sublime that dazzles it, and ourselves. A voice rises up here, beyond the sea, beyond the singer, beyond Stevens, for it is more than those voices. What rises up is a voice neither natural nor human, yet Stevens cannot tell us, or know himself, what such a voice might be. Our clue must come through the second crossing of the poem, which moves toward greater expressiveness as opposed to mimesis, moves back partly to a world of sight and moves also to an internalization of the spirit. Why? Because, though the voice that is great within us cannot be our own, we are under the transgressive necessity of being able to locate it nowhere else. This necessity is the most vital implication of the poem's next stanza:

> It was her voice that made
> The sky acutest at its vanishing.
> She measured to the hour its solitude.
> She was the single artificer of the world
> In which she sang. And when she sang, the sea,
> Whatever self it had, became the self
> That was her song, for she was the maker. Then we,
> As we beheld her striding there alone,
> Knew that there never was a world for her
> Except the one she sang and, singing, made.

In this movement back toward *ethos* or Fate, the *topos* of Resemblance and dissimilarity is evoked and results in the major presentation of the poem's central metaphor, the singer as "single artificer of the world." "The sky acutest at its vanishing" is a Shelleyan trope, reminding us of a world in which sounds are keenest where demarcations are ghostliest, as in the realm of the skylark, flying too high to be seen, with its song so acute or keen that it barely can be heard. The singer herself is therefore very Shelleyan and has the same relation to the world she makes as Shelley's Emilia has to "Love's rare Universe" in *Epipsychidion*. This stanza is the poem's attempted sublimation of its deepest intentions or desires for utterance, and like all such metaphors it "fails." This is not poetical failure so much as it is argumentative or topical failure, for the sublimating metaphor tries to emphasize the resemblance between inner voice and outer ocean, at the expense of the dissimilarity. Stevens perspectivizes desperately, in the Nietzschean manner, to evade the fiction of the human self. Did the sea become the singer's self, when it "became the self / That was her song"? Whitman hovers overtly here, as he has been hovering covertly throughout the poem. What song can the woman be singing if it is not a song of herself?

The answer comes shrouded in the poem's third crossing, which I have called the Crossing of Identification, that is, of introjection. But to characterize the third crossing, we need to examine the poem's last full stanza, after which we can attempt to interpret its most famous passage, the five-line coda. With the last full stanza, Ramon Fernandez as anti-Romantic inquisitor enters the poem, but only to be admonished:

> Ramon Fernandez, tell me, if you know,
> Why, when the singing ended and we turned
> Toward the town, tell why the glassy lights,
> The lights in the fishing boats at anchor there,
> As the night descended, tilting in the air,
> Mastered the night and portioned out the sea,
> Fixing emblazoned zones and fiery poles,
> Arranging, deepening, enchanting night.

Power returns, as the final *pathos* of a transumptive vision, making the twilight into a Romantic aurora, a fresh earliness of seeing. And time re-enters the poem also, with the "when" of the song's ending. Somewhere in the background there does

survive a trace of Wordsworth's *Solitary Reaper,* a girl who sang
as if her song could have no ending. Stevens' singer stops, but
her lingering idea of order triumphs over both the pale and
unknowing Fernandez and the Stevens who knows too well the
fear of a calm darkening among water lights. Here the water
lights flame rather than darken, in the aftereffect of song. These
lights transume the darkness, by reversing the Whitmanian
night and sea, the world of the mother and of the sleepers. In
lines of Tennysonian glamor, the lights accomplish Hoon's
project of adding Paterian strangeness to beauty. The *topoi* of
this final stanza are Antecedents and Consequences, with the
song as the prime instance of the former and the action of the
lights as the latter. In the Crossing of Identification, Stevens introjects the singer's solitude and freedom, and projects, casts
forth away from him, the ocean and the night, the Whitmanian
cosmos that is his poetic origin and that he fears will be his poetic end or aim. Mimesis vanishes in this final crossing, and the
sense of sight displaces the hearing that held on to the sea's cry
despite all of Stevens' protestation. But the third mark of disjunctiveness, internalization, is reversed, as Stevens turns toward an external world again, in the harbor of Key West.

There remains the coda, which may be regarded as a key sig-
nature for all of the stronger poems in *Ideas of Order:*

> Oh! Blessed rage for order, pale Ramon,
> The maker's rage to order words of the sea,
> Words of the fragrant portals, dimly-starred,
> And of ourselves and of our origins,
> In ghostlier demarcations, keener sounds.

"Blessed" here almost takes its French meaning of "wounded,"
since it distinguishes the formalist's rage *for* order from the
poet's rage *to* order. "Words of the sea" reminds us again of
Whitman's *Word Out of the Sea,* the word being of course
"death." "Words of the sea" represent a universe of death, and
the maker's rage to order is an assertion of the power of the poetic mind over the sea, or such a universe. But the syntax here
is revelatory in its movement. The maker's rage to order words
of the sea in ghostlier demarcations and in keener sounds is a

Shelleyan rage to order. Stevens is closer to Keats in the aspiration to order words of the fragrant portals, dimly-starred, which recalls *Peter Quince*'s "fitful tracing of a portal" and goes back to Keatsian visions of charmed magic casements. The third rage to order is Wordsworthian, recalling Wordsworth's ambition to speak of nothing more than what we are, but also Whitmanian, since no better description of Whitman could be made than to name his ambition as a rage to order words of himself, and of his origins, in ghostlier demarcations, keener sounds. But, finally, this coda is Stevens' true response to the anxieties of influence and of reduction that had diminished and then halted his poetry from 1922 until 1934.

The words, whether of the sea, the portals, ourselves, or our origins, are not Stevens' own words, as he belatedly had recognized. Yet a strong poet must have a word of his own, a stance of his own. *Ideas of Order* searches for such a stance, without quite finding it, but its ambitions toward the word are more modest. To order the words of anteriority in ghostlier demarcations is to undo the intertextual contexts to a limited degree, but they cannot be undone wholly. To order the words of the literary tribe in keener sounds is the ambition of every poet, and like Tennyson before him Stevens largely succeeded in this. But the poem *The Idea of Order at Key West*, despite all its strength, remains equivocal and perhaps impossible to interpret fully in at least two respects, and these are nearly antithetical to each other. The poem affirms a transcendental poetic spirit yet cannot locate it, and the poem also remains uneasily wary about the veritable ocean, which will rise up against Stevens yet again in *The Man with the Blue Guitar*.

No other poem in *Ideas of Order* stands near in eminence to this one, but the book has other brilliant pieces, notably *Evening without Angels*, *Farewell to Florida*, and *A Postcard from the Volcano*. If we invoke an insight of Kenneth Burke's and ask what Stevens was trying to do for himself by composing *The Idea of Order at Key West*, we could answer by the results, the heightened poetic productivity of 1935–36 and the writing of *The Man with the Blue Guitar* in 1937. The *Blue Guitar* marks the advent of Stevens' true mode, the longer poem or sequence in the form of variations upon a theme. In *Ideas of Order*, the precursor of this mode is the very uneven *Like Decorations in a Nigger Cemetery*, where the unfortunate title intends to reveal Stevens' continued irony toward his own poems. Helen Vendler points to *Thirteen Ways of Looking at a Blackbird* in *Harmonium* as Stevens' first attempt at so frankly disjunctive a kind of poem. Disjunction is indeed the issue, but it was so also in the High Romantic crisis-poem, as I tried to show in my first chapter. Stevens' principal difference from his precursors Wordsworth and Whitman is that he emphasizes his disjunctiveness and makes of his crossings overt rather than hidden placements of meaning. Stevens writes a poetry centered on the *aporia* between rhetoric as persuasion and rhetoric as a system of tropes, and in a curious way this centering became a guarantee of his poetic importance.

Thirteen Ways in 1917 itself returns to *Domination of Black*, the powerful lyric of 1916 that I shall discuss in Chapter 14. As the black becomes there the color or trope of *ethos* or Fate, so in *Thirteen Ways* it also serves as the emblem of Ananke, of Fate conceived as Necessity, where again Emerson is the likeliest origin for Stevens. Section VIII seems to me the revelation of the poem's disjunctiveness:

> I know noble accents
> And lucid, inescapable rhythms;
> But I know, too,
> That the blackbird is involved
> In what I know.

What the poet knows is poetry, *materia poetica* and poetry being the same thing for Stevens. But there is no *materia poetica* without the domination of the blackbird, for the blackbird is Stevens' first thinker of the First Idea. And so he mixes in everywhere, including the union of a man and a woman. He is our knowledge, to use Stevens' very American idiom, not just that it is snowing but that it is going to snow. In *Like Decorations*, he figures as the opposite of the superb and exuberant manifestation of the chanting Whitman, anti-apocalyptic bard of the joyful and loudly shouting sun. Against the Power of

Whitmanian pathos, the *ethos* of blackness makes its demystifying appearance:

> It was when the trees were leafless first in November
> And their blackness became apparent, that one first
> Knew the eccentric to be the base of design.

Palpably this is an *illusio*, the irony that means the opposite of what it says, since "eccentric" here is a figuration for "mortal." Vendler's general comment on *Like Decorations* is not likely to be bettered: "Stevens' true subject in *Decorations* becomes the complexity of mental response as he gives intimations, in these fifty stanzas, of almost all possible reactions to the decay that is the topic of the poem." This might be modified by saying that the *topoi* in *Like Decorations* never get beyond Contraries and Contradictories, out of which rhetorical ironies constantly are generated. Hence the total disjunctiveness of a sequence that undoes all its own synecdoches before they can establish themselves, since so continuously ironical a thinking becomes, over fifty sections, a kind of allegory of allegorization, in which an otherness is always intended. Here are the last four sections:

> The sun is seeking something bright to shine on.
> The trees are wooden, the grass is yellow and thin.
> The ponds are not the surfaces it seeks.
> It must create its colors out of itself.
>
> Music is not yet written but is to be.
> The preparation is long and of long intent
> For the time when sound shall be subtler than we ourselves.
>
> It needed the heavy nights of drenching weather
> To make him return to people, to find among them
> Whatever it was that he found in their absence,
> A pleasure, an indulgence, an infatuation.
>
> Union of the weakest develops strength
> Not wisdom. Can all men, together, avenge
> One of the leaves that have fallen in autumn?
> But the wise man avenges by building his city in snow.

The first of these seems the most positive, as though the sun were Walt or Hoon, except that this is a sun of poverty, compelled to make its tropes from its own *materia poetica*, and so is reduced to being a synecdoche for the self-undermining nature of desire. The second is spookily reminiscent of Emerson's deprecation of all poetry yet written in favor of a poetry that could never be written. The third, rather morose (for Stevens) in its solipsism, puts in question what "infatuation" can mean beyond the self's ambiance. Finally, the quatrain that ends the sequence seeks to oppose to a revolutionary Shelleyan *pathos*, in respect to the fiction of the leaves, only the *ethos* of the Snow Man's reduction. Perhaps the irony is intended to be Nietzschean, but it fails of Nietzsche's pungency, as we are left uncertain of both Power and Fate in the two modes of strength and wisdom. All men, together, or any man in solitude can avenge a fallen leaf only through apocalyptic thought, but that is hardly the Nietzschean notion of repetition as the will's revenge against time. The Snow Man's wisdom is closer to the Nietzschean *Amor Fati*, but unlike that embrace of Necessity it does not melt into nihilism, in which only nothing stands for nothing. If there is a central formulation in *Like Decorations*, then it is section XII:

> The sense of the serpent in you, Ananke,
> And your averted stride
> Add nothing to the horror of the frost
> That glistens on your face and hair.

The sense of the serpent in the Platonic or Shelleyan or Emersonian Necessity, here or in *The Auroras of Autumn*, is a sense of seasonal cycle. But, as again Vendler precisely observes, Ananke here is "the strict, the final, the intrinsic, the limiting, the temporal." The horror of the frost is presented by Stevens as final and intrinsic, but these qualities belie the figuration of the serpent. It will not be until he writes the *Blue Guitar* that Stevens discovers how to reconcile his defensive resort to disjunctiveness with the demands for continuity (however illusive) of a long poem.

Like Decorations, for all its inventiveness, is one of the failures of *Ideas of Order*, together with such poems as *Lions in Sweden*, *Winter Bells*, and *A Fish-Scale Sunrise*, all of them also purely ironic exercises in repetition. In happy contrast, one of Stevens' own favorites, *How to Live. What to Do* (CP, 125–26), is probably the best shorter poem to be omitted from *The Palm at the End of the Mind:*

> Last evening the moon rose above this rock
> Impure upon a world unpurged.
> The man and his companion stopped
> To rest before the heroic height.
>
> Coldly the wind fell upon them
> In many majesties of sound:
> They that had left the flame-freaked sun
> To seek a sun of fuller fire.
>
> Instead there was this tufted rock
> Massively rising high and bare
> Beyond all trees, the ridges thrown
> Like giant arms among the clouds.
>
> There was neither voice nor crested image,
> No chorister, nor priest. There was
> Only the great height of the rock
> And the two of them standing still to rest.
>
> There was the cold wind and the sound
> It made, away from the muck of the land
> That they had left, heroic sound
> Joyous and jubilant and sure.

That is pure hyperbole or the American Sublime, remarkable for its repressive force, for its prolepsis of Stevens' late image of the Rock, excessive and tantalizing escape from disjunctiveness. As in the Key West chant, this heroic sublimity is put in question by its uneasy withdrawal from a reductive reality, here "the muck of the land / That they had left." The poem is a triumph of the Will-to-Power, but the triumph is somewhat diminished when read against a poem like *Meditation Celestial & Terrestrial* (*CP*, 123–24), a page away from it in *Ideas of Order:*

> The wild warblers are warbling in the jungle
> Of life and spring and of the lustrous inundations,
> Flood on flood, of our returning sun.

Day after day, throughout the winter,
We hardened ourselves to live by bluest reason
In a world of wind and frost,

And by will, unshaken and florid
In mornings of angular ice,
That passed beyond us through the narrow sky.

But what are radiant reason and radiant will
To warblings early in the hilarious trees
Of summer, the drunken mother?

Stevens has, in this book, no answer to such a question, which betrays a nostalgia not so much for a lost world in *Harmonium* as for a world this poet never had, though I do not doubt that much in him poignantly had wanted it. That is surely the underlying point of the contrast between *Sailing after Lunch* and *Farewell to Florida*, the poem written to replace it as the first poem in the public edition of *Ideas of Order*. Both of these are poems "about" the Romantic, but the bad faith of *Sailing after Lunch* is not redeemed by its halfhearted attack upon Emerson's American Romantic image of the transparent eyeball in the poem's final two stanzas:

It is least what one ever sees.
It is only the way one feels, to say
Where my spirit is I am,
To say the light wind worries the sail,
To say the water is swift today,

To expunge all people and be a pupil
Of the gorgeous wheel and so to give
That slight transcendence to the dirty sail,
By light, the way one feels, sharp white,
And then rush brightly through the summer air.

The "pupil / Of the gorgeous wheel" is also the middle of the Emersonian eyeball, producing the solipsistic vision that causes one "to expunge all people." The huge transcendence of the Emersonian transparency has diminished to a "slight transcendence," and the "sharp white" of one's feelings prophesies another Emersonian crisis-epiphany, the "being of the solid of white" in the second section of *The Auroras of Autumn*. "Where my spirit is I am" lightly parodies Jehovah and the Coleridgean Primary Imagination, preparing for the more serious parody in *Notes*, Part III, VIII. It hurts Stevens that the word "romantic" should have turned *pejorative*, yet he adds to the hurt by his own anxiety of influence. A year later, in 1936, he could replace this poem with the Spenserian–Shelleyan high rhetoric of *Farewell to Florida*:

> Go on, high ship, since now, upon the shore,
> The snake has left its skin upon the floor.
> Key West sank downward under massive clouds
> And silvers and greens spread over the sea. The moon
> Is at the mast-head and the past is dead.
> Her mind will never speak to me again.
> I am free. High above the mast the moon
> Rides clear of her mind and the waves make a refrain
> Of this: that the snake has shed its skin upon
> The floor. Go on through the darkness. The waves fly back.

The great serpent Ananke is turning the year into autumn, and the high ship of Stevens' poetry is urged to the North, away from Florida and from summer, away from the idea of creative solitude at Key West. "Her mind" is the mind of Florida, which is to say, the mind of *Harmonium* and of its revival in *Ideas of Order*. But more than the waves fly back:

> Her mind had bound me round. The palms were hot
> As if I lived in ashen ground, as if
> The leaves in which the wind kept up its sound
> From my North of cold whistled in a sepulchral South,
> Her South of pine and coral and coraline sea,
> Her home, not mine, in the ever-freshened Keys,
> Her days, her oceanic nights, calling
> For music, for whisperings from the reefs.
> How content I shall be in the North to which I sail
> And to feel sure and to forget the bleaching sand . . .

It is so erotic a stanza that the reader needs to keep reminding himself that this Florida, as a state of mind, is a trope of pathos, a synecdoche for desire and not desire itself. "The leaves in which the wind kept up its sound" is another rejoinder to the Snow Man, who would not hear any misery in the sound of the wind, in the sound of a few leaves. "Her home, not mine, in the ever-freshened Keys, / Her days, her oceanic nights, call-ing / For music" evokes the singer at Key West, with whom, however imaginary she was, we now see that Stevens fell in love. Here, in a poem where desire immediately undoes every irony, we know how to take the poet's assertion of his coming contentment in the North and how to read a stanza like the next one, where "hated" means "loved too much," and where that "Farewell" is wild with all regret:

> I hated the weathery yawl from which the pools
> Disclosed the sea floor and the wilderness
> Of waving seeds. I hated the vivid blooms
> Curled over the shadowless hut, the rust and bones,
> The trees like bones and the leaves half sand, half sun.
> To stand here on the deck in the dark and say
> Farewell and to know that that land is forever gone
> And that she will not follow in any word
> Or look, nor ever again in thought, except
> That I loved her once . . . Farewell. Go on, high ship.

The vision in the final stanza *is* of a total leaflessness, and yet, for the first time in this poem, the rhetoric of going on becomes persuasive:

> My North is leafless and lies in a wintry slime
> Both of men and clouds, a slime of men in crowds.
> The men are moving as the water moves,
> This darkened water cloven by sullen swells
> Against your sides, then shoving and slithering,
> The darkness shattered, turbulent with foam.
> To be free again, to return to the violent mind
> That is their mind, these men, and that will bind
> Me round, carry me, misty deck, carry me
> To the cold, go on, high ship, go on, plunge on.

The overt theme is that of *Owl's Clover*, the poet's ambivalent response to social disorder and the Marxist challenge, but the true *topos* is Freedom or Emersonian wildness, the *aporia* in whose midst lies the possibility of meaning. There is only the binding, whether by the mind of the summer or of the winter vision. Freedom is *Amor Fati*, the worship of the Beautiful Necessity, the rather grim resolve to plunge on.

Yet that is hardly either the dominant or the lasting impression of *Ideas of Order* as a book. What persists is the note of the American Sublime, a hyperbole overthrowing the ironies that attempt to work a catachresis upon it. This persistence of the dominant can be rendered by a cento of passages:

> One likes to practice the thing. They practice,
> Enough, for heaven. Ever-jubilant,
> What is there here but weather, what spirit
> Have I except it comes from the sun?

◇   ◇   ◇

> But how does one feel?
> One grows used to the weather,
> The landscape and that;
> And the sublime comes down
> To the spirit itself,
>
> The spirit and space,
> The empty spirit
> In vacant space.
> What wine does one drink?
> What bread does one eat?

◇   ◇   ◇

> Be thou the voice,
> Not you. Be thou, be thou
> The voice of angry fear,
> The voice of this besieging pain.
>
> Be thou that wintry sound
> As of the great wind howling,
> By which sorrow is released,
> Dismissed, absolved
> In a starry placating.

◇   ◇   ◇

. . . Evening, when the measure skips a beat
And then another, one by one, and all
To a seething minor swiftly modulate.
Bare night is best. Bare earth is best. Bare, bare,
Except for our own houses, huddled low
Beneath the arches and their spangled air,
Beneath the rhapsodies of fire and fire,
Where the voice that is in us makes a true response,
Where the voice that is great within us rises up,
As we stand gazing at the rounded moon.

Stevens denied that the "ever jubilant" weather was a symbol, but of course as synecdoche it is, and as he said, "The state of the weather soon becomes a state of mind" (*L,* 349). The Sublime ambition here, and in the other passages, derives from *Song of Myself:* to be a physical being in a physical world, while acknowledging, as Whitman did when truest, that one celebrates "the empty spirit / In vacant space." Though the Shelleyan "Be thou me" becomes, in 1935, "the voice of this besieging pain," and the "thou" be reduced to a wintry sound, still the word is spoken, and by it "sorrow is released." "Bare earth is best," and yet "the voice that is great within us rises up," beautifully betraying still its family resemblance in the tribes of the imagination, its carry-on from Shelley and from Whitman, persistent questers after the Sublime.

Any consideration of *Ideas of Order* ought not to conclude without glancing at its three beautiful and plangent elegies for Stevens' own poetic self, *Sad Strains of a Gay Waltz* (which might be called *Hoon's Last Stand*), *Anglais Mort à Florence,* and *A Postcard from the Volcano. Sad Strains* celebrates mournfully the vanishing of Hoon's vision, under the pressures of the social theme that was to draw forth from Stevens *Owl's Clover,* his largest failure. Yet it ends in an intimation that Stevens, as harmonious skeptic, may yet redeem his own work, if not the time. The little elegy for an imaginary English High Romantic dead at Florence is Stevens' saddest and most elegant version of Wordsworth's *Immortality* ode and is another anticipation of *The Auroras of Autumn,* particularly in its lament for a time of lost glory, "before the colors deepened and grew small." *A Postcard,* the best of these laments, achieves the most mature balance in *Ideas of Order*, between the pride of a poet's belief that in dying he leaves behind a legacy that alters "the look of things" and the final transumptive or projective undoing of *Harmonium*'s great Whitmanian trope of the sun. *Ideas of Order* can be thought of as concluding, majestically but despairingly, with the poet's confession of his temporal defeat. Any belated Romantic, whether Shelley, Whitman, or Stevens, leaves us a final image of himself and his creation as

> A spirit storming in blank walls,
>
> A dirty house in a gutted world,
> A tatter of shadow peaked to white,
> Smeared with the gold of the opulent sun.

The strong rhetoric here is at variance with the sentiment, and the title's bitter image of the Sublime poet as a man who mails us postcards from the volcano curiously predicts the poet of *Esthétique du Mal* nearly a decade later, the poet who "could describe / The terror of the sound because the sound / Was ancient." It might have seemed, in 1936, that Stevens was again at an impasse, but soon after he was to be able to write:

> Here I inhale profounder strength
> And as I am, I speak and move
>
> And things are as I think they are
> And say they are on the blue guitar.

6 *The Man with the Blue Guitar*

The Stevens who matters most, and will go on mattering, is the poet of *Notes toward a Supreme Fiction* (1942) and the series of strong poems that followed it, *Esthétique du Mal* (1944), *Credences of Summer* (1946), *The Owl in the Sarcophagus* (1947), *The Auroras of Autumn* (1947), *An Ordinary Evening in New Haven* (1949), *The Rock* (1950), and the twenty or so astonishing late lyrics that came after *The Rock* in the final five years of Stevens' life. The peculiar centrality of *The Man with the Blue Guitar* (1937) in Stevens' canon is that it is the threshold to this major phase of his work. Though, in some respects, the nervy, apparently improvisatory manner of the *Blue Guitar* represents a triumph over its poet's literary anxieties, the poem itself is dwarfed by what was to come. As readers we need to be generous enough to restore some of the poem's vivacity by reading it against the *Comedian* rather than against the intricate splendors of *Notes* and the *Auroras*.

The *Comedian*, as we saw, was the satyr-romance closing out the tradition that goes from *Alastor* through *The Wanderings of Oisin*, very much a British tradition. But the *Blue Guitar* is a very American poem, and deliberately so. Its precursor poem is *Song of Myself*, which is also the model, but again through misprision, of *Notes*. There is a movement, in Stevens, hidden always, yet unmistakable, from a repressed concern with *The Sleepers* and the *Sea-Drift* pieces, on to *Song of Myself*, and then back to *The Sleepers* in *The Owl in the Sarcophagus* and finally to *When Lilacs Last in the Dooryard Bloom'd* in *The Rock*. I've discussed Whitman in relation to the *Comedian* and to *Ideas of*

Order, but I want now to introduce *The Blue Guitar* through a fuller examination of this subtlest and most elusive of really crucial intertextual relationships between Stevens and other poets. A juxtaposition of two passages, from *Song of Myself*, section 2, and *Blue Guitar*, xx, can begin this examination, though the juxtaposition rather diminishes Stevens, who seems skinny if not puny alongside the superbly exuberant, the Sublime Walt, whose superior rhetorical power is accompanied so uncannily by a suppleness of dialectic:

> The smoke of my own breath,
> Echoes, ripples, buzz'd whispers, love-root, silk-thread, crotch
>   and vine,
> My respiration and inspiration, the beating of my heart, the
>   passing of blood and air through my lungs,
> The sniff of green leaves and dry leaves, and of the shore and
>   dark-color'd sea-rocks, and of hay in the barn,
> The sounds of the belch'd words of my voice, loos'd to the
>   eddies of the wind,
> A few light kisses, a few embraces, a reaching around of arms,
> The play of shine and shade on the trees as the supple boughs
>   wag,
> The delight alone or in the rush of the streets, or along the
>   fields and hill-sides,
> The feeling of health, the full-noon trill, the song of me rising
>   from bed and meeting the sun.

◇   ◇   ◇

> What is there in life except one's ideas,
> Good air, good friend, what is there in life?
>
> Is it ideas that I believe?
> Good air, my only friend, believe,
>
> Believe would be a brother full
> Of love, believe would be a friend,
>
> Friendlier than my only friend,
> Good air. Poor pale, poor pale guitar . . .

    This section of the *Blue Guitar* can remind us of the epigraph to *Evening without Angels* that Stevens took from the contemporary Italian philosopher Mario Rossi: "The great interests of man: air and light, the joy of having a body, the voluptuousness of looking." We could regard this as an apt epigraph for all of Stevens' poetry, and for all of Whitman's as well. Air heads the list of man's great interests, because there is no belief possible. In the absence of faith, air is the only friend. But that is Stevens. Whitman finds a closer substitute for belief in his own breath, the passing of air through his lungs. Still, this self-intoxication directly follows an invocation of the air as beloved friend:

> The atmosphere is not a perfume; it has no taste of the
>   distillation, it is odorless,
> It is for my mouth forever, I am in love with it,
> I will go to the bank by the wood and become undisguised and
>   naked,
> I am mad for it to be in contact with me.

Even here, Whitman does not say he is mad for himself to be in contact with the air. He remains central. He is the cynosure. Stevens cannot achieve such self-confidence, but his dilemmas and his resources in the *Blue Guitar* are in their crucial respects difficult to distinguish from Whitman's in *Song of Myself*. The dilemmas of Stevens, in *Ideas of Order*, could find no resolution in a long poem, *Like Decorations* constituting the closest approach to one, but so deliberately disjunctive as scarcely to have been a sequence, let alone a long or longer poem. The question now to be answered is: what led Stevens, on whatever level of consciousness or intention, to the Whitmanian model for the *Blue Guitar*, assuming that I am correct in seeing the poem as a variant upon the Whitmanian model? A. Walton Litz makes the useful observation that the 1935 sequence or long poem *Owl's Clover* "stands in the same relation to *Ideas of Order* as *The Comedian* does to *Harmonium*." The failure of *Owl's Clover*, incontrovertibly Stevens' poorest performance, is an element that helped precipitate the change in mode that gave Stevens the *Blue Guitar*.

Stevens might as well have called *Owl's Clover* by the title he once ventured, *Aphorisms on Society*, as the poem is his one full-scale invocation of the social muse, his rather desperately mistaken attempt to mix it up with the Marxists. By temperament Stevens was incapable of formulating any social vision less archaic than the one he had inherited from his family and his social class. He had written only the first section of *Owl's Clover* when he read an attack on the first edition of *Ideas of Order* by the then-Marxist critic Stanley Burnshaw. Roused, Stevens visited upon Burnshaw the same unhappy immortality that Blake gave to the trooper Scholfield and Joyce to Gogarty under the grand name of Malachi Mulligan. Part II of *Owl's Clover*, probably its best section, is *Mr. Burnshaw and the Statue*, the response of Stevens to Burnshaw's observation that "*Ideas of Order* is the record of a man who, having lost his footing, now scrambles to stand up and keep his balance." In a letter commenting on the poem, Stevens paraphrased his argument: "The only possible order of life is one in which all order is incessantly changing. Marxism may or may not destroy the existing sentiment of the marvellous; if it does, it will create another" (*L*, 291–92).

Unfortunately, Stevens could not maintain this level of commentary, whether in the poem or in prose. *Mr. Burnshaw and the Statue* is impressive wherever Stevens is able to repress his social and poetic anxieties into his own variety of the American Sublime, but much is left unrepressed, until the poem, like the rest of *Owl's Clover*, collapses into a hysteria of bad wit. I find it difficult to accept a passage like this as being by the poet of *The Auroras, Notes, An Ordinary Evening*, and *The Rock:*

> A solemn voice, not Mr. Burnshaw's says:
> At some gigantic, solitary urn,
> A trash can at the end of the world, the dead
> Give up dead things and the living turn away.
> There buzzards pile their sticks among the bones
> Of buzzards and eat the bellies of the rich,
> Fat with a thousand butters, and the crows
> Sip the wild honey of the poor man's life,
> The blood of his bitter brain; and there the sun
> Shines without fire on columns intercrossed,
> White slapped on white, majestic, marble heads
> Severed and tumbled into seedless grass,
> Motionless, knowing neither dew nor frost.

Can we define the badness of this? The solemn voice is uncomfortably close to Stevens' own elegiac tone, and the reader need not be a Marxist to reflect that his heart is not moved by the sorrows that make Stevens so pompously solemn. Stevens was forgetting again the Whitmanian lesson of Hoon and of the woman at Key West, which was, "Chant to yourself in solitude." We can see now what John Jay Chapman first saw and memorably said, that Whitman truly addressed only himself, that *Song of Myself* is a great *esoteric* poem, because the poet in Whitman was too wise to join the man Whitman in the self-deceiving mystification that he could sing to the masses in their own language. Stevens, as man, hardly wanted to make such an attempt, but he came to an impasse as a poet whenever he failed to repress the anxiety of not making the attempt. I think that this is where the power of the *Blue Guitar* is to be located, for the poem continually reflects upon an audience that makes the wrong demands upon a poet, yet it centers always upon Stevens' own earlier self.

Stevens contrasted *Owl's Clover* and the *Blue Guitar* by saying that the effect of *Owl's Clover* was to isolate poetry by emphasizing the opposition between things as they are and things imagined, while the *Blue Guitar* dealt with the conjunctions between things as they are and things imagined. But Stevens' contrast is as rhetorically misleading as it is thematically accurate, since the language of *Owl's Clover* is conjunctive, while the *Blue Guitar* is marked throughout by a pervasive rhetorical disjunctiveness. Helen Vendler, here as elsewhere Stevens' most astute rhetorical critic, admirably summarizes the poem's style:

> After indulging in the grandiose paragraphs of *Owl's Clover*, Stevens seems to have set himself the problem . . . of making a long poem out of the fewest possible words. . . . The monotonous continuo of a strumming guitar appears in the repetitive downbeat of "things as they are" and "the blue guitar" (with all their variations) as well as in the insistent resurgence of other talismanic phrases.

I would add to this that much of the effect of *The Man with the Blue Guitar* depends upon the interplay of a minimal vocabulary and a disjunctive movement between figurations, a discord founded upon only a very few notes. Where I will suggest a disagreement with Vendler is in her notion that the *Blue Guitar* "could be rearranged internally without loss," because I find in this poem, as in *Song of Myself* or the *Comedian* or *Notes* or the *Auroras*, the characteristic ordering of the post-Enlightenment crisis-poem. This is the pattern of ratios and of crossings in *The Man with the Blue Guitar*:

I–IV	*Clinamen*, or dialectic irony of presence and absence
Crossing of Election	
V–VI	*Tessera*, or synecdochal reversal
VII–XVII	*Kenosis*, or metonymic isolation and emptying out
Crossing of Solipsism	
XVIII–XXI	
	Daemonization, or the hyperbolical Sublime
XXII–XXVII	
	Askesis, or sublimating metaphor
Crossing of Identification	
XXVIII–XXXIII	*Apophrades*, or transumptive balance between projection and introjection

That is, of course, the merest grid, but the *Blue Guitar*, with its highly disjunctive rhetoric and its minimal diction, does little to evade or conceal this traditional design, which is only to say that despite its surface buoyancy the poem depicts crisis in Stevens' poetic career, as did the *Comedian* and *The Idea of Order at Key West*, and as the *Auroras* and *The Rock* will do during the final years. Yet this is truly the happiest of Stevens' crisis-poems, because the crisis is resolved less ambivalently than it had been earlier or was to be again.

Section I–IV are the poem's opening swerve away from its own origins, which have little to do with Picasso's painting "The Old Guitarist" and much to do with Romantic poetry, particularly with Shelley in his final year, 1822, writing poems to Jane Williams, one entitled *With a Guitar, To Jane*, and another celebrating her song as she played the guitar, to her lover, and revealed "some world far from ours, / Where music and moonlight and feeling / Are one." Both poems, with their star and moon imagery, are echoed in *Mr. Burnshaw and the Statue:*

> In a mortal lullaby, like porcelain,
> Then, while the music makes you, make, yourselves,
> Long autumn sheens and pittering sounds like sounds
> On pattering leaves and suddenly with lights,
> Astral and Shelleyan, diffuse new day.

Critics have misread this, weakly, as an attack upon Shelley, which the context alone would reveal to be unlikely, and which Stevens, in a letter, clearly disowns, in a strong tribute to the harmonious skeptic among his Romantic precursors: "The astral and Shelleyan lights are not going to alter the structure of nature. Apples will always be apples, and whoever is a ploughman hereafter will be what the ploughman has always been. For all that, the astral and the Shelleyan will have transformed the world" (*L*, 367).

Shelley and Stevens shared a preference for azure or blue as the color of the imagination, and we can say that whereas Picasso's guitar is brown a Shelleyan guitar is necessarily blue. A Shelleyan guitar, of course, is not at all interested in playing things as they are, but rather sings the secrets either "of an elder day" or "of some world far from ours." Stevens had invoked the astral and Shelleyan lights that shone upon Jane Williams and her guitar, in order to contrast "pure poetry" to the Marxist reductions of Mr. Burnshaw. In *The Man with the Blue Guitar*, Stevens himself picks up the Shelleyan instrument, not to put Shelleyan lights into question but to fashion a defense of poetry adequate to 1937. As a guitarist, Stevens is only a shearsman, a tailor patching both the world and the hero, for his starting point is the *ethos* of limitation, or poetry confined to the area of poetry. He begins as any poet must, with the insistence that "things as they are / Are changed upon the blue guitar." Behind his poem's opening is the opening of Shelley's *Defence of Poetry*, which is never far away at any point in the poem. The blue guitar is also Shelley's Æolian lyre:

Man is an instrument over which a series of external and internal impressions are driven, like the alternations of an ever-changing wind over an Æolian lyre, which move it by their motion to ever-changing melody. But there is a principle within the human being, and perhaps within all sentient beings, which acts otherwise than in a lyre, and produces not melody alone, but harmony, by an internal adjustment of the sounds and motions thus excited to the impressions which excite them. It is as if the lyre could accommodate its chords to the motions of that which strikes them, in a determined proportion of sound; even as the musician can accommodate his voice to the sound of the lyre.

Stevens' *clinamen* is his regretful reaction formation against this Shelleyan kind of skeptical confidence in the poet's power to create harmony as well as melody. *The Man with the Blue Guitar* picks out a melody, but no more than that. His audience asks for the Whitmanian impossible, a transcendence through "a tune beyond us" yet a tune that is "ourselves." As shearsman, Stevens recalls the grim final line of the *Comedian:* "So may the relation of each man be clipped." Section III plays upon what Stevens believed he recalled as a Pennsylvania farm custom: nailing up a hawk to frighten off other hawks.

> Ah, but to play man number one,
> To drive the dagger in his heart,
>
> To lay his brain upon the board
> And pick the acrid colors out,
>
> To nail his thought across the door,
> Its wings spread wide to rain and snow,
>
> To strike his living hi and ho
> To tick it, tock it, turn it true,
>
> To bang it from a savage blue,
> Jangling the metal of the strings . . .

Absent here, as Stevens commented, is man. What does it mean "to express man in the liveliness of lively experience, without pose" (*L*, 783), and to do it exactly, when by inherent limitation you cannot "play man number one," you cannot reach to man through art? The negations of total absence and total presence precipitate Stevens into the desperation of section IV, where the irony is completed and we realize that the poet cannot play things as they are. Between the buzzing of the feelings and the buzzing of the guitar there is a gap that Stevens, and his poem, need to close or at least to cross.

The first crossing or disjunction concerns Stevens' election or vocation: is he still a poet, is anyone still a poet? A synecdochal rhetoric, noble and nostalgic, strikingly changes the poem's tonality, with section v:

> Do not speak to us of the greatness of poetry,
> Of the torches wisping in the underground,
>
> Of the structure of vaults upon a point of light.
> There are no shadows in our sun
>
> Day is desire and night is sleep.
> There are no shadows anywhere.
>
> The earth, for us, is flat and bare.
> There are no shadows. Poetry
>
> Exceeding music must take the place
> Of empty heaven and its hymns,
>
> Ourselves in poetry must take their place,
> Even in the chattering of your guitar.

It is worth remarking that Stevens' favorite moment in the day was earliest morning, when the light begins but the sun is not yet over the horizon. This is the moment called, in *The Rock*, III, "the difficult rightness of half-risen day." A letter written four months before Stevens' death, to a young Korean poet in New Haven, beautifully catches this "difficult rightness":

Well, then, greetings from all us rabbits. I say that because the rabbits are definitely out of their holes for the season; the robins are back; the doves have returned from Korea and some of them sit on our chimney before sunrise and tell each other how happy they are in the most melancholy tones. Robins and doves are both early risers and are connoisseurs of daylight before the actual presence of the sun coarsens it. [L, 879]

The greatness of poetry, enhanced by Orphic torches in Hades, is not to be spoken of to ourselves, who are connoisseurs of daylight. The guitar chatters, yet it is the way to the only heaven we can visualize in such uncoarsened daylight. Poetry is here the synecdoche for all that could be transcendent, yet this transcendence can change nothing, cannot repair our mutilations. Poetry makes a new *topos*, a place of *pathos*, yet the placing is defensively a reversal. The divine has become a dew so redundant that it looks like smoke, and art seems final in contrast, but the art here gives only a touch more space. This movement of the poem ends with an uneasy "composing of senses of the guitar," an antithetical completion that invites a further and immediate emptying out, which it forthwith receives in the longest movement of the poem, the metonymic and very Whitmanian *kenosis* of sections VII–XVII.

One of the poem's subtlest laments begins this movement:

> It is the sun that shares our works.
> The moon shares nothing. It is a sea.
>
> When shall I come to say of the sun,
> It is a sea; it shares nothing;
>
> The sun no longer shares our works
> And the earth is alive with creeping men,
>
> Mechanical beetles never quite warm?
> And shall I then stand in the sun, as now
>
> I stand in the moon, and call it good,
> The immaculate, the merciful good,
>
> Detached from us, from things as they are?
> Not to be part of the sun? To stand
>
> Remote and call it merciful?
> The strings are cold on the blue guitar.

Here is Stevens' own paraphrase, useful chiefly because he names the accurate defense, isolation, which dominates the emptying out of his poetic self:

I have a sense of isolation in the presence of the moon as in the presence of the sea. If I could experience the same sense in the presence of the sun, would I speak to the sun as I so often speak to the moon, calling it mercy and goodness? But if I could experience the same sense in the presence of the sun, my imagination grows cold at the thought of such complete detachment. I do not desire to exist apart from our works and the imagination does not desire to exist apart from our works. [L, 362]

As almost always, Stevens' verse and his prose paraphrase have an uneasy intertextual relationship, since the verse exudes a psychic necessity for the defense of isolation and the prose denies any desire for such a defense. Isolation defends by destroying context, yet without context there can be no poem, leaving the strings cold on the blue guitar. The poetic instinct that is being isolated, defensively, is the High Romantic desire for the confrontations of the Reason rather than the subject-object knowings of the mere understanding. The isolating progresses, by metonymic cataloging, in the following sections, VIII and IX, which Stevens said showed that "the dull world is either its poets or nothing" (L., 363). Poetry is the "lazy, leaden twang" of the guitar, yet it limits the storm's chaos but in IX is limited itself by the weather that Stevens calls reality. Section X contemplates, with polemical zeal, the reduction of the hero in an unpoetic society and is perhaps the least interesting section in the poem. Stevens compensates with the uncanny section XI:

Slowly the ivy on the stones
Becomes the stones. Women become

The cities, children become the fields
And men in waves become the sea.

It is the chord that falsifies.
The sea returns upon the men,

The fields entrap the children, brick
Is a weed and all the flies are caught,

> Wingless and withered, but living alive.
> The discord merely magnifies.
>
> Deeper within the belly's dark
> Of time, time grows upon the rock.

This empties the world out so thoroughly that we wonder how the poem can bear to go on. Stevens said that time here meant "life" and the rock meant "the world," which is a weak misreading at best. The rock is close to being the terrible mother, whether of Whitman or Stevens' *Madame La Fleurie*, and time is just time, or repetition. I don't subscribe to Vendler's characteristically bleak view of *The Man with the Blue Guitar* as "a duet with the undertaker," but the movement from sections VII through XVII is mercilessly exuberant in its undoings. In XII, the orchestra of people in the mass reduces to the timid breathing of the insomniac poet, who himself reduces to his art. In XIII, Hoon returns, to be debased into the apotheosis of blue as "the amorist Adjective aflame," a phrase that must have hurt Stevens. After all this negativity, the poem has the wisdom to relent, briefly, in XIV, before an extraordinary descent to a nadir in XV–XVII. As one analytical beam after another lights up the sky, and yet the sea and shore remain recalcitrant to our "scientific" understanding, the poet wages his *polemos* against the "German chandelier," the baroque overelaborateness of the rival disciplines of thought. The image for poetry is again the Emersonian one from *Society and Solitude:* "A scholar is a candle which the love and desire of all men will light." But this pride of the poet cannot abide, and Stevens' most radical undoing of his own residual idealism follows, in a deconstructive eloquence surpassing his earlier enterprises in decreation.

Picasso had tried to define the difference between earlier paintings and his own work by calling past painting a total amount (sum or hoard) of additions and his painting a total amount of destructions. This is the starting point of section XV, where the destruction culminates in the metonymic "spot" which is a parody of Stevens himself reduced to the First Idea of man:

Is this picture of Picasso's, this "hoard
Of destructions," a picture of ourselves,

Now, an image of our society?
Do I sit, deformed, a naked egg,

Catching at Good-bye, harvest moon,
Without seeing the harvest or the moon?

Things as they are have been destroyed.
Have I? Am I a man that is dead

At a table on which the food is cold?
Is my thought a memory, not alive?

Is the spot on the floor, there, wine or blood
And whichever it may be, is it mine?

The disabling fear is that Stevens himself is only another
"hoard of destructions," who can hear words as words, but no
longer can see and feel the veritable harvest or the actual moon.
In the next lyric, mother earth transcends even her own terrors
to become oppressive stone, grudging us even a good death and
abandoning the distressed and naturalistic Stevens "to chop the
sullen psaltery," which he paraphrased weakly as "to write poetry with difficulty" (*L*, 360). To sing such psalms as the lyrics
of the *Blue Guitar* is to "place honey on the altars and die," a
line that would have graced Keats's *Fall of Hyperion*.

At the exact midpoint of his sequence, section XVII, Stevens
completes his *kenosis*, the total emptying out of his poetic spirit,
his share in the ultimate imaginative godhead of the makers:

The person has a mould. But not
Its animal. The angelic ones

Speak of the soul, the mind. It is
An animal. The blue guitar—

On that its claws propound, its fangs
Articulate its desert days.

> The blue guitar a mould? That shell?
> Well, after all, the north wind blows
>
> A horn, on which its victory
> Is a worm composing on a straw.

We can observe again Stevens' retreat from his own merci-lessness by a juxtaposition of this text with his prose para-phrase, so much gentler in its implications:

> The person has a mould = the body has a form. All men have es-sentially the same form. But the spirit does not have a form. What would the form of the spirit be, if the form of the north wind is no more than that of a worm composing on a straw, to judge from the fact that, even at its deadliest, it blows with little or no sound? [L, 360]

The lyric polemicizes against "the angelic ones," believers in Christ or in Plato, and yet it knows it is angelic about poetry. If the blue guitar is another animal, then it is the firecat of *Earthy Anecdote* (1918), Stevens' version of Blake's Tyger, bristling in the way of the poet. Or it is the lion of *Poetry Is a Destructive Force* (1938):

> The lion sleeps in the sun.
> Its nose is on its paws.
> It can kill a man.

Either way, the guitar lacks a human form divine. If it has a form, if it is body or person as well as force or spirit—that is, if it can be incarnated in a poet—what form could that tortoise-shell of a lyre have anyway? What form does the greater force of the north wind have, since its victory over our utterances is only the small sound of a worm composing on a straw, in the great silences of a cosmos conceived wholly materialistically? Behind Stevens' north wind is Shelley's prayer to the west wind, when he urged it to be, through his poet's lips, the trum-pet of a prophecy to unawakened earth. Halfway through his poem, Stevens has despaired of it and has arrived at the mid-crossing that I have called the Crossing of Solipsism, the negative moment or breaking of form that is at once *logos* and *aporia*, and that precedes a sudden mounting into a personalized Counter-Sublime.

This *daemonization* is the labor of xviii through xxi, where the American precursors, Emerson and Whitman, make a hovering re-entrance, culminating in the vision of the Transcendentalist mountain, Chocorua, brother to Emerson's Monadnoc and Thoreau's Wachusett, and in 1943 to reappear in the exalted poem *Chocorua to Its Neighbor*, one of Stevens' clearest victories over his own ironic evasions.

It is useful to consider the sequence of xviii–xxi with initial emphasis upon the crossing from xvii to xviii:

> The blue guitar a mould? That shell?
> Well, after all, the north wind blows
>
> A horn, on which its victory
> Is a worm composing on a straw.
>
> A dream (to call it a dream) in which
> I can believe, in face of the object,
>
> A dream no longer a dream, a thing,
> Of things as they are, as the blue guitar
>
> After long strumming on certain nights
> Gives the touch of the senses, not of the hand,
>
> But the very senses as they touch
> The wind-gloss. Or as daylight comes,
>
> Like light in a mirroring of cliffs,
> Rising upward from a sea of ex.

There is a movement here from a mimetic theory of poetry to an expressive theory, attended by greater internalization of the self and by a sensory transposition from hearing, first to touching and then to seeing, a clarified seeing in the mode of Stevens' "difficult rightness." The disjunction is abrupt, from a metonymic reification to an hyperbolical transcendence. Or, as Stevens said, in one of his stronger paraphrases: "The imagination takes us out of (Ex) reality into a pure irreality. One has this sense of irreality often in the presence of morning light on cliffs which then rise from a sea that has ceased to be real and is therefore a sea of Ex." (L, 360).

Can we locate more precisely the triumphant solipsism or isolation that allows Stevens to cross into the pure irreality of his Sublime, which is to say, can we identify exactly what it is that he represses so strongly as to free his sense of his own glory? What revives Hoon within him?

The object marks the limit of solipsism, and when Stevens says that his dream is "no longer a dream" then the universe of death or object-world has yielded to the poet's asserted power of mind. Repression here is of everything in consciousness that admits dualism. The particular repression is of the awareness that one's own hand writes the poem, strums the guitar. The poem does not ensue from "the very senses as they touch / The wind-gloss," which would be a revival of Shelley's High Romantic trope. What follows is the Shelleyan or Blakean antithetical desire of xix, where the trope of *pathos* or Power, "the lion in the lute," attempts to outface the *ethos* of nature and Fate, "the lion locked in stone":

> That I may reduce the monster to
> Myself, and then may be myself
>
> In face of the monster, be more than part
> Of it, more than the monstrous player of
>
> One of its monstrous lutes, not be
> Alone, but reduce the monster and be,
>
> Two things, the two together as one,
> And play of the monster and of myself,
>
> Or better not of myself at all,
> But of that as its intelligence,
>
> Being the lion in the lute
> Before the lion locked in stone.

This is again the repressive force of the Emersonian–Whitmanian American Sublime, which defeats Necessity only by
joining itself to Necessity. Inevitably, as in Whitman, there is a
descent from such an identification in xx, which we examined
earlier. Stevens' *daemonization* attains its climax in the imagery
of xxi, which ascends Chocorua only to descend into the abyss
of "the flesh, the bone, the dirt, the stone," returning the poem
to its next movement, the sublimating metaphors of xxii
through xxvii.

What is probably the best-known section of the *Blue Guitar*,
xxii, is also the most problematic:

> Poetry is the subject of the poem,
> From this the poem issues and
>
> To this returns. Between the two,
> Between issue and return, there is
>
> An absence in reality,
> Things as they are. Or so we say.
>
> But are these separate? Is it
> An absence for the poem, which acquires
>
> Its true appearances there, sun's green,
> Cloud's red, earth feeling, sky that thinks?
>
> From these it takes. Perhaps it gives,
> In the universal intercourse.

Stevens observed of this lyric that "poetry is the spirit, as the
poem is the body" (*L*, 363), which itself is a formula for sublimation or the return of the dualism overcome in xviii through
xxi. Ultimately derived from Coleridge, Stevens' formula sets
imagination as "inside" in perspectivizing relation to reality as
"outside," and perspectivism is the mark of nearly all the imagery of xxii through xxvii. The "universal intercourse" of xxii,
the "Dichtung und Wahrheit" of xxiii, and the poem in the
mud of xxiv are all variations upon this theme, which is epi-
tomized in the metaphor "a hawk of life," where the hawk is

the inside term of poetic vision, seizing upon the world as its object. The next three lyrics, xxv through xxvii, instructively trace Stevens' self-defeating attempt to celebrate metaphor until at the close of xxvii, in the demon image, he completes his awareness that metaphor has failed him.

"He held the world upon his nose" begins the wild whirl of xxv, and though Stevens charmingly said that "he" could be Copernicus, Columbus, Alfred North Whitehead, or whoever, "he" appears to be Stevens himself as strong poet, flinging the world about at will, in a somewhat heavy and even desperate gaiety. An elegiac intensity replaces this fervor in the Whitmanian lyric xxvi, which recalls the vision of the last stanza of *Sunday Morning* and prophesies *Auroras*, vi. This is the cosmos of Whitman's *Sea-Drift* and of Emerson's *Seashore:*

> The world washed in his imagination,
> The world was a shore, whether sound or form
>
> Or light, the relic of farewells,
> Rock, of valedictory echoings,
>
> To which his imagination returned,
> From which it sped, a bar in space,
>
> Sand heaped in the clouds, giant that fought
> Against the murderous alphabet:
>
> The swarm of thoughts, the swarm of dreams
> Of inaccessible Utopia.
>
> A mountainous music always seemed
> To be falling and to be passing away.

Stevens somberly said of this, "We have imagined things that we have failed to realize" (L, 364), and his lyric is an authentically American elegy, a study of the nostalgias. But this mood is uneasy and cannot prevail. The movement of *askesis* culminates in a rejection of perspectivizing, through an act of self-parody in which

> The iceberg settings satirize

The demon that cannot be himself,
That tours to shift the shifting scene.

With this satirical realization, Stevens reaches the threshold
of his poem's last crossing, the Crossing of Identification that
takes place between the poet as demonic tourist and the poet as
a native in this world. I judge the peculiar strength of *The Man
with the Blue Guitar* to inhere in its final movement, XXVIII
through XXXIII, which is the first full instance of a triumphant
use of a metaleptic or transumptive conclusion in Stevens'
major poetry. That is, in these final half-dozen lyrics, Stevens
introjects his own poetic future and projects or casts out his poetic past, at the knowing expense of any poetic resolution in the
present moment. This final recovery begins with an acknowl-
edgment that the precursors are part of Stevens' world, where
"the wave / In which the watery grasses flow" is Whitman's
identifying trope and "the wind in which the dead leaves blow"
is Shelley's. Yet just here, in a world of anterior images, of *other
minds*, Stevens is able to affirm that he inhales profounder
strength. Indeed he even approaches what will be the great resolution of *Notes* in his declaration "And as I am, I speak and
move." This self-reliance intensifies in XXIX, where the "Fran-
ciscan don" performs the same function as the rabbi does elsewhere in Stevens, expressing a sense of a spirituality that is
very much part of this world. It does not matter, we are now
told, that the poet's "shapes are wrong and the sounds are
false," for a confidence has been achieved that this poet will
now be more himself. Though he has learned not "to play man
number one" on his guitar, he now will evolve a man for us, a
man who is a possible poet, himself, as Whitman was a fictive
self evolved by a poem. Yet this man will be only a puppet,
"the old fantoche," a resident of the banal suburb of Oxidia,
which at last is revealed to be a version of Olympia, but only as
the soot of fire is also the fire.

With this affirmation of *pathos*, Stevens movingly relaxes into
the surprising lyric geniality of XXXI, where the social theme
that strained *Owl's Clover* is set aside as the repetition of a droll
affair. It nears the end of winter, and Stevens listens for the

shriek of the pheasant that will announce the return of the spring to Hartford. "It must be this rhapsody or none," and Stevens is now content to choose what he can get. Out of such contentment come the power and pride of the great chant of XXXII, the poem's penultimate section:

> Throw away the lights, the definitions,
> And say of what you see in the dark
>
> That it is this or that it is that,
> But do not use the rotted names.
>
> How should you walk in that space and know
> Nothing of the madness of space,
>
> Nothing of its jocular procreations?
> Throw the lights away. Nothing must stand
>
> Between you and the shapes you take
> When the crust of shape has been destroyed.
>
> You as you are? You are yourself.
> The blue guitar surprises you.

This is major Stevens, prophesying the opening sections of *Notes*, five years later, and Stevens is immensely moving even in his paraphrase when he explains "You are yourself" as "being oneself being so not as one really is but as one of the jocular procreations of the dark, of space. The point of the poem is, not that this can be done, but that, if done, it is the key to poetry, to the closed garden, if I may become rhapsodic about it, of the fountain of youth and life and renewal" (*L*, 364).

Neither the verse nor the prose sounds much like part of a duet with the undertaker, and we need not search for irony where something better is offered to us, that something better being *surprise*. The blue guitar surprises Stevens as it surprises us, and we ought to remember that to be "surprised" means to be captured or to be taken hold of without warning. Stevens' poem suddenly has seized its poet and its reader together, and taught both the Whitmanian lesson of serious play, of the jocular procreation of the me myself out of the dark and out of the madness of space.

Nothing in Stevens up to this time is so majestic and persuasive as the final lyric of *The Man with the Blue Guitar:*

> That generation's dream, aviled
> In the mud, in Monday's dirty light,
>
> That's it, the only dream they knew,
> Time in its final block, not time
>
> To come, a wrangling of two dreams.
> Here is the bread of time to come,
>
> Here is its actual stone. The bread
> Will be our bread, the stone will be
>
> Our bed and we shall sleep by night.
> We shall forget by day, except
>
> The moments when we choose to play
> The imagined pine, the imagined jay.

We are naming realities in the dark, and therefore "that generation's dream" refers to every generation, always illusively seeking "time in its final block, not time / To come." But when the false lights are cast away, with the past, then we know that true time is always to come, and always dialectical, "a wrangling of two dreams." Introjecting the bread of time to come, the poet surrenders the present with the somber knowledge of an absence in reality: "Here is its actual stone," which is also the necessity of forgetting by day, except in the making of poetry. But this is no longer the playing of the guitar that opened the poem. No shearsman, no patcher can will those negative yet saving moments which give us the green of the imagined pine, the blue of the imagined jay. "Imagined" here has achieved a transumptive freshness. We are very near to the "ever-early candor" of *Notes* and to the celebration of that candor as "an elixir, an excitation, a pure power." The poet who had written *The Man with the Blue Guitar* had weathered his long crisis, and at fifty-eight was ready to begin again.

7 *Parts of a World*

Parts of a World (1942) is Stevens' most underrated book. It comprises most of his work between *The Man with the Blue Guitar* and *Notes toward a Supreme Fiction* and includes at least fifteen superb shorter poems and two accomplished long poems, *Extracts from Addresses to the Academy of Fine Ideas* and *Examination of the Hero in a Time of War*. *Extracts* is much the finer poem, and this chapter will concentrate upon it and on the half dozen shorter poems in the book that seem to me essential for any reader of Stevens: *A Rabbit as King of the Ghosts, The Poems of Our Climate, The Man on the Dump, Mrs. Alfred Uruguay, Asides on the Oboe,* and *The Well Dressed Man with a Beard*. But *Parts of a World* justifies its title; it is a noble synecdoche of a book and gives us astonishing imaginative richness, more than did *Ideas of Order* if several touches less than *Harmonium*. This judgment is so apparently eccentric, given the contours of Stevens criticism to date, that a little polemic seems in order. Helen Vendler and Joseph Riddel, two of the canonical critics of Stevens, agree upon little else, but both of them rate *Parts of a World* rather low. Vendler comments that, all through the book, "one side or another of Stevens' expressiveness seems to be restrained, ignored, or falsified, in violent seesaws of effort," while Riddel says that the book "has a forbidding singleness of tone, of a world without variety and hence life." Stevens proleptically answered his critics in the final line of *Parochial Theme*, the first poem in the book, which reads, "Piece the world together, boys, but not with your hands." Or, as he said earlier in the poem:

This health is holy, this descant of a self,
This barbarous chanting of what is strong, this blare.

But salvation here? What about the rattle of sticks
On tins and boxes? What about horses eaten by wind?

The first two of these lines are deliberately the purest Whitman, or else a parody of his holy descant of self, his blaring chant that Santayana had called "the poetry of barbarism." The last two lines are equally Whitmanian, but downward-turning, as Whitman frequently was. Stevens said of *Parochial Theme* that it meant "there is no such thing as life; what there is is a style of life from time to time" (*L*, 435). I would broaden this to a defense of *Parts of a World*. There is no such thing as a world in a book of poems; what there is is the style of a world from time to time. *Parts of a World* catches that style for 1937 through 1942, in the United States, and is clearly superior to any other American poetry of those prewar and then early-war years.

War, as A. Walton Litz observes, is the unifying theme of *Parts of a World*, whether it be war between the sky and the mind or between nations. But mostly I think it is between the sky and the mind, as it always is in Stevens. Not long after he finished the *Blue Guitar*, Stevens recorded a major battle in the war between being-without-consciousness and consciousness-without-being and titled it *A Rabbit as King of the Ghosts*. He considered it one of his favorites among his own poems, and I think we can surmise why. For Stevens, it must have represented both a return of the repressed, a kind of expansive letting go, and also the great danger of letting go. There is no critical agreement on the *Rabbit* poem and there isn't likely to be one, ever, as the reading of the poem depends upon a judgment as to its tonality. How ought this to be recited?

The difficulty to think at the end of day,
When the shapeless shadow covers the sun
And nothing is left except light on your fur—

There was the cat slopping its milk all day,
Fat cat, red tongue, green mind, white milk
And August the most peaceful month.

To be, in the grass, in the peacefullest time,
Without that monument of cat,
The cat forgotten in the moon;

And to feel that the light is a rabbit-light,
In which everything is meant for you
And nothing need be explained;

Then there is nothing to think of. It comes of itself;
And east rushes west and west rushes down,
No matter. The grass is full

And full of yourself. The trees around are for you,
The whole of the wideness of night is for you,
A self that touches all edges,

You become a self that fills the four corners of night.
The red cat hides away in the fur-light
And there you are humped high, humped up,

You are humped higher and higher, black as stone—
You sit with your head like a carving in space
And the little green cat is a bug in the grass.

The rabbit is the Sublime or Transcendental consciousness-without-being in Stevens, while the cat is his mere being-without-consciousness. Whose voice do we hear in the poem, which is to say, what is it in Stevens that speaks to the rabbit or grandly repressive consciousness in him? No simple answer is possible, and so the tone is ambiguous. I suggest that it is an ironic hysteria, the hysteria being in mimicry of or in sympathy with the more authentic hysteria of the rabbit. The largest clue to the poem is the repetition of the Emersonian–Whitmanian formula "for you." "Everything is meant *for you* / . . . The trees around are *for you*, / The whole of the wideness of night is *for you*." This echoes Emerson's famous address to his countrymen at the close of *Nature:* "Know then that the world exists for you. For you is the phenomenon perfect." Stevens' "for you, / A self that touches all edges" parodies also the Emerson of *Circles:* "There is no outside, no inclosing wall, no circumference to us." Whitman's curious half-parody, half-repetition of the Emersonian "for you" in *As I Ebb'd with the Ocean of Life* is part of this context also: "Just as much for us that sobbing dirge of Nature." Stevens, too, rather involuntarily, and probably unknowingly, both parodies and repeats Emerson. The rabbit of consciousness-without-being is the tendency within Stevens to seek an expansion of the self, beyond all bounds, and everything in Stevens that fears such expansiveness speaks the poem as an ironic warning. Yet the rhetoric of the poem is primarily hyperbolic, and the rabbit wins his Pyrrhic victory.

The poem opens in the difficult and negative moment of a consciousness seeking to be utterly free of being, free of "that moment of cat," free "to feel that the light is a rabbit-light," or an inner light made outer. What is the "it" of "It comes of itself" except the afflatus that Emerson, following the Swedenborgians, called "Influx" or "the Newness"? The rabbit is Hoon again, himself the compass of that sea, in whom all directions find their home. But the language is not Hoon's Whitmanian self-celebration. It is the language of hysteria rising to an apocalyptic pitch of consciousness, as the red cat of being vanishes. "And there you are humped high, humped up, / You are humped higher and higher" until you are a stone divinity, an Aztec or Mayan carving. Mount that high up, and your sense of your own mere being indeed is shrunk to a bug in the grass, but you have gone quite mad.

How can we connect this poem to the cosmos of *The Man with the Blue Guitar?* Why is not Chocorua, in lyric xxi, another rabbit as king of the ghosts? The rabbit is no lion in the lute, even though the cat may be the lion locked in stone. The American Sublime so beautifully touched in the *Blue Guitar* was no more a resting place for Stevens than it had been for Emerson, Whitman, or Dickinson, or for Stevens' younger contemporary Hart Crane. If we consider the progression of *Tea at the Palaz of Hoon, The Idea of Order at Key West, The Man with the Blue Guitar*, xxi, and then its culmination in *A Rabbit as King of the Ghosts*, do we confront the defeat of Stevens' return to the triad of power, will, and vitality? The language of desire, possession, and power seems to defeat Stevens whenever it becomes too unrestrained in him, yet his poetry all but died in the decade 1924–1934, when he evaded such language. Stevens could not live with the Sublime, as a poet, and he could not live without it and still be a poet.

I don't find it useful to distinguish between a true and false Sublime in Stevens, as Vendler attempts to do, because the Sublime seems to me neither true nor false but only there or not there. When it is not there, Stevens is quick to turn upon himself with intense alienation. The poems written directly after *A Rabbit* show the malaise of this absence. In the bitter *United Dames of America*, the Emersonian vision of the central man as poet is parodied again by the fiction of the leaves, as our faces, like leaves in the wind, repeat a "circling round a central face / And then nowhere again." Against the Transcendentalist image of the giant, Stevens sets his poem of *The Dwarf*, "the final dwarf of you, / . . . Neither as mask nor as garment but as a being," a dark epilogue to the year in which the *Blue Guitar* had been composed. The next year, 1938, though a rich one for Stevens' poetry, shows a continuous and mounting reductive reaction against the American Sublime and its Transcendentalist drive toward expanded consciousness-without-being. The sinister *Weak Mind in the Mountains* records a nightmare, and the yielding to nightmare's teachings, in the spirit's slumber, yet the poem ends poignantly with a flickering of the Sublime:

> Yet there was a man within me
> Could have risen to the clouds,
> Could have touched these winds,
> Bent and broken them down,
> Could have stood up sharply in the sky.

"Could have" is the revelatory formula, where "could" does not mean the possibility of the will becoming operative but something much more limited, something closer to a desperate wistfulness. This wistfulness is what Stevens called "the never-resting mind" in one of his most nearly perfect shorter works, the Keatsian meditation with the very American title of *The Poems of Our Climate*:

Clear water in a brilliant bowl,
Pink and white carnations. The light
In the room more like a snowy air,
Reflecting snow. A newly-fallen snow
At the end of winter when afternoons return.
Pink and white carnations—one desires
So much more than that. The day itself
Is simplified: a bowl of white,
Cold, a cold porcelain, low and round,
With nothing more than the carnations there.

This is Stevens' *Ode on a Grecian Urn* with "a bowl of white, / Cold, a cold porcelain" replacing Keats's "Cold Pastoral" that teases us out of thought. But Stevens, always acting the Snow Man, has been cold a long time. He has arranged his still life so as to make "the light / In the room more like a snowy air / Reflecting snow." Hence the choice of a brilliant or shining bowl, reminding us that "brilliant" means "full of light," and hence also the emphasis upon the clarity of the water and upon the pink and white as chosen colors. The intended effect is not a dead-of-winter Snow Man's vision but a slight upward turning: fresh snow, winter's end, lengthening of afternoon and so delaying of the twilight. The subtlest play here may be on the choice of flower, carnations, with their etymological hint of human flesh, which prompts the *illusio* of "one desires / So much more than that," where "more" means "less," and where "desires" flickers with the ghost of its etymological meaning, "to shine." So the opening irony, or alternation of imagistic presence and absence, offers itself as perhaps Stevens' most ineluctable swerve away from poetic origins. If I am correct in my surmise that Stevens' true precursor, like Williams', was a composite Keats / Whitman figure, just as Eliot's was Tennyson / Whitman, and Pound's Browning / Whitman, then the *clinamen* here ought to be away from a Keatsian text like the *Grecian Urn* but in a Whitmanian direction. Stevens says that "one desires / So much more than that" because his ostensible desire here is for "complete simplicity," but such "simplicity" is a trope for reduction or decreation, with the aim of arriving back at a fresh version of the Whitmanian "me myself." Where Keats deprecated "identity" or the "sole self," Whitman and Stevens quest for the powerful press of themselves.

With the movement to "The day itself / Is simplified," we are at the poem's first crossing, as its rhetoric disjunctively passes from irony to synecdoche, to the "cold porcelain, low and round" as a trope of Power. Just as the brilliant bowl is microcosm, so the cosmos or whole of the day is seen in the First Idea of whiteness. "How clean the day when seen in its idea," we might say, impressed by Stevens' power in so washing his bowl in the remote cleanliness of a heaven that we and our images are expelled. However, Stevens is throwing away neither the lights nor the definitions, as his next stanza evidences:

> Say even that this complete simplicity
> Stripped one of all one's torments, concealed
> The evilly compounded, vital I
> And made it fresh in a world of white,
> A world of clear water, brilliant-edged,
> Still one would want more, one would need more,
> More than a world of white and snowy scents.

The "vital I" is compounded evilly only because it is compounded at all. To be stripped of all one's torments, in this context, is to have one's poethood emptied out, until the ever-early candor is completed in the vision of "a world of clear water, brilliant-edged." Stevens does not allow himself much of the Sublime here, yet it creeps in by negation in the litotes or understatement of the stanza's close. Wanting and needing reflect a poverty that provokes the Sublime, and there is a ghostly crossing between the metonymy of "a world of white" and the litotes of "More than a world of white and snowy scents," with their evocation of the carnations. A curious return to the title becomes the dominant trope of the last stanza:

> There would still remain the never-resting mind,
> So that one would want to escape, come back
> To what had been so long composed.
> The imperfect is our paradise.

Note that, in this bitterness, delight,
Since the imperfect is so hot in us,
Lies in flawed words and stubborn sounds.

The Snow Man began with a trope of *ethos,* "a mind of winter" that vainly sought to ward off all tropes of *pathos.* The poems of our climate necessarily must be more varied than an exclusively wintry mind could hope to compose. Here, "never-resting" and "escape" are metaphors, inner turnings that perspectivize against the outer world, which is "what had been so long composed." But these metaphors vanish in the great line that is itself the poem's third crossing, its Oedipal disjunction of identification: "The imperfect is our paradise." We can suspect that Stevens' adage remembers Browning's praise of imperfection, and yet the anteriority of the line belongs more largely to Keats and to Whitman, whom Stevens introjects in his poem's final three lines. "This bitterness" is the imperfect earth, and the final lines are a prolepsis of the great passage that will conclude *Esthétique du Mal* six years later. "The imperfect is so hot in us" because we desire the perfection of a perpetual earliness and freshness, as the woman did in *Sunday Morning.* "Delight" is poetry's delight, and yet Stevens substitutes for the "keener sounds" that concluded his striding Key West meditation the "stubborn sounds" of this still-life piece. "Flawed words" mean all words, the flaw being belatedness, and here Stevens has not the strength to reverse the anteriority of his rhetoric. In some sense, *The Poems of Our Climate* comes to rest in a final implication that "in the way you speak / You arrange, the thing is posed, / What in nature merely grows." I quote from *Add This to Rhetoric,* a kind of footnote to the greater poem, and sharing with that still-life vision the Emersonian insight that everything that is not natural is rhetorical, which means that only the Not-Me, including the body, is free of rhetoric, while the soul itself "lies in flawed words and stubborn sounds." The play upon "lies" here is the poem's finest moment. Delight lies *to us* in flawed words and stubborn sounds, and also delight lies or inheres in such words and sounds.

This wordplay can introduce Stevens' other strong poem of

1938, the superbly bitter comedy of *The Man on the Dump*, where the verbal exuberance is at considerable variance with the poem's self-disgust, nowhere more so than in its mad apotropaic litany played upon the sacred word of *Harmonium*, which is "dew":

> The green smacks in the eye, the dew in the green
> Smacks like fresh water in a can, like the sea
> On a cocoanut—how many men have copied dew
> For buttons, how many women have covered themselves
> With dew, dew dresses, stones and chains of dew, heads
> Of the floweriest flowers dewed with the dewiest dew.
> One grows to hate these things except on the dump.

The dew of *Harmonium* was a synecdoche for everything in nature that still could be thought of as pure or refreshing, or rather for something that has not yet come into nature, a dew that might be, a dew associated with the sun not as a god but as a god might be. The motto for such dew is Nietzsche's wistful admonition "Try to live as though it were morning." The reader of *Harmonium* is now asked by Stevens to undergo the Emersonian wildness of attaining freedom by yielding to the *antithetical* motto "Everything that can be broken should be broken," and so what dissolves here is the fiction of the dew. We think back to so many splendors of this fiction in Stevens: to Crispin, for whom the spring came "irised in dew and early fragrancies"; to the Nietzschean "heavenly fellowship / Of men that perish and of summer morn," whose origin and whose purpose only "the dew upon their feet shall manifest." But mostly there is the Keatsian wonder of "the immense dew of Florida" beheld in *Nomad Exquisite*, a dew still being reflected in *Parts of a World*, as when the peaches in *A Dish of Peaches in Russia* (*CP*, 224) are full "of fair weather, summer, dew, peace"; or more grandly in the strong doctrinal poem *Asides on the Oboe*, where we will see that "the philosophers' man alone still walks in dew." The palinode of the fiction of the dew in Stevens is not in *The Man on the Dump*, which no more bids farewell to the dew than *Farewell to Florida* left Florida behind. It is in *The Rock* section of the *Collected Poems*, in the sinister *Madame La Fleurie*, that our waiting mother, the earth, destroys us by this fiction of fecundity: "His crisp knowledge is devoured by her, beneath a dew."

In *The Man on the Dump*, after eight appearances of dew in six lines, Stevens says, "One grows to hate these things except on the dump"; what he means is much the same as when, in *Farewell to Florida*, he says that he "hated" the weathery yawl and the vivid blooms he has abandoned. What is actually hated in the *Dump* poem is our *mimesis* of the dew, copying it or covering ourselves with its representation. Here Stevens is playing with the rather dangerous notion that you can write a poem which is "about" hating your own poems. A poet like Robinson Jeffers is always inadequate in such a posture, and even Marianne Moore is not very convincing when she allows herself to say, "I too dislike it." Several critics have juxtaposed *The Man on the Dump* with a passage in a preface that Stevens wrote to Williams, when Stevens says of the contemporary Romantic: "He happens to be one who still dwells in an ivory tower, but who insists that life would be intolerable except for the fact that one has, from the top, such an exceptional view of the public dump" (*OP*, 256).

The intertextual relation here is nearly one of blank opposition, as the poem, and Stevens, find the dump to be quite intolerable. *The Man on the Dump* is a later version of *The Snow Man*, but without the rhetorical restraint that dignified that reduction to a First Idea. Stevens is his own Childe Roland in this poem, and the dump is his own dark tower. To Stevens, as defeated quester, day creeps down and moon creeps up. Certainly the overt burden is belatedness, which this time Stevens does not bother even to conceal: "The freshness of night has been fresh a long time." Cornelius Nepos reads so easily that he used to be a standard text for learning Latin; morning and day have become standard texts also, too easy for the fastidious Stevens. But his is a knowing fastidiousness, and so we return to his disgust at his, and everyone else's, mimesis of the dew.

If you reject mimesis, then you cross over to an expressive theory of poetry, but that is here only a crossing "between that disgust and this." Nature is on the dump, and nature-to-come will be there. Stevens opts for the crossing; between disgusts, "One feels the purifying change. One regrets / The trash." Does one? Or does one merely substitute tropes of *ethos* for tropes of *pathos*, images of Fate for images of Power? The negative moment of substitution takes place, with deliberate grotesquerie, "to the bubbling of bassoons," and as "one looks at the elephant-colorings of tires." Even as he bubbles and colors, Stevens says that "everything is shed," and so he does not believe himself, nor do we believe him, when he insists that a reduced moon is the moon itself and that a reduced self is a true man, not an image of man. The emptiness of the sky in which we see the moon rise is no less a trope than all the rejected images were.

It is scarcely a triumph over Stevens when I note his knowing and wise refusal of his own decreations. I think that Stevens' best critics have underestimated somewhat the peculiar dialectical complexities of the poem's famous final stanza:

> One sits and beats an old tin can, lard pail.
> One beats and beats for that which one believes.
> That's what one wants to get near. Could it after all
> Be merely oneself, as superior as the ear
> To a crow's voice? Did the nightingale torture the ear,
> Pack the heart and scratch the mind? And does the ear
> Solace itself in peevish birds? Is it peace,
> Is it a philosopher's honeymoon, one finds
> On the dump? Is it to sit among mattresses of the dead,
> Bottles, pots, shoes and grass and murmur *aptest eve:*
> Is it to hear the blatter of grackles and say
> *Invisible priest;* is it to eject, to pull
> The day to pieces and cry *stanza my stone?*
> Where was it one first heard of the truth? The the.

Frank Doggett takes "the truth" here without irony:

With all this centering of reality upon the self, the moment of a specific experience becomes the only verity, the only available identification for truth, that otherwise mythical abstraction. The truth is "the the," as this poet puts it in *The Man on the Dump*, speaking of what he believes while beating on the old tin can, the lard pail of poetry. The specific experience, the *the*, that certain instant of light that is *this* instant, includes the reflective life of the mind as well as the life of the senses.

Helen Vendler, as always, is both warier of Stevens' rhetoric and rather eager to find Stevens accepting his own reductiveness: " 'That which one believes' is 'the truth,' and Stevens suspects that truth is not a transcendence, but merely oneself. Oneself is the dump out of which must be constructed apt eves, invisible priests, and stanzas." A. Walton Litz sums up the stanza as rejecting "the evasions of the nightingale in favor of the grackle, a poetry of the irreducible minimum, 'The the.' "

Whether one accepts any of these three readings ought to depend upon an understanding of the disjunctiveness of Stevens' rhetoric generally and particularly in the final stanza of *The Man on the Dump*. I myself would say that "The the" is not a specific experience or a present moment, not oneself in any anti-Transcendental sense, and not a poetry of the irreducible minimum. "The the" is any object whatsoever, outside the self, which is in the process of being taken up again into language. Or, ironically, "The the" is a necessarily failed fresh attempt to avoid figuration, another incipient realization that there are no proper meanings in the language of poetry. Vendler is right when she says of the questions of this stanza that they function "more as hints than as easily answerable rhetorical questions," that is, they function as suggestions. But suggestions of what?

One clue is provided by those blattering grackles, who were cracking their throats of bone in the negative exuberance of *Banal Sojourn* nearly twenty years earlier. A step further on, and Stevens had become the man whose pharynx was bad. In *The Man on the Dump*, he is in no danger of becoming that man of the bad pharynx again. He may be beating an old tin can or lard pail, all right, but that is an American way of making music, and there certainly is a belief, Keatsian and Whitmanian, for which he is beating out his poem. The self that he wishes to get near, through his music, is not without a transcendental element. The suggested answer to the six not-quite-rhetorical questions turns out to be a unanimous if always hesitant "yes." Yes, it is oneself, a superior self. Yes, as in *Autumn*

Refrain, another poem juxtaposing grackles and nightingales, the nightingale did torture, pack, and scratch the ear, heart, and mind of Stevens, for this is Keats's bird, teaching Stevens his American belatedness. Yes, the poet's ear does solace itself in peevish birds, in the poems of precursors. And it is after all peace, it is a honeymoon from cognition, that the dump of anterior images affords Stevens. But it is also a grotesque fate, to murmur *aptest eve* amidst the detritus; to say *invisible priest* in response to parodistic birds (when elsewhere one defines the poet as the priest of the invisible), and even to lament *stanza my stone*, against all life, when the poet himself destroys the life of the day. Last, and most strenuously, it is indeed there that one first heard of the truth, when with a heightened sense of self one emulated Whitman by returning to the object, any object, in the manner though hardly in the tone of a poem like *Crossing Brooklyn Ferry. The Man on the Dump* is one of those poems that make us understand why Stevens thought Hemingway an important poet; beneath the toughness of rhetoric and of stance is the American High Romantic, perpetually at work reconstructing itself.

I neglect many other fine shorter poems of 1938–40, in order to do justice to a longer poem I greatly love, the extravagant *Extracts from Addresses to the Academy of Fine Ideas*, in which Stevens most certainly is no longer on the dump. He stands in front of a mad convocation and prophesies the opening manner of his masterpiece, *Notes toward a Supreme Fiction*, where a rather rococo scholar-poet addresses the reader-as-ephebe. Here we are the speaker's cronies, charmingly called "my beards," as though we were so many *idiots savants*, like the speaker himself. But the poem's concerns are not mockeries, and the fantastification results from Stevens' poetic anxieties as he directly confronts the ambition of bringing his language to bear upon truth and upon evil, though both in his rather special sense. Truth here, and throughout *Parts of a World*, comes into existence in the gap between concept and percept, while evil is what it will be in *Esthétique du Mal*, the pain and suffering endemic in the nature of things.

We can see Stevens, in the poems written between *The Man*

on the Dump and *Extracts*, recognizing that the truth, in a poem, is identical with what in *Notes* he would call "the hum of thoughts evaded in the mind." In *On the Road Home*, the denial of the concept of truth renders "the fragrance of the autumn warmest, / Closest and strongest." *The Latest Freed Man*, "having just / Escaped from the truth," is thereby granted a Nietzschean vision of the sun, not as a strong man but as a strong man might be. Again, in *Connoisseur of Chaos*, the first speaker, who knows that to impose an order is to bring about another chaos, tells us persuasively that there is only, at last, a chaos or "the immense disorder of truths." Some such realization informs *The Sense of the Sleight-of-Hand Man*, with its tentative assertion, "It may be that the ignorant man, alone, / Has any chance to mate his life with life." These poems culminate in *Man and Bottle* and *Of Modern Poetry*, the duo that Stevens first published together under the title *Two Theoretic Poems*. Both poems have been overpraised, on the basis of particularly weak misreadings, which have interpreted them as typical Modernist manifestos against Romanticism. *Man and Bottle*, though neatly turned, is only a simplistic footnote to *The Snow Man*. The "mind of winter," itself a trope of *ethos*, returns as the Snow Man is exalted into the "great poem of winter." But, this time, Stevens tropes his irony against his own reductiveness, as the wintry mind destroys everything that is more valuable than its destruction enables it to find. What is it that "will suffice" if it must do without "an old affair with the sun, / An impossible aberration with the moon, / A grossness of peace"?

Of Modern Poetry, the other "theoretic" text, is a weak poem, inaccurate about past poetry and mistaken about itself. Yet it is a useful poem, through its implicit definition of this poet's truth as being "what will suffice." The strength of *Extracts*, as a poem, is that it goes so far in defining what truth might be sufficient if the process of writing strong poems is to go on. Santayana, as he often was elsewhere, is the guide for Stevens in the opening passages of *Extracts*, as Doggett first demonstrated. In his *Realms of Being*, Santayana attacked the idealizing habit that replaces the material world by language until "the poor human soul walks in a dream through the paradise of truth, as a child might run blindly through a smiling garden, hugging a paper flower." Stevens' hyperbolical lecturer adumbrates Santayana's trope, yet also recalls his precursor in Stevens, the elegant monologist of *Le Monocle de Mon Oncle:* "Shall I uncrumple this much-crumpled thing?" Here the lecturer states the point more directly:

> A crinkled paper makes a brilliant sound.
> The wrinkled roses tinkle, the paper ones,
> And the ear is glass, in which the noises pelt,
> The false roses—Compare the silent rose of the sun
> And rain, the blood-rose living in its smell,
> With this paper, this dust. That states the point.

Yet the point is more ironical than it is in Santayana. The blood-rose of sun and rain is living, while the paper is dust, but the living rose is silent, and the paper-as-poem makes more than one kind of brilliant sound. Blood and paper roses alike, in any case, cannot suffice. Paper cannot restore us to an Eden "beyond the knowledge of nakedness," and the world of rain and sun "is an unbearable tyranny." Paper delivers us to the prison-house of language, to the concept; rain and sun imprison us in the percept, and so "The false and true are one." Stevens-as-mad-lecturer, remembering the Keatsian "cold porcelain" of *The Poems of Our Climate*, orates against Keats's motto "I see, and sing, by my own eyes inspired," while admonishing Keats as his Academy's Secretary for Porcelain, his scholar of Grecian Urns:

> The eye believes and its communion takes.
> The spirit laughs to see the eye believe
> And its communion take. And now of that.
> Let the Secretary for Porcelain observe
> That evil made magic, as in catastrophe,
> If neatly glazed, becomes the same as the fruit
> Of an emperor, the egg-plant of a prince.
> The good is evil's last invention. Thus
> The maker of catastrophe invents the eye
> And through the eye equates ten thousand deaths
> With a single well-tempered apricot, or, say,
> An egg-plant of good air.

Evil, as elsewhere in Stevens, takes no moral meaning but is the pain and suffering that we endure from nature alone. Catastrophe here is the process of figurative substitution that *is* poetry, its constant turning over and breaking of illusory forms, its neat glazing of evil into magic. The kernel is the curiously Emersonian adage that "the good is evil's last invention." But it is astonishing that Stevens then should modulate from this compensatory bitterness to a rhetoric of solace, though the solace is itself not deceived:

> Be tranquil in your wounds. The placating star
> Shall be the gentler for the death you die
> And the helpless philosophers say still helpful things.
> Plato, the reddened flower, the erotic bird.

Plato, flower, and bird alike teach eros, helpful though itself helpless. Despite the colors of irony, the great trope of Whitman as wound-healer, as patient nurse and hospital consoler of wounded soldiers, has entered the poem in the grand pathos of "Be tranquil in your wounds"; and with the entrance of this greatest of Stevens' hidden influences, the tone of *Extracts* changes massively and prevails in its change for the remaining six sections of the poem. It is no accident that section III begins with a variation upon the most central of all Emersonian–Whitmanian figurations, the American poet-prophet as a preacher of what is to be:

> The lean cats of the arches of the churches,
> That's the old world. In the new, all men are priests.
>
> They preach and they are preaching in a land
> To be described. They are preaching in a time
> To be described. Evangelists of what?

The polemic, exactly as it will be three to four years later, in *Esthétique du Mal* and in shorter poems like *The Lack of Repose* and *The Creations of Sound*, is against Eliot and his followers, yet is kept implicit by the device of referring to Eliot as "X, the pernoble master." In *The Creations of Sound*, X or Eliot is massively (and prophetically) dismissed as "an obstruction, a man / Too exactly himself," a palpable irony against a poet who asserted that his verse excluded mere personality. More crucially, Stevens follows Whitman as against Eliot on the issue of the American poet as orator:

> Tell X that speech is not dirty silence
> Clarified. It is silence made still dirtier.
> It is more than an imitation for the ear.
>
> He lacks this venerable complication.
> His poems are not of the second part of life.
> They do not make the visible a little hard
>
> To see.

I think that Stevens here ventures the crucial formula for American Romantic poetry, including even Eliot, Pound, and Williams at their infrequent best: it must make the visible a little hard to see, which is one of the great achievements of Whitman and Dickinson, and of Frost, Stevens, Hart Crane after them, and is still the gathering achievement of Robert Penn Warren, Elizabeth Bishop, John Ashbery, A. R. Ammons, and our other distinguished contemporaries who maintain this major tradition of our verse. In *Extracts*, III, Stevens is at once polemical and characteristically cautious. The right time for the American poet-priests is neither the Age of Emerson nor what I suggest we might begin to call the Age of Stevens (or shall we say the Stevens Era?), but is, introjectively, "a time / To be described." Stevens offers two answers to his authentic or open question "Evangelists of what?" One answer would be a central man and a central woman, but since Stevens rather desperately exclaims, "If they could!" that answer clearly would have been in what Emerson wistfully called the Optative Mood. The darker answer is itself two more questions, both historically unanswerable:

> Or is it the multitude of thoughts,
> Like insects in the depths of the mind, that kill
> The single thought? The multitudes of men
> That kill the single man, starvation's head,
> One man, their bread and their remembered wine?

This is a Transcendentalist despair, *not* an anti-Transcendentalism, as canonical criticism of Stevens continues to insist. The paradox of the passage is writ large in Emerson's rhapsodic essay *The Poet*, with its contradictory insistences that the poet must be at once part of the commonal or Dionysiac and wholly individualized or Apollonian. Though this was also the Whitmanian impasse, Stevens still chooses the new world against the old world tradition as maintained by Eliot, leanest of cats:

> The lean cats of the arches of the churches
> Bask in the sun in which they feel transparent,
> As if designed by X, the per-noble master.
> They have a sense of their design and savor
> The sunlight. They bear brightly the little beyond
> Themselves, the slightly unjust drawing that is
> Their genius: the exquisite errors of time.

The sun is the Christian God, but the basking cats or Eliotics only *feel* transparent, mistaking their sense of their own design for the emblem of transcendence. But the supposed transcendence, "the little beyond / Themselves" is merely a misprision of tradition, a "slightly unjust drawing," and the culmination of the section is Nietzschean. Error, or the swerve from origins, is the true strength of Eliot also; his poems are among "the exquisite errors of time."

It is fascinating that the next "extract," section IV, opens more in the mode of Robert Frost than of Stevens, though it becomes Stevensian enough before it concludes. Indeed, it is another of Stevens' multiform variations upon *The Snow Man*. There, the listener heard "the same wind / . . . blowing in *the* same bare place." Here, first, "The wind blew in *the* empty place," but then Stevens revises to, "The winter wind blew in *an* empty place—." The difference frees Stevens from reductiveness:

> There was that difference between the and an,
> The difference between himself and no man,
> No man that heard a wind in an empty place.
> It was time to be himself again, to see
> If the place, in spite of its witheredness, was still
> Within the difference.

Stevens critics consistently and weakly misread this passage, which in fact is a palinode of *The Snow Man* and which goes on to turn against that winter abstraction or reduction with humanizing force:

> the abstraction would
> Be broken and winter would be broken and done,
> And being would be being himself again,
> Being, becoming seeing and feeling and self,
> Black water breaking into reality.

This is no longer a reductive "reality" but closer to what Stevens, in *Notes*, would term a "discovered" one. Two phases of "himself" coexist in section IV, with "no man" as the middle term in the dialectic and the second "himself" *aufgehoben* into a higher repetition. Characteristically, Stevens is embarrassed by his own affirmativeness, and he compensates immediately by descending into the swirl of section V, where the man with the blue guitar returns, in the shape of the surviving philosophic assassin in Stevens, to sing a song of consolation, and yet admittedly a failed song, unable to find the right sound to match the inner music:

> Of the assassin that remains and sings
> In the high imagination, triumphantly.

Something of this confessed limitation still abides in section VI, which is the least impressive part of *Extracts*, primarily in contrast to its superior revision in the splendid canto XXIII of *An Ordinary Evening in New Haven*: "The sun is half the world, half everything, / The bodiless half." Still, section VI contains a remarkable clarification of the poem's crucial *aporia*, the gap between percept and concept, a clarification that shows us again how for Stevens (as for Emerson, Whitman, and Dickinson) the percept belongs to *ethos* or Fate, and the concept to *pathos* or Power:

> He wanted that,
> To face the weather and be unable to tell
> How much of it was light and how much thought,
> In these Elysia, these origins,

This single place in which we are and stay,
Except for the images we make of it,
And for it, and by which we think the way,
And, being unhappy, talk of happiness
And, talking of happiness, know that it means
That the mind is the end and must be satisfied.

Is this a dualism or a monism? The question is as unanswerable as it was for Emerson, who had to confess that "a believer in Unity, a seer of Unity, I yet behold two." Stevens' swerve here away from origins is that his man facing Elysia *wanted* to be unable to tell Fate from Power, light from thought. Perhaps Stevens is most himself when he implicitly follows William James (as several critics, including Doggett and Frank Lentricchia, have stressed) in the pragmatic pluralism that is a kind of realistic modification of the Emerson of the essays *Experience* and *Montaigne or the Skeptic*, as here in the next section of *Extracts*:

What
One believes is what matters. Ecstatic identities
Between one's self and the weather and the things
Of the weather are the belief in one's element,
The casual reunions, the long-pondered
Surrenders, the repeated sayings that
There is nothing more and that it is enough
To believe in the weather and in the things and men
Of the weather and in one's self, as part of that
And nothing more.

Canonical inquisitors somehow can read this as meaning the opposite of what it means and so continue to give us a rather skinny Stevens, who somehow finds what will suffice without believing anything whatsoever. What does it mean to believe in the weather? Well, what is weather for an American poet? New England weather is infamous for its variety, and my own principal complaint about Connecticut, after a quarter-century in New Haven, is that the state has too much weather. Stevens could not get enough of it. The root of "weather" means "to blow," and that is what the weather does in Stevens' poetry; it blows right through, fulfilling the ancient function of inspiration. Here is Stevens in a hushed prose piece called *Connecticut*, one of the last things he wrote:

> The man who loves New England, and particularly the spare region of Connecticut, loves it precisely because of the spare colors, the thin light, the delicacy and slightness and beauty of the place. The dry grass on the thin surfaces would soon change to a lime-like green and later to an emerald brilliance in a sunlight never too full. When the spring was at its height we should have a water-color, not an oil, and we should all feel that we had had a hand in the painting of it, if only in choosing to live there where it existed. Now, when all the primitive difficulties of getting started have been overcome, we live in the tradition which is the true mythology of the region and we breathe in with every breath the joy of having ourselves been created by what has been endured and mastered in the past. [*OP*, 295]

That is Stevens at seventy-five, close to death, breathing in with every breath the joy of the weather and the place, himself at the end having become one of the poems of our climate. In the beautiful poem of the year before, *A Clear Day and No Memories*, he finally had said, "Today the mind is not part of the weather." But until then, he mixed mind and weather, not wanting to know how much of the weather came from the light of his own mind, the breath of his own spirit. Not knowing was a sacred ignorance, "the exactest poverty," the gap or void out of which his imagination could rise. The imagination rises in section VIII, the concluding movement of *Extracts*, with a humanistic dignity and interpretive power surpassing anything previous in Stevens. For the first time he becomes what he afterward frequently was to be; he becomes what criticism scarcely so far credits him with having been, a sage and seer, who chants persuasively a possible wisdom:

>   How can
>   We chant if we live in evil and afterward
>   Lie harshly buried there?

How can poetry be written if we cannot come to terms with the pain and suffering of our natural or given condition? That would be the proper meaning, if living in evil were not for

Stevens a figuration for the refusal to accept and welcome change, for a failure to live with the weather. Accepting change means accepting death as the final form of change, which is again to accept death as the mother of beauty and so also as the mother of the innocence of earth. Stevens mounts to a defense of his art even as he finds his faithless faith in natural change:

> If earth dissolves
> Its evil after death, it dissolves it while
> We live. Thence come the final chants, the chants
> Of the brooder seeking the acutest end
> Of speech: to pierce the heart's residuum
> And there to find music for a single line,
> Equal to memory, one line in which
> The vital music formulates the words.

The "residuum," as earlier in *Autumn Refrain* and later in *An Ordinary Evening*, is for Stevens a positive emblem, the rock of our human nature, the substance that prevails in us even after valuable parts have been abstracted or withdrawn. "The acutest end of speech" is a prolepsis of the superb stanza XIX of *Chocorua to Its Neighbor*, three years later:

> To say more than human things with human voice,
> That cannot be; to say human things with more
> Than human voice, that, also, cannot be;
> To speak humanly from the height or from the depth
> Of human things, that is acutest speech.

Here is the first sounding of Stevens' acutest speech, in the final figuration of *Extracts*, acutely moving because it *is* a metaleptic trope and not merely a proper statement:

> Behold the men in helmets borne on steel,
> Discolored, how they are going to defeat.

The helmeted men ride the discolored steel of their tanks, but the men are discolored too, ill troped by war, which is a dehumanizing mimicry of the true war between sky and mind. All such men, on whatever side, are projected as going to defeat, but "we demand Victory," as Emerson said for all his descendants, "a success to the senses as well as to the soul." It is with something of that implicit pride in the act of reintrojecting his own imaginative calling that Stevens concludes one of his most vital and prophetic longer poems, his true prelude to *Notes*.

I myself am much less moved by *Examination of the Hero in a Time of War*, the other longer poem in *Parts of a World*, which seems to me as much a failure as *Owl's Clover*. And yet it merits at least a brief account, partly because it is the direct prelude to *Notes toward a Supreme Fiction* and partly because Stevens prided himself upon the poem. In one of his death-poems, *As You Leave the Room*, equivalent to Whitman's *Good-Bye, My Fancy*, Stevens affirmed his own vitality through four of the many poems he had written:

> That poem about the pineapple, the one
> About the mind as never satisfied,
>
> The one about the credible hero, the one
> About summer, are not what skeletons think about.

Credences of Summer is the only poem here which is not surprising, though *Someone Puts a Pineapple Together* is, to a true Stevensian, a kind of final test for the ephebe. But the two *Parts of a World* poems, *The Well Dressed Man with a Beard* and *Examination of the Hero*, are hardly what I would expect to have been the choice of the author of *Notes*, *The Auroras*, *An Ordinary Evening*, and *The Rock*. The clue appears to be affirmation or celebration, as all four poems share the spirit of the jaunty opening lines of *The Well Dressed Man*:

> After the final no there comes a yes
> And on that yes the future world depends.

Examination of the Hero evidently was intended to support the second sentence of Stevens' rather unnerving prose statement on the poetry of war: "In the presence of the violent reality of war, consciousness takes the place of the imagination." In his *Adagia*, Stevens stated this better: "In the presence of extraordinary actuality, consciousness takes the place of imagination" (*OP*, 165). War seems to me only a trope in *Examination of the Hero*, which remains firmly in the Emerson–Whitman tradition of testing out the poet as hero or as central man. The soldier who speaks the opening lines of the poem is Stevens himself, still fighting the old war of the imagination, ostensibly against the sea and the sky but actually against time and time's agent, language. One can add that this is a particular Stevens, examining the *Nachträglichkeit* of his own poetry and consciously fighting against his own past reductiveness, but ambivalently and uneasily. So he opens by asserting, "Force is my lot," but this trope of power is countered rapidly by an allusion to *The Sun This March*, the poem that twelve years before had ended, tentatively, six years' total silence. In that poem, he had cried out, "Cold is our element and winter's air / Brings voices as of lions coming down." Yet the Snow Man's universe is dispersed spiritually "by a wind that seeks out shelter from snow," a wind of *pathos*. This is "the will opposed to cold" and to "fate / In its cavern," Power against fatal *Ananke*, the common god.

All through the poem the authentic *stigmata* of the hero belong to the poet alone, and to Stevens most of all, starting with the dialect of his Pennsylvania Dutch ancestors in stanza II. The captain or "man of skill" turns out to be a master of tropes, "creator of bursting color / And rainbow sortilege." His armory is eloquence:

> All his speeches
> Are prodigies in longer phrases.
> His thoughts begotten at clear sources,
> Apparently in air, fall from him
> Like chantering from an abundant
> Poet, as if he thought gladly, being
> Compelled thereto by an innate music.

Granted that the poem goes on too long, we can surmise the cause for these repetitions that are not incremental enough. The hero is not a person, and so he is not a poet; he is a feeling, an image, an idea, but alas he never does become a poem. For fifteen stanzas, Stevens evades the inevitable, the Emersonian or Whitmanian conclusion that is nevertheless his own, his only, his final conclusion, that the poetic self has nothing to celebrate save its own possible glory. Every trope having failed him (or he it), Stevens comes to his final stanza, the only one in the poem worthy of him:

> Each false thing ends. The bouquet of summer
> Turns blue and on its empty table
> It is stale and the water is discolored.
> True autumn stands then in the doorway.
> After the hero, the familiar
> Man makes the hero artificial.
> But was the summer false? The hero?
> How did we come to think that autumn
> Was the veritable season, that familiar
> Man was the veritable man? So
> Summer, jangling the savagest diamonds and
> Dressed in its azure-doubled crimsons,
> May truly bear its heroic fortunes
> For the large, the solitary figure.

The hero is summer, when the world is largest. Autumn is the veritable season exactly as the sea at Key West is the veritable ocean, or familiar man the veritable man, because we fall into so reduced a mode of apprehension. Summer is overdressed and oxymoronic, in azure-doubled crimsons, but in many senses it may truly bear, bring forth as well as sustain and be able to tolerate, a vision of poetic heroism.

Stevens probably was wrong about the merits of *Examination of the Hero*, but at least the poem does seem to have cleared the ground for *Notes toward a Supreme Fiction*, written soon after it, and *Notes* is truly Stevens' poem about the credible hero. But a more interesting cure or clearing of the ground also took place late in 1940 and in 1941, with the writing of a dialectical triad of poems equivalent to the triad nearly twenty years before of *The Man Whose Pharynx Was Bad*, *The Snow Man*, and *Tea at the Palaz of Hoon*. This later triad is composed of *Mrs. Alfred Uruguay*, *Asides on the Oboe*, and *The Well Dressed Man with a Beard*, respectively playing the dialectical roles of reduction, expansion, and invention, whereas *Pharynx* was crisis, *The Snow Man* reduction, and *Hoon* expansion. In the later dialectic, to be triumphant in *Notes*, Stevens has altered his stance, as an analysis of these three *Parts of a World* poems should indicate.

Mrs. Alfred Uruguay is a comic masterpiece, in a mode that Stevens never developed, a quest-romance not so much parodied, as in the *Comedian*, as raised to an unparalleled pitch of sardonic irreality. Mrs. Uruguay is no interior paramour; she is the reductionist in Stevens personified, but personified as she might be in James or Wharton. Her name, as Northrop Frye noted, is meant to suggest the city of Montevideo, the mount of vision she is determined to take by a laborious cure of the ground. But though she is sublimely funny as a reductionist, she is also very formidable, for she represents what Stevens now knows to be the most dangerous element in his own poetic mind, the Snow Man tendency that says no to everything in order to get at itself. The reductive fallacy can be defined as the notion that we cannot know what someone or something really is until we know the very worst that someone or something is or can be. Applied to poetry, this is indeed to wipe away moonlight like mud.

Mrs. Uruguay is an apostle of the total leaflessness, except for the idea of her own elegance, which she cannot surrender even to sacred reductiveness. She climbs the mount of vision all dressed in velvet, though in the pure good of theory she would wish to ride naked. The very likable donkey is Sancho Panza to her Don Quixote, as inexorably "she approached the real, upon her mountain, / With lofty darkness," which is her Sublime contribution to the quest. We too wish for a falsifying bell, but that would spoil this anecdote since "her no and no made yes impossible," and any bell on her dark road upward would be a happily falsifying yes.

Yet that is only one half of this mad poem, the other half belonging to the figure of the youth as a virile poet, the ephebe as reborn Apollo who ruhes past her down the mountain, remorselessly abandoning "the real" even as she seeks it. She is all *ethos*, the limitation of Fate; like the horse he rides, he is "all will," the *pathos* of Power. She presumably seeks the martyrs' bones, relics of those who attained the mount of vision before her. He is the "figure of capable imagination," a noble synecdoche personified, though "no chevalere and poorly dressed," the poverty of costume representing his eros, his need of the imagination he pursues, the idea of the sun upon which he is intent. His vision is expansionist yet capable, and his blindness is itself an enabling act. Stevens, and we ourselves as readers, are moved by the young man, but Stevens and the reader are more in sympathy with the donkey, with the bells and midnight forms, with the moonlight, and with the charm of the reductive dowager's velvet. The rider's "phosphorescent hair" marks him as being in the tradition of the youth with flashing eyes and floating hair that Coleridge fears to become at the close of *Kubla Khan*, the youth who like Keats in *The Fall of Hyperion* has been *daimonic* enough to re-enter the earthly paradise. Mrs. Uruguay seeks the real because the mountaintop is indeed outside and above her. The youth scorns the real, and out of those who have died seeking it he creates, in his mind, his own eventual victory: "The ultimate elegance: the imagined land." "Elegance" is a final irony against Mrs. Uruguay, who had identified herself with elegance, presumably in its Paterian or etymological sense of "chosen out" or "selected"; so we can interpret "the ultimate elegance" as a seeking after evidence of election. This lovely poem's ultimate elegance is that both Mrs. Uruguay and the youth are equally outrageous, each just as elected a quester as the other. To pursue the middle path of invention or discovery is to wish for a falsifying bell, but such a statement takes us beyond this poem and into the doctrinal text *Asides on the Oboe*, with its curious balance between transcendental expansiveness and what Stevens hoped to distinguish as a separate mode of discovery.

The deliberately offhand title suggests an anxiety in Stevens, because he is starting to make a definitive formulation and he is wary of finalities. But "It is time to choose," and the mythologies being obsolete Stevens chooses a crucial Nietzschean notion, though he tries to defend himself against Nietzsche by taking his ideas at second hand (through Hans Vaihinger's *The Philosophy of "As If"*) and by assimilating Nietzsche to Whitman's presentation to the self. The philosophers' man alone who still walks in dew is not Zarathustra but the ephebe of *Out of the Cradle Endlessly Rocking,* and also the central man and human globe of Emersonian tradition, at once mimetic and

expressive ("responsive / As a mirror with a voice") and recalling Emerson's lament in *Experience:* "Temperament also enters
fully into the system of illusions and shuts us in a prison of
glass which we cannot see. There is an optical illusion about
every person we meet." Emerson's ambivalence is also Stevens',
but Doggett is probably right in finding a closer parallel in
Schopenhauer, who before Nietzsche had demystified the inner
self as being a mere fiction: "As soon as we . . . seek for once
to know ourselves fully by means of introspective reflection, we
are lost in a bottomless void; we find ourselves like the hollow
glass globe, from out of which a voice speaks whose cause is not
to be found in it."

And yet because belief is final in this known fiction of the
self, the Emersonian emblem of transcendence, "the transparence of the place," is possible; and as Emerson had prophesied,
such a self must be a poet's, "and in his poems we find peace."
Stevens' acute anxiety at his own affirmativeness is rarely more
noticeable than in part II of the poem, where the glass man is
fictively "cold and numbered" yet cries with the vital voice of
the dew, and puns brilliantly in "Thou art not August unless I
make thee so." The possible poet, abstracted from the anteriority of poetic tradition, has an actual erotic effect, but only
upon the mind. Yet we live in the mind, as Stevens kept saying, and *Asides on the Oboe* becomes a more elevated and convincing poem when, in its third part, it engages the problem of
a world whose erotic intensities have been mutilated by pain
and suffering:

> One year, death and war prevented the jasmine scent
> And the jasmine islands were bloody martyrdoms.
> How was it then with the central man? Did we
> Find peace? We found the sum of men. We found,
> If we found the central evil, the central good.
> We buried the fallen without jasmine crowns.
> There was nothing he did not suffer, no; nor we.

The jasmine here is likelier to be Southern American than
East Indian; for Stevens it is a residue of the image of Florida,
the venereal soil of *Harmonium.* We can read "jasmine islands"

as a trope for Stevens' poetry of earth, his celebration of the marriage of flesh and air. As Emerson and Whitman discovered in the American Civil War, there is no central man if there is no peace. With the expansive or Transcendental vision impaired, Stevens substitutes a subtler if more modest discovery:

> It was not as if the jasmine ever returned.
> But we and the diamond globe at last were one.
> We had always been partly one. It was as we came
> To see him, that we were wholly one, as we heard
> Him chanting for those buried in their blood,
> In the jasmine haunted forests, that we knew
> The glass man, without external reference.

It is worth noting that this is one of Stevens' most American stanzas. Eros is projected, and an identity with the Transcendent poetic self is introjected, in a transumptive trope that abolishes all possibility of putting the will into present time. The effect is Whitmanian, as we hear a universal bard chanting for all of us, for who is not one of "those buried in their blood," even while supposedly alive, and everyone is "in the jasmine haunted forests," studying the nostalgias of lost erotic longings. Yet there is a final knowledge here, and it is of the self, "without external reference," which is a muted anticipation of *It Must Give Pleasure*, VIII, the climax of *Notes*, when the self proclaims its majesty, "I have not but I am and as I am, I am," and then confirms this Hoon-like glory by dismissing "these external regions" as being relevant only to Cinderella-like wish-fulfillments.

I conclude this account of *Parts of a World* by turning to *The Well Dressed Man with a Beard*, the only short poem upon which Stevens congratulated himself at the end. Like so much of Stevens, the poem has a hidden origin in Whitman's *Sleepers*, where the poet wanders all night in his vision, "bending with open eyes over the shut eyes of sleepers." Stevens seems to have assimilated, repressively, the opening of *The Sleepers* to the opening of the most poignant of Whitman's poems, *The Wound-Dresser*, where the poet has a proleptic vision of himself telling future children how he nursed the wounded in Washington hospitals during the Civil War:

An old man bending I come among new faces,
Years looking backward resuming in answer to children.

The imageries of *The Wound-Dresser* and *The Sleepers* seem to combine in *Extracts*, and the passage of the woman waiting for her lover toward the end of Part 1 of *The Sleepers* is repressively echoed in Stevens' *Poem with Rhythms*, composed just before *The Well Dressed Man with a Beard*. What does the title mean? A man with a beard, to an American poet, tends to mean God, Uncle Sam, or the prophetic Walt, or some combination thereof, but of course neither Jehovah nor Whitman can be called well dressed. I suspect that an idealized version of Stevens' own father gets into the mix also, both here and in *The Auroras of Autumn*, since the elder Stevens was a man of splendidly affirmative temperament until he was let down by a business associate. The charm of *The Well Dressed Man with a Beard* is that it celebrates "yet one, / One only, one thing" that is not an actual thing but rather affirmative language itself, the eloquence of "a speech / Of the self that must sustain itself on speech." It is "a petty phrase" that sweetens the meadow, honeys the heart, greens the body. Most striking is the culminating object of this celebration:

The form on the pillow humming while one sleeps,
The aureole above the humming house . . .

Doggett relates this humming or living self to a passage in Bergson's *Creative Evolution*, which "suggests that the subjective self cannot conceive of a void or absence of self." But the humming, I think, is more Stevens' misprision of Whitman than of Bergson. Two years before, Stevens had written a wild poem, *The Woman That Had More Babies than That* (*OP*, 81–83), which he felt was not worthy of being in *Parts of a World*. The poem is Stevens' most obsessive variation upon *Out of the Cradle*, for the woman is Whitman's fierce old mother crying for her castaways. And these are her castaways, poets like Whitman and Stevens:

The children are men, old men,
Who, when they think and speak of the central man,

Of the humming of the central man, the whole sound
Of the sea, the central humming of the sea,
Are old men breathed on by a maternal voice.

So humming while sleeping is one with the central murmuring or humming of the sea in Whitman. This purchases affirmation at a high price, for it was just this Whitmanian identification that Whitman himself transcended in the 1855 *Song of Myself*, only to fall back into it in the 1860 *Leaves of Grass*. And it was again this identification that Hoon transcended when he declared, "I was myself the compass of that sea," or that Stevens was moved to declare when he chanted of the woman at Key West that "she sang beyond the genius of the sea." I think this is why Stevens does not end *The Well Dressed Man with a Beard* with the image of the aureole or crown of light above the central, because humming, house of the mind, for that would not suffice. He remembered the poem thirteen years later, as "the one / About the mind as never satisfied," as though the poem's true subject inhered in its final line: "It can never be satisfied, the mind, never." It cannot be satisfied with a central humming because it wants to assert its power, its *pathos*, over the humming of the sea, and no assertion can convince it of a finality in that exercise of its will. Powerful as *Parts of a World* was, Stevens could not be satisfied with it. He went on to *Notes toward a Supreme Fiction*, his truly central humming, where a more capable idea of the hero appears as "the major man." This man, as we will see, called forth a subtler music of thought from his maker. Of him, *Notes* says that he is "the object of / The hum of thoughts evaded in the mind," and for him Stevens commanded a stronger muse: "My dame, sing for this person accurate songs."

8 Notes toward a Supreme Fiction

The eight lines that stand at the start of *Notes toward a Supreme Fiction* are no more addressed to the muse or interior paramour than they are to Henry Church. Not that I am going to propose any other candidate for the "you," because evidently Stevens himself never encountered such a candidate. The muse, or the one of fictive music, in Stevens as in Whitman, was the mother as an ultimate, metaleptic trope of *pathos*, a felt presence and power. But the "you" of these lines is neither an inspiring force nor a maternal presence.

> And for what, except for you, do I feel love?
> Do I press the extremest book of the wisest man
> Close to me, hidden in me day and night?
> In the uncertain light of single, certain truth,
> Equal in living changingness to the light
> In which I meet you, in which we sit at rest,
> For a moment in the central of our being,
> The vivid transparence that you bring is peace.

Stevens felt love for his wife and daughter, as he had for the family into which he was born. The "you" here must be a synecdoche which includes all familial passions yet transcends them. Transcendence, indeed, seems to me the tenor of this octave, culminating as it does in "the central," "the vivid transparence," and "peace." Five year later, in 1947, elegizing Henry Church in the hushed Whitmanian splendors of *The Owl in the Sarcophagus*, Stevens mythologized peace most memorably, but that was "peace after death, the brother of sleep," and the peace he celebrates here, though momentary, is very much of this life. This "peace" is what is celebrated in *Parts of a World*, particularly in *Asides on the Oboe* and *Extracts*, and clearly it is a peace that comes from reading and writing poems. *Extracts* beautifully speaks of stanzas and of chants of final peace, a finality attained within this life. I do not think it a limitation but rather a precision that Stevens writes to his own poetry in these lines, that the "you" is simply the text, *Notes toward a Supreme Fiction*. The Emersonian vocabulary of "central" and "transparence" suits an address to a pattern of tropes by a trope, by a consciousness willing to confront the alarming possibility that consciousness itself may be only another trope in a wilderness of tropes.

Notes is a notoriously elusive text to write commentaries upon, and I myself am no longer particularly happy with what I have written about it in the past or with nearly anyone else's commentary either. It is all too easy to underestimate how labyrinthine the poem is in its subtle evasions and in its preternatural rhetoricity, its excessively acute awareness of its own status as text. Stevens had the uncanniness and the persistence to get about a generation ahead of his own time, and he is still quite a few touches and traces ahead of ours. His major phase, from 1942 to his death in 1955, gave us a canon of poems themselves more advanced *as interpretation* than our criticism as yet has gotten to be. My theoretical emphasis in these chapters has been on finding a critical procedure for describing disjunctions or crossings in the rhetoric of poetry, because Stevens is the most advanced rhetorician in modern poetry and in his major phase the most disjunctive.

I need another theoretical *excursus* before entering the text proper of *Notes*, in order again to bring together psychology and rhetoric as aids in the reading. The most problematic element in *Notes* is what it calls "later reason," the equivalent of Freud's *Nachträglichkeit*, "deferred meaning," a difficult notion that both Jacques Lacan and Jacques Derrida have illuminated, in rather different ways. But I want to start here, not with the Freudian "after-the-event" or "retroactive meaningfulness" or perhaps just plain "aftering," but with the Wordsworthian afterimage.

168

Coleridge, in *Biographia Literaria*, had written of "distinct recollection, or as we may aptly express it, *after-consciousness*." Thomas McFarland has traced Coleridge's "after-consciousness" to the *nachempfinden* or "after-perceiving" of the metaphysician Tetens, who was the source of Coleridge's formulation of the Primary Imagination, a formulation that Stevens parodies in the supreme moment of *Notes*. How much Stevens had read of Freud we don't know, but I suspect not much, and I suspect it doesn't matter, because Stevens, with his natural "realism," is also a naturally Freudian poet. Freud had acknowledged, "The poets were there before me," and we can add now that they were there after him also, whether they had read him or not. Freud and Stevens share the common ancestry that I shall trace in my concluding chapter, a tradition that went from classical rhetoric to associationist psychology to Romanticism, with Freud and modern poetry as the inheritors in the fourth phase of this progression. The afterimage, with its curious blend of percept and concept, is as crucial in Freud as in the poets. The view of object-representation that Freud carried over into his central essay *The Unconscious* (1915) is identical with the associationist view that he stated in 1891 in *On Aphasia:*

> The word, then, is a complicated concept built up from various impressions, that is, it corresponds to an intricate process of associations entered into by elements of visual, acoustic and kinesthetic origins. However, the word acquires its significance through its association with the "idea" (concept) of the object, at least if we restrict our consideration to nouns. The idea, or concept, of the object is itself another complex of associations composed of the most varied visual, auditory, tactile, kinesthetic, and other impressions. According to the philosophical teaching, the idea of the object contains nothing else; the appearance of a "thing," the "properties" of which are conveyed to us by our senses, originates only from the fact that in enumerating the sensory impressions received from an object we allow for the possibility of a large series of new impressions being added to the chain of associations (John Stuart Mill).

Though this is now hopelessly outmoded, it remained Freud's theory of language down to the end. Not only did Freud thus hold fast to an associationist view of language, but in some sense he remained an associationist psychologist, despite the efforts of Jacques Lacan and his followers to demonstrate the opposite. Wherever Freud discovers two or more psychical events to be in series, he calls any connection between the events "associationist." Freud's swerve away from associationist origins (he had translated Mill) came about through his speculations upon belatedness, speculations that began with his realization that associations functioned through what he called path-breakings. Precisely as Wordsworth got beyond associationism through a dialectic that took him from haunts or spirit of place, through a re-cognition, and on to a recognition, even so Freud worked out a path that led from memory traces, impressions, experiences undergoing a belated revision, into a new meaning of augmented psychical effectiveness. *Nachträglichkeit* is thus Freud's *logos*, his reason or later reason which constructed the force of the otherwise illusory past, or rather of what was heterogeneous in that past and so required contextualization through deferred meaningfulness. Another word for Freud's revisionary *logos* is "maturation," provided that we rid ourselves of any notion that maturation is necessarily a process involving temporal continuity.

Stevens, whose whole art is an aftering that battles belatedness, returns to Wordsworth (and to Whitman) in the patterns of his *Nachträglichkeit*. For Stevens, an image is an obsession or a haunting, part percept and part concept, or we might say *ethos* as "haunt," and so he tries to demystify it by a reduction to its First Idea, a Fate or reality supposedly beyond further reduction. But, in the next stage of his dialectic, he undergoes a re-cognition of the First Idea (itself an "imagined thing" or image) and then finds he is in danger of being dehumanized by this Freedom of substitution, since substitution *is* its own meaning, as though to-put-into-question was what would suffice. Thus Stevens moves on to a fresh recognition or retroactive meaningfulness of the First Idea as a *potentia* (both Power and passion) or *pathos*, or as he says in his very Wordsworthian language, as the fiction that results from feeling.

The origins of *Notes toward a Supreme Fiction* cannot be fixed, whether in "sources" beyond Stevens, or in Stevens' own earlier writings. In some clear sense, he had been writing notes toward a supreme fiction in every poem he had attempted from the start, and the crucial word in his title is surely *toward*, which means "in the direction of" but also "rather before in time" and also "as a way of achieving." The stance of *toward* is prospective, as in the marvelous close of *Song of Myself*, where Walt is up ahead of us, and we have to go toward him, as he stops somewhere waiting for us. Stevens is in the questing stance of Whitman's reader, rather than in Whitman's own pioneering, and yet *Notes* can be termed the *Song of Myself* of our time, in preference to such strong rivals as the *Cantos, Paterson,* and *The Bridge,* and such worthy descendants as Ashbery's *Three Poems* and Ammons' *Sphere.* Whitman is the best aid to reading *Notes* that I know, and so I will cite him more often than certain other indubitable predecessors of the poem among the philosophers: Schopenhauer, Nietzsche, James, Santayana. There is a considerable conceptual debt to Valéry, but I have discussed this relationship in *Poetry and Repression* and I will do little more than revisit it here.

One of the seeds of *Notes* is a poem that Stevens must have internalized early, Whitman's poignant *There Was a Child Went Forth.* It may even be parodied, perhaps unknowingly, in *It Must Change,* IV, which is, however, so suspiciously close that we may be encountering unconscious allusion, since the passage ends by sounding like Hart Crane, owing to the common ancestral figure:

> The partaker partakes of that which changes him.
> The child that touches takes character from the thing,
> The body, it touches. The captain and his men
>
> Are one and the sailor and the sea are one.
> Follow after, O my companion, my fellow, my self,
> Sister and solace, brother and delight.

Whitman had, as he said, a terrible doubt of appearances which tended to intensify as he moved from 1855 to 1860 and beyond. *There Was a Child Went Forth,* like *Song of Myself,* is a poem of the first edition, 1855, and keeps the terrible doubt within the confines of a larger faith in the First Idea, or "the first object" as Whitman calls it:

> There was a child went forth every day,
> And the first object he look'd upon, that object he became,
> And that object became part of him for the day, or a certain
>   part of the day. . . .

◇

> Affection that will not be gainsay'd, the sense of what is real,
>   the thought if after all it should prove unreal,
> The doubts of day-time and the doubts of night-time, the
>   curious whether and how,
> Whether that which appears so is so, or is it all flashes and
>   specks?

The child or future poet is Stevens' ephebe, the figure of the youth as virile poet, to cite the title of one of the two essays (really prose-poems), that Stevens wrote at about the time he wrote *Notes*. The first of these, *The Noble Rider and the Sound of Words*, is a disaffected essay, even complaining about the income tax, but it warms up as it moves along and says some things that the reader of *Notes* benefits for having heard. Here is a relevant cento:

It is one of the peculiarities of the imagination that it is always at the end of an era.

His own measure as a poet, in spite of all the passions of all the lovers of the truth, is the measure of his power to abstract himself, and to withdraw with him into his abstraction the reality on which the lovers of truth insist. He must be able to abstract himself and also to abstract reality, which he does by placing it in his imagination.

What makes the poet the potent figure that he is, or was, or ought to be, is that he creates the world to which we turn incessantly and without knowing it and that he gives to life the supreme fictions without which we are unable to conceive of it.

For the sensitive poet, conscious of negations, nothing is more difficult than the affirmations of nobility and yet there is nothing that he requires of himself more persistently, since in them and in their kind, alone, are to be found those sanctions that are the reasons for being and for that occasional ecstasy, or ecstatic freedom of the mind, which is his special privilege. [*NA*, 22, 23, 31, 35]

We may gloss these statements as saying, respectively, that "Modernism" is an illusion; that "abstract," for Stevens as for Valéry, is not opposed to "concrete" but means "to separate out from," as in Valéry's aphorism "Man fabricates by abstraction"; that the perceptual world is, as Nietzsche said, an invention or primordial poem of mankind; that Stevens knows his function as poet is to attain the Transcendental freedom of ecstasy, the wildness of seeing and knowing that is the root of the word "nobility."

The Figure of the Youth as Virile Poet is a stronger, more vatic Emersonian–Paterian prose-poem or rhapsody, and no cento could be adequate to the force of its eloquence. Yet here too there is one crucial *topos* for the reader of *Notes:* "The pleasure is the pleasure of powers that create a truth that cannot be arrived at by the reason alone, a truth that the poet recognizes by sensation. The morality of the poet's radiant and productive atmosphere is the morality of the right sensation" (*NA*, 58).

If this sentence were to be inserted into the "Conclusion" of Pater's *Renaissance*, it would be wholly homogeneous with that context. For the reader of *Notes*, the sentence helps define the "pleasure" of *It Must Give Pleasure*, and reminds also of the Paterian origins of Stevens' emphasis upon perception, solipsism, and the flux of sensations. *Notes* is a late Romantic poem, Paterian and Whitmanian, a text expounding the dilemma of a tradition grown profoundly self-conscious of its vexed relations to time and to language. On the verge of starting *Notes*, in February 1942, Stevens wrote to his exegete, Hi Simons, a letter of commentary on the *Noble Rider* essay and on a cryptic poem in *Parts of a World* entitled *On an Old Horn*. The remarks on *The Noble Rider* defensively outline the hidden rationale for the reduction to a First Idea, and are more interesting in themselves than as an explanation of the essay:

When a poet makes his imagination the imagination of other people, he does so by making them see the world through his eyes. Most modern activity is the undoing of that very job. The world has been painted; most modern activity is getting rid of the paint to get at the world itself. Powerful integrations of the imagination are difficult to get away from. I am surprised that you have any difficulty with this, when the chances are that every day you see all sorts of things through the eyes of other people in terms of their imaginations. This power is one of the poet's chief powers. [L, 402]

Modern poetry, Stevens says, undoes a painted world; he does not say that modern poetry in turn can apply only another coat of paint. Not to see through the eyes of others is of course the prime Emersonian–Whitmanian injunction, and Stevens adds nothing to the admonition. But he illuminates the three notes toward his supreme fiction. It must be abstract, because that will undo previous poets' jobs of paint. It must change, so as to avoid being only a single paint job of one's own, if that can be done. It must give pleasure, but what is pleasure for a strong poet, ultimately, if it is not the pleasure of priority in one's invention? Here is Stevens, in the same letter to Hi Simons, commenting upon *On an Old Horn*, quite a bad poem for which Stevens nevertheless harbored fondness:

If you understand the body of the poem, of course you understand the title. Animals challenge with their voices; birds comfort themselves with their voices, rely on their voices as chief encourager, etc. It follows that a lion roaring in a desert and a boy whistling in the dark are alike, playing old horns: an old horn, perhaps the oldest horn. [L, 404]

There is a bird booming in *On an Old Horn*, but there is no lion. Stevens is anticipating or perhaps even starting to draft *It Must Be Abstract*, v, which opens, "The lion roars at the enraging desert." There had been plenty of lions in Stevens before this: the poet as lion-in-the-lute confronting reality as lion-in-the-stone in the *Blue Guitar;* the lion sleeping in the sun of *Poetry Is a Destructive Force;* the majestic images of *Lions in Sweden;* most memorably, the winter air of *The Sun This March* bringing voices as of lions coming down. Like the later lions in *Puella Parvula* and *An Ordinary Evening in New Haven*, all these are emblems of the poetic Will-to-Power, stemming perhaps from

Nietzsche's *Zarathustra*. The lion of *It Must Be Abstract* is a fundamentalist of the First Idea, as we will see in context. But Stevens himself, though not in *Notes*, was in some danger of being such a fundamentalist, as *On an Old Horn* and his comments upon it show. A hidden origin of *Notes* is Stevens' deep need not to play the oldest horn, not to comfort himself by imposing his own temperament upon reality. It was because he had written *Notes* that two years later, in *Esthétique du Mal* (1949), he could celebrate his liberation from his own wintry reductiveness: "How cold the vacancy / When the phantoms are gone and the shaken realist / First sees reality."

Let us begin a closer consideration of the text of *Notes* by deciding whether we can trust Stevens to define for us his poem's purpose. In a letter (December 8, 1942) to Henry Church he stated it in language that oddly mixes Coleridge ("willingly suspend disbelief") and William James ("will to believe"):

There are things with respect to which we willingly suspend disbelief; if there is instinctive in us a will to believe, or if there is a will to believe, whether or not it is instinctive, it seems to me that we can suspend disbelief with reference to a fiction as easily as we can suspend it with reference to anything else. . . .

I have no idea of the form that a supreme fiction would take. The *Notes* start out with the idea that it would not take any form: that it would be abstract. Of course, in the long run, poetry would be the supreme fiction; the essence of poetry is change and the essence of change is that it gives pleasure. [*L*, 430]

The supreme fiction of the poem *Notes* finally is revealed, in the poem, to be a certain ecstasy or satisfaction that the poet himself experiences, a certain consciousness of an expanded self that goes beyond the fiction he has made. Stevens' purpose in the poem's text, like Whitman's, is to define himself, not poetry, so that we cannot trust his asserted aim any more than we can trust his asserted freedom from poetic origins. His language when he talks about his poem tends to be Santayana's, but not when he talks *within* his poem. Santayana closes *Interpretations of Poetry and Religion* by defining poetry as being "religion without practical efficacy and without metaphysical illusion." We will find Stevens, at the climax of *It Must Give Pleasure,* so experiencing a sense of his own fictive power as to achieve a pragmatically efficacious joy, and in the strength of that joy he will re-entertain some traditional metaphysical illusions. His closeness both to Santayana and to his own stated purpose is much greater at the poem's start, then at its finish, but that is the achievement of the poem.

The familiar desire to be stripped of all metaphysical illusion begins *It Must Be Abstract* and governs the first five cantos of the poem, which can be regarded as its initial *illusio* or *clinamen* away from Romantic tradition. In Valéry's dialogue *Eupalinos, Or the Architect,* Phaedrus speaks to Socrates of a rhapsody of Eupalinos in praise of seaports, "these noble, half-natural constructions," which then goes on to praise the constructions of art as transcending the half-natural: "Admirable theaters they are, in truth; but let us place above them the edifices of art alone! It is necessary to abstract oneself from the spells of life and from immediate enjoyment, even if for this purpose we must make a stern effort against ourselves. What is most beautiful is of necessity tyrannical."

Valéry's use of "abstract" can remind us that the root meaning of the word is to move or withdraw away from something, so that *It Must Be Abstract* means in effect *It Must Be Antithetical,* in the Nietzschean sense of "antithetical" that Yeats adopted in *A Vision,* which is essentially *contra Naturam.* With this as context, let us consider the opening lines of *It Must Be Abstract:*

> Begin, ephebe, by perceiving the idea
> Of this invention, this invented world,
> The inconceivable idea of the sun.
>
> You must become an ignorant man again
> And see the sun again with an ignorant eye
> And see it clearly in the idea of it.

"Ephebe" is the ancient Greek for "upon early manhood," for the young citizen of Athens who is out on garrison duty from age eighteen to twenty, after which he comes home to full citizenship. Here in *Notes*, the ephebe is the young poet or young scholar, the potential full citizen of the republic of letters. The voice we hear is a half-mocking, half-oracular voice, the slightly mad professor's voice that opened *Extracts from Addresses to the Academy of Fine Ideas*, a voice that I suspect Stevens adapted from Nietzsche, who used it with high deliberateness for similar effects. Stevens had employed the notion of ephebe first in a rejected poem of 1939, *Life on a Battleship*, which is almost wholly a mockery. Here in *Notes* the address to the ephebe modulates until it becomes almost wholly serious, so that after *Notes*, in *An Ordinary Evening*, xiii, "The ephebe is solitary in his walk," the word's tonality is beyond any trope of the ironic.

The voice that opens *It Must Be Abstract* presents us, as its ephebe, with a riddle: we are to begin our abstraction from the given, or merely "natural," by an act of perception. But what we are to perceive is Nietzsche's "primordial poem of mankind," the whole of our perceptual and sensible world, as the idea or conception it is. And yet this conception is inconceivable; to be seen and not to be thought. Hence the second tercet: to resee the sun *in* the idea of the sun, the ephebe must reduce to a primordial ignorance. In what sense? "Ignorance," in Stevens, does not mean lack of knowledge, but what it finally means in the late poem *Saint John and the Back-Ache:* "The little ignorance that is everything, / The possible nest in the invisible tree," or ignorance as an abstraction or a fabrication in Valéry's sense. The ephebe thus descends from the great admonitions in *The Blue Guitar*, xxxii: "Throw away the lights, the definitions, / And say of what you see in the dark / That it is this or that it is that, / But do not use the rotted names." To see the sun clearly in the idea of it was once to see Phoebus Apollo, but now the solar chariot is junk. Stevens genially demonstrates that to be a poet you must keep naming the sun, when his kenning "gold flourisher" suddenly substitutes for the sun just after he insists the sun must bear no name. This sun is still the sun celebrated not as a god, Phoebus, but as a god might be, which is the old project for the sun in Stevens. But the might-be has been reduced now from the Optative Mood to the First Idea, or being "in the difficulty of what it is to be."

We might say that Stevens had been writing about the First Idea for a quarter of a century before he wrote *Notes*, so that it is a kind of shock to come upon him handling the notion explicitly in *It Must Be Abstract*, II. Peirce had used the heliotrope as an illustration of an idea of Firstness, and Stevens had written an odd little poem, *Gubbinal*, using the same image just before he wrote *The Snow Man*. A "gubbinal" is presumably a celebration of a world of gubbinses, or barbarous people:

> That strange flower, the sun,
> Is just what you say.
> Have it your way.
>
> The world is ugly,
> And the people are sad.
>
> That tuft of jungle feathers,
> That animal eye,
> Is just what you say.
>
> That savage of fire,
> That seed,
> Have it your way.
>
> The world is ugly,
> And the people are sad.

We might say that this poem expresses a fundamentalism, indeed an ennui of the First Idea, as Stevens gives in to the Mrs. Alfred Uruguay within himself and perhaps satirizes Peirce in the process. *Gubbinal* is the precise contrary of *The Brave Man*, written twelve years later, where that brave man, the sun, walks without meditation. By 1942, Stevens has learned to avoid both extremes, and canto II begins with a remarkable wariness as to the limits of reduction:

> It is the celestial ennui of apartments
> That sends us back to the first idea, the quick
> Of this invention; and yet so poisonous

Are the ravishments of truth, so fatal to
The truth itself, the first idea becomes
The hermit in a poet's metaphors,

Who comes and goes and comes and goes all day.
May there be an ennui of the first idea?
What else, prodigious scholar, should there be?

I doubt that the ironic opening trope of canto II could be understood without reference to a not particularly inspiring passage in *The Noble Rider and the Sound of Words:*

The way we live and the way we work alike cast us out on reality. If fifty private houses were to be built in New York this year, it would be a phenomenon. We no longer live in homes but in housing projects. . . . It is not only that there are more of us and that we are actually close together. We are close together in every way. [*NA*, 18]

And so on. It seems a waste that the poet of *Notes* should tell us what is no news, but this is his "celestial ennui of apartments," the ennui induced in him by unwanted intimacy. It is then a socially induced dissatisfaction that sends Stevens back to an ultimate reduction, but this distaste for that which undermines the supposed nobility of the spirit is not wholly un-Nietzschean. Such a reaction remains aesthetic, though we are rightly a little uneasy when Stevens ascribes his motive for metaphor, the living core or essence of his fresh idea of the sun, to his distaste at being surrounded by apartment-dwellers. Fortunately, he soon returns to the ennui of the First Idea. "Poverty" as imaginative need is the kernel of the rest of canto II, centering on "desire" or the *pathos* of the poet's will discovering that to live with the first idea alone is to have "what is not." The throwing away is a refreshment, which is a dark irony, since what is being thrown away, the First Idea, itself had been intended as a refreshment. Stevens may be playful, yet seriously so, in describing desire, at winter's end, observing not only the emergence of the blue woman of early spring, but seeing also the myosotis, whose other name is "forget-me-not." Desire, hearing the calendar hymn, repudiates the negativity of the mind of winter, unable to bear what Valéry's Eryximachus had called "this cold, exact, reasonable, and moderate consideration of human life as it is." The final form of this realization in Stevens comes in 1950, in *The Course of a Particular*, in the great monosyllabic line "One feels the life of that which gives life as it is." But even Stevens cannot bear that feeling for long. As Eryximachus goes on to say in *Dance and the Soul*:

A cold and perfect clarity is a poison impossible to combat. The real, in its pure state, stops the heart instantaneously. . . . [. . .] To a handful of ashes is the past reduced, and the future to a tiny icicle. The soul appears to itself as an empty and measurable form. —Here, then, things as they are come together, limit one another, and are thus chained together in the most rigorous and mortal fashion. . . . O Socrates, the universe cannot for one instant endure to be only what it is.

Valéry's formula for reimagining the First Idea is, "The idea introduces into what is, the leaven of what is not." This "murderous lucidity" can be cured only by what Valéry's Socrates calls "the intoxication due to acts," particularly Nietzschean or Dionysiac dance, for this will rescue us from the state of the Snow Man, "the motionless and lucid observer." Dance, in Stevens as in Yeats, is always a Nietzschean trope, but Stevens is uneasy with it and does not adopt Valéry's hint in *Notes*. We might expect a dance in canto III, but what we get is a fabulistic chant:

> We say: At night an Arabian in my room,
> With his damned hoobla-hoobla-hoobla-how,
> Inscribes a primitive astronomy
>
> Across the unscrawled fores the future casts
> And throws his stars around the floor. By day
> The wood-dove used to chant his hoobla-hoo
>
> And still the grossest iridescence of ocean
> Howls hoo and rises and howls hoo and falls.
> Life's nonsense pierces us with strange relation.

This is the very first of the fifteen or so fables that are the true glory of *Notes*, and like the others it is wild and free enough *not* to illustrate the doctrinal text that it is meant to illustrate, here the first twelve lines of canto III, with their praise of poetry's "candor" (used not in its common meaning of "frankness of expression" but in its etymological meaning of "whiteness," that is, the First Idea). The fables of *Notes* need much turning over; Stevens said of this one that "the Arabian is the moon; the undecipherable vagueness of the moonlight is the unscrawled fores: the unformed handwriting" (*L*, 433). We can be more precise than Stevens; the Arabian is the moon as erotic stimulus to a poet aged sixty-three, who reacts with a necessary bitterness. Robert Buttel printed an early lyric by Stevens (1909) in which the poet's "golden strings"

> Resound in quiet night,
> To an Arab moon above,
> Easing the dark senses need,
> Once more, in songs of love.

This bad little poem may echo a bad and once popular poem by Francis Thompson, *Arab Love-Song*, which opens with a rather baroque image: "The hunchèd camels of the night / Trouble the bright / And silver waters of the moon." Stevens is likelier to be recalling his own lyric, or Thompson's, than Wordsworth's dream-Arab of *The Prelude*, V, for Stevens' moony Arab leads to a reverie not on saving imagination from the abyss but on the failure of the erotic imagination. We say: the moon shines upon me in my bed and by synesthesia sets up a horrid variant on the song of the wood-dove, bird of Venus, making that voice of the turtle not a hoobla-hoo, but a hoobla-how, the "how" crassly referring to one's own sexuality. But since sexual anxiety is a mask for the fear of death, the damned parody of the *Waldtaube* by the moonlight is also the unformed handwriting of the future; just how much future is there for one at age sixty-three? The moon is not only astronomer (*not* astrologer), knowing more than one knows oneself, but *he* is replete with potency; so full of light and power that carelessly he "throws his stars around the floor." Once one lived an erotic life by day; the authentic chant of the wood-dove used to be heard, but no more; now vain desire rises to torment one only by night. Yet now, day and night, the synesthesia of the iridescent ocean still goes on; still reality rises and falls, howling a derisive or fearful "hoo," mocking the lack of the same rhythm in oneself. This is life's nonsense: the waning of sexuality, the continued mockery of desire, the endless motions and noises of the sea. It pierces us with strange relation: our story yet not our story; related to us, yet not related. By the time we have passed from "hoobla-hoobla-hoobla-how" through "hoobla-hoo" to just "hoo," we have lost all continuity, because the middle term provided by the bird of Venus has dropped out.

This bitter fable cannot be reconciled with the Coleridgean idealization of poetry it was meant (supposedly) to adumbrate or illustrate:

> The poem refreshes life so that we share,
> For a moment, the first idea . . . It satisfies
> Belief in an immaculate beginning
>
> And sends us, winged by an unconscious will,
> To an immaculate end. We move between these points:
> From that ever-early candor to its late plural
>
> And the candor of them is the strong exhilaration
> Of what we feel from what we think, of thought
> Beating in the heart, as if blood newly came,
>
> An elixir, an excitation, a pure power.
> The poem, through candor, brings back a power again
> That gives a candid kind to everything.

The poem of the Arabian certainly was candid, and brings back a candid kind to everything, all right, but was it a poem that "refreshes life"? Helen Vendler elegantly observes that if the passage is taken in sequence "we have had twelve lines of iridescence, and now we are given eight lines of grossness." I would add that the first twelve lines economically sum up Stevens' "system": "that ever-early candor" is the reduction or First Idea, and "its late plural" is (as Kermode first noticed) any single First Idea *and* its reimagining. Yet the fable that follows is only a First Idea; we might call it *the* First Idea of eroticism in old age, and Stevens is too much the realist to ruin his fable by any vain reimaginings.

Stevens commented on canto IV that in it "Descartes is used as a symbol of the reason. But we live in a place that is not our own; we do not live in a land of Descartes; we have imposed the reason; Adam imposed it even in Eden" (*L*, 433). Stevens is still writing his poem in this comment; that is, in the language of *The Noble Rider* he is still being evasive, capable of resisting or evading the pressure of the reality of this last degree, with the knowledge that the degree of today may become a deadlier degree tomorrow. Earlier in *The Noble Rider*, Stevens showed us that we must read canto IV as opening, "The first idea was not our own. Adam / In Eden was the father of Freud," on the basis of: "Boileau's remark that Descartes had cut poetry's throat is a remark that could have been made respecting a great many people during the last hundred years, and of no one more aptly than of Freud, who, as it happens, was familiar with it and repeats it in his *Future of an Illusion*" (*NA*, 14). Freud, substituted for Descartes, centers our sorrow not in the abyss between subject and object but in Eve making air the mirror of herself. In *Three Academic Pieces*, Stevens evasively attempted to reduce narcissism to the inside / outside metaphor of Romanticism when he said: "Narcissism itself is merely an evidence of the operation of the principle that we expect to find pleasure in resemblances" (*NA*, 80). The poetic anxiety here stems from any strong poet's displacement of primal narcissism into his own self-delighting imagination. This anxiety is the genuine antecedent of "this" in canto IV's key tercet:

> From this the poem springs: that we live in a place
> That is not our own and, much more, not ourselves
> And hard it is in spite of blazoned days.

"Blazoned days" are days at once proclaimed and adorned, days that herald our Power rather than our Fate. The poverty announced here as poetry's cause despite blazoned days finds its final formula in *The Auroras of Autumn*: "An unhappy people in a happy world," a world not themselves or their own, a world fallen away from the power of Hoon's solitude or that of the woman at Key West. Condemned to the fate of mimics, reducing to First Ideas that were contrived before us, we are in Stevens' peculiar version of Hell, which is always a theatre of the grotesque imposed upon the whole of the terrestrial cosmos. The air, reflecting nothing, serves as bare board for the stage; the wings are bright and dark, dawn and dusk, providing light mixed with shade for tragedy, and rose color for comedy, but it does not matter whether the play is tragic or comic, since our imagination can add nothing to what is. The abysmal instruments, ocean and weather, reduce our imposed meanings to peeps or pips, as though we were so many birds.

The imposition of meaning, here by animals upon reality, is the topic of canto v, the last in the poem's opening movement of limitation, or getting down to a First Idea. We have seen Stevens evolving the image of the lion roaring at the desert in his comments upon the poem *On an Old Horn*, and I think we can regard this image as the negative emblem of the poem *Notes*; that is to say, as the emblem of Stevens' critique of his own earlier reductiveness, since what the image reveals is that the First Idea only dehumanizes. The poet as Snow Man might aspire, at best, to be a voice coloring the world. To have a mind of winter, or of any season, is to breach the darkness with blares or to snarl at summer thunder or sleep through winter snow:

> But you, ephebe, look from your attic window,
> Your mansard with a rented piano. You lie
>
> In silence upon your bed. You clutch the corner
> Of the pillow in your hand. You writhe and press
> A bitter utterance from your writhing, dumb
>
> Yet voluble dumb violence. You look
> Across the roofs as sigil and as ward
> And in your centre mark them and are cowed . . .
>
> These are the heroic children whom time breeds
> Against the first idea—to lash the lion,
> Caparison elephants, teach bears to juggle.

Vendler comments aptly that the rhetoric of *Notes* is both celebratory and minimized, so that this authentic praise of the ephebe grants him both "triumph and deprecation." Stevens' own comment is celebratory in its implications: "What I mean by the words 'sigil and ward' is that the person referred to looks across the roofs like a part of them: that is to say, like a being of the roofs, a creature of the roofs, an image of them and a keeper of their secrets" (*L* 434).

The ephebe, whose place and whose very instrument are not his own, is presented in all his poverty, for the secrets of the roofs are all dualisms, all imbalances between subject and object, concept and percept. Though the bitter utterance of the ephebe has an unheroic origin, it *is* uttered word by word, its "dumb violence" is at least voluble, and not a lion's roar. The dumbfoundering abyss between subject and object, of which the roof is (in Stevens) the emblem, affrights the ephebe, and yet the ephebi are "the heroic children" bred by time against the First Idea's impositions. Poetry may be only a circus act, and yet that too reimagines the First Idea. In this bitterness and imaginative need, Stevens reaches the midpoint of *It Must Be Abstract*, and also, I would say, its Crossing of Election, its negative moment of moving from ironic thinking or the *illusio* of the First Idea to synecdochal thinking, where the *tessera* or symbol is the giant of the weather or major man. In this first crossing, Stevens confirms his own poetic strength, as he moves away from mimetic images of presence and absence to the weather as expressive image of the macrocosm. And, surely we can add, he moves *Notes* into its proper greatness, for nothing in his earlier poetry is quite of the subtle splendor of canto VI:

> Not to be realized because not to
> Be seen, not to be loved nor hated because
> Not to be realized. Weather by Franz Hals,
>
> Brushed up by brushy winds in brushy clouds,
> Wetted by blue, colder for white. Not to
> Be spoken to, without a roof, without
>
> First fruits, without the virginal of birds,
> The dark-blown ceinture loosened, not relinquished.
> Gay is, gay was, the gay forsythia

And yellow, yellow thins the Northern blue.
Without a name and nothing to be desired,
If only imagined but imagined well.

My house has changed a little in the sun.
The fragrance of the magnolias comes close,
False flick, false form, but falseness close to kin.

It must be visible or invisible,
Invisible or visible or both:
A seeing and unseeing in the eye.

The weather and the giant of the weather,
Say the weather, the mere weather, the mere air:
An abstraction blooded, as a man by thought.

As is almost always the case with Stevens' comments upon
Notes, his remarks here give us a weak misreading:

This was difficult to do & this is what it means: The abstract does
not exist, but it is certainly as immanent: that is to say, the fictive abstract is as immanent in the mind of the poet, as the idea of God is immanent in the mind of the theologian. The poem is a struggle with the
inaccessibility of the abstract. First I make the effort; then I turn to
the weather because that is not inaccessible and is not abstract. The
weather as described is the weather that was about me when I wrote
this. There is a constant reference from the abstract to the real, to and
fro. [*L*, 434]

Where canto VI relies upon the two crucial aspects of weather—
which are always the presence and absence of wind and sun, or
movement and light, visible and invisible dialectically linked—
the comment devalues the weather, saying that the poet turns
to it only because it is an accessible reality. But Stevens turns
to the idea of the weather precisely as the religious man turns to
the idea of God, which is to say that for him the weather is not
just a trope for the supreme fiction but is itself as much of that
fiction as poetry is or can be. It may be that the world does not
present itself as a poem every day, but still poetry and *materia
poetica* are the same thing, every day, and for Stevens the prime
materia poetica is the weather.

The poignance of canto VI comes from the *pathos* of *Nachträglichkeit*, or the purchase of Power at the cost of knowledge. Power is gained as the image of a giant personifies not the will to change but a will to stop willing, to yield oneself to the weather. It is not so much the absence of perceiving subject which is striking in the opening lines of the canto as it is the uncertainty of the fiction or of the abstraction as saving withdrawal. What is being withdrawn from what? If the lines referred to God as the supreme fiction of the theologians, then they would be agnostic. God is not to be seen, therefore not to be known or made real, therefore not to be loved or hated. But Stevens, as prophet of a supreme fiction that finds its poem in the weather, is searching for evidences of his own continued election as poet. And Stevens is no Hals, who painted people as though they lived in a place that was their own, and even more themselves. There is a turning against the self in Stevens' beautiful synecdoche of the weather, because for Stevens the prime poetic evil was the unpleasure of a conscious belatedness. The fiction, idea of poetry and/or of weather, is not to be addressed by Stevens as though he were Wordsworth, who to the open fields spoke a prophecy.

Stevens, in the difficulty of canto VI, begins as an ephebe again; he is another heroic child bred by time "against the first idea." He too looks as sigil and as ward, from under and across the roofs, and only thus, as indoor poet, addresses the weather, weather by Stevens and not by Franz Hals. This is weather not quite revealed, its "ceinture loosened, not relinquished," and the lyrical burst of forsythia does not persuade the weather to yield a fuller sight. The weather, like the sun, must bear no name; being confronted, it saves the poet from that sense of not-having that is the beginning of desire. Be it idea-of-poem or idea-of-motion-and-light, this fiction, since abstracted, is only imagined, but, Stevens proudly adds, "imagined well." He proceeds to demonstrate that truly he is no ephebe in the extraordinarily haunting lines beginning "My house has changed a little in the sun," where the emphasis falls strongly upon "has." This change may be "false flick, false form," a *pathos* added to the fiction, yet this is "falseness close to kin," an error or trope that has Necessity in it. As nature draws near again, with the magnolias' fragrance, Stevens dares a tercet that his detractors happily quote agianst him:

> It must be visible or invisible,
> Invisible or visible or both:
> A seeing and unseeing in the eye.

Like his Dutch ancestors in their religion, so Stevens in believing in the weather grants it a reality consisting of the visible and the invisible, both or either, and then for the first time in the canto admits to an agent of perception. Yet both the seeing and the unseeing are *in* the eye, rather than by it, and the implication is the Emersonian–Blakean one that the eye altering would alter all. The weather, like the poem, is not to be seen and yet can be seen in change, even as *A Primitive Like an Orb*, six years later, will end by putting it:

> That's it. The lover writes, the believer hears,
> The poet mumbles and the painter sees,
> Each one, his fated eccentricity,
> As a part, but part, but tenacious particle,
> Of the skeleton of the ether, the total
> Of letters, prophecies, perceptions, clods
> Of color, the giant of nothingness, each one
> And the giant ever changing, living in change.

This is "the giant of the weather," who is the reimagining, even as the "mere weather" is the First Idea, but an idea or abstraction blooded, as a man by thought, not as a Snow Man.

I have commented at some length on canto VI, for it is the only genuinely difficult lyric in *It Must Be Abstract*. The remaining cantos of the first part of *Notes* trace an evolution from the giant of the weather through visonary "moments of awakening" to the "crystal hypothesis" of major man, who is celebrated first as an abstraction and then as a Chaplinesque being presented to the ephebe as a reduced idea of man who must be made, indeed confected, into the ultimate elegance of the imagined hero. These four cantos, VII–X, are difficult only in the single issue of Stevens' uneasiness at his own humanism or his lack of humanism. Canto VII gives a reduction of the Paterian privileged moment or secularized epiphany to "moments of awakening, / Extreme, fortuitous, personal," moments that put all received structures of ideas into question, but by no means in the name of a more human potential. The next canto, the fable of the MacCullough, was glossed by Stevens with considerable unease of spirit:

The gist of this poem is that the MacCullough is MacCullough; MacCullough is any name, any man. The trouble with humanism is that man as God remains man, but there is an extension of man, the leaner being, in fiction, a possibly more than human human, a composite human. The act of recognizing him is the act of this leaner being moving in on us. [*L*, 434]

The MacCullough is MacCullough as Hoon was the son of Old Man Hoon. Yes, but Ramon Fernandez did not turn out to be two common Spanish names, and MacCullough was the name of a hardheaded clan, producing eminent political economists, geologists, and even the American Secretary of the Treasury when Stevens was a student at Harvard. That is to say, we expect Whitman and not MacCullough to be experiencing poetic incarnation while lounging by the sea. Where the Mac-Cullough sits, there is the head of the table, was Emerson's way of saying it. Unlike Viollet-le-Duc, Stevens is not interested in that kind of restoration in which you put false fronts on edifices. Even the First Idea, though imagined, is a thing; that is, the First Idea is man, the earth, or the sun washed clean by being taken up into the imagination. Stevens denied the influence of Nietzsche here, but a Stevensian denial of infuence, whether Nietzschean or Whitmanian, is merely a confirmation of how unconvincing Stevens' notions of influence are. The fictive leaner being belongs to the cosmos of *Also Sprach Zarathustra*, and his is just as much an authentically rational humanism as Nietzsche's was. In the MacCullough we confront Whitman assimilated to Nietzsche, an American Over-Man, a grand trope or noble synecdoche of Power, power that compounds the ocean as universe of death, and language: "power of the wave, or deepened speech."

Kermode, with the best eye yet for Stevens' affiliations, compares canto IX to a late idealization by Whitman, *When the Full-grown Poet Came.* Stevens, like Whitman, was not quite that full-grown poet, fulfiller of Emerson's most outrageous prophecies. Canto IX both heralds the full-grown poet as major man and makes it impossible to describe him or recognize him if ever he comes. His origin is not apotheosis; he comes "from reason," yet most indirectly, being "the object of / The hum of thoughts evaded in the mind." We cannot see him, we cannot think him, we cannot name him, and yet "he is, he is, / This foundling of the infected past." The Emersonian, apocalyptic dismissal of history could go no further, and the Optative Mood could not be more stressed: "The hot of him is purest in the heart."

As the qualifications keep piling on in Canto X, the reader (any reader) may grow weary of a prophecy that cannot stop deconstructing itself. We too cry out with Stevens, "Who is it?" and despite the captiousness of the ironists and canonical critics, we do receive an answer, or at least a challenge as good as an answer:

> What rabbi, grown furious with human wish,
> What chieftain, walking by himself, crying
> Most miserable, most victorious,
>
> Does not see these separate figures one by one,
> And yet see only one, in his old coat,
> His slouching pantaloons, beyond the town,
>
> Looking for what was, where it used to be?
> Cloudless the morning. It is he. The man
> In that old coat, those sagging pantaloons,
>
> It is of him, ephebe, to make, to confect
> The final elegance, not to console
> Nor sanctify, but plainly to propound.

By now, each of us is a rabbi, frustrated by the endlessly qualifying Stevens into the full fury of "human wish." It is a rhetorical challenge for Stevens that he imposes upon us, as readers, what Whitman imposes upon us in *Crossing Brooklyn Ferry*, the necessity for finishing his poem, *It Must Be Abstract*, by making our own transumptive trope, by abstracting from this tramp figure, at once Whitmanian and Chaplinesque, "the final elegance." To "propound" is to "propose," and it is our burden to put our own version of major man forward for consideration. To "confect" need not be to make candy but simply to prepare by a mixture of ingredients, and so Stevens concludes the first of his three major *Notes* with an admonition that is rather less ironic than it sounds. He then goes on to visions beyond irony in the rest of the poem.

It Must Change is more exuberant than *It Must Be Abstract*, reflecting Stevens' momentary but profound relief at being almost free of reductiveness. "Almost," because while Stevensian "change" ultimately does take the force of the word's etymological meaning, which is to "curve" or "bend," Stevens was affected all too strongly by modern philosophers of the flux: Bergson, Whitehead, Santayana, James. These speculators may not have made of change just another reduction, but Stevens tends to whenever he follows one of them too closely. When he is most himself, his vision of change is Lucretian and Shelleyan, as in the final canto of *It Must Change*:

> The west wind was the music, the motion, the force
> To which the swans curveted, a will to change.

Yet *It Must Change*, though it continually confronts Shelley, is no *Ode to the West Wind*. Its first five cantos feature change as an undoing, or metonymic emptying out of the invented world, while its second five cantos present us with the puzzle of change as a repression into the daemonic force of an American Sublime. Between the two halves, in the disjunction that follows the elegy for the planter in canto v, and the sublime mockeries of "bethou" in canto vi, intervenes the greatest of Stevens' Crossings of Solipsism, as the poet rises up again into the creative solitude of the mountain-minded Hoon.

Cantos I through IV are all poetic successes, yet what most needs commentary in them can be served best by a juxtaposing cento of their problematic moments: "It means the distaste we feel for this withered scene / Is that it has not changed enough. It remains, / It is a repetition." "Is spring a sleep?" "Nothing had happened because nothing had changed." "In solitude the trumpets of solitude / Are not of another solitude resounding." The burden of this cento, not surprisingly, is reduction, particularly when cyclic repetition *is* the reduction, when eros and life go round and go round and round. Stevens' own erotic bitterness is powerfully implied, as it was with the Arabian moonlight, yet we ought to see that such bitterness is itself an assertion. Stevens, unlike Eliot, does not allow sexual bitterness to pass into disgust; he affirms, however wryly, and with whatever distaste for mere repetitiveness.

Helen Vendler, commenting on canto I, justly praises Stevens for his unmatched "expertise in presenting several images at once, first in their repetitiveness and then in their change." His distaste, whether contemplating his booming bees and Italian girls, or this withered scene in wintry Hartford, is that nature cannot change enough to please him, which by implication more interestingly means that his own fictive consciousness is also too much of a repetition. It is Stevens whose memory of spring after spring gives *this* spring its deferred meaningfulness, and so it is Stevens who is his own worst enemy. Except for the poet and his addiction to *Nachträglichkeit*, there would be no question of returning and no reason to insist on "death in memory's dream." The malaise of Stevens' own comment makes it more than usually beside the point: "We cannot ignore or obliterate death, yet we do not live in memory. Life is always new; it is always beginning. The fiction is part of this beginning" (*L*, 434). *Contra* the prose Stevens, can we not say that his poem's text presents the beginning as part of the fiction? Who but a consciousness aware that consciousness may be a verbal fiction would think spring a sleep? Surely, there is a defensive triumph of isolation when Stevens surmounts his own sense of Fate to take the new-come bee's booming as a metonymy of beginning rather than resuming? Stevens perhaps fears for himself the fate of the statue of the General Du Puy. The solar chariot is junk, every image is on the dump, and the only change the statue ever will know is the final transformation into rubbish. Is there any difference between the formula "nothing had happened because nothing had changed" and the formula I devised at the start of this book: "Everything that can be broken should be broken"?

I think that formula, or whatever similar version of an American Orphism each reader makes for himself, is the justification for the canto of embraces that follows, where every coming together is still a limitation, still a leading up to the possible freedom of solitude. The key lines about solitude rely upon the strange use of the word "copulars"; doubly strange, first because "copular" is an adjective, and second because a copula, though in Latin it means a "link" or "bond," in English just means a verb that identifies the subject and predicate of a sentence with each other, the verb almost always being some form of "be." Stevens is playing upon the verb "copulate," which is from the same *copula* for link or bond. "Cold copulars" linguistically can join just about anything to anything else, which ought to make us a little suspicious of all the dependencies, origins, embraces, forthcomings, and claspings together that cluster in this canto.

What can it mean to say that winter and spring are cold copulars? "Cold copulars" is a trope, but what trope, and what does the figuration substitute for, which is to ask, I think, what other trope does it undo? Stevens is defending against his own trope, "Yet the General was rubbish in the end," since rubbish is rubble and even rubbings, that which has been rubbed down because it could no longer change. To avoid being rubbish, one must change, and the origin of change is the dependency of cold copulars upon one another, the need for every substantive to be joined together with its antithesis in a plural substantive. The origin of change is thus love, yet this is love in its First Idea, akin to Freud's powerfully reductive observation that man must love in order to avoid becoming sick. "Cold copulars" substitutes as a metonymic undoing of "rubbish," which means that something had happened because something had changed. That is why Stevens wins the release of his *kenosis*, so that he is moved to proclaim: "In solitude the trumpets of solitude / Are not of another solitude resounding." And that is why he is able to soften so beautifully into elegy, first in the six lines alluding to Whitman's *There Was a Child Went Forth*, and then in the marvelous lament for the planter that is one of the triumphs of *Notes*, the summation of major Stevens in canto v.

This lyric takes up its stance where Stevens never ceased to be celebratory, in the state of mind, not of nature, that he identified with his sojourns in Florida and Cuba. The apotheosis of this state is in the sublimely crazy poem of 1947, *Someone Puts a Pineapple Together*; its first text in Stevens goes back to *Sunday Morning* in 1915. Stevens said of canto v that "it is one of the things in the book that I like most." When he came to state its meaning, he was a touch colder to his planter in prose than he had been to him in verse:

> What it means is that, for all the changes, for all the increases, accessions, magnifyings, what often means most to us, and what, in a great extreme, might mean most to us is just as likely as not to be some little thing like a banjo's twang. . . . I suppose that it is possible to say that the planter is a symbol of change. He is, however, the laborious human who lives in illusions and who, after all the great illusions have left him, still clings to one that pierces him. [*L*, 435]

I think the revelatory word is "pierces," which in Stevens always has the strongest of auras, in that it is his verb for a sensation against which no defense can work. The planter was a man who could be pierced, could be affected, by his islands or, as Stevens translates them, his illusions. Vendler praises Stevens for tact in his negative praise of the planter, yet I am not certain that Stevens' diffidence here is not in itself an irony directed against the poet's own excessive tact. I find more elegy in canto v than either the poet or his critic care to acknowledge. Stevens is afraid of being too moved here, but he *is* very moved, and his rhetoric persuades us to be immensely moved:

> He thought often of the land from which he came,
> How that whole country was a melon, pink
> If seen rightly and yet a possible red.
>
> An unaffected man in a negative light
> Could not have borne his labor nor have died
> Sighing that he should leave the banjo's twang.

Far from being a symbol of change, the planter shows that "there is a substance in us that prevails." The planter *is* Stevens, or so much like him as to make no difference, though this is the Stevens of *Harmonium*, and even just one aspect of *Harmonium:* the celebration of the poetry of earth. On that wide water inescapable, the planter fabricated a world of tropes or colors, like Whitman walking his beaches, making "his patter of the long sea-slushes." Of the island or illusion transcendentally "beyond him," the planter had made a poem like a mountain, had put together "a pineapple pungent as Cuban summer," and in that erotic atmosphere had stationed the piercing vision not of Yggdrasil but of "the great banana tree," a true tree of life. Having made all this, and brooded upon the melony motherland of his origins, the planter fitly can be elegized as a hero of the imagination. Stevens too was an affected man in a positive light, a man who had borne much labor, with persistence and power, but who died more sublimely, not so much sighing that he should leave the banjo's twang but listening intently to a song: "Beyond the last thought."

We have reached the midpoint of *It Must Change*, and indeed of *Notes*, and in the radical disjunctiveness between "Sighing that he should leave the banjo's twang" and "Bethou me, said sparrow, to the crackled blade," we negotiate, with Stevens, a grand Crossing of Solipsism, a concealed confrontation with the death of love and with the continued awareness of the reality of external nature and of other selves. Has any strong poet ever disliked birdsong as much as Stevens did? Vendler, in a discerning commentary on canto VI, finds "the true center of revulsion in the canto [to be] the anger at the inevitable exhaustion of religious myth. Though the celestial and ecclesiastical are theoretically used as metaphorical vehicles to illustrate the tedium of the natural, actually *they* are the true subject of the poem."

There is certainly a figurative relation between Stevens' authentic distaste for Christianity and his violence against the birds, but another element in Stevens' complex hyperbole is also here. I think the element is an erotic bitterness, which is always involved in Stevens' ornithological polemics. The elegized planter fabricated, by abstraction, a world of trees and colors; his making of that world was a changing process of love, and the world he made kept changing until it suffered death with him, as the final form of change. But the world of birdsong knows no change, and its eros is also a "granite monotony." Stevens' largest *clinamen* away from his prime precursor, Whitman, is to refuse the musical shuttle that comes out of the mockingbird's throat. His own commentary on canto VI for once does not fall short of the intensity of his own text:

> There is a repetition of a sound, ké-ké, all over the place. Its monotony unites the separate sounds into one, as a number of faces become one, as all fates become a common fate, as all bottles blown by a glass blower become one, and as all bishops grow to look alike, etc. . . .
>
> In the face of death life asserts itself. Perhaps it makes an image out of the force with which it struggles to survive. Bethou is intended to be heard; it and ké-ké, which is inimical, are opposing sounds. Bethou is the spirit's own seduction. [*L*, 438]

The "Bethou" mockery, if it is a mockery, in Stevens, goes back to *Mozart, 1935* in *Ideas of Order,* where Shelley's "Be thou me, impetuous one!" had been turned not against Shelley but against those who in 1935 demanded of the poet that he invoke only the social muse. In canto VI, the "bethou" suffers a falling away, from the "heavenly gong" that transcends the "single text" of the ké-ké, until it suffers becoming "a sound like any other." The point is precisely Shelleyan, rather than anti-Shelleyan, since both poets lament the absorption into the natural cycle of the language that would transcend cycle. If an unchanging fiction gives no pleasure, an unchanging love ceases to be love, and Stevens' hyperbolic trope for eros-as-monotony is the choir of birds. But to reach this trope he crossed via a violent disjunction, and much can be learned about his text by studying the crossing. The banjo's twang, like the guitar's plucking, is a metonymy for the proud solitude of Stevens' art; the Shelleyan "Bethou me" is a hyperbole for the intense personal confrontations between mind and nature in the Sublime. As the crossing is made a movement occurs from the expressive to the mimetic, from the more internalized to the less internalized, and from a vastation of sight to a monotony of sound. This is a crossing to the Sublime that wounds, that takes away rather than adds strength, and there is also a repression of the hard-earned lessons of Stevens' earlier poetic career and its vicissitudes. Something is amiss with the *topos* of change, and I think that cantos VII through X of *It Must Change* labor to correct a malaise in Stevens' experience of the Sublime. That is why cantos VII and VIII defend Stevens' ideas of eros, and why IX and X are written in defense of poetry, with Shelley's *Ozymandias* the climax of VII–VIII, and his west wind rising up again as the culmination of IX and X.

Canto VII is a variation upon Whitman's elegy for his own poetic self under the guise of an elegy for Lincoln, *When Lilacs Last in the Dooryard Bloom'd*. Stevens seems to be mocking the *Lilacs* elegy, uneasily, in the *Comedian*, just before the presentation of Crispin's four egregious daughters:

> All this with many multings of the man,
> Effective colonizer sharply stopped
> In the door-yard by his own capacious bloom.
> But that this bloom grown riper, showing nibs
> Of its eventual roundness, puerile tints
> Of spiced and weathery rouges, should complex
> The stopper to indulgent fatalist
> Was unforeseen.

This is also the mode of the rather nasty *Harmonium* poem, *Last Looks at the Lilacs* (*CP*, 48), where the Whitmanian bloom is reduced to "the bloom of soap / And this fragrance the fragrance of vegetal," and the Whitmanian "great star early droop'd in the western sky in the night" is merely "the cool night and its fantastic star." But *Notes* makes an admiring and positive use of Whitman's poem, inaugurating a strain in Stevens that will intensify through the rest of his poetic career. *Chocorua to Its Neighbor* and *The Owl in the Sarcophagus* are part of this story, as we will see, but so are *Things of August*, IV, and above all else *The Rock*, but that is to run too far ahead. Though critics until now have interpreted *It Must Change*, VII, as irony, that is a weak misreading of a thoroughly Whitmanian hyperbole, the American Sublime as a democratic eros:

After a lustre of the moon, we say
We have not the need of any paradise,
We have not the need of any seducing hymn.

It is true. Tonight the lilacs magnify
The easy passion, the ever-ready love
Of the lover that lies within us and we breathe

An odor evoking nothing, absolute.
We encounter in the dead middle of the night
The purple odor, the abundant bloom.

The lover sighs as for accessible bliss,
Which he can take within him on his breath,
Possess in his heart, conceal and nothing known.

For easy passion and ever-ready love
Are of our earthy birth and here and now
And where we live and everywhere we live,

As in the top-cloud of a May night-evening,
As in the courage of the ignorant man,
Who chants by book, in the heat of the scholar, who writes

The book, hot for another accessible bliss:
The fluctuations of certainty, the change
Of degrees of perception in the scholar's dark.

Stevens is returning (consciously, I think) to the earliest of
his invocations of the Whitmanian mother-muse, *To the One of
Fictive Music*, of 1922, where the second stanza celebrates our
"earthy birth" in terms akin to the hyperboles here. So extreme
is this hyperbolic rhetoric, with its quasi-mockery of sound patterns and repetitions of the formula "The easy passion, the
ever-ready love," that the reader is tempted to doubt Stevens'
authentic, serious, and indeed outrageous celebratory force.
But he means it all right, just as Whitman did, for this is the
rhetoric of Transcendentalist eros, not so much an exaggeration
as a heaping up in order to suggest a true "beyond." The
scholar of the closing tercets is Emerson's American scholar,

and the eros is an eros of belatedness; impatient, more promiscuous in thought than in fact, and heartened by the courage of its own ignorance, which takes on an intentional meaning that is not pejorative.

When hyperbole, by catachresis, is compounded with irony, in the next canto, we enjoy the disconcerting and by now famous confrontation between Nanzia Nunzio and Shelley's shattered Sphinx. Nanzia Nunzio is Stevens' version of a Transcendentalist heroine-messenger like Margaret Fuller, off on her quest to accept the Universe. But she has the reductive spirit of Mrs. Alfred Uruguay, as she divests herself of necklace and stone-studded belt, prepared to proclaim that elegance must suffer like the rest:

> I am the spouse, divested of bright gold,
> The spouse beyond emerald or amethyst,
> Beyond the burning body that I bear.
>
> I am the woman stripped more nakedly
> Than nakedness, standing before an inflexible
> Order, saying I am the contemplated spouse.
>
> Speak to me that, which spoken, will array me
> In its own only precious ornament.
> Set on me the spirit's diamond coronal.

This is the error of being a fundamentalist of the First Idea, and the Shelleyan reply is properly High Romantic:

> Then Ozymandias said the spouse, the bride
> Is never naked. A fictive covering
> Weaves always glistening from the heart and mind.

It "weaves always glistening" because it must change; nakedness (even if Nanzia Nunzio and Mrs. Uruguay were to strip down) is precisely what cannot change, which is to say that nakedness is not a fiction. The fictive status of poetic language is the burden of canto IX, which is an enigmatic and self-doubting text, more so than I think Stevens could have intended. Kermode points to the influence of Valéry's speculations on poetic language, and this seems right, but Stevens weakly misreads Valéry by insisting that the poet is beyond language, a Transcendentalist and very American dream. Yet Stevens moves us here by the honesty of his own doubt. It is wholly Emersonian that Stevens posits an oratory at our "bluntest barriers," our ultimate limitations, which is a kind of speech opposed to poetry-as-writing, a speech indeed of the direct will and so "only a little of the tongue." This is the Emersonian emphasis upon the poet as transcending his own poetry, upon an ideal or possible orator who will destroy all limitations. What is least convincing is the declaration in the canto's final lines, where Stevens speaks of himself as if he were Whitman (or, in our time, Williams), when in fact he was wholly of those who speak "the imagination's Latin."

It Must Change concludes with a grace note, one of Stevens' most persuasive lyrics. The poet sits on a park bench, in a place of trance, his Theatre of Trope, and watches the swans go through their changes to the music of the west wind, destroyer and preserver. What emerges from the scene is the conviction of the necessity of the antithetical, the Nietzschean justification for art, which is that without it we would perish from the truth. This invented world depends upon "the freshness of transformation," but this is "the freshness of ourselves"; the poet is the only transforming agent. Yet time sets the limits for that agency, and the poet only projects, as the canto ends. "Time will write them down," and that "down" takes on a grimly directional meaning.

The rhetorical pattern of *It Must Give Pleasure* is a little at variance with that of the first two parts of *Notes*. Here the dialectical movements of *ethos* or Fate, and *pathos* or Power, occupy four cantos each, rather than five. Cantos IX–X of *It Must Give Pleasure* fall together with the coda, addressing the soldier, as an epilogue not only to *Notes* but to all of Stevens' canon between 1915 and 1942.

Despite several recent attempts to baptize Stevens' poetry by neo-Christian critics, a proper translation of *It Must Give Pleasure*, as of the rest of Stevens, could be: Christianity, as an unchanging fiction, has ceased to give pleasure, in that it has ceased to give poetry. The pairing of cantos I and II opposes devotional verse, as "a facile exercise," to the weather, "the blue woman." But the polemic is genial because Stevens is now so triumphantly at ease in his rhetoric. He allows the devotional mode six lines of apparent splendor before he inserts the qualification "This is a facile exercise." The emphasis falls on the contrast between "facile exercise" and "difficultest rigor," in which the rigor is the mode of *Nachträglichkeit*, the retroactive meaningfulness that comes from reasoning about things with a later reason. But pleasure, for Stevens, as I said earlier, is a strong poet's pleasure, which is priority, and his protest against those who "sing jubilas at exact, accustomed times" hardly has any priority. Hugh Kenner, out of his general distaste for Stevens, unamiably observes that Stevens, like every agnostic, wished to believe that he was the first agnostic. I suspect that the burden for Stevens, here as elsewhere, is simply Whitman, who does have the American priority in opposing poet to priest or mystic, though that was really just priority in verse, since as usual Emerson had done it already in prose. Stevens says that St. Jerome, presumably through his translation of the Psalms, "begat the tubas," but his true opponent would appear to be the as-it-were-original supreme fiction, Jehovah, "bleakest ancestor" of the word that was also a light. "More than sensual mode" evokes from Stevens a polemic resembling Pater's defense of his secularized epiphanies against the *logos* of Coleridge:

> But the difficultest rigor is forthwith,
> On the image of what we see, to catch from that
>
> Irrational moment its unreasoning,
> As when the sun comes rising, when the sea
> Clears deeply, when the moon hangs on the wall
>
> Of heaven-haven. These are not things transformed.
> Yet we are shaken by them as if they were.
> We reason about them with a later reason.

This is a superb instance of Stevens' *Nachträglichkeit*, his re-imagining of First Ideas. If he knew Hopkins' poem about a nun taking the veil, his "heaven-haven" here is parodistic. The

Paterian element I find crucial; the pleasure of priority in perception combines with the sensual mode of the irrational moment to dispute all exact, accustomed times. This is the pleasure developed in the ravishing canto II, of which Stevens remarked, "The more exquisite the thing seen, the more exquisite the thing unseen," and "The sense of reality makes more acute the sense of the fictive" (L, 444–45). As in canto v of It Must Change, this hymn of "the blue woman" is a late revision of Sunday Morning. Stevens even remarked that the blue woman was "the weather of a Sunday morning early last April when I wrote this" (L, 444). His muse now finds that "it was enough / For her that she remembered." The emphasis upon cold clarity recalls the early Pater, of the Winckelmann essay, with his embryonic formula for the peculiar and privileged moment of vision: "To realise this situation, to define, in a chill and empty atmosphere, the focus where rays, in themselves pale and impotent, unite and begin to burn."

Stevens follows his marvelous celebration of April's blue with the "unending red" of canto III, a grim lyric that is his equivalent of Yeats's Second Coming and which, like Yeats's apocalyptic lyric, goes back to Shelley's underrated sonnet, Ozymandias, with which Stevens had played already in canto VIII of It Must Change. It is grotesque that Stevens should envision his Ozymandias as a Jehovah-statue in the African or South American wilderness, and yet the total effect of the stanza is menacing rather than merely sardonic. Stevens may not have realized that he had written a Nietzschean history of Judaism and of Christianity here, in miniature, a history out of On the Genealogy of Morals. In his curious commentary (letter to Hi Simons, January 28, 1943), Stevens says of the Christ or "dead shepherd" of this canto, that it "was an improvisation. What preceded it in the poem made it necessary, like music that evolves for internal reasons and not with reference to an external program" (L, 438). We can interpret this as meaning improvisation became necessary in religion, when Jehovah as an unchanging fiction ceased to give pleasure. I recall here again my American Gnostic formula in the opening chapter, "Everything that can be broken should be broken"; or, as Stevens goes on to say in his commentary, "What the spirit wants it creates, even if it has to do so in a fiction." Stevens, as Vendler shows, is much more interested in the colossal head of his Jehovah than in his Orphic Christ, who is a less successful invention. But the two tropes are in series anyway; as unchanging fictions they cannot be rescued from their belatedness by any later reason, being forms of Fate and not of Power.

Not that the marriage trope of canto IV goes beyond them though, since sadly this seems to me now only a metaphoric self-deception, the last desperate stand in Stevens of a familiar Romantic figure of the reconciliation of mind and nature. Yet Stevens half knows this when he oxymoronically calls his maiden Bawda, recalling not only the "bawds of euphony" in *Thirteen Ways* but also the euphonic "bawdiness, / Unpurged by epitaph, indulged at last" of *A High-Toned Old Christian Woman*, the *Harmonium* poem that opened with the prophetic assertion "Poetry is the supreme fiction, madame." It is only a sublimating fantasy when Stevens too hopefully says that "we make of what we see . . . / a place dependent on ourselves." That is to have forgotten: "From this the poem springs: that we live in a place / That is not our own and, much more, not ourselves." Canto IV wistfully hints at a Wordsworthian reciprocity between mind and nature, but the lyric wavers and breaks because for once Stevens does not qualify enough. I suspect that this failure can be accounted for by realizing how disjunctive the rhetoric is between "They were love's characters come face to face" and the robust "We drank Meursault, ate lobster Bombay with mango / Chutney," which brings us to the third and last crossing of *Notes*, its Crossing of Identification. But I shall describe this crossing only after an account of what was waiting on the other side.

If there is a center in Stevens' constantly decentering canon, it is *Notes*, and the thematic and rhetorical center of *Notes*, if such a poem can have one, is the figure of the Canon Aspirin. He is not a figure upon whom criticism has achieved a consensus, and this is as it should be. Stevens himself seems to have been rather friendly to his creation, judging by the commentary in his letter of March 29, 1943, to Hi Simons:

The sophisticated man: the Canon Aspirin, (the man who has explored all the projections of the mind, his own particularly) comes back, without having acquired a sufficing fiction, —— to, say, his sister and her children. His sister has never explored anything at all and shrinks from doing so. He is conscious of the sensible ecstasy and hums laboriously in praise of the rejection of dreams etc.

For all that, it gives him, in the long run, a sense of nothingness, of nakedness, of the finality and limitation of fact; and lying on his bed, he returns once more to night's pale illuminations. He identifies himself with them. He returns to the side of the children's bed, with every sense of human dependence. But there is a supreme effort which it is inevitable that he should make. If he is to elude human pathos, and fact, he must go straight to the utmost crown of night: find his way through the imagination or perhaps to the imagination. He might escape from fact but he would only arrive at another nothingness, another nakedness, the limitation of thought. It is not, then, a matter of eluding human pathos, human dependence. Thought is part of these, the imagination is part of these and they are part of thought and of imagination. In short, a man with a taste for Meursault, and lobster Bombay, who has a sensible sister and who, for himself, thinks to the very material of his mind, doesn't have much choice about yielding to "the complicate, the amassing harmony." (How he ever became a Canon is the real problem.) [L, 445]

Let us start with how this flawed but authentic hero of the imagination ever became a canon. A canon is a priest serving in a cathedral, or simply a religious bound by vows, hence the word from the late Latin *canonicus*, one living under a rule, from *canon* meaning "rule" or "measuring rod." But the name "the Canon Aspirin" would fit only the ecclesiastical world of Ronald Firbank. Why "Aspirin"? Though Kermode ascribes the name to being an "expert in sedation" I hold to my earlier notion that the Canon is an apocalyptic cure for our headache of unreality, just as Saint John in Stevens' *Saint John and the Back-Ache* is the apocalyptic cure for the back-ache of fallen human history. But there is more to be said about why the canon and why Aspirin.

In *Description without Place*, written three years after *Notes*, "description is revelation" and is also "the book of reconciliation, / Book of a concept only possible / In description, canon central in itself, / The thesis of the plentifullest John." The latter is the apocalyptic John who confronts the back-ache. A "canon central in itself" to be found in "description" is not a rule but rather a visionary argument. In the 1954 poem *Conversation with Three Women of New England* (*OP*, 108–09), we encounter the Vichian adage "The author of man's canons is man, / Not some outer patron and imaginer," where "canon" means human self-definition. The Canon Aspirin is not an ecclesiastic but a High Romantic fallen angel, a morning star, and his name "Aspirin" probably plays upon the archaic meaning of "aspires," the *anders-streben* of Pater's "*All art constantly aspires towards the condition of music*," or the upward-rising of Blake's "On what wings dare he aspire." In his great flight, the Canon, like Milton's Satan winging through the abyss, *falls upward*, in that condition of psychic extravagance which Binswanger names *Verstiegenheit*. "Aspire" goes back to the Latin for "breaking upon, desiring, favoring," and I think we can translate "the Canon Aspirin" as the self-defining, self-describing human desire for a beyond, even if that beyond turns out to be an abyss.

In the company of the sophisticated canon we have enjoyed "lobster Bombay with mango / Chutney." Unfortunately, lobster Bombay is devoured nowhere else in Stevens' verse, but there is a fair amount of mango consumed, and the contexts are worth some consideration. In *Certain Phenomena of Sound*, written soon after *Notes*, we are to be given mango dressed with white wine, sugar, and lime juice, so as to prepare us to hear a narrative that will be "a sound producing the things that are spoken," which is a kind of visionary romance. Earlier, in a stanza rejected from *The Blue Guitar*, rather lively skeletons sit on a wall and drop red mango peels as the guitarist plays. Later, in *The Rock*, Stevens' major elegy for his own poetic self, the mango is given a vital emphasis:

> The rock is the habitation of the whole,
> Its strength and measure, that which is near, point A
> In a perspective that begins again
>
> At B: the origin of the mango's rind.

We can say, at the least, that the mango is visionary food for Stevens, perhaps his equivalent of Coleridge's "honey-dew." As

I am reading so minutely and madly, to clear the Canon Aspirin's good and visionary name, I note that his first action is that of declaiming. Vehement oratory has a special place in Stevens' poetry. *Notes* earlier had sought to defend, moderately, "the romantic intoning, the declaimed clairvoyance" as being appropriate idiom for apotheosis, while still insisting that "apotheosis is not / The origin of the major man," which indeed will be the one test that the Canon Aspirin will fail, since he will attempt apotheosis. We can say then that the Canon Aspirin is the High Romantic poet, Stevens' heroic precursor, whom Stevens hopes to surpass, since Stevens has learned that the composite precursor is not so easily reduced or dismissed. I will not review all the uses of "declaim" in Stevens, but highly relevant ones are "the actor that will at last declaim our end" in *United Dames of America*, "subtler than look's declaiming" in *The Owl in the Sarcophagus*, and, most remarkably, "a vacant sea declaiming with wide throat" in *Puella Parvula*. High Romantic rhetoric is what declaims in Stevens, and while it makes him very anxious he knows that the imagination, like the Canon Aspirin, needs to be indulged.

I go back now to Stevens' commentary on the Canon, who is said by his maker to be sophisticated in all the ways of consciousness but who has not found what he quested after, what would suffice, a supreme fiction. This is our clue, for this is why, in the greatest moment of his poetry, Stevens will abstract himself from the Canon Aspirin, in order to proclaim his own momentary incarnation of a supreme fiction, which will turn out not to be poetry or a poem but, as in Emerson and Whitman (and Wordsworth), to be a poet, to be a fiction of the self, or the poetic self as a transumption, an audacious trope undoing all previous tropes. With all this as prelude, I am ready to return now to the Crossing of Identification and subsequently to interpret the texts of the Canon Aspirin, cantos v through viii of *It Must Give Pleasure*.

Canto iv, the "mystic marriage in Catawba," remained more of a limitation than a restitution of meaning, since its interpretation of itself is governed by·*Nachträglichkeit*. It is only by reasoning "of these things with later reason" that Stevens persuades himself that he makes of what he sees, or rather *has seen*, a place dependent on himself; and it is only that belated self-persuasion which makes possible the fable of the mystic marriage of the great captain and the maiden charmingly and paradoxically called Bawda. But this is Stevens' version of the High Romantic inside / outside, mind / nature metaphor; like all such metaphors it "fails," as all endlessly elaborating perspectivisms necessarily fail. It is instructive to compare the failure of this metaphoric lyric, *It Must Be Abstract*, IV, with the success of the metonymic lyric *It Must Change*, IV, the embrace of winter and spring as "cold copulars." The point is not that Stevens is happier in the more "realistic" mode of contiguities but that he belatedly realizes the authentic burden of Romantic metaphor, which is to "fail" so as to prepare a path for the restitutions of Romantic metaleptic reversal, the mode of transumption.

The Crossing of Identification here is thus from the metaphor of the mystic marriage to the metalepsis of the fable of the Canon Aspirin, whose "failure" is of a very different kind, as I will show. Where *It Must Give Pleasure*, I, III, and IV, emphasized sound rather than sight, an expressive aesthetic rather than a mimetic one, and a relative externalization of the self, the emphases in cantos v through VIII are all in the opposite modes. Stevens moves toward a projection or casting away of the Canon Aspirin (though very ambivalently) and toward an introjection of a Newness or Transcendental Selfhood, a more-than-Sublime influx, in which momentarily he becomes God-like. What the rhetorical and topological disjunction between cantos IV and V shows us is that Stevens, unlike Wordsworth and Whitman, will not as yet come to terms with his own death, which is the true issue of the final two cantos of *Notes* and of its epilogue, as I think we will see.

Stevens' exuberance of invention, in cantos v through VIII, is so powerful as to be bewildering. It not only fights off his own capacity for commentary but resists almost too successfully the intelligence of all commentators. The difficulties are of transumptive figuration, that is, of tropes undoing prior tropes, and the text needs to be put in question at nearly every phrase if something more than a weak misreading is to result. Hoping to offer a strong misreading, I want to venture upon a very full account of these four cantos.

The Canon Aspirin is the High Romantic or Transcendentalist expansionist *in Stevens himself*, which is to say, he is Stevens aspiring most wildly and most freely after drinking Meursault, and eating Lobster Bombay with mango chutney. So exalted, he declaims, "Of his sister, in what a sensible ecstasy / She lived in her house." If the Canon Aspirin is the Romantic poet in Stevens, at once a morning star and a new Apollo or potential idea of the sun, then his sister is the muse, or the one of fictive music, an idea of the moon of the imagination. This is why she has two daughters, "one of four, and one of seven," the four weeks and the seven days together reminding us that the moon traditionally is called "the Mother of the Months" (as she is, for instance, in Shelley's *Witch of Atlas*, a poem from which Stevens quoted to me the one time I met him). She is of course not only "sister and solace" but companion, fellow, self, brother, delight, as the Whitmanian catalog of *It Must Change*, IV, itemized. But she goes a long way back in Stevens, back to 1922, when he wrote *To the One of Fictive Music*, in which she was even more Whitmanian: "Sister and mother and diviner love, / And of the sisterhood of the living dead." Her house is the cosmos, and when the Canon praises her for "sensible ecstasy" he plays upon the last line of *The Greenest Continent*, V, in *Owl's Clover*: "to feel / The ecstasy of sense in a sensuous air" (*OP*, 56). But she is a chastened muse, and her widowed ecstasy is now more sensible than sensuous, as reflected in the way she dresses her daughters, "appropriate to / Their poverty." They are the weeks and days as we live them, their chief characteristic being imaginative need, and they contrast sharply with Crispin's four gaudy and egregious daughters. The most ascetic and reductive of muses, their mother, rejects dreams for them, but more dangerously she also rejects poetry:

> With Sunday pearls, her widow's gayety.
> She hid them under simple names. She held
> Them closelier to her by rejecting dreams.

The words they spoke were voices that she heard.
She looked at them and saw them as they were
And what she felt fought off the barest phrase.

The Canon Aspirin, having said these things,
Reflected, humming an outline of a fugue
Of praise, a conjugation done by choirs.

That reflection and humming are done "laboriously," as Stevens cunningly remarked, since the Canon is necessarily less admiring of so reductive a stance than he admits to being. The Canon, like his ancestors in the Wordsworthian Solitary and the Poet of *Alastor*, has not found a fiction that suffices, but at least he has explored the range of his own mind, whereas "his sister has never explored anything at all and shrinks from doing so." Unable to accept "a sense of nothingness, of nakedness, of the finality and limitation of fact," that is to say of the First Idea as ultimate *ethos* or Fate, the Canon dreams a heroic dream. For "a point, / Beyond which fact could not progress as fact," might as well be a mere, dreamless sleep, or as Stevens says it in one of his *Adagia:* "To be at the end of fact is not to be at the beginning of imagination but it is to be at the end of both" (*OP*, 175). The Canon internalizes, as any strong Romantic poet must:

Thereon the learning of the man conceived
Once more night's pale illuminations, gold

Beneath, far underneath, the surface of
His eye and audible in the mountain of
His ear, the very material of his mind.

What the eye beholds and the ear receives is the very material of the mind, since the theory of imaginative perception, in Stevens as in Whitman, is Lucretian. An Epicurean or Paterian materialism is the metaphysic of the universe of dream through which the Canon flies in the shape of a Miltonic angel, though the children and the Canon's relation of pathos to them suggest more precisely the phantasmagoria of Whitman's *Sleepers*. In that flight, the Canon–Angel reaches a point directly antithetical to his sister's: "a point / Beyond which thought could not

progress as thought." Such a point, at "the utmost crown of
night," may be a dreamless death. Confronted by a choice between two modes of imagelessness, the Canon truly becomes a
strong poet by choosing "to include the things / That in each
other are included, the whole, / The complicate, the amassing
harmony," which we can assume is the fiction that will suffice,
the supreme fiction of Romantic poetry.

But Stevens, always ambivalent about Romanticism, disengages from the Canon in canto VII, because the Canon no
sooner chooses than "he imposes orders as he thinks of
them, / As the fox and snake do," or as the lion does when he
roars at the enraging desert. To use the language of the essay
Imagination as Value (1948), the Canon's Romanticism becomes a
failure of the imagination when the liberty of the mind is
evaded by him. The Canon "builds capitols," which in Stevens
are emblems of failed creativity. So, in 1944, he explained the
Harmonium poem *Anecdote of Canna* as "an aspect of the idea that
the imagination creates nothing" (*L*, 465). In the poem the
tropical flowers fill the terrace of the capitol in the dreams of
"X, the mighty thought, the mighty man," yet these are merely
the same canna that can be observed in the daybreak of reality.
Again, in the *The Auroras of Autumn*, VI, Stevens sees a phantasmagoria dispelled, with the image "A capitol, / It may be, is
emerging or has just / Collapsed." The ancestor image, as so
often, is taken from Emerson, in a great passage of 1846 from
the Journals, on the poet as the Central Man: "The Poet should
install himself and shove all usurpers from their chairs by elec-
trifying mankind with the right tone, long wished for, never
heard. The true centre thus appearing, all false centres are suddenly superseded, and grass grows in the Capitol."

Building capitols, the Canon has forgotten that his mission is
to include reason yet to project beyond it. Sardonically observing the Canon's "statues of reasonable men, / Who surpassed
the most literate owl, the most erudite / Of elephants," Stevens
at first is amused and amusing. But not for long:

> But to impose is not
> To discover. To discover an order as of
> A season, to discover summer and know it,

To discover winter and know it well, to find,
Not to impose, not to have reasoned at all,
Out of nothing to have come on major weather,

It is possible, possible, possible. It must
Be possible. It must be that in time
The real will from its crude compoundings come,

Seeming, at first, a beast disgorged, unlike,
Warmed by a desperate milk. To find the real,
To be stripped of every fiction except one,

The fiction of an absolute—Angel,
Be silent in your luminous cloud and hear
The luminous melody of proper sound.

There is an interpretive problem here in determining Stevens' tone. Vendler reads the tone as desperation, and says of this passage that in it "repetitive, accumulative, and hysterical affirmations mount in a crescendo conveying the fear which is their origin." That there is an anxiety of influence at the origin here I do not doubt, and I myself called this a dignified desperation in a commentary written some years ago. But I would dissent now both from Vendler and from my earlier self. Repetitive and accumulative the rhetoric certainly is here, but it is too controlled to be hysterical, and Stevens is too shrewd and too sure of himself, at this point, to be desperate. He *is* overinsistent, because he is arguing against his own reductiveness, but his insistence is upon the possibility of a middle path between reduction and expansion, between Mrs. Uruguay and the rabbit as king of the ghosts. To come on major weather, or the giant, out of nothing or the First Idea, it must be possible to reimagine the First Idea. When the real *will* come (like Emerson and Whitman, Stevens is prophesying), it will seem, at first, not very attractive, indeed "a beast disgorged, unlike, / Warmed by a desperate milk." There will be something desperate about the real-to-be, but not about ourselves. The tone that I read is excited Power, as Stevens commands his own creation, the angel conceived by the Canon as one of "night's pale illuminations," to be silent and to hear Stevens himself proudly declaiming "the luminous melody of proper sound."

This melody is the great canto VIII, upon which the whole of *Notes* comes to rest:

> What am I to believe? If the angel in his cloud,
> Serenely gazing at the violent abyss,
> Plucks on his strings to pluck abysmal glory,
>
> Leaps downward through evening's revelations, and
> On his spredden wings, needs nothing but deep space,
> Forgets the gold centre, the golden destiny,
>
> Grows warm in the motionless motion of his flight,
> Am I that imagine this angel less satisfied?
> Are the wings his, the lapis-haunted air?
>
> Is it he or is it I that experience this?
> Is it I then that keep saying there is an hour
> Filled with expressible bliss, in which I have
>
> No need, am happy, forget need's golden hand,
> Am satisfied without solacing majesty,
> And if there is an hour there is a day,
>
> There is a month, a year, there is a time
> In which majesty is a mirror of the self:
> I have not but I am and as I am, I am.

What am I to believe? What kind of a question is this, open or rhetorical? And which of these words is to be emphasized: what? am? I? Believe? "I" is the answer, and the question is rhetorical, implying the single answer "I am to believe in a fiction of the self, in a trope of myself." It is not surprising that only a few months after writing this canto Stevens should have written *Chocorua to Its Neighbor*, for he had linked the imagery of what became this canto to Chocorua in section XXI of the *Blue Guitar* some five years before. There "his self, not that gold self aloft" is declared "a substitute for all the gods," and the solitude of the self was compared to "the shadow of Chocorua." But Stevens had become more audacious, for there "one's self and the mountains of one's land" are "without magnificence" but here one's self is majestic.

"Am I that imagine this angel less satisfied?" The emphasis in this wholly rhetorical question is upon "less," and the answer is: "No, I am more satisfied than the angel I have imagined." But what does "satisfied" mean here? To be satisfied is to have one's needs or desires fulfilled, and even to have accomplished the will's revenge against time and so against time's mocking statement "It was." But etymologically it means to make something suffice, to make enough, and the root *sa* appears ominously also in the words "sad," "sated," and "satire." To be satisfied is to be sated and to be sad, to be self-satirized, and we can recall Freud's melancholy reflection that for the human psyche there can be no satisfaction in satisfaction anyway. And Stevens is well warned; his *Extracts* had insisted that "the mind is the end and must be satisfied," but his *Well-Dressed Man with a Beard* had ended with the great line "It can never be satisfied, the mind, never." What could suffice? No reductive quests had found the answer, and just as clearly the Canon's expansive quest, culminating in the leaping downward of his angel, had not sufficed either. But if the angel forgets God and heaven, "the gold centre, the golden destiny," and is warmed by his purely fictive flight, and thus achieves, through repression, a satisfaction, then Stevens can achieve a satisfaction also. This is the satisfaction of knowing that the wings and the stone-haunted air, the place not the angel's own, are both evidences of what the essay *Imagination as Value* was to call the power of the poet's mind over the possibilities of things, that is to say, over reality.

The authentic difficulties of canto VIII commence with the next question: "Is it he or is it I that experience this?" Why does Stevens ask such a question? What is it to ask such a question? What is "this"? I do not think there are answers except by way of two intertextual juxtapositions, one, which Kermode first suggested, with *The Prelude*, XIV, 91–120, and the other with Whitman's *By Blue Ontario's Shore*, section 18. The Wordsworth passage in its conclusion attains its meaning only by an intertextual juxtaposition with *Paradise Lost*, V, 483–90, where Raphael discourses to Adam on the "gradual scale sublim'd" which distinguishes human from angelic faculties, a passage crucial also for Coleridge's formulation of the Secondary Imagination. But intertextuality must be kept within some limits if a critical discourse is to sustain itself, so I will confine this juxtaposition to Stevens and Wordsworth and then to Stevens and Whitman. Here are the crucial lines, for Stevens' passage, in Wordsworth; lines which constitute a *pathos* of absolute poetic self-recognition, or as Wordsworth says, which concern "the power, which . . . is the express / Resemblance" of the higher Reason or poetic imagination. Stevens' Hoon had said, "I was myself the compass of that sea." Wordsworth's solitary bards deal

> With the whole compass of the universe:
> They from their native selves can send abroad
> Kindred mutations; for themselves create
> A like existence; and, whene'er it dawns
> Created for them, catch it, or are caught
> By its inevitable mastery,
> Like angels stopped upon the wing by sound
> Of harmony from Heaven's remotest spheres. . . .

◊

> Such minds are truly from the Deity,
> For they are Powers; and hence the highest bliss
> That flesh can know is theirs—the consciousness
> Of Whom they are, habitually infused
> Through every image and through every thought.

The Canon Aspirin is Stevens' kindred mutation; the Angel he dreams is stopped upon the wing by Stevens' luminous melody of proper sound, by the complicate, the amazing harmony of canto VIII. Wordsworth's "highest bliss" of poets is Stevens' more modest "expressible bliss," and the nature of the two joys is the same—"the consciousness / Of Whom they are" and "I have not but I am and as I am, I am." Wordsworth's power of self-recognition verges upon a divination; Stevens as heir of Emerson and Whitman audaciously crosses over into it. Jehovah's *ehyeh asher ehyeh*, "I am that I am," is replaced by Stevens' "as I am, I am." What comes just before in Stevens has been misread rather weakly: "I have not but I am" is a confession not of loss but of the influx of power. During that time when the self can behold itself accurately as being majestic, the ego does not possess nor is it possessed, but it simply is. One no longer says, "I have my body" because, for a time, "I am my body." In this triumphant solitude, the self disengages from the Cinderella-like wish-fulfillments that obsess it when the shadow of an external world comes near again:

> These external regions, what do we fill them with
> Except reflections, the escapades of death,
> Cinderella fulfilling herself beneath the roof?

"Beneath the roof" is to be back in a subject-object, internal-external, dualizing cosmos, where reflections give back the self as the death instinct, or as Freud said, the world "beyond the pleasure principle." But in the time of canto VIII, we are *in* the world of the pleasure principle, the world of the supreme fiction or of the solitary self as mortal god. But what time is that? Not so much the time of making a poem as the time of having made it, seen it fail, and only *then* stepping back from it and proclaiming one's greater freedom and satisfaction, greater than those of the fiction one has made. Stevens smiles his work to see, and only when the time of majesty is past does he return to the post-midnight world of Cinderella. Troping upon *The Prelude*'s great closing tropes of angel and of the poet's divinating self he accomplishes a transumption of the founder of his tradition. In this large figure of a figure, Stevens has projected death, introjected a momentary earliness, and realized again that whether he stands in majesty or in phantasmagoria he stands in a mirror world, a world of force and not of presence. But that means he knowingly stands and lives in the mind and not in the world, since his Saint John tells the Back-Ache that "the world is presence and not force. / Presence is not mind." So late in tradition, the price of a transumptive allusion is a total surrender of what Emerson and Whitman had fought to preserve, the fiction of a Transcendental consciousness in which the ontological and empirical selves could fuse together.

Closer even than Wordsworth to Stevens' climactic chant is a great self-recognition of Whitman's, in section 18 of *By Blue On-*

tario's Shore. Here is Whitman asking the Stevensian questions and implying a more-than-Stevensian triumphant answer:

> I will confront these shows of the day and night,
> I will know if I am to be less than they,
> I will see if I am not as majestic as they,
> I will see if I am not as subtle and real as they,
> I will see if I am to be less generous than they,
> I will see if I have no meaning, while the houses and ships have
>   meaning,
> I will see if the fishes and birds are to be enough for
>   themselves, and I am not to be enough for myself.

Stevens approximates this confrontation, and he too says to his fiction: "Copious as you are I absorb you all in myself, and become the master myself."

Notes has a deliberate coda, Stevens' direct and overtly personal address to the soldier of reality, who is anyone that fights for the mind in the "war between the mind / And sky." But there is a less deliberate coda in cantos IX and X, which is more revelatory of what is still unresolved in Stevens and I think more interesting as poetry than the quite moving, rather Whitmanian *envoi* to the soldier. The distasteful birdsong of *It Must Change*, VI, returns, but Stevens is better fortified now against the cyclic repetitions of mere nature. A curious tolerance manifests itself in the poet, who for the first time can contemplate the pleasure of merely circulating as being indeed a pleasure, "the way wine comes at a table in a wood," an image of contentment that will be amplified later in *A Primitive Like an Orb*. "Pleasure" now means to be a master of repetition, and to master repetition you must accept it.

That is one partial satisfaction; what suffices in canto X is much subtler. The earth, affectionately addressed as "Fat girl," is enough and more than enough, as curiously she could never have been in *Harmonium* and as she was not to be again during the final phase of the group of poems called *The Rock*. By the pragmatic test of which Stevens became the supreme lyrist, experience itself has got to be enough. But Stevens never stays philosophic for very long; he is himself only when he is most evasive. I think that the beauty of canto x, surely the most relaxed and good-humored of Stevens' lyrics, is itself the result of a knowing evasion, the evasion of Stevens' true muse, the Whitmanian fierce mother of fictive music, by this homely, earthly nurse of a summer night in which a poem is born:

> Fat girl, terrestrial, my summer, my night,
> How is it I find you in difference, see you there
> In a moving contour, a change not quite completed?
>
> You are familiar yet an aberration.
> Civil, madam, I am, but underneath
> A tree, this unprovoked sensation requires
>
> That I should name you flatly, waste no words,
> Check your evasions, hold you to yourself.
> Even so when I think of you as strong or tired,
>
> Bent over work, anxious, content, alone,
> You remain the more than natural figure. You
> Become the soft-footed phantom, the irrational
>
> Distortion, however fragrant, however dear.
> That's it: the more than rational distortion,
> The fiction that results from feeling. Yes, that.

This is the gentlest of all Stevens' ironies, since *he* is making the evasions and *he* is refusing to name his muse flatly, as he will name her in the great creative desperation of *The Auroras of Autumn*. The "irrational" here is the "later reason" of *Nachträglichkeit* come into a wholly matured operation. As in *A Primitive Like an Orb*, xii, the poet even allows himself the triumphant snap of a "That's it," a richly earned positive moment which is essentially Nietzschean, recognizing as it does that the pleasure of art ensues from a willing error, a more than rational distortion, an evasion of the truth, because the truth either is or becomes death. The ultimate trope of *pathos* is "the fiction that results from feeling," a lie against time, or rather against time's unflickering "It was." In the highest of good humors, with a

Nietzschean gaiety, Stevens returns to the mock-academic world of the opening of *Notes*, but with a rhetorically saving difference:

> They will get it straight one day at the Sorbonne.
> We shall return at twilight from the lecture
> Pleased that the irrational is rational,
>
> Until flicked by feeling, in a gildered street,
> I call you by name, my green, my fluent mundo.
> You will have stopped revolving except in crystal.

9 *Transport to Summer*

"Transport" means to carry from one place (or season) to another or else to enrapture, to carry away. The book *Transport to Summer*, since it reprinted *Notes*, has to be regarded as Stevens' strongest single volume. Yet, even without *Notes*, it contains four major long poems: the greatly underrated, almost hushed poem of rapture, *Chocorua to Its Neighbor;* the polemical *Esthétique du Mal*, which does move the poet from one stance to another; the intensely visionary *Description without Place*, another carrying to elsewhere, to difference; most beautiful of these, *Credences of Summer*, where the rapture of the destination has been attained and begins to be modulated into loss. I will here concentrate upon these four poems and will consider the book's shorter poems for the most part only when they help define the difficulties and values of the major texts. But I will begin with an exception, a powerful poem of middle length, *Dutch Graves in Bucks County*, one of Stevens' rare overtly personal statements.

Holly Stevens has documented the genealogical obsession that formed so large an element in the poet's consciousness during the decade 1942–1952. *Dutch Graves in Bucks County* is the finest single product of Stevens' intense preoccupation with his ancestors, and it is a surprising result of such speculation, being anything but a study of the nostalgias. Indeed, I have chosen to lead off this chapter with it because it is so pugnacious and polemical a stand against the past and is as strongly an Emersonian text as any Stevens wrote. Its dialectic is precisely Emerson's: "Fate is the present desperado" is the formula of the poem's *ethos;* Power or *pathos* appears as the force of "an instinctive incantation" and as "the will of what is common to all men"; while *logos* or meaning enters negatively in the bitter question "What is this crackling of voices in the mind, / This pitter-patter of archaic freedom, / Of the thouands of freedoms except our own?" This pattern comes as no surprise, but the open expression of Stevens' deepest creative anxieties is startling: all through the poem he keeps insisting that his ancestors, in their death, know what he does *not* know, despite his over-protestations. The dead know "that the past is not part of the present," "that this time / Is not an early time that has grown late," "that your children / Are not your children, not your selves," and "that a new glory of new men assembles." Such a vision, set so desperately against time's "it was," must lead to a vision of a terrible freedom: "Freedom is like a man who kills himself / Each night." Moved by the *pathos* of his own vision, seeing himelf as dead, this most continuously eloquent of all American poets suddenly achieves an eloquence piercing and extraordinary even for him:

> This is the pit of torment that placid end
> Should be illusion, that the mobs of birth
> Avoid our stale perfections, seeking out
> Their own, waiting until we go
> To picnic in the ruins that we leave.

This is to recapitulate *A Postcard from the Volcano*, but in a fiercer tone. Urgent in his will not to be belated, Stevens yet concludes here with one of his most ambivalent tropes, perhaps beyond interpretation:

> Time was not wasted in your subtle temples.
> No: nor divergence made too steep to follow down.

The first line tropes upon an eloquent passage in *The Greenest Continent* of the discarded *Owl's Clover:* "The temple of the altar where each man / Beheld the truth and knew it to be true" (*OP*, 54). The second recalls the Whitmanian *Stars at Tallapoosa*, where "The lines are straight and swift between the stars" and where Stevens comments, "These lines are swift and fall without diverging." The swerve of divergence, absent at Talla-poosa, is attributed by Stevens to his individualistic ancestors, but not so steeply as to alienate him from his heritage. He, like they, beheld and knew his own truth, and he seems to be hint-ing that his divergence from tradition will not prevent those coming after from finding a continuity with him. But such an interpretation is not consistent with "the pit of torment that placid end / Should be illusion, that the mobs of birth / Avoid our stale perfections, seeking out / Their own." Stevens ap-pears to be alluding, ironically, to the speech of Oceanus in Keats's *Hyperion* where that sage accepts the truth that the "stale perfections" of the vanquished Titans must yield to the upstart Olympians: "So on our heels a fresh perfection treads, / A power more strong in beauty, born of us / And fated to excel us, as we pass / In glory that old Darkness." To pass from Keats's "fresh perfection" to Stevens' "stale perfec-tions" is to confront a darker anxiety of belatedness than even Keats had known and had labored to overcome.

It Must Change remains the formula of everything vital in *Transport to Summer*, from the need for fresh perfections in *Dutch Graves* through *The Motive for Metaphor*, on to the magnifi-cent speech of Chocorua. *Chocorua to Its Neighbor* returns Ste-vens to some of the obsessive images of the *Blue Guitar*, images he has in common with and perhaps derives from Shelley, one of the pervasive presences always haunting Stevens' poetry, together with Keats and Whitman, as well as the *antithetical* triad of Pater, Nietzsche, and Emerson. *The Motive for Metaphor* is remarkably like Shelley's late lyric *To Night* on the deep level of *stance*. Shelley, rising and seeing the dawn, sighs for night: "When light rode high, and the dew was gone, / And noon lay heavy on flower and tree." This is "the weight of primary noon" from which Stevens shrinks in *The Motive for Metaphor*, still "desiring the exhilarations of changes." Stevens' love for that moment in the day when light has come but the sun has not yet risen above the horizon is a thoroughly Shelleyan pas-sion, related to all of Shelley's visions of the morning star fad-ing in the dawn light. I have commented on this moment al-ready in my chapter on the *Blue Guitar*, relating it to what *The*

Rock will call "the difficult rightness of half-risen day" and to the letter of April 1, 1955, that ends: "Robins and doves are both early risers and are connoisseurs of daylight before the actual presence of the sun coarsens it" (*L*, 879).

Chocorua to Its Neighbor is a morning-star poem, astral and Shelleyan, stationed in the difficult rightness of that moment when the day is half risen, when "there are no shadows in our sun" and when "daylight comes, / Like light in a mirroring of cliffs," to cite two memorable tropes from the *Blue Guitar*. It is thus no accident that the poem of Chocorua develops section XXI of the *Blue Guitar*, written six years before it. The earlier poem celebrated "one's shadow magnified" as a substitute for all the gods, comparing it to "the shadow of Chocorua / In an immenser heaven, aloft." *Chocorua to Its Neighbor* meditates a "prodigious shadow" that arrives in freedom and of whom the mountain says, "He was not man yet he was nothing else." Stevens critics have neglected *Chocorua* because the poem has *Notes* on the one side of it and the other three long poems of *Transport to Summer* coming after it, and all four of these seem more central in Stevens' work. I myself would set *Chocorua* as high as *Esthétique du Mal, Description without Place*, and *Credences of Summer*. Kermode has remarked that "*Chocorua* is not one of the better poems, and moves too slowly," but a patient series of rereadings will find the poem's immense strength to reside in the almost hovering effect that it uncannily conveys, a hovering in and over the Sublime.

Chocorua is written in the five-line unrhymed stanzas that Stevens uses also in *Credences*, and in *To an Old Philosopher in Rome*. Isabel MacCaffrey observes that this stanza in Stevens is associated with a tone less aphoristic than that of *Notes, An Ordinary Evening*, and the other long poems in blank terza rima, but also more assertive than that of blank-verse paragraphs, as in *Esthétique*. Of all Stevens' longer poems, *Chocorua* is the most unreservedly affirmative, though what it affirms is neither simple enough nor sufficiently palpable to bear reduction. This is hardly surprising in a poem which purports to be the discourse of one mountain to another. American poetry is replete with talking mountains, from Emerson and Thoreau on to Ammons, who seems to have more of them than anyone else ever did. Chocorua is Stevens' one speaking mountain, yet mountains move and are eloquent elsewhere in him, I suppose because they are associated with Nietzschean solitude (which may be why the Paterian–Whitmanian Hoon is called "mountain-minded" in *Sad Strains of a Gay Waltz*). Stevens is never more of a myth-maker than in *Chocorua to Its Neighbor*, where the very idea of the poem, one mountain talking to another about the vision of a transcendental form, more-than-human though human, an Over-Man, is an idea that belies Stevens' description of himself as an "anti-mythological" poet. *Chocorua to Its Neighbor* makes a good contrast to Auden's *In Praise of Limestone*, one of the most overrated poems of the century, which actually makes a covert attack upon Stevens that *Chocorua* more than answered in advance. Auden says of his landscape that it "calls into question / All the Great Powers assume; it disturbs our rights. The poet, / Admired for his earnest habit of calling / The sun the sun, his mind Puzzle, is made uneasy / By these solid statues which so obviously doubt / His antimythological myth." We may wonder just who is being made uneasy by whom in Auden's lines, even as we describe the new mythology being worked out in *Chocorua to Its Neighbor*.

Chocorua begins with a hushed stanza of definition and division that declares its own synecdochal rhetoricity and that says what it is to be an Emersonian mountain in New Hampshire. The ultimate ancestor poem is Emerson's *Monadnoc*, but as in the climax of *Notes* the immediate father 'text is Whitman's very Emersonian versification of his 1855 "Preface" as *By Blue Ontario's Shore*, or to give it its original synecdochal title, *Poem of Many in One*. In section 19, Whitman has a vision: "Strange large men, long unwaked, undisclosed, were disclosed to me." The opening and closing stanzas of *Chocorua* are dominated by this image of largeness, but the largeness of the beginning belongs to the mountains, who thus are able "to perceive men without reference to their form." In the final stanza, the mountains perceive the Over-Man or "prodigious shadow" as being large in reference to his form, which leads Chocorua to the Emersonian realization of a beyond, of a transcendental realm of presences greater than the mountain's sense of reality.

Chocorua's anecdote is plotless, but accumulative in its eloquence. What is accumulated is a vision, which takes place at the end of night but before the morning comes, at the transitional time that Shelley loved, when "the crystal-pointed star of morning" rises and lights the snow into a congenial setting for the spirit of freedom. Shelley's *Two Spirits: An Allegory* is an exact parallel, yet Stevens' poem moves the Shelleyan emphasis on vision into the more extreme doctrine of "to see was to be," which is Emersonian. As "the figure in / A poem for Liadoff" the prodigious shadow suggests another poem in *Transport to Summer*, the somewhat surrealistic *Two Tales of Liadoff* (*CP*, 346), where the Russian composer's posthumously performed arpeggios "at a piano in a cloud" are associated with a mad town's crowding of itself into a rocket, which explodes "in an ovation of resplendent forms." *Chocorua to Its Neighbor* is another ovation of resplendent form, but its crucial resplendent form is "the self of selves," the prime fiction of American Romanticism, belated and apocalyptic: "Blue's last transparence as it turned to black."

As we would expect, this being finds his *logos* or meaning in "solitude" and "freedom" (stanza IX), and when he speaks he resumes the imagery common to Emerson, Whitman, and Stevens:

> "The moments of enlargement overlook
> The enlarging of the simplest soldier's cry
> In what I am, as he falls. Of what I am,
>
> The cry is part. My solitaria
> Are the meditations of a central mind.
> I hear the motions of the spirit and the sound
> Of what is secret becomes, for me, a voice
> That is my own voice speaking in my ear.
>
> There lies the misery, the coldest coil
> That grips the centre, the actual bite, that life

> Itself is like a poverty in the space of life,
> So that the flapping of wind around me here
> Is something in tatters that I cannot hold."

That soldier's cry had been echoing in Stevens' poetry for a long time and had been assimilated to two Whitmanian images, the cry of the maternal sea and the wounded and fallen soldiers of *Drum-Taps*. The crucial revelation in the speech of Stevens' giant or central man is that life itself, spirit, is imaginative need, Emersonian "poverty," in the larger context of the space of life. Life too lives in a place that is not its own and, much more, not itself. But Chocorua, admiring follower of the central man, praises him as possessing what Dickinson called "adequate desire." The central man is force and power, the human dream of a transcending "beyond," our idea of the hero, epitome of other heroes celebrated in stanzas XVII–XVIII. Pausing to consider the role of the hero, Chocorua suddenly declaims the apologia of Wallace Stevens, the credo of his eloquence:

> To say more than human things with human voice,
> That cannot be; to say human things with more
> Than human voice, that, also, cannot be;
> To speak humanly from the height or from the depth
> Of human things, that is acutest speech.

It is clear after this that the titan to whom we listen in this rapt poem is Stevens himself, hardly the poet as presented to us by most of his critics but a great affirmer, lineal heir of Emerson and even more of "an American bard at last," Whitman.

Yet, as is endemic in Stevens, there is a diminishment in this poem's last movement, its remaining seven stanzas. The qualifications begin to be asserted; the shadow "is an eminence, / But of nothing, trash of sleep that will disappear" by day. Even the oracular final stanza qualifies its Whitmanian sense of the large by enclosing, between the two uses of large, "If nothing more than that, for the moment." But the final vision is "of human realizings, rugged roy," and we end by recognizing a rare triumph in Stevens of the language of desire, possession, and power.

Though Stevens dodged the word "humanism," much of his

poetry of 1943–46 is a humanistic polemic, of which the major text is *Esthétique du Mal* of 1944. In a letter to John Crowe Ransom, Stevens worried about the sequence's title as being not quite accurate, and added, "I am thinking of aesthetics as the equivalent of aperçus, which seems to have been the original meaning" (L, 469). Stevens thus follows Pater in returning "aesthetic" to its root meaning of "perceptiveness," and I suspect his uneasiness about the title came from the Baudelairean implications of *mal*, implications mostly irrelevant to a poem in which what is perceived is not so much willed or chosen evil as necessary evil, the pain and suffering inseparable from a consciousness of self in a post-Christian or Nietzschean world. Nietzsche seems to me the presiding intelligence of this sequence, though this is Nietzsche assimilated to Emerson and Pater, Whitman and Keats, assimilations fecund and inevitable for Stevens to have made.

Esthétique du Mal, though an uneven long poem or sequence, has no section without its own greatness; yet the sections are so various as to make us see again how subtly diverse Stevens' poetry was. We need not seek a single argument as moving through the whole of the sequence, but the antagonist remains constant, however concealed: Eliot and his school, who had appeared in *Extracts*, III, as "the lean cats of the arches of the churches / . . . As if designed by X, the per-noble master." Eliot as X, per-noble master, is the subject of *The Creations of Sound*, a very pugnacious poem written just before *Esthétique du Mal*. Though Eliot had insisted upon poetry as an escape from personality, which means *ethos* as an escape from *pathos*, Stevens ironically categorizes him as "an obstruction, a man / Too exactly himself." Against Eliot, Stevens presents the vision of the fictive self of *Notes:* "intelligent / Beyond intelligence, an artificial man / At a distance." But this is not yet a palpable hit, compared to what follows:

> Tell X that speech is not dirty silence
> Clarified. It is silence made still dirtier.
> It is more than an imitation for the ear.

He lacks this venerable complication.
His poems are not of the second part of life.
They do not make the visible a little hard

To see nor, reverberating, eke out the mind
On peculiar horns, themselves eked out
By the spontaneous particulars of sound.

We do not say ourselves like that in poems.
We say ourselves in syllables that rise
From the floor, rising in speech we do not speak.

This is the will or the power of personality against the character or limitation of fate, an argument from a naturalistic bias, which says that sound is like earth. Frank Doggett usefully comments that "silence or non-being is the basic condition: like air it lies all about, enveloping the individual sounds; and sound is like sediment or dirt, even the sound of poetry." Sound must labor to "make the visible a little hard / To see," as Eliot's poems tend not to do. By writing *The Creations of Sound*, Stevens commits himself to an even more intense Emersonianism than before, for a poetry that tries to differentiate itself from the visible earth of which it is too knowingly a part and that rises "in speech we do not speak," as a kind of interior oratory, fulfills the Transcendentalist program.

Stevens was too reticent and cunning to speak out overtly against Eliot, but this polemic haunts his letters as well as his verse and goes back, I think, to the reception of *Harmonium*, and possibly even before. In 1920, he wrote Harriet Monroe that he had just received a copy of Eliot's volume, *Ara Vos Prec*, upon which his only comment was, "It contains nothing, I think, that I had not seen before" (*L*, 217). This reserved attitude was not much changed by the juxtaposition of the rival receptions of *The Waste Land* and of *Harmonium*, Stevens' volume coming out just nine months after Eliot's. Holly Stevens accurately notes (*L*, 241) of *Harmonium* that "the book was received rather indifferently by the public and the critics, who were largely reserving their accolades for T. S. Eliot and *The*

Waste Land." Stevens, meditating on scholars of the supreme fiction, remarked of Eliot in a letter to Henry Church: "It is possible that a man like T. S. Eliot illustrates the character, except that I regard him as a negative rather than a positive force" (*L*, 378). Later on Stevens began to be a little more explicit. A letter to William Van O'Connor, in 1950, corrects a false attribution to Stevens of an homage to Eliot by Allen Tate, and then adds, "After all, Eliot and I are dead opposites and I have been doing about everything that he would not be likely to do" (*L*, 677). In 1954, a general denial of all influence, made to Richard Eberhart, expanded into a specific testiness toward what Stevens evidently regarded as a school of Mannerism: "I . . . have purposely held off from reading highly mannered people like Eliot and Pound so that I should not absorb anything, even unconsciously" (*L*, 813). *Esthétique du Mal*, sent off to Ransom's *Kenyon Review* as a riposte to the adversary camp, meets directly the challenge of Eliot's assertion that the Romantics and naturalists had an inadequate vision of evil.

At the midpoint of *Esthétique du Mal*, in section VIII, Stevens presents us with his central polemic:

> How cold the vacancy
> When the phantoms are gone and the shaken realist
> First sees reality. The mortal no
> Has its emptiness and tragic expirations.
> The tragedy, however, may have begun,
> Again, in the imagination's new beginning,
> In the yes of the realist spoken because he must
> Say yes, spoken because under every no
> Lay a passion for yes that had never been broken.

The inspiring force here is Nietzsche's *The Gay Science*, as it is so often in Stevens, and "The tragedy, however, may have begun again" is a probable reference to Nietzsche's crucial *Incipit tragoedia*, which opened the final section of *The Gay Science* in its first edition, a section that serves also as the start of *Zarathustra*. "The tragedy begins" is a Nietzschean formula that follows an affirmation of the eternal recurrence, and it is related to Nietzsche's *Amor Fati* and his tremendous Yes-saying. Section 377 of *The Gay Science* celebrates the secret wisdom of those to whom Nietzsche can say, "The hidden Yes in you is stronger than all Nos and Maybes that afflict you and your age like a disease." This is precisely Stevens' "yes" that is "spoken because under every no / Lay a passion for yes that had never been broken." The Nietzschean mark is on *Esthétique du Mal* from its beginning, since the opening section participates in the heroic irony of section 283 of *The Gay Science*, where "preparatory human beings" are urged to live dangerously: "Build your cities on the slopes of Vesuvius!" The "he" of cantos I–III is not one of the "preparatory" Nietzscheans but is rather more like the American aesthetes Trumbull Stickney and George Cabot Lodge, the Harvard poets of Stevens' generation who took their promise off with them to the Continent and who thus anticipated Eliot's exile. Stevens' attitude toward this poet is wholly oblique, since his own Crispin is a self-critique of some of the same tendencies, particularly of the attempt to avoid nostalgia or sentimentalism by studying the nostalgias, by becoming an analyst of one's own sentimentality. Nietzsche's polemic against pity and self-pity in *The Gay Science* and in *Zarathustra* again seems to be Stevens' point of departure, and it would be bitterly ironic if Helen Vendler were correct in her negative judgment that Stevens' poem is unsympathetic because of his own sense of self-pity.

Pain is the *Mal* of sections I–III, yet this is the pain of the aesthete, coolly studied, suitable to a sensibility that "could describe / The terror of the sound because the sound / Was ancient." Aesthetic distance is so strong in the first two sections as to make their attitude virtually indescribable, though their deliberate preciosity is clear. Both can be summed up in an adage of Stevens': "In the end, the aesthetic is completely crushed and destroyed by the inability of the observer who has himself been crushed to have any feeling for it left" (*OP*, 172). The poet of the opening sections has not yet reached such an end, but he is on his way. That way is repression, and what is forgotten is the Shelleyan lesson taught in a poem like *Mont Blanc*, which is that the only thing we can learn by confronting nature is nature's indifference, which translates as our freedom. That is: "How that which rejects it saves it in the end," where "it" is our pain and the rejecting agent is nature.

"His firm stanzas" of section III refer not to the aesthete's poetry but evidently to Dante, to whom the rest of the poem says farewell, even as it says farewell to Christianity and to its overhuman god, rejected here in a Nietzschean dismissal of pity. Stevens' poetry of earth returns in the celebration of the health of the world, the honey of common summer. But the six occurrences of "as if" remind Stevens, and us, that this hymn to the earth is only a seeming, which belies the major recognition of *Notes:* that we live in a place not ours and not ourselves, that we live in Emerson's Not-Me. An Emersonian recognition, indeed the doctrine of the essay *Experience*, is the pith of the next section, the first in the poem where we can feel that Stevens is his strong self again:

> The genius of misfortune
> Is not a sentimentalist. He is
> That evil, that evil in the self, from which
> In desperate hallow, rugged gesture, fault
> Falls out on everything: the genius of
> The mind, which is our being, wrong and wrong,
> The genius of the body, which is our world,
> Spent in the false engagements of the mind.

"Evil" here approaches its root meaning, which is one with the imagery of the Sublime: "under, up from under, over." This in turn leads to the grimmer meanings of "evil" by way of "exceeding the proper limit." "That evil in the self" is the instinct for the Sublime, or the defense of repression, an unconsciously purposeful forgetting that both safeguards and aggrandizes the self. "Evil," "fault," "wrong," and "false" in this passage are all versions of what Nietzsche calls "necessary error." Stevens' rhetoric is nearly an antithetical triumph as he hymns the "desperate hallow, rugged gesture" of engagements of the mind as inevitable as they must be false, where "engagements" takes on nearly its full range of possible meanings: betrothals, obligations, appointments, employments, simply being in gear, and, surely most vitally, battles or confrontations.

If we go back in section IV, we confront Stevens' overt anxiety about his own potential for sentimentality, or for Whitmanian elegiac intensities, nostalgias for the quartet of night, death, the mother, and the sea. Against such a potential are set "B." (who may be Brahms, "his dark familiar") and a Spanish horticulturist (one Pedro Dot), who are presented as true precursors of Stevens. "B." played "all sorts of notes" or "in an ecstasy of its associates, / Variations in the tones of a single sound, / The last, or sounds so single they seemed one." That is not much of a description of Brahms but a palpable insight into *Notes toward a Supreme Fiction*, just as the horticulturist is also portrayed as reducing to a First Idea and then reimagining it. He "rescued the rose / From nature, each time he saw it, making it, / As he saw it, exist in his own especial eye."

Having identified himself with the genius of misfortune, Stevens is freed to be (for him) amazingly tender in the next section, one of the gentlest in all his work:

> Within what we permit,
> Within the actual, the warm, the near,
> So great a unity, that it is bliss,
> Ties us to those we love. . . .

◊

> Be near me, come closer, touch my hand, phrases
> Compounded of dear relation, spoken twice,
> Once by the lips, once by the services
> Of central sense, these minutiae mean more
> Than clouds, benevolences, distant heads,
> These are within what we permit, in-bar
> Exquisite in poverty.

"Exquisite in poverty" is the formula meant to defend this chant against the critical accusation that it is too sentimental a consolation. I do not think that the judgment of any critic here can be purely cognitive in its determinations, and I for one am very moved. But Stevens, no doubt fortunately, enters into a very different mode in section VI where his genius for the fantastic gives us the now famous fable of the hungry big bird and the sun in clownish yellow, also hungering. To call the sun "reality" or "nature" or "day" and the bird "imagination" or "the mind" or "night" does not seem particularly helpful as interpretation. Rhetorically, the sun is a trope of *pathos* or Power, while the boney bird is a trope of *ethos* or Fate, so that the fable becomes an epitome of Stevens' rather desperate quest for the *logos* of Freedom, for the "meaning" of his Solitude. The sun too has a Transcendental poverty, the need for a beyond and for a refusal of time ("space is filled with his / Rejected years"). But the insatiable bird, as Ananke, cannot stop and is curiously redeemed by being in a place somehow his own and even himself, in the landscape of the sun. We could read the fable by remembering Quintilian's formula that *ethos* and *pathos* are two degrees of the same thing, and so we could translate by saying that character and personality at last are one, except that Stevens ends by giving us something more startling:

> The sun is the country wherever he is. The bird
> In the brightest landscape downwardly revolves
> Disdaining each astringent ripening,
> Evading the point of redness, not content
> To repose in an hour or season or long era
> Of the country colors crowding against it, since
> The yellow grassman's mind is still immense,
> Still promises perfections cast away.

That is to say, the sun wins, by converting the bird to the sun's desire to be even more summery, evading the redness of autumnal decline. For the sun, as in *Like Decorations*, turns out to be Walt the grassman, and as he says in the great, grassy section 6 of *Song of Myself*: "All goes onward and outward, nothing collapses."

What follows is the poignant "How red the rose that is the soldier's wound," which would be in place in *Drum-Taps*. Vendler makes a serious, indeed a massive, case against this lyric, when she says:

It surely means that Stevens has averted his mind from the visual scene and has fixed it not on experience but on pious value. It is a betrayal of Stevens' most ambitious aesthetic to name death a summer sleep, to call a wound a rose, to palliate finality by a stroking hand, and to blur the tragic outline by a spell of Parnassian language.

It is difficult to argue against so severe and ascetic a vision of the Sublime, doubtless a true as against a false Sublime, but Stevens simply was *not* as heroically severe as this severest of all his critics. The imagination, as he said, needs to be indulged, and like Whitman he indulged it. Certainly Stevens passes a fiction upon himself in his elegiac mode, and this fiction is less than a supreme one, but to reject the elegiac Stevens is to lose *The Owl in the Sarcophagus*, *To an Old Philosopher in Rome*, and *The Rock*, as well as this Whitmanian chant for the soldier of time. Such a loss, like the death of Satan, would be another tragedy for the imagination. To deny Stevens either his Whitmanian consolations or his Nietzschean yea-sayings is to keep the Dionysiac tragedy of the will's revenge against time from recurring again, and that is precisely what Stevens declines to do in the central section, VIII, upon which I commented earlier. Stevens' most ambitious aesthetic may be the reduction to a First Idea, but his more human aesthetic was the reimagination of the First Idea. His way of saying this is the pith of section IX, where he declines to be left with nothing but comic ugliness or a lustred nothingness, the latter being all that the severest criticism finds worthy of him. Stevens takes his stance with the Canon Aspirin rather than the Canon's sister:

> Effendi, he
> That has lost the folly of the moon becomes
> The prince of the proverbs of pure poverty.
> To lose sensibility, to see what one sees,
> As if sight had not its own miraculous thrift,
> To hear only what one hears, one meaning alone,
> As if the paradise of meaning ceased
> To be paradise, it is this to be destitute.
> This is the sky divested of its fountains.

Effendi means "master," in the sense of "authentic one," and Stevens is most moving when he dreads the loss of his authentic freedom, which is the Emersonian conviction that a paradise of heretofore unknown meaning waits upon the American poet. Whitman still hovers in the poem, and I propose that the "he" of section x is an amalgam of Whitman and of Stevens. Indeed, the mother of section x is unquestionably Whitman's fierce old mother, the ocean of *Out of the Cradle* and *As I Ebb'd*; and the innocence of living, to be developed more beautifully in the *Auroras*, is a wholly Whitmanian innocence.

The glory of *Esthétique du Mal* is in its final third, since four of the last five sections (excluding xiv, an uneasy throwback to the anti-Marxist polemic of *Owl's Clover*) are among Stevens' most eloquent meditations, matching in depth, sonority, and passionately sustained argument the great passage concluding section iv. It is worth pondering that, at his most eloquent, Stevens now begins to dare phantasmagoria, in the wild vision of section xi, but this is phantasmagoria tempered by a de-idealizing social realism, as in the brutally placed "poor, dishonest people." As "a man of bitter appetite," accepting only the Nietzschean lordship of "the gaiety of language," Stevens is able to transform the brilliant closing lines of Keats's *Ode on Melancholy* into a transumptive credo all his own.

> The tongue caresses these exacerbations.
> They press it as epicure, distinguishing
> Themselves from its essential savor,
> Like hunger that feeds on its own hungriness.

The Stoic flavor here is a kind of tonic to the spirit, yet the final trope returns to section vi, the fable of the sun and the bird, Transcendentalist in its temper. This curious blend of restraint and Emersonianism is at work in the gnomic section xii, where Stevens writes one of his strongest critiques of his own exaltations of solitude. The first stanza asks an open question; which kind of knowledge is more desperate when one wills what one knows to be true, knowledge of self or knowledge of others? Instead of answering this question, the second stanza shows that both knowledges are destructive and yet shows also that both knowledges are inescapable unless one chooses a total ignorance of being alone. That ignorance is no longer praised by Stevens, for such solitude has ceased to be a mode of freedom, except as freedom from pain, the pain that is the *mal* of this poem. For Stevens, another crucial self-recognition is recorded in the rhetorical question that ends the section, a question that must be answered, "no lover, no woman," despite whatever knowledge has been attained.

Section XII, for all its dialectical twistings, is Stevens' rather direct disclosure of self and the self's anxieties. The opening of XIII, lucid and unhappy with its own insight, also hints at autobiography:

> It may be that one life is a punishment
> For another, as the son's life for the father's.
> But that concerns the secondary characters.
> It is a fragmentary tragedy
> Within the universal whole. The son
> And the father alike and equally are spent,
> Each one, by the necessity of being
> Himself, the unalterable necessity
> Of being this unalterable animal.
> This force of nature in action is the major
> Tragedy.

Again, this is Nietzsche's rather affirmative notion of tragedy, though assimilated to a Freudian context. When Stevens goes on to declaim, "This is destiny unperplexed, / The happiest enemy," he is overtly Nietzschean. The same spirit almost saves section XIV, but Stevens' polemic is too political and so too narrow. With the great chant of XV, the final section, Stevens returns to his strength, directed here against the neo-Christianity of Eliot and the American Southern agrarians. It is illuminating to juxtapose with the final section two shorter polemical poems that are companions to *The Creation of Sound*, one being *The Lack of Repose*, where the young man is Tate or Warren or some other member of their group, "One of the gang, / Andrew Jackson Something." The other, more profound, is *Somnambulisma*, a belated manifesto for the revival of the Emersonian American scholar. In *The Lack of Repose*, Stevens charmingly praises himself for not finding his individual talent within tradition:

And not yet to have written a book in which
One is already a grandfather and to have put there
A few sounds of meaning, a momentary end
To the complication, is good, is a good.

We can surmise that any volume at all by Eliot is the book
that Stevens has never written. The complication is the Eliotic
account of tradition, and the curious half-echo of Frost's momentary stay against confusion may acknowledge another contemporary rival who nevertheless is on the Transcendentalist
side. Stevens' restlessness, which is actually a choice between
rival traditions—Emerson against Poe, Whitman against Eliot,
Nietzsche against Wagner—finds its decisive emblem in the
"thin bird" that never settles in *Somnambulisma:*

Without this bird that never settles, without
Its generations that follow in their universe,
The ocean, falling and falling on the hollow shore,

Would be a geography of the dead: not of that land
To which they may have gone, but of the place in which
They lived, in which they lacked a pervasive being,

In which no scholar, separately dwelling,
Poured forth the fine fins, the gawky beaks, the personalia,
Which, as a man feeling everything, were his.

Eliotic or Ransomian "tradition" is the "geography of the
dead" that Stevens declines to join, a death-in-life ("the place in
which they lived") that can be averted only by the solitary
American scholar. The scholar's resource is to feel not less than
everything and to express his feelings in a Hoonian pouring
forth of fine fins, gawky beaks, personalia, or the whole of *Harmonium.* This is the spirit that is poured forth in section xv of
Esthétique, which is Stevens at his strongest:

The greatest poverty is not to live
In a physical world, to feel that one's desire
Is too difficult to tell from despair. Perhaps,
After death, the non-physical people, in paradise,
Itself non-physical, may, by chance, observe
The green corn gleaming and experience

> The minor of what we feel. The adventurer
> In humanity has not conceived of a race
> Completely physical in a physical world.
> The green corn gleams and the metaphysicals
> Lie sprawling in majors of the August heat,
> The rotund emotions, paradise unknown.

Twenty-two years after *The Waste Land,* Stevens gives us his passionate rejection of Eliot's vision and perhaps his rejoinder to the achieved forms of that vision, as published together in *Four Quartets* in 1943, the year before *Esthétique* was written. Eliot is pre-eminently the poet who felt that his desire was too difficult to tell from despair and who chose instead an ancient hope of paradise. Stevens' rejection of "the metaphysicals" extends also to Eliot's essay *The Metaphysical Poets,* though Stevens plays upon nearly every possible meaning of "the metaphysicals." But Stevens' argument transcends his polemic against the Waste Landers and is directed against his own Romantic tradition also, against Keats and Whitman, who despite their adventures in humanity are seen as having failed to conceptualize strenuously enough. Precisely Emersonian, Stevens' contention is that poetry has not yet rendered "the rotund emotions, paradise unknown," and that this failure *is* "the thesis scrivened in delight, / The reverberating psalm, the right chorale." And yet Stevens cannot conclude there, where Emerson does tend to conclude. Like Keats and Whitman, he needs to go beyond a holding hard to this poverty, and like his naturalistic precursors he attempts the quest through sight and sound and feeling, while knowing that even these will not suffice:

> One might have thought of sight, but who could think
> Of what it sees, for all the ill it sees?
> Speech found the ear, for all the evil sound,
> But the dark italics it could not propound.
> And out of what one sees and hears and out
> Of what one feels, who could have thought to make
> So many selves, so many sensuous worlds,
> As if the air, the mid-day air, was swarming
> With the metaphysical changes that occur,
> Merely in living as and where we live.

Stevens' characteristic "one" verges here upon being an irony, a trope for "the evilly compounded, vital I." A Nietzschean distrust of the subject as being only another fiction, or a fear that the ego is an outworn trope, compels Stevens to avoid "I" or "he" throughout this climactic passage. "Ill" and "evil" here are the *mal* of the poem's title, and take their final significance from the nineteenth aphorism of Book One of *The Gay Science:*

Evil.—Examine the lives of the best and most fruitful people and peoples and ask yourselves whether a tree that is supposed to grow to a proud height can dispense with bad weather and storms; whether misfortune and external resistance, some kinds of hatred, jealousy, stubbornness, mistrust, hardness, avarice, and violence do not belong among the *favorable* conditions without which any great growth even of virtue is scarcely possible. The poison of which weaker natures perish strengthens the strong—nor do they call it poison.

Here the dark italics are "evil" itself and "favorable." Stevens' misprision of Nietzsche is to give "the metaphysical changes" as a trope substituting for "the strong." As the poem is *Esthétique du Mal*, one thinks first of *aesthesis*, "perception," but one is stopped by the ill of seeing, where "ill" takes its etymological force of "bad." What then of the final finding of the ear? Speech fails because it cannot propound its own dark italics, which we can interpret as whatever assumes an independent function within the main text or speech, or simply the roman of speech equals signification while the italics constitute meaning. Stevens had ended *It Must Be Abstract* by demanding that the ephebe confect the final elegance out of the Whitmanian Chaplinesque tramp figure, "not to console / Nor sanctify, but plainly to propound." If he retreats from that ambition here, it is because, momentarily, he feels less poverty. Perhaps we do live in a place not our own, and much more, not ourselves, yet merely in living as and where we live we fulfill the injunction "It Must Change." The fiction that results from feeling is not less pathetic fallacy or trope of pathos by being recognized as such, yet Stevens is, for a moment again, remarkably free of anxiety about being self-deceived. "So many selves, so many sensuous worlds": where there are so many, does it matter that they are all errors, since errors are necessary for life? Stevens seems so determined not to let it matter that he refuses to end the stanza with the question mark that "who could have thought to make" warrants. Writing to Ransom, in whose *Kenyon Review* the sequence was to appear, he is a touch defiant at omitting the question mark: "The last poem ought to end with an interrogation mark, I suppose, but I have punctuated it in such a way as to indicate an abandonment of the question, because I cannot bring myself to end the thing with an interrogation mark" (*L*, 469).

The question is abandoned because Stevens has been "touched suddenly by the universal flare / For a moment, a moment in which we read and repeat / The eloquences of light's faculties." This epiphany, the final lines of *The Pure Good of Theory*, is the transport proper of *Transport to Summer*. The two main texts of that transport are *Description without Place* and Stevens' particular favorite among his longer poems, *Credences of Summer*. *Description without Place* is nobody's particular favorite and is never going to be, since it is apparently Stevens at his most arid. But it would be a masterpiece for most other modern poets and even for Stevens it is replete with passages that no critic willingly could let die. The puzzle of the poem is why he wrote it. Vendler wittily calls it "an ode to the Adjective" or to "the moment when the characters of the author take on for a moment life of their own, as his adjectives become the principles of their action." In a letter, Stevens stated what he thought to be his theme. "We live in the description of a place and not in the place itself" (*L*, 494). This formulation goes back, via *Notes* and its "that we live in a place / That is not our own and, much more, not ourselves" to Emerson's *Nature* (in *Essays, Second Series*), which connects the lament that "our music, our poetry, our language itself are not satisfactions, but suggestions" to the realization that "we are encamped in nature, not domesticated." In Stevens' intention, then, *Description without Place* began as a note to *Notes*. But it became something very different as it proceeded, something precisely not naturalistic but apocalyptic, and that curious metamorphosis into the theme of an antithetical revelation is what made the poem surprising and important, and more prophetic of Stevens' last phase than anything in *Notes* or in the rest of *Transport to Summer*.

The origins of *Description without Place* go back seven years to 1938, to *The Latest Freed Man* in *Parts of a World*. The latest freed man rises at six so as to escape from "the truth" or the tiresome old descriptions of the world, and is content to say that the morning is color and mist and that the sun is "the strong man vaguely seen." Freedom is "being without description," but this is just a First Idea of freedom or "being an ox." Everything may be bulging, blazing, big in itself, yet freedom without description is a dehumanizing reduction, though momentarily it may exhilarate, because it seems to be a Nietzschean vision of the sun, not as a god but as a man-god might be. *Description without Place* is a reimagining of *The Latest Freed Man*, and so by "description" Stevens now means a redescription. "It is possible," he begins, reminding us of the "It is possible, possible, possible. It must / Be possible," of *Notes*. What is possible here is that the mind's images may be realized, that tropes may be as well as seem. By the third section, the possibility has become even more prodigious:

> There might be, too, a change immenser than
> A poet's metaphors in which being would
>
> Come true, a point in the fire of music where
> Dazzle yields to a clarity and we observe,
>
> And observing is completing and we are content,
> In a world that shrinks to an immediate whole,
>
> That we do not need to understand, complete
> Without secret arrangements of it in the mind.

This Paterian passage culminates the vision of that *andersstreben* in which the world has become a poem and the poem has become music. "Description" has begun to approach what Nietzsche called "perspectivism," a doctrine that hints we perceive fictions because we ourselves are fictive selves. This is the

basis of the remarkable opening of section IV, a vision of
Nietzsche that has no source in Nietzsche:

> Nietzsche in Basel studied the deep pool
> Of these discolorations, mastering
>
> The moving and the moving of their forms
> In the much-mottled motion of blank time.
>
> His revery was the deepness of the pool,
> The very pool, his thoughts the colored forms,
>
> The eccentric souvenirs of human shapes,
> Wrapped in their seemings, crowd on curious crowd,
>
> In a kind of total affluence, all first,
> All final, colors subjected in revery
>
> To an innate grandiose, an innate light,
> The sun of Nietzsche gildering the pool,
>
> Yes: gildering the swarm-like manias
> In perpetual revolution, round and round . . .

This passage triumphs over the perspectivism of Romantic
metaphor, since we cannot say where the inside and the outside
are located in such a reverie. In apposition, a parable of Lenin
returns us to a subject-object world, but without troubling Stevens, who goes on to a purely visionary account of "description":

> It is an expectation, a desire,
> A palm that rises up beyond the sea,
>
> A little different from reality:
> The difference that we make in what we see
>
> And our memorials of that difference,
> Sprinklings of bright particulars from the sky.
>
> The future is description without place,
> The categorical predicate, the arc.

> It is a wizened starlight growing young,
> In which old stars are planets of morning, fresh
>
> In the brilliantest descriptions of new day,
> Before it comes, the just anticipation
>
> Of the appropriate creatures, jubilant,
> The forms that are attentive in thin air.

In Stevens, the palm has progressed from the unreal "cloudy palm / Remote on heaven's hill" of *Sunday Morning*, through the naturalistic "big-finned palm / . . . angering for life" of *Nomad Exquisite* to this "palm that rises up beyond the sea, / A little different from reality." That little difference, at the end, will expand into the large difference of "the palm at the end of the mind" that stands "on the edge of space." Here the palm preludes that final revelation, for it is a self-generated particular that leads Stevens to another of his very personal visions of the difficult rightness of half-risen day, to the light he loves before the sun comes to coarsen the dawn. Blake's Minute Particulars, Keats's *Bright Star* sonnet, Tennyson's Hesper–Phosphor variation of evening and morning stars (from *In Memoriam*) and Shakespeare's "bright particular star" all come together in a jubilant celebration of the vagaries of individual seeing. Section VI carries this self-exaltation further by making Stevens his own St. John the Divine, reading his description of the world as revelation, as the text of reconciliation.

When the poem's final section proclaims that this curious sense of description is a theory of the word, we are tempted to resist such self-conscious grandeur until suddenly Stevens charmingly undermines himself:

> It is a world of words to the end of it,
> In which nothing solid is its solid self.

This is like Emerson's disarming insinuations that nature is only one vast trope and that we are tropes also. So strengthened by our relaxation in wariness, Stevens ends the poem with a wholly Emersonian transumption. All of anteriority is projected as "description without place, a cast / Of the imagination," and the future is introjected as a poem still to be written, one that "must portend, / Be alive with its own seemings, seeming to be / Like rubies reddened by rubies reddening." This outrageous final trope evades tautology by suggesting an incremental repetition and conveys both an image of the process that is Stevens' poetry and the characteristic coloring that Stevens associates with autumnal change and finally with autumnal decay.

Stevens himself was grateful for *Credences of Summer*, a gratitude we share in turning from the astringent *Description without Place* to the warmer splendors of this greater work. But the tone and meanings of *Credences* have been much in dispute among critics, and there is something equivocal about the poem that stimulates sharp disagreements among its readers. Kermode said that "it is an example of that incantatory power, the tone of rapture, Stevens sometimes brings to meditation, and is undoubtedly one of the great poems. The subject is total satisfaction, the moment of total summer." Against this may be placed the summary given by Vendler:

Credences of Summer, as its title betrays, is the creed of the believer rather than the certain projection of the prophet or the divided commentary of the skeptic, but its intention cannot all command the strings. Its initial impetus of praise and involvement, resolutely kept in the original moment, is maintained through the first three cantos, but from then on the oneness with the here and now diminishes, until by the end of the poem Stevens is at an inhuman distance from his starting point.

A third judgment, balanced between these polarities, is made by Isabel MacCaffrey:

Stevens has, therefore, established conditions of maximum difficulty in which to assert the imagination's power. Winter, "the nothing that is," cannot satisfy us for long, however scrupulously we submit to it; its perfect ineloquence invites the imagination's additions. But summer offers a rival rhetoric; its richness "must comfort the heart's core," its eloquence silences our speech.

I think this last judgment is the most accurate; *Credences* is a celebratory poem, but the celebration is thwarted by the rival eloquence of mere nature, which resists being reimagined. Even as his ancestor Wordsworth was defeated at the start of *The Prelude* when he tried to make a present joy the matter of his song, so Stevens becomes muted when he tries to sing in face of the living object. Stevens is able to get started without "poverty," without a reduction to a First Idea, but then finds that he can't keep going, and so *Credences* grows more and more dark from its fourth on to its final canto.

Yet that is only part of the story, for a different sorrow infiltrates the poem, also, a sorrow that intensifies until it becomes authentic crisis in *The Auroras of Autumn*. Stevens begins to discover, in *Credences*, that he has been paying a psychic and poetic price for the characteristic procedures of his poetry, procedures that had triumphed in *Notes*. The motto for *Credences* could be Emerson's Law of Compensation: "Nothing is got for nothing." Stevens himself realized that *Credences* represented a different imaginative period from that of *Notes*, and he remarks in a letter some of the affinities shared by *Credences*, the *Auroras*, and *An Ordinary Evening* as all being part of a different vision than the vision of *Notes* (*L*,636–37). This later vision sought what Stevens oddly called "a final accord with reality" (*L*, 719), a curious hope for the theorist of *It Must Change*. Just as *Credences* is not quite as joyous as it seemed to Kermode (though it is still more cheerful than Vendler allows), even so *An Ordinary Evening* is a great deal more buoyant than criticism has judged it to be, while the *Auroras* can be said to move from fear and anxiety to a freshened sense of "innocence" and so of life's possibilities. It remains worth saying that *Credences* is the most naturally Keatsian of Stevens' poems and that it would like to have been rather more celebratory than finally it was.

Credences begins with a stanza that is a drum-roll of rhetorical self-confidence, a five-line single sentence reminding us that Stevens tends to affirm through his syntax:

> Now in midsummer come and all fools slaughtered
> And spring's infuriations over and a long way
> To the first autumnal inhalations, young broods
> Are in the grass, the roses are heavy with a weight
> Of fragrance and the mind lays by its trouble.

The poet is sixty-eight, and the trouble his mind lays by appears to have been desire. "All fools slaughtered" would include one's own earlier self as it had been on All Fools' Day, at the start of April's green. The infuriations of spring, for those well past meridian, are over, and yet it is still a long way to what will be the occasion of the *Auroras*, "the first autumnal inhalations." Surrounded by a triumphant nature, the mind considers its own less triumphant comfort, the moment of sublimation that is held in the "this" of "It comes to this and the imagination's life." Whether the heart's disasters were ended is put in question by the "must" of "must comfort," yet Stevens seems ready enough to accept a second-best in the fulfillment of others, a pattern in which Coleridge excelled but which comes hard to any American poet whatsoever.

Canto II begins as a variation upon the penultimate section of the *Blue Guitar* and the start of *Notes*. The ignorant eye is to burn away the tropes and false names and thus is to give us an unvarnished sun. But there is a difference, because this is the sun of midsummer, which resists both the rigors of reduction and the ardors of reimagining. We now confront the sun "in its essential barrenness" or "the barrenness / Of the fertile thing that can attain no more" or, as canto III puts it, "the refuge that the end creates." Canto III marks a new limit for Stevens' imagination, and its tone begins to ebb in self-confidence. Yet the reader sees, with canto III, that all of the first three cantos of the poem present him with an *illusio*, an irony or discontinuous allegorical movement almost always saying the opposite of what it means. The old man on the tower, a kind of anti-Yeatsian figure, neither reads nor writes a book, because he is beyond poetry, having absorbed the total affluence of "green's green apogee." Stevens says that the old man, a version of himself, is "appeased" yet he means the opposite, in this fresh *clinamen* away from Keatsian tradition. To have a mind of midsummer is to write no more poetry, because one has been absorbed as part of "a feeling capable of nothing more."

Canto IV, which was one of Stevens' two favorites in the poem (the other being canto VII), is the synecdochal antithesis to cantos I–III, and is one of Stevens' finest lyric achievements:

> One of the limits of reality
> Presents itself in Oley when the hay,
> Baked through long days, is piled in mows. It is
> A land too ripe for enigmas, too serene.
> There the distant fails the clairvoyant eye
>
> And the secondary senses of the ear
> Swarm, not with secondary sounds, but choirs,
> Not evocations but last choirs, last sounds
> With nothing else compounded, carried full,
> Pure rhetoric of a language without words.
>
> Things stop in that direction and since they stop
> The direction stops and we accept what is
> As good. The utmost must be good and is
> And is our fortune and honey hived in the trees
> And mingling of colors at a festival.

"Festival" is itself an antithetical primal word in Stevens' poetry, a word that evokes a defensive turning-against-the-self or a curious kind of masochistic awareness in so massively confident a psyche. Though we use "festival" to mean "feast" or "celebration," deriving our usage from a Latin word for joyousness, its Indo-European root *dhes* has a general religious significance that allies "festival" to such antithetical words as "final," "fanatic," "theism," and "enthusiasm." Something of an uncanny, rather negative quasi-religious flavoring is felt each time Stevens uses "festival" in a poem. It occurs first in the *Comedian*, where Crispin, in Yucatan, finds "that earth was like a jostling festival / Of seeds grown fat, too juicily opulent." In the *Blue Guitar*, XXIX, the poet sits in a cathedral, reads "a lean Review," presumably of new poetry and criticism, and opposes these degustations, or fresh relishings, to the religious heritage, to "the past and the festival." This polemic is carried forward in *Esthétique du Mal*, V, where the "fire of the festivals" belonged to the time "before we were wholly human and knew ourselves." Here, in *Credences*, IV, the sense of satisfaction is severely put into question when the canto comes to rest upon the word "festival" as the final form of the supposed "utmost." Looking ahead, "festival" attains its Stevensian nadir in the *Auroras*, V, when the poet whips up his spirits until he can proclaim, "We stand in the tumult of a festival," but then reacts bitterly with rhetorical questions: "What festival? This loud, disordered mooch?" Only in his final use of the word, in *An Ordinary Evening*, x, does Stevens seem to soften its negative force, though ambiguously:

> So that morning and evening are like promises kept,
> So that the approaching sun and its arrival,
> Its evening feast and the following festival,
>
> This faithfulness of reality, this mode,
> This tendance and venerable holding-in
> Make gay the hallucinations in surfaces.

Returning to *Credences*, IV, we can see the canto as Stevens' beautiful and wholly momentary acceptance of, or resignation to, his defeat by nature, by the "pure rhetoric of a language without words." Canto IV is haunted by Keats's *Ode to Autumn* and by Keats's hidden source in Shakespeare's "Ripeness is all." Stopped by such powerful influencers, Stevens subsides yet finds his defense in the single counterthrust of "festival" which restores the sense of enigma and allows for the poem's middle movement in the next pair of contraries, cantos v and vi. But I want to look back to the disjunction or crossing between cantos I–III and IV, before going on to v and vi and the crossing between them.

The Crossing of Election has no clearer example in Stevens than in the gap between "By a feeling capable of nothing more" and "One of the limits of reality / Presents itself in Oley." Here the disjunction itself holds the *aporia* or dilemma of Stevens' poethood, so uneasily balanced between a natural fulfillment that makes poetry superfluous and an eloquence of sight and sound that makes fulfillment suspect, or perhaps makes it part of the nostalgia of defeat, in the sentiment of a false spirituality. Either way, the crossing is negotiated with something less than ease, and that sense of a barely managed transition contributes to the felt precariousness of the ostensibly triumphant canto IV.

Credences continues to follow the Wordsworthian crisis-poem model of revisionary ratios in the interplay of cantos v and vi, with v being the *kenosis* or metonymic emptying out of the poet's power and vi responding to this ebb with a daemonic countermovement into a freshly repressive Sublime. No better epitome of a poetic *kenosis* could be adduced than the juxtaposition of "One day enriches a year" with the contrary question "Or do the other days enrich this one?" with its suggestion that the day of rich completion impoverishes the rest of the year. Even so, the heroic woman or man may not add to the common wealth, as Emerson insisted, but rather may subtract from all other persons. The canto's crucial metonymy is "the more than casual blue" that at once belongs to the day of midsummer and to the imagination that adequately hopes to confront "green's green apogee." Again, there is a malaise felt here, though Stevens goes on to proclaim the day of midsummer as enrichment for the rest of the year, indeed as the figure of capable imagination who rushed down the road past the reductive Mrs. Uruguay. But Stevens overprotests the enrichment, in a premature hyperbole that would be more in place in canto vi. This time, I find it difficult to dispute Vendler when she calls this both a blustering and a false solution.

The relative failure of canto v makes all the more crucial the Crossing of Solipsism that is located between "The youth, the vital son, the heroic power" and "The rock cannot be broken. It is the truth." In *Credences*, the rock fills the role of the serpent in the *Auroras*, an emblem of fatal Ananke, Necessity. Crossing from the hero or day-of-days to the rock means a crossing into the solitude of the American sublime, with its great images of height, as in *Chocorua*. The best commentary on the hyperbole of height in Stevens is by Stevens, who, in the essay *Imagination as Value*, associated the imagery of height with Nietzsche: "Height in itself is imaginative. It is the moderator of life as metempsychosis was of death. Nietzsche walked in the Alps in the caresses of reality" (*NA*, 150). Let us name the rock of summer as one of the caresses of reality, or what Stevens in canto vi calls "things certain sustaining us in certainty." Why does Stevens insist, of this truth that cannot be broken, that "it is not / A hermit's truth nor symbol in hermitage"? There is a backward refrence here to the second canto of *It Must Be Abstract*, where Stevens warned that

> so poisonous
>
> Are the ravishments of truth, so fatal to
> The truth itself, the first idea becomes
> The hermit in a poet's metaphors,
>
> Who comes and goes and comes and goes all day.

There is also an anticipation of *Things of August*, with its vision of "a text of intelligent men / At the centre of the unintelligible, / As in a hermitage," and of the development of that vision in the very late lyric *The Hermitage at the Center*. In *Credences*, VI, the emphasis is upon the rock not being a First Idea, or hermit's truth, and so not a reduction but rather "the visible rock, the audible," a Necessity that somehow sustains us. Halfway through summer, Stevens seeks a solitary certitude in his half-green, half-blue mountain, which is itself a hyperbolical figuration for his poem. For this *is* his largest credence rising out of his knowledge of summer, his own *Poem That Took the Place of a Mountain*. Here is his late poem of that title, which we can see now is actually about *Credences of Summer:*

> There it was, word for word,
> The poem that took the place of a mountain.
>
> He breathed its oxygen,
> Even when the book lay turned in the dust of his table.
>
> It reminded him how he had needed
> A place to go to in his own direction,
>
> How he had recomposed the pines,
> Shifted the rocks and picked his way among clouds,
>
> For the outlook that would be right,
> Where he would be complete in an unexplained completion:
>
> The exact rock where his inexactnesses
> Would discover, at last, the view toward which they had
>   edged,

> Where he could lie and, gazing down at the sea,
> Recognize his unique and solitary home.

This ends in the Whitmanian vision of the *Sea-Drift* pieces, yet it exudes the confidence and gratitude that composing *Credences* seems to have instilled in Stevens. The poem "about summer," as he called it in *As You Leave the Room*, is really about arriving at "the exact rock," which is a precisely defined Ananke and which in turn becomes the subject of *The Auroras of Autumn*.

When *Credences* crosses from canto V to canto VI, it crosses away from the fictive hero and toward the image of the rock. This is almost too final a Crossing of Solipsism, as it propels Stevens into a still greater inwardness, so that the culminating hyperbole of canto VI speaks of the color of Stevens' own imagination as "the extremest light / Of sapphires flashing from the central sky, / As if twelve princes sat before a king." This is to bring the zodiac within the poetic self, but whether such an incongruous Sublime representation is appropriate here is disputable.

The final movement of *Credences* juxtaposes canto VII, with its Romantic inside / outside metaphor of singers confronting nature, and cantos VIII–X, a transumption of Romantic tradition, of the earlier cantos of *Credences*, and of much previous poetry by Stevens. We can surmise why canto VII was one of Stevens' favorites:

> Far in the woods they sang their unreal songs,
> Secure. It was difficult to sing in face
> Of the object. The singers had to avert themselves
> Or else avert the object. Deep in the woods
> They sang of summer in the common fields.
>
> They sang desiring an object that was near,
> In face of which desire no longer moved,
> Nor made of itself that which it could not find . . .
> Three times the concentered self takes hold, three times
> The thrice concentered self, having possessed
>
> The object, grips it in savage scrutiny,
> Once to make captive, once to subjugate

Or yield to subjugation, once to proclaim
The meaning of the capture, this hard prize,
Fully made, fully apparent, fully found.

"They" are the Romantics, but Stevens also, who sings of summer in the common fields, who desires a near object that stops desire, and who fears the self-generated delusions of ungratified desire. Indeed, "they" are all poets whatsoever, and MacCaffrey is accurate in judging canto VII not to be a disparagement of the imagination but rather to show that "*all* songs are 'averted,' oblique." In the final seven lines of canto VII, Stevens ceases to speak primarily of all poets and speaks instead largely of himself, for the triple process he describes is the dialectic of his own poetry. The first "savage scrutiny" of the object makes it captive, through abstraction or reduction. In the process of subjugating or yielding to subjugation, the implicit fear of dehumanization enters, to be alleviated by "the meaning of the capture," the reimagining that proclaims the taking up of the First Idea into the mind. "This hard prize, / Fully made, fully apparent, fully found" is the First Idea as reimagined thing, "half sun, half mind," percept and concept come together in Stevens' version of the Romantic image.

Between this triple rhythm of creation and the Shelleyan blowing of morning's trumpet, *Credences* weathers its Crossing of Identification, as Stevens moves toward the acceptance of his own death. "What is possible" is the divided mind of the poet aware of its own cry as clarion, as the only trumpet of a prophecy that remains past midsummer, where all prophecy begins to age into mortality. Canto IX, one of the subtlest of Stevens' lyrics, ironically observes the whole sequence's complex of emotions fall apart, in anticipation of the fall of the season. From the sweets and tribulations (*douceurs*, / *Tristesses*) of summer as "the fund of life and death," we pass to the bird's sound as parody of the trumpet, presaging the winter to come, a casting into doubt of many of the qualified raptures of earlier cantos.

It is appropriate that the poem's most problematic canto should be its last, as Stevens strives to close on a note not wholly estranged from celebration. By seeing himself as "an inhuman author," Stevens means something like "not yet wholly human," that is, not yet knowing himself wholly, beyond illusion. He does not mean that he has come to an inhuman distance from his own fictions. The deliberate contrast here is between Stevens' gaudy dressing of his summer personae, and the poverty-dominated dressing of her daughters by the Canon Aspirin's sister in *Notes*. His creatures wear "appropriate habit for / The huge decorum" of midsummer and of his fictive universe. Summer's whole, as Stevens contrives it, is still to live where motley is worn, yet the mood is one

> In which the characters speak because they want
> To speak, the fat, the roseate characters,
> Free, for a moment, from malice and sudden cry,
> Complete in a completed scene, speaking
> Their parts as in a youthful happiness.

To be free, for a moment, is still freedom, and so it is a completion. Perhaps nothing else by Stevens ends so poignantly as *Credences*, since the last we hear of his personae is that they are "speaking / Their parts as in a youthful happiness," and yet all that we know of a youthful happiness is that it must grow old and sad.

10 *The Auroras of Autumn*

In his later sixties, Stevens began to write with an uncanny clairvoyance that critics have been slow to apprehend. The immediate difficulty of the poems in the volume *The Auroras of Autumn* (1950) veils their intensifying affirmations. Any grouping of Stevens' masterpieces among the longer poems ought to include the title poem, *The Auroras of Autumn* (1947), *The Owl in the Sarcophagus* of the same year, *A Primitive Like an Orb* (1948), and *An Ordinary Evening in New Haven* (1949). The length, complexity, and importance of *An Ordinary Evening* are such that the poem deserves the full analysis that it will be afforded in Chapter 12. Here I will center upon the other three major poems of 1947–49, but a few of the shorter poems in the *Auroras of Autumn* volume are of crucial importance also: *Large Red Man Reading*, *Imago*, *Saint John and the Back-Ache*, *Puella Parvula*, and *Angel Surrounded by Paysans*. So is a not wholly successful longer poem or sequence, *Things of August* (1949). As he approached seventy, Stevens found new strength, and yet it was the strength of persistence and of persistent eloquence. He did not solve the dilemmas and recurrent crises of his poetry, nor did he transcend them, but he compelled himself to render his struggles with them in a finer tone.

Stevens' three finest poems, to me, are *Notes*, the *Auroras*, and *An Ordinary Evening*, and I do not know how to judge among them, as they are remarkably different works. *Notes* is a discovery that is also a confirmation; it is not a crisis-poem, though its form is a large-scale parody of the crisis-lyric. *An Ordinary Evening* is a majestic *performance;* the instrument has been perfected, realities have been accepted and tolerated, and the master for a last time shows the full range of what he is capable of doing. But the *Auroras* is a crisis-poem, the culmination of that Wordsworthian tradition and the most directly personal and even dramatic of all Stevens' poems. Its advantage over *Notes* and *An Ordinary Evening* is in compression; it is only a third the length of the others, and much of its apparent difficulty results from its economy. The longer a reader stays with it, the more it reveals of the clearest and most adequate design of all Stevens' long poems. Granted that closure is always an illusion, I find that the *Auroras* sustains the illusion better than any other poem written, in English, in our century.

There are possible "sources" for Stevens' figuration of the auroras in Wordsworth's *Prelude,* in Emerson's essay *The Poet,* and in Dickinson's lyric *Of Bronze – and Blaze – The North – Tonight,* but the true point of origin for Stevens is Shelley, whose *Ode to the West Wind* is much involved here. Even more involved is the rhapsodic *Mont Blanc,* where Shelley confronts his equivalent of the northern lights, battles his version of Necessity, and ends by denying that Mont Blanc is a spell of light or false sign or symbol of malice. Watching the auroras, Stevens re-enacts the central Romantic confrontations between the power of a poet's mind and the object-world or universe of death. This had always been the problem of Stevens' poetry, and *Notes* had been a hard-won solution but a victory that could not prevail. *The Auroras of Autumn* is packed with allusion to Stevens' own poetry, as if the poet's lifelong anxieties had flooded upon him again all at once. The major allusion, partly repressed, is "Farewell to an idea . . . ," which introduces cantos II–IV, where "an idea" is the superb invention of *Notes,* the idea of reimagining the First Idea. But an account of that tragic synecdoche of farewell must wait until after the intricacies of canto I are explored in all their ironic subtlety.

The poem's title is as much part of canto I as the title *Mont Blanc* is part of section I of Shelley's poem. In both cases, we might be troubled to know the poem's "subject" without the title. Stevens does not mention the northern lights directly until "these lights" in line 14, and Shelley more audaciously has no reference to the Ravine of Arve until he begins his second stanza. *The Auroras of Autumn* is a beautiful interplay of a title, revising the meaning both of the auroras and of the season of autumn. Stevens expects us to have seen the aurora borealis or at least to know what it looks like. I myself came to a better understanding of his poem's first canto after watching a particularly brilliant display of the auroras on Block Island during an August twilight in 1974. Rather like the auroras Stevens described, these flashed on and off at a high altitude, as multicolored lights in the northern sky, and their coilings from the horizon to the zenith's height unmistakably resembled a giant, many-folded serpent, with its head at the zenith. Stevens plays upon the auroras' supposed cause, in charged particles of solar origin, when he implicitly associates the auroras with an ultimately menacing First Idea, since for Stevens all First Ideas necessarily are ideas of the sun. He avoids any associations with the dawn, partly by emphasizing, again implicitly, the secondary meaning of autumn as the time of ripeness verging upon descent, autumn as fall.

"This is where the serpent lives, the bodiless": the poem's first line refers us back to earlier appearances of the serpent as Ananke, emblem of Necessity, in Stevens, who may have taken the emblem from Nietzsche's Zarathustra, or from Shelley. Section XII of *Like Decorations*, in 1935, is clearly an ancestor of *The Auroras of Autumn:*

> The sense of the serpent in you, Ananke,
> And your averted stride
> Add nothing to the horror of the frost
> That glistens on your face and hair.

Another poem, *The Bagatelles the Madrigals* (*CP*, 213), again associates the serpent with "winter's meditative light." The largest presage in Stevens, though, is *The Greenest Continent*, IV, in *Owl's Clover*, where the poet presents what he absurdly asserts to be the heaven or rather "no heaven" of Africa, "the black sublime" or "heaven of death" where "the serpent might be-

come a god, quick-eyed, / Rising from indolent coils," "a part
of a northern sky." A terrible vision of a throne even more directly prophesies the *Auroras:*

> a throne raised up beyond
> Men's bones, beyond their breaths, the black sublime,
> Toward which, in the nights, the glittering serpents climb,
> Dark-skinned and sinuous, winding upwardly,
> Winding and waving, slowly, waving in air,
> Darting envenomed eyes about, like fangs,
> Hissing, across the silence, puissant sounds.
> Death, only, sits upon the serpent throne. [*OP*, 54–55]

That is the ultimate meaning of the serpent of the *Auroras*,
death, because the serpent is the emblem of the necessity of
change and the final form of change is one's own death. So,
when Stevens opens *The Auroras of Autumn* with the declaration
"This is where the serpent lives," the "this is" (which is repeated five times more in canto i) refers again back to *Notes* with
its "From this the poem springs: that we live in a place / That is
not our own and, much more, not ourselves," or as canto x of
the *Auroras* will put it, we are "an unhappy people in a happy
world." "This is" in *Auroras*, i, means the place where we live,
the serpent's nest, but the repetitions of "this is" make a meaning akin to Nietzsche's when he speaks of the will's revenge
against time, and time's "It was." "This is" will turn into "it
was."

No other longer poem by Stevens opens or proceeds with the
deliberate, personal drama of *The Auroras of Autumn* or so po-
tently fosters the illusions of unity and closure. As crisis-poem,
the *Auroras* follows rather faithfully the High Romantic model.
I mapped the poem's ratios in *A Map of Misreading*, but will map
it again here so as to indicate its disjunctions or crossings,
where much of its meaning is collected.

Canto i is a dark irony of *ethos* or Fate, while cantos ii–iv are
a combined synecdoche, where the major trope of *pathos* or self-
mutilating power is, in each canto, the elaboration of the opening motto: "Farewell to an idea." The Crossing of Election,
confronting the possible death of poetry, comes between i and

II, where the reader must handle the *aporia* that bridges the aboriginal vision of "the Indian in his glade" and the first image of the abandoned reimagining of a reduction: "A cabin stands, / Deserted, on a beach. It is white."

The poem's second movement juxtaposes the *kenosis* or poetic undoing of canto V with the daemonic Counter-Sublime of canto VI. Within the juxtaposition there intervenes the Crossing of Solipsism, or Stevens' facing of the death of love, here in the poignant context of the family romance. The disjunction is acute, as we pass from "There is no play. / Or, the persons act one merely by being here" to "It is a theatre floating through the clouds." From defending the self through a regression that, quite disastrously, does not work, Stevens moves to a powerful repression that does work, until at the end of canto VI the repression works so well as to reach a fresh crisis of actual fear.

In the poem's final movement of ratios, canto VII works as a sublimating metaphor against the introjecting triad of trope-undoing tropes or transumptions of cantos VIII–X. The sharpest of the poem's rhetorical disjunctions occurs in the Crossing of Identification between "a flippant communication under the moon" and "There may be always a time of innocence. / There is never a place." For here, Stevens most acutely meets, and perhaps partly overcomes, his horror of his own death. But, as with the other crossings, analysis must wait upon the systematic reading of the poem that follows. I return therefore to the opening lines and to their strategy of ironic abstraction or reduction. The scene of canto I, as of the more overt canto II, is the beach-world, established by Whitman as the proper American *topos*, the place where the Poetical Character is incarnated and also where the poetic self is emptied out, voided, the symbolic actions, respectively, of *Out of the Cradle* and *As I Ebb'd*. But Stevens mentions the sea only in the ninth line of canto I, and after that not at all in the rest of his poem. Its place is taken, throughout, by the auroras, and by the auroras' ally, the sea-wind, which continues to blow "as sharp as salt" all through the poem, just as the lights go on flashing throughout the poem.

Why does Stevens follow the strategy of Shelley's *Mont Blanc* in not explicitly describing his "natural" subject until he first has given an account of his internalization of the natural phenomenon? Shelley's purposes are more complex and philosophical, whereas Stevens, I think, means to begin with the irony that he has been all too successful in having taught himself how to reduce all perception to a First Idea or, as canto II grimly puts it, to "being of the solid of white, the accomplishment / Of an extremist in an exercise." The exercise is abstracting to the First Idea, or the Snow Man's Pyrrhic victory; the extremist is Stevens himself, as observer and as poet; the "accomplishment" is the intolerable congealing of what should have been "that ever-early candor" into a universal blank of whiteness, as horrifying here as it is in Melville's meditation upon the whiteness of his whale. Whitman, in *As I Ebb'd*, spoke of nature there in sight of the sea darting upon him, to sting him, because he had dared to open his mouth to sing at all. Stevens implicitly, in canto I, shows nature, in the serpentine shape of the auroras, taking advantage of the old poet, to sting his sight with an astonishing display of its "artistic" powers, not because he has dared to be a poet but because he has dared to become a poet by questing after a First Idea, or earliest seeing of the thing itself. "Let us see then who shall be master!" nature seems to say, in sending against Stevens not the sunrise she sent against Whitman or against Wordsworth but the even more awesome false dawn of the northern lights. "Try this for a First Idea!" nature says in effect. We will see Stevens trying and failing to reimagine this shattering First Idea, and knowing a potentially annihilating fear as a result.

A contrast with Wordsworth is instructive for cantos I and II, even as contrasts with Emerson, Dickinson, and Whitman will be useful for the American sublime of canto VI, and the American sublimating flippancy of canto VII. Here is Wordsworth in Book V of *The Prelude*, finding in the auroras an emblem of his own childhood strength of imagination:

> ye whom time
> And seasons serve; all Faculties to whom
> Earth crouches, the elements are potter's clay,
> Space like a heaven filled up with northern lights,
> Here, nowhere, there, and everywhere at once.

Wordsworth associates the language of desire, power, possession with the auroras, and makes of the lights a noble synecdoche for imagination and for God. "Here, nowhere, there, and everywhere at once" would make a better translation of *ehyeh asher ehyeh* than "I Am That I Am" does. Stevens' flashing lights reverse Wordsworth's synecdoche, for in canto I they signify the absence, rather than the presence, of the poet's Secondary Imagination. For Stevens, the auroras are an ironic allegory, the largest trope of *ethos*, or limitation of Fate, he has brought into his poetry. The flashing of the serpent body without the skin suggests the imagery of the final chorus in Shelley's *Hellas* but more immediately recalls Stevens' own *Farewell to Florida*, the introductory poem in the public edition of *Ideas of Order*. As emblem, it is therefore ambiguous, since it says change but may mean change or death. In *Farewell to Florida*, it mostly does mean change, but here in canto I of the *Auroras* it means death, or at least the death of the poet's ability to respond to a natural challenge.

Emphasized in the first tercet is our dubious status as the intended object of the starry-eyed serpent, "fatal Ananke, the common god," as Stevens once called him. But this emphasis immediately is placed in doubt by the next tercet, with its triple, open questionings:

> Or is this another wriggling out of the egg,
> Another image at the end of the cave,
> Another bodiless for the body's slough?

The first line, if answered positively, would make of the auroras-serpent another Orphic rebirth, a new mythological beginning for this antimythological poet. The second line, more exhaustedly, would make of the serpent only another illusory image, copy of a copy, in Plato's cave. The third line, most exhaustedly, would find in the serpent an old man's scary wish-fulfillment, to escape the prison of the body's decay. However, the third tercet dismisses all three questions, clarifying the "this is" as the whole of the visible scene. The auroras nest below as well as above, "tinted distances" indicating the dominance of the great lights. Therefore, fields, hills, and pines as well as sky come together in the ironic or dialectical trope that juggles presence and absence: "form gulping after formlessness, / Skin flashing to wished-for disappearances." Whose wish? Already Stevens either cannot or will not battle his fresh immersion in the greatest poverty; already he feels, or fears that he feels, that his desire is too difficult to tell from despair. For the serpent body to flash without the skin is at once an image of the lights and an image of despair that may be the last residue of an old man's desire.

It is all the more heroic that Stevens should declare at just such a point: "This is the height emerging and its base." Referentially, this line pertains to the figuration of the serpent's head and tail in the panoply of the northern lights, but ironically it signifies also the zenith and nadir of continuing desire. A purposiveness without purpose begins to emerge:

> These lights may finally attain a pole
> In the midmost midnight and find the serpent there,
>
> In another nest, the master of the maze
> Of body and air and forms and images,
> Relentlessly in possession of happiness.
>
> This is his poison: that we should disbelieve
> Even that.

Would it be less poisonous if Stevens had written "that we should *believe* / Even that."? Either way the nest and the happiness never will be ours. The sense of loss grows as Stevens studies the nostalgias, in a passage that might have moved the author of *Huckleberry Finn*:

> His meditations in the ferns,
> When he moved so slightly to make sure of sun,
>
> Made us no less as sure. We saw in his head,
> Black beaded on the rock, the flecked animal,
> The moving grass, the Indian in his glade.

This is not the auroras-serpent but a snake seen perhaps in childhood, and certainly in a world other than the incessant

"This is." The Indian in his glade lives in a place his own and, much more, himself, and Stevens seems to be recalling a blazoned day. Much tonal uncertainty in the first canto is resolved in these gently nostalgic closing lines that do not alter the essential figuration of the poem's opening, which is that Stevens ironically says change yet means death.

It is difficult to conceive of a more adequate dialectical image of presence and absence than the auroras-serpent, but fittingly Stevens tends to portray so overwhelming a presence mostly in terms of absence. "There was a project for the sun and is," according to *Notes*, but we apprehend almost instantly that Stevens has no project for the auroras, the most intimidating of First Ideas, because it seems to be its own First Idea and to resist becoming "an imagined thing." Or, to cite *Notes* again, the auroras are a strong instance of those "abysmal instruments [that] make sounds like pips / Of the sweeping meanings that we add to them." Stevens adds no meanings to the auroras in canto I; it is enough that implicitly they threaten him with the irony of an ultimate *ethos* that he had spent a poetic lifetime soliciting. His search for an enabling act of the mind, for a figuration of capable imagination, now yields him in the auroras too sufficient an image or "mythology of modern death."

Between the aboriginal nostalgia of the close of canto I, and the chilled synecdoches of waning power in II–IV, Stevens fails to negotiate a Crossing of Election. "Farewell to an idea" is a dirge of Wordsworthian dimensions, a lament here not for an absent gleam but for the driving away of tropes and colors by the glare of the auroras, which begin now to perform a sinister function akin to the whiteness of Shelley's *Mont Blanc* or to the blinding light given off by the chariot in *The Triumph of Life*. Canto II is at once a triumph of Stevens' art and a tolling of the human loss exacted by that art. Stevens had said "farewell" before in his poetry; indeed, in some sense he always had been saying farewell to some aspect of self or experience, and he went on with such elegiac intensities until the end in *Of Mere Being*. "Farewell" for Stevens is what in *Blue Guitar*, XXVI, he called "valedictory echoings," Whitmanian echoings of the beach-world of the *Sea-Drift* poems. For Stevens as for Whitman, "The world washed in his imagination, / The world was a shore, whether sound or form / Or light, the relic of farewells, / Rock, of valedictory echoings, / To which his imagination returned, / From which it sped."

Stevens' imagination returns, in canto II, to the beach and contemplates with dread what *Notes* triumphantly had termed "that ever-early candor." This poem, *The Auroras of Autumn*, savagely parodies *Notes* by showing how "the poem, through candor, brings back a power again / That gives a candid kind to everything." Candor is reduced to whiteness: of the beach cabin, the flowers against the wall, and finally everything that is visible in the "this is." *Examination of the Hero* had spoken of "a white abstraction only, a feeling / In a feeling mass, a blank emotion, / An anti-pathos," while *Holiday in Reality* (*CP*, 312–13) had opened, "It was something to see that their white was different, / Sharp as white paint in the January sun." *Auroras*, II, develops all these prefigurations into an extraordinary fantasia upon the trope of whiteness. The deserted cabin's whiteness prompts the odd triple explanation 1) that everyone customarily whitewashes beach cabins; 2) that the New England ancestral theme of attempting a purity in one's recreations is involved; 3) that an infinite course of entropy has attained its consequence. A movement from unthinking custom to a consciousness of moral ancestry to a sense of natural entropy is suggestive of the natural history of our sensibilities as we are compelled to engage forebodings of our own death. What follows is a sharper movement in the same pattern, an awareness of death gaining with every phrase:

> The flowers against the wall
> Are white, a little dried, a kind of mark
>
> Reminding, trying to remind, of a white
> That was different, something else, last year
> Or before, not the white of an aging afternoon,
>
> Whether fresher or duller, whether of winter cloud
> Or of winter sky, from horizon to horizon.
> The wind is blowing the sand across the floor.

Emerson, in his essay *The Poet*, cites the Orphic hymns speaking of hoariness as "that white flower which marks extreme old age." Stevens' Orphic flowers possess consciousness, intend Stevens as their object, and mark a difference that is a crisis, a difference in whiteness. The white of an aging afternoon is related to the cold sea-wind heralding seasonal change but more crucially to an authentic crisis of vision, one that the poet knows to have been self-induced:

> Here, being visible is being white,
> Is being of the solid of white, the accomplishment
> Of an extremist in an exercise . . .

This passage plays against *Esthétique du Mal*, XIII, where the visible is established as "a zone of blue and orange / Versicolorings." But here, on the beach, Stevens fails to make the visible a little hard to see. Instead, he congeals it as an opaque blank, the solid of white, and this is indeed his accomplishment. As poet he is the extremist, and the exercise is his characteristic reduction to a First Idea, performed here all too successfully and with fearful consequences:

> The season changes. A cold wind chills the beach.
> The long lines of it grow longer, emptier,
> A darkness gathers though it does not fall
>
> And the whiteness grows less vivid on the wall.
> The man who is walking turns blankly on the sand.
> He observes how the north is always enlarging the change,
>
> With its frigid brilliances, its blue-red sweeps
> And gusts of great enkindlings, its polar green,
> The color of ice and fire and solitude.

"Blankly" is the central word of this superb passage and reverberates against the many "blanks" in Stevens' poetry, both before and after *The Auroras of Autumn*. The ancestral passages, as I've indicated before, are in Coleridge and in Emerson, who began as Coleridge's ephebe. Stevens, walking the beach, might as soon say, "And still I gaze—and with how blank an eye!" or even "The ruin or the blank that we see when we look at nature is in our own eye." Closer still to his "turns blankly" and "solid of white" is the meditation of Emerson near the end of *Nature:* "We make fables to hide the baldness of the fact and conform it, as we say, to the higher law of the mind. But when the fact is seen under the light of an idea, the gaudy fable fades and shrivels."

The fact of the auroras proposes itself as a literal light that is its own First Idea, and what fades and shrivels is the fable of reimagining. A peculiar force is assumed by the two allied lines that are complete sentences in themselves: "The wind is blowing the sand across the floor" and "The man who is walking turns blankly on the sand." To turn blankly is to trope vainly or write poetry without purpose, in a state of "This is," where the wind and the auroras dominate and the wind and auroras themselves are allied as "gusts of great enkindlings." As the season changes, the lights of the north enlarge the change, reminding us that the root of the word "change," *skamb*, means "curve" or "bend," since this enlarging is a serpentine coiling of brilliances. Canto II ends fittingly upon the word "solitude," which is more intensely dehumanized, from a trope for freedom into a vertigo of solipsism, than it is anywhere else in Stevens. The contrast is to *It Must Change,* IV, with its triumphant, more Emersonian and Whitmanian solitude.

> In solitude the trumpets of solitude
> Are not of another solitude resounding;
> A little string speaks for a crowd of voices.
>
> The partaker partakes of that which changes him.
> The child that touches takes character from the thing,
> The body, it touches. The captain and his men
>
> Are one and the sailor and the sea are one.
> Follow after, O my companion, my fellow, my self,
> Sister and solace, brother and delight.

From that visionary zenith, Stevens in five years has moved to the "polar green" of this nadir, to the Coleridgean Antarctic sheen of "the color of ice and fire and solitude." Having failed his own vision, he turns "naturally" or all too humanly to a

summoning up of the imagos of the mother and father in cantos
III–IV, where "Farewell to an idea" is extended into further ex-
plorations of the failure of the power of the mind to assert itself
over the auroras and the wind, synecdoches of the universe of
death (and of language). But the idealized images of Stevens'
own parents, which endure their own crises in cantos III and IV,
do not fail Stevens to the same degree as he has failed himself in
canto II. So he is compelled to the bitterness of canto V, where
both imagos are made to sustain a very grim emptying out and
Stevens' own poetic gift necessarily undergoes a *kenosis* together
with the muse, his mother, and the affirmative force or passion
for yes, his father.

"Farewell to an idea" at the opening of canto III therefore
means something like "Farewell to the idea of my being able to
reimagine the First Idea of my mother," that is, "The mother's
face, / The purpose of the poem." Stevens, at sixty-eight, returns to the house of his childhood, as a house "of the mind and
they and time," where "the mind" means memory, "they" the
poet and his brothers, and "time" all the time there ever was,
because time never will be again. Canto III, more even than
Notes, demonstrates so oddly original a mode of writing as to
make critical description very difficult. We have been slow to
see that memory is a kind of thinking, particularly in post-
Romantic poetry. Stevens' peculiar originality, in *The Auroras of
Autumn*, *The Rock*, and other late poems, is to show us the dissolving of memory as the falling, apart and away, of poetic
thinking. "Transparence," the gift of the mother, had entered
Stevens' poetry out of Emersonian tradition, where it had been
an emblem of inspired perception. For Stevens it makes a triad
with place and innocence, and sometimes he seems to regard it
as a kind of vivid sleep. Canto III begins with the admission that
the purpose of any poem, or at any rate of the Stevensian
poem, is to recover the memory of the mother's face. Perhaps
the most poignant lines in all of Stevens are these in which the
poetic will and the memory of the mother dissolve together:

> It is the mother they possess,
> Who gives transparence to their present peace.
> She makes that gentler that can gentle be.

And yet she too is dissolved, she is destroyed.
She gives transparence. But she has grown old.
The necklace is a carving not a kiss.

The soft hands are a motion not a touch.
The house will crumble and the books will burn.

It is the language of *pathos*—of desire, possession, and power—but what it represents is the inability of language to restitute the loss of memory, *when memory itself grows old,* when mind has been thinking by and through memory for too long a time. The keepsake of the mother's necklace is now only a carving when held in the hands and no longer recalls her kiss. Tactile memory of her has been emptied out, and the house of the mind therefore crumbles. The agency of the undoing which rhetorically converts synecdoches to metonymies, is necessarily the auroras, the boreal night that leaves the rooms of memory unlit and illuminates only the windows, the eyes of the aging poet. There is also a transformation of three-dimensional memory into a two-dimensional façade, as depth abandons the mind. This first and most primal of imagos yields to the wind, to the invincible sound with which language no longer dares to compete.

"Farewell to an idea" sounds again, but now it provokes the yea-sayer in Stevens, the imago of his confident and optimistic father, who was something of a poet too and a hearty celebrator of life's purposes. As befits the paternal imago, Jehovah gets mixed into the picture of the mind, and so does the Canon Aspirin, himself a Sublime psychic expansionist and affirmer. There is very little ambivalence toward this figuration of the father, either in canto IV or canto V, but there is a considerable distancing between father and son, and a rhetorical shading off from the father as noble synecdoche in IV to the father as a regressive image and metonymizer in V. Celestial and terrestrial paternal antics and flamboyances will not suffice, despite Stevens' considerable nostalgias in IV. The Jehovah-like father, with burning bushes for eyes, is too near allied to "a lasting visage in a lasting bush" of *It Must Give Pleasure*, III. He is therefore simply not available, too distant from relevance: "He says yes / To no; and in saying yes he says farewell." Where Stevens passively must suffer the north's perpetual enlargement of the change, the father "measures the velocities of change," but the difference is that, after all, the father, like God, is dead. But he remains impressive nevertheless, being agile in the mode of the Canon Aspirin and like the Canon a High Romantic Idealist in his epistemology:

> He assumes the great speeds of space and flutters them
> From cloud to cloudless, cloudless to keen clear
>
> In flights of eye and ear, the highest eye
> And the lowest ear, the deep ear that discerns,
> At evening, things that attend it until it hears
>
> The supernatural preludes of its own,
> At the moment when the angelic eye defines
> Its actors approaching, in company, in their masks.

This passage goes back to the Canon Aspirin's reconceivings of reality, though with a losing difference:

> Thereon the learning of the man conceived
> Once more night's pale illuminations, gold
>
> Beneath, far underneath, the surface of
> His eye and audible in the mountain of
> His ear, the very material of his mind.

The Canon, as transumptive form of the American scholar, conceives through learning and falls into imposing only later, but the father imposes orders from the start, which is to say that the Canon is rather like Shelley, whereas the father is an amateur poet in Reading, Pennsylvania. His angelic eye defines its own company of maskers, but unlike Shelley's they cannot choir it with the naked wind. Yet the father is one's own father, "of motion the ever-brightening origin," or the one of fictive will, and so attached is Stevens to this imago that he requires the strenuous and bitter canto v to dissolve this final trope of Power.

We can describe the father in canto v as a failed Prospero, a fetcher of pageants but one who then cannot dissolve his own airy fictions at will. Helen Vendler is a touch too harsh when she says, "The autumnal wind has blown pretenses away, and the creator-father becomes, in consequence, the object of contempt." Rather, the father is a failed translator, of desire into fiction, which is why the father's poetic failure is compared to the work of Châtillon, who was a sixteenth-century Huguenot humanist, a doctor expelled from Geneva for heresies from Calvinism, heresies exalting the will, and whose passion for yes led him to translate the Hebrew Bible into Latin and French. Châtillon may be the subject of *The Doctor of Geneva*, who in that *Harmonium* poem confronts the Pacific without awe:

> He did not quail. A man so used to plumb
> The multifarious heavens felt no awe
> Before these visible, voluble delugings.

Châtillon (wherever Stevens had read about him) becomes a curious, hidden emblem for the poetry of Stevens' father:

> Among these the musicians strike the instinctive poem.
> The father fetches his unherded herds,
> Of barbarous tongue, slavered and panting halves
>
> Of breath, obedient to his trumpet's touch.
> This then is Chatillon or as you please.
> We stand in the tumult of a festival.

The "unherded herds" are the amateur poems of Garrett Stevens; the metonymies of barbarous tongue and breath, obedient to the father's trumpet, suggest the notion of translation from the holy tongue into the barbarous vernacular and suddenly give Wallace Stevens his absurdly and significantly recondite allusion to Châtillon as a scamp of the heretical will. But the word "festival," whose darkness for Stevens I traced in the last chapter, suggests in turn a total undoing of the father's optimism and of the son's poetry:

> What festival? This loud, disordered mooch?
> These hospitaliers? These brute-like guests?
> These musicians dubbing at a tragedy,

A-dub, a-dub, which is made up of this:
That there are no lines to speak? There is no play.
Or, the persons act one merely by being here.

I do not hear contempt for the father's vision in this, but certainly there is dismay at the savage disparity between the yea-saying and the world of the reality principle. With a double desperation, *The Auroras of Autumn* arrives at its midpoint as a poem, which is also its Crossing of Solipsism, again not to be negotiated successfully. Either there is no play, no lines to speak, but only death, or else our existence here is only a play anyway, a fantastic performance in which we too are brutelike guests. Between these realizations and the Sublime opening of canto VI the rhetorical disjunction is quite absolute, despite the thematic link from play to theatre.

It is a theatre floating through the clouds,
Itself a cloud, although of misted rock
And mountains running like water, wave on wave,

Through waves of light. It is of cloud transformed
To cloud transformed again, idly, the way
A season changes color to no end,

Except the lavishing of itself in change,
As light changes yellow into gold and gold
To its opal elements and fire's delight,

Splashed wide-wise because it likes magnificence
And the solemn pleasures of magnificent space.

The movement is from mimetic to expressive, from hearing to sight, and from internalization to externalization, and it is sharp enough to suggest that the loss of the imagos has exposed Stevens to a death of love, to a greater solipsism than even he can sustain. Just this augmented degree of solitude is the force that is repressed in canto VI, where Stevens achieves his grandest realization of the American Sublime. The auroras are seen in a vision as a theatre of cloud, misted rock, and mountains transforming into oceans, with all this metamorphic cycle moving through light even as the seasons move through the year. This is to see the auroras as the epitome of nature and of art alike, changing in a purposeless purpose because such lavishing pleases it, and yet the change is idle. So detached a Sublime startles Stevens into a phantasmagoria in which a partial return of the repressed takes place, but only as the prelude to a greater repression:

> The cloud drifts idly through half-thought-of forms.
>
> The theatre is filled with flying birds,
> Wild wedges, as of a volcano's smoke, palm-eyed
> And vanishing, a web in a corridor
>
> Or massive portico. A capitol,
> It may be, is emerging or has just
> Collapsed. The denouement has to be postponed . . .

This passage, the most irrealistic in all of Stevens, is the poet's challenge of his own powers of invention, a challenge that provokes the Sublime response of canto VI's last two tercets, which attempt to repress the negative emblems of this theatre of the auroras. The wedgelike birds mock Stevens' naturalistic synecdoche of the Floridian palm, while the corridor and the capitol deliberately allude to the Canon Aspirin's collapse into the imposition of orders: "Next he builds capitols and in their corridors, / Whiter than wax, sonorous, fame as it is." When Stevens concludes here that "the denouement has to be postponed," he declines to join himself to the Canon's errors of imposition, and so he calls into question his vision of the auroras as a cloud-theatre of the Sublime. What follows is the most strenuous single moment in all his poetry, a true test for Stevens and for his reader. Just this one and only time in the poem, Stevens defies the auroras or attempts to defy them. He turns against them his linguistic and psychological discipline of a lifetime, by seeking to reduce the northern lights as though they were only another illusion. Since any First Idea is finally an idea of an idea, or a new troping of the sun, Stevens seeks to show that the auroras are "nothing" unless and until they are "contained" by being imagined in his mind. Thus they would be unnamed, and their menace to the poet would be destroyed. So once it would have been, as here in *Blue Guitar*, XXXII:

> Throw away the lights, the definitions,
> And say of what you see in the dark
>
> That it is this or that it is that,
> But do not use the rotted names.
>
> How should you walk in that space and know
> Nothing of the madness of space,
>
> Nothing of its jocular procreations?
> Throw the lights away: Nothing must stand
>
> Between you and the shapes you take
> When the crust of shape has been destroyed.

Stevens would adjure himself, then, not to use the rotted names of the auroras and to perceive the inconceivable idea of the auroras. But *this time* he is not able to cry triumphantly, "How clean the auroras when seen in their idea." Instead, having prepared himself for this great battle of the mind against the sky, he opens the door of his house, his entire consciousness, to find that the whole sky is on fire, as the auroras triumphantly quell his challenge and reduce him to fear:

> This is nothing until in a single man contained,
> Nothing until this named thing nameless is
> And is destroyed. He opens the door of his house
>
> On flames. The scholar of one candle sees
> An arctic effulgence flaring on the frame
> Of everything he is. And he feels afraid.

It is one thing to say, in the *Final Soliloquy of the Interior Paramour*, "How high that highest candle lights the dark," but it would be quite another thing to say, "How high that highest candle lights the aurora borealis." The scholar, as Emerson said in *Society and Solitude*, is that single, that one candle, a Pascalian thinking reed, a frail frame against this sublimity of flares, par-

ticularly when the scholar or poet harbors as his deepest fear
the notion that this great effulgence itself *is thinking*, that it has,
or rather is, an intelligence. "I felt afraid," the poet of *Domination of Black* had said, thirty years before, when he "saw how
the night came." When the scholar of one candle feels afraid, at
the close of canto VI, it is because "a fantastic effort has failed,"
in the phrase of a later poem, *The Plain Sense of Things*. His
daemonic force momentarily abated, Stevens turns in canto VII
to the search for sublimation, the quest for a metaphor that his
newest poverty requires.

The first half of canto VII consists of three rhetorical questions, all of which imply an unhappily positive answer. The
first is the culmination of one of Stevens' deepest obsessions:

> Is there an imagination that sits enthroned
> As grim as it is benevolent, the just
> And the unjust, which in the midst of summer stops

> To imagine winter?

Shelley could have asked this question of the nameless Power
behind Mont Blanc, or of the nameless Spirit that moved in the
west wind. But Stevens is haunted here as much by Keats as by
Shelley. As far back as 1910, he was quoting a passage of Keats
that is the clear precursor of the speculations of canto VII:

> It is a flaw
> In happiness, to see beyond our bourn.—
> It forces us in summer skies to mourn,
> It spoils the singing of the Nightingale.

Stevens quoted these lines from the *Epistle to John Hamilton
Reynolds* in a letter to his wife (*L*, 167). The lines just preceding
are the model for the questions in canto VII:

> Or is it imagination brought
> Beyond its proper bound, yet still confin'd,
> Lost in a sort of Purgatory blind,
> Cannot refer to any standard law
> Of either earth or heaven?

Like Keats, Stevens is dealing with the "material sublime,"
but his musings turn more in the Lucretian direction of Shel-

ley's meditations upon Necessity. Stevens' enthroned imagination is a kind of Epicurean god, remotely benevolent, but grimly presiding over just and unjust alike. Why does such an imagination stop in midsummer to imagine winter? Since Stevens has identified the auroras with that imagination, the answer must be the auroras' idle liking for change and for magnificence in change. Hence Stevens adds the next question, which confirms the identity of auroras and inhuman imagination, and gives us also a curious insight into the nature of the auroras, a nature that is not our own and yet sometimes is manifested in Romantic poets:

> When the leaves are dead,
> Does it take its place in the north and enfold itself,
> Goat-leaper, crystalled and luminous, sitting
>
> In highest night?

In *Someone Puts a Pineapple Together*, written earlier in the same year as the *Auroras*, Stevens posited three planets, sun, moon, and the imagination, and called the third "man and his endless effigies." Later in the *Pineapple* poem, Stevens spoke "of the tropic of resemblances, sprigs / Of Capricorn or as the sign demands." Capricorn, the goat-leaper, tenth sign of the zodiac, though a constellation of the southern hemisphere, is assigned to the auroras in what Stevens was to call the planet on the table, the book of the whole of *Harmonium*. Enfolded like a serpent, robed in the northern lights, the tropic of resemblances takes on a sinister splendor in the third rhetorical question:

> And do these heavens adorn
> And proclaim it, the white creator of black, jetted
> By extinguishings, even of planets as may be,
>
> Even of earth, even of sight, in snow,
> Except as needed by way of majesty,
> In the sky, as crown and diamond cabala?

This is surely the most Gnostic supposition in Stevens' poetry up to this point, though even darker notions were to come in still later poems. One of Stevens' rare Biblical echoes, of the Psalmist's insistence that the heavens proclaim the glory of

God, is followed by the remarkable play upon two meanings of "jetted." The white lights of the auroras are jetted or propelled outward by the energy obtained from the extinguishings of planets, but also the black skies are made blacker by the action of the auroras in sacrificing planets to the need of the lights for more and more majesty. The crucial line is "Even of earth, even of spirit, in snow," which returns to *The Snow Man*, with a new explanation for the very solitary purpose of that seminal poem. Stevens too jetted the auroras by the extinguishings of his sight, in snow; by his consent to having a mind of winter. Beholding nothing, nothing himself, he diminished so as to augment the majesty of the imagination enthroned in the auroras. A diamond cabala is a kind of spectral emanation from the self rather than a majesty that mirrors the self. Though cabala ultimately means "reception" (in the sense of a secret tradition), Stevens seems to mean by it a sublimating knowledge that takes the place of our instinctual fulfillments. Cabala here possibly means something like *askesis*, or what Nietzsche called "the ascetic spirit," and appears peculiarly as a human sublimation in the passage following:

> It leaps through us, through all our heavens leaps,
> Extinguishing our planets, one by one,
> Leaving, of where we were and looked, of where
>
> We knew each other and of each other thought,
> A shivering residue, chilled and foregone,
> Except for that crown and mystical cabala.

This is very close to an orthodox Freudian theory of poetry, since this "crown and mystical cabala" would be precisely a poem like *The Snow Man* or *A Postcard from the Volcano*, which indeed is echoed here, as *The Snow Man* was earlier. The poet who sends the postcard before the volcano flames says that "with our bones / We left much more, left what still is / The look of things." Yet Stevens cannot abide in this ascetic spirit, in a sublimation both Nietzschean and Freudian. Even the auroras, leaping through us, reducing us to an intolerable First Idea of ourselves, cannot leap without our perception and our will:

But it dare not leap by chance in its own dark.
It must change from destiny to slight caprice
And thus its jetted tragedy, its stele

And shape and mournful making move to find
What must unmake it and, at last, what can,
Say, a flippant communication under the moon.

This is the most surprising passage in *The Auroras of Autumn*, and perhaps in all of Stevens, for who could have foretold that the sinister splendor of the auroras would be undone by "Say, a flippant communication under the moon" (where "flippant" evidently does not so much mean "pert" but takes its archaic sense of "voluble" or "talkative"). Between that surprising line, and "There may be always a time of innocence," Stevens successfully gets over his poem's Crossing of Identification, his hidden confrontation of death as the most violent of rhetorical disjunctions, here between a flippant communication and a time of innocence. How are we to explain this most peculiar and drastic of nontransitions? To answer first another query: why dare the aurora borealis not leap by chance in its own dark? Vendler excels the other critics of Stevens, here as elsewhere, by at least confronting the question, though she does not give Stevens high marks in her answer. She says: "The only force regulating the leaper is its necessary polarity. . . . It is hard to imagine what might undo the aurora borealis, as the aurora 'undid' summer," and she adds that Stevens' undoing of the spell of the lights is an imposed order, not a discovered one. She thus chastises Stevens precisely as he himself chastisingly disengaged from the Canon Aspirin.

But Stevens is neither imposing nor discovering an order but rather uncovering a disorder, which is the dependence of any hypostasis upon our wildness, our light caprice of freedom, if there is to be meaning of any kind. "Caprice" is a curious word, related to Capricorn as goat-leaper, since it derives from the Italian *capriccio*, "head with hair standing on end," and so horror or whim, in the sense influenced by *capra*, goat. A goat-leaper is therefore already a caprice, and not a destiny; it is an inclination or *clinamen* to make a change. Linguistically, this is what Stevens means when he says of the aurora borealis that it dare not leap by chance in its own dark, as if it truly were Ananke. It is not a necessity at all, moving by laws of its own, but an interplay, an endless decentering of itself. As for its jetted tragedy, blackened and propelled outward by our extinguishings, this is merely a "stele," an inscribed slab or sculptured stone in the face of a building. Here the building is the cosmos, and the flaring auroras are therefore only a kind of commemorative tablet whose shape and mournful making alike are subject to change, to whim, to an unmaking by man as the only maker of meaning, and by way of any flippant communication under the moon. Shelley ends *Mont Blanc* by saying to the mountain or the Power behind the mountain: "And what were thou, and earth, and stars, and sea, / If to the human mind's imaginings / Silence and solitude were vacancy?" This is to celebrate, implicitly, the imagination as the "violence from within," fighting the war of the mind against the sky. Stevens does not go so far, fearing to impose order, like Shelley or his surrogate the Canon Aspirin, but his "flippant communication" that unmakes the auroras is an imaginative gesture of a Shelleyan kind, though not a very wholehearted one.

The final movement of *The Auroras of Autumn* is the transumption carried out by cantos VIII–X, where any reading must depend upon the interpretation of the equivocal term "innocence," which Stevens uses as a metalepsis or "far-fetched" trope for fresh imaginative possibility, for the potential of going on as a poet, or rather for an introjection of, or identification with, such potential. "Innocence" as a projection or casting out of death can be traced back to the root of the word, *nek*, which is rather remote from our current meaning of being uncorrupted by malice or evil, yet is closer to the older meaning of harmlessness. Since the ambiance of cantos VIII–IX is Whitmanian, as all visions of the mother in Stevens tend to be, their use of "innocence," like Whitman's, may go back ultimately to the Emersonian center, the chant of the Orphic poet in the final chapter of *Nature*: "A man is a god in ruins. When men are innocent, life shall be longer, and shall pass into the immortal as gently as we awake from dreams. Now, the world would be insane and rabid, if these disorganizations should last for hundreds of years. It is kept in check by death and infancy."

In Stevens, the dialectical relationship between innocence and autumn goes back to *Like Decorations*, XLIV:

> Freshness is more than the east wind blowing round one,
> There is no such thing as innocence in autumn,
> Yet, it may be, innocence is never lost.

The very late poem *One of the Inhabitants of the West* (*CP*, 503–04) ends with a bodiless reader of a text reading quietly: "So much guilt lies buried / Beneath the innocence / Of autumn days." The central text for this trope in Stevens is, necessarily, *Esthétique du Mal*, where the student of the nostalgias encounters

> the last nostalgia: that he
> Should understand. That he might suffer or that
> He might die was the innocence of living, if life
> Itself was innocent. To say that it was
> Disentangled him from sleek ensolacings.

Here innocence is again dialectical and involves holding the imagination open to death much in the manner of Whitman at the end of *The Sleepers*. Stevens is a touch too anxious, in canto VIII, and his "pure principle" of a time of innocence come again is perhaps as desperate as Nietzsche's affirmation of the eternal recurrence, at least in *Zarathustra*. What counts about the time of innocence is that "it is visible," not so much the twice-repeated insistences that it exists and that it is. It is visible precisely because Stevens now has the courage to identify it with the auroras of autumn:

> So, then, these lights are not a spell of light,
> A saying out of a cloud, but innocence.
> An innocence of the earth and no false sign
>
> Or symbol of malice.

This is the most radical instance in Stevens of the undoing of an earlier trope by a later play upon it. The auroras, whose glare had been opposed to the mother's face, now join the in-

nocent mother as part of an innocence of the earth. The cost is
high and means not only the emptying out of present time and
place but the acceptance of death as what may come tomorrow
and what must be seen as being part of the family:

> The rendezvous, when she came alone,
> By her coming became a freedom of the two,
> An isolation which only the two could share.
>
> Shall we be found hanging in the trees next spring?
> Of what disaster is this the imminence:
> Bare limbs, bare trees and a wind as sharp as salt?
>
> The stars are putting on their glittering belts.
> They throw around their shoulders cloaks that flash
> Like a great shadow's last embellishment.
>
> It may come tomorrow in the simplest word,
> Almost as part of innocence, almost,
> Almost as the tenderest and the truest part.

The first tercet appears to refer to the same moment in Stevens' courtship of his wife that is portrayed later in *The Rock:*

> The meeting at noon at the edge of the field seems like
>
> An invention, an embrace between one desperate clod
> And another.

But the air has not yet been emptied out of Stevens' memories,
here in the *Auroras,* and the poet thus celebrates a freedom that
was also a solitude of two, only to confront the imminent possibility of a wintry death both for himself and for his wife. This
realization makes all the more effective the penultimate tercet of
canto IX, with its marvelous contrast of the human disaster of
death, "disaster" being a back-formation from "ill-starred," and
the glory of the stars attiring themselves as for battle or brave
display and yet in the likeness of "a great shadow's last em-
bellishment." After this splendor, the canto ends in massive
Whitmanian simplicity, where the word may be any word that
returns one, as at the end of *The Sleepers,* to the tenderest and

truest presence that is at once death, the night, and the mother.

Stevens could have ended his poem there, but he chose not to seek an illusory closure in so elegiac a strain. There is nothing else in him like the jocular procreations of canto x, though the model for this coda appears to be the address to the soldier that serves as the coda to *Notes*. But the earlier coda was elegiac; this is a poetic apologia that concludes by returning us to the wind and to the flaring auroras that we now see have never been absent from the poem. Stevens moves to mitigate the turning against his own self that, in canto II, had caused him to speak of "the accomplishment / Of an extremist in an exercise." This extremity, the whole poem of *The Auroras of Autumn*, is to be read to the congregation as a meditation on the central text: "An unhappy people in a happy world," a text that darkens the formula of *Notes*, "that we live in a place / That is not our own." But the never-failing genius of poetry reveals its limitation, through the evasive interplay of Stevens' grammar and syntax:

> In these unhappy he meditates a whole,
> The full of fortune and the full of fate,
> As if he lived all lives, that he might know,
>
> In hall harridan, not hushful paradise,
> To a haggling of wind and weather, by these lights
> Like a blaze of summer straw, in winter's nick.

We all of us are "these unhappy," a synecdoche or broken part of "the full of fortune and the full of fate," which only the imagination, "as if he lived all lives," might know. But what would then be known? The poem's closing tercet does not attempt to tell us this "what," for Epicurus himself, ultimate founder of Stevens' truest tradition, said that the "what" was unknowable. Whitman, in *Song of Myself*, 6, said that he could not answer the child's question *What is the grass?*, for "I do not know what it is any more than he." The imagination of Stevens knows *by* these lights of the aurora borealis; knows *in* a hag-ridden place and not a paradise; knows *to* a haggling of the wind; and most of all knows *in* the nick of winter, in the crucial notch or moment that is a final crossing. But the lights go up like a blaze of summer straw, reminding us of Wordsworth's light of sense that goes out but with a flash that reveals the invisible world. All that the flash reveals to Stevens is change and ourselves as the origin of the meaning of change. On the threshold of a beyond, Stevens bends back and refuses the advice he gave more than thirty years earlier to his Blanche McCarthy:

> Look in the terrible mirror of the sky.
> Oh, bend against the invisible; and lean
> To symbols of descending night; and search
> The glare of revelations going by!

Stevens left us no deeper or more eloquent search of the glare of such revelations than *The Auroras of Autumn*. It is conservative to say that no other twentieth-century poem in English takes us further or more powerfully into the mode of the Sublime.

11 *The Auroras of Autumn:*
Shorter Poems

Besides *An Ordinary Evening in New Haven*, the subject of Chapter 12, the great achievement of the volume *The Auroras of Autumn* is the elegy for Stevens' best friend, Henry Church. *The Owl in the Sarcophagus* is a poem of authentic difficulty, a work curiously hieratic and reserved, even for Stevens. As he said, it is not personal in tone, though it was written in a frame of mind induced by Church's death. Rather, it is hushed, gentle, immensely dignified, and like all strong elegies more a meditation upon the poet's own consciousness than a lament or a song of loss that involves another self.

Part of the difficulty of the *Owl* is that it is Stevens' most intensely visionary or transcendental poem, its only rival in this respect being the pre-elegy for Santayana, *To an Old Philosopher in Rome*, though certain cantos of *An Ordinary Evening* touch upon this visionary realm, as do some of the final lyrics. Its ancestor, in a troubling but indisputable way, is Whitman's astounding poem *The Sleepers*, but the influence is very much repressed; if my way of theorizing is at all accurate, that repression is the cause of Stevens' power here in the Sublime mode.

The first canto of the *Owl* both presents and defines a vision of three immortal forms—sleep, peace, and the mother—that move among the dead. Canto II, with only four tercets, is a direct tribute to Henry Church. Then follow three cantos: six tercets for sleep, nine for peace, and six again for the mother, after which the poem concludes with a four-tercet coda that comments upon the mythological status of the poem's own imagery. This curious pattern is unique among Stevens' longer poems and suggests that the center for him is the figuration he calls "peace," as close to a savior as ever he celebrated, whether here or in the hushed prefatory lines to *Notes*, where he closed his address to his poem by the grateful assertion "The vivid transparence that you bring is peace."

A sarcophagus in this poem does not appear to mean a stone coffin or flesh-eating stone but rather the mind's false vision of modern death as making the whole of earth seem such a stone. The owl, traditionally the goddess of wisdom's bird that flies forth in the darkness, may not stand so much for wisdom as for the "central things" it represents in two poems in *Parts of a World*. Here are the first two stanzas and then the closing stanza of *On the Adequacy of Landscape* (*CP*, 243–44):

> The little owl flew through the night,
> As if the people in the air
> Were frightened and he frightened them,
> By being there,
>
> The people that turned off and came
> To avoid the bright, discursive wings,
> To avoid the hap-hallow hallow-ho
> Of central things, . . .
>
> ◇   ◇   ◇
>
> So that he that suffers most desires
> The red bird most and the strongest sky—
> Not the people in the air that hear
> The little owl fly.

In *Woman Looking at a Vase of Flowers* (*CP*, 246–47), the little owl within the woman is urged to host "an affirmation free from doubt," the affirmation being the movement of nature's inhuman colors into "the form and the fragrance of things / Without clairvoyance, close to her," that is, the inhuman making choice of a human self, as at the close of the poem *Of Ideal Time and Choice*. On these models, the title *The Owl in the Sarcophagus* means the transformation of our vision of death from merely being swallowed up by the stone of earth to a realm where a central and humanizing discursiveness can operate, as in the flight of the little owl.

The visionary forms that Stevens sees moving about the night, quieting the dead, are akin to the figure of Whitman wandering all night in his vision in *The Sleepers* and quieting the restless ones:

> I stand in the dark with drooping eyes by the worst-suffering
>   and the most restless,
> I pass my hands soothingly to and fro a few inches from them,
> The restless sink in their beds, they fitfully sleep.

As he pierces the darkness, "new beings appear" to Whitman. He does not name them; Stevens does, as sleep, peace, and the mother, chosen because these are "the forms of dark desire," as they are in Whitman. But Whitman *sees* himself moving through the night; Stevens equivocally calls his forms visible, but only "to the eye that needs, / Needs out of the whole necessity of sight." What is "the whole necessity of sight" for Stevens? Later, in *The Plain Sense of Things*, it is the eye's plain version that "had to be imagined as an inevitable knowledge, / Required, as a necessity requires." How can the plain sense of things allow for transcendental or visionary forms? That question will be the burden of Stevens' last phase, to which *The Owl in the Sarcophagus*, more even than *The Auroras of Autumn*, is the prelude. Stevens says of his three mythological forms that they do not move in our space and time, but "in an element . . . / In which reality is prodigy." When, in the second canto, Stevens gives a vision of the mind of Henry Church, he portrays his friend as questing to see the forms of thought not only in their lustre as it is but also "in harmonious prodigy to be." In *Three Academic Pieces*, written just before the *Owl*, Stevens says of nature that "its prodigy is not identity but resemblance and its universe of reproduction is not an assembly line but an incessant creation" (*NA*, 73). The vision of death in the *Owl* is then an image of a world of resemblance to this one, but even this is not so much death as it is but rather *death as it will be.* And such a vision invokes Whitman at his most magnificent, in a passage of the elegy for Lincoln that also haunted Eliot in *The Waste Land:*

> Then with the knowledge of death as walking one side of me,
> And the thought of death close-walking the other side of me,
> And I in the middle as with companions, and as holding
>   the hands of companions,
> I fled forth to the hiding receiving night that talks not.

To walk *between* the knowledge of death and the thought of death is to walk in a liminal state, to be within what is problematic in the *meaning* of death, which is that it is the only event where the crossing between thought and knowledge will be beyond communication. Stevens peers over the threshold and says of the forms he sees that they "are not abortive figures, rocks, / Impenetrable symbols, motionless," where "rocks" is the crucial term, in another anticipation of *The Rock*, the poem in which that motionless, impenetrable symbol or abortive figure is most fully adumbrated. Emerson, in the 1838 Notebooks, had penetrated the figure of the rock, which for him was "a rock of diamonds," another text for myriad interpretations: "And presently the aroused intellect finds gold and gems in one of these scorned facts, then finds that the day of facts is a rock of diamonds, that a fact is an Epiphany of God."

Perceiving the apocalyptic forms of sleep, peace, and memory or the mother of the muses, Stevens makes a difficult distinction between the thought of those three, which is dark because it is desire, and the sight of them, which is a lustre. This distinction allows the tribute to Church in the poem's second canto, where Church is seen as being akin to the planter of *Notes* or to Stevens himself, another celebration of the poetry of earth:

> There came a day, there was a day—one day
> A man walked living among the forms of thought
> To see their lustre truly as it is
>
> And in harmonious prodigy to be,
> A while, conceiving his passage as into a time
> That of itself stood still, perennial,

Less time than place, less place than thought of place
And, if of substance, a likeness of the earth,
That by resemblance twanged him through and through,

Releasing an abysmal melody,
A meeting, an emerging in the light,
A dazzle of remembrance and of sight.

The triple emphasis upon a particular day marks this as
being possibly the day of Church's death, his passage into "an
element not the heaviness of time." It is true that Stevens says,
"A man walked *living* among the forms of thought," but that
"living" may be a trope conveying the strength of Church, who
as an enthusiast for philosophy had engaged deeply in the study
of death. The forms of thought, being sleep, peace, and memory the mother, move in a realm that is "thought of place," a
version of Stevens' apocalyptic "description without place."
Twanged by resemblances, even as the planter sighed to leave
the banjo's twang, Church encounters something like "the luminous melody of proper sound" with which Stevens stopped,
upon the wing, the angel dreamed by the Canon Aspirin.
"Dazzle" is the key word in the canto, presumably meaning the
quality or act of being blinded or blinding with intense light.
Stevens may be playing on the root meaning, which is "vanish," as in the stupefaction of being in a daze. We can recall
Description without Place:

There might be, too, a change immenser than
A poet's metaphors in which being would

Come true, a point in the fire of music where
Dazzle yields to a clarity and we observe,

And observing is completing and we are content,
In a world that shrinks to an immediate whole,

That we do not need to understand, complete
Without secret arrangements of it in the mind.

But "a dazzle of remembrance and of sight" remains a trope
and not a clarity, remains an emerging in purely a metaphorical

lustre. What Church sees, in canto III, is a series of character-istic Stevensian images: foldings, whiteness, robings, a moving mountain, violet, wind on water. For Stevens, foldings are part of the hieratic panoply of the divine or its substitutes, as in the "voluminous master folded in his fire" of *Notes*, or as in the "giant, on the horizon" of *A Primitive Like an Orb*, who is "vested in the serious folds of majesty." The whiteness is the familiar reduction to a First Idea, or an ever-early candor. Rob-ings, also a hieratic emblem, recall a passage in *The Greenest Continent* (OP, 52–60) from *Owl's Clover* that seems to be linger-ing in Stevens' language here:

> The heaven of Europe is empty, like a Schloss
> Abandoned because of taxes . . . It was enough:
> It made up for everything, it was all selves
> Become rude robes among white candle lights,
> Motions of air, robes moving in torrents of air,
> And through the torrents a jutting, jagged tower,
> A broken wall—and it ceased to exist.

The curious echoes of Yeats's *Leda and the Swan* betray what is, for Stevens, an uncharacteristic impatience, a flirtation with apocalyptic yearnings, provoked by despair at what seems the end of Europe. Something of this apocalyptic quality lingers in the third canto of the *Owl*, but chastened, as befits the world of sleep as brother and as father. There, the image of "many rob-ings, as moving masses are," suggests something of Whitman's Blake-like phantasmagoria in *The Sleepers*, where, however, the robings characteristically are removed:

> The sleepers are very beautiful as they lie unclothed,
> They flow hand in hand over the whole earth from east to west
>   as they lie unclothed.

The flowing is what Stevens seems to have appropriated for his even more startling phantasmagoria, as his sleeper, like a moving mountain, drifts through day and night. Visions of a moving mountain haunted Stevens and were to culminate in *The Auroras of Autumn*, with "mountains running like water, wave on wave." Rock and water and air were one entity in his imagination, whenever he tried to see ultimates. Here, in the third canto, the ultimate of sleep is seen as a giant body enfolded in a violet and vexed water, curiously like Whitman's "beautiful gigantic swimmer" of *The Sleepers,* with the large difference that Stevens' giant is beyond death, having entered and then gone through the condition of fire that transcends the identity of rock, water, and air:

> Sleep realized
> Was the whiteness that is the ultimate intellect,
> A diamond jubilance beyond the fire,
>
> That gives its power to the wild-ringed eye.

The last trope here is plainly Emerson's, with "wild" meaning "free," and the repressed allusion being to the opening of *Circles:* "The eye is the first circle; the horizon which it forms is the second." Sleep, fully real, is the ultimate ever-early candor, a first cognition of whiteness. "A diamond jubilance beyond the fire" echoes a passage in *The Witch of Atlas* that Stevens could quote from memory, on the diamond beauty of fire that lies just beyond our perceptive powers. "Power," for Stevens as for Emerson, is again *potentia,* the possibility of a more restoring sleep than ever we have known:

> Then he breathed deeply the deep atmosphere
> Of sleep, the accomplished, the fulfilling air.

Peace, in canto IV, provides a more difficult vision, in one of Stevens' most eloquent passages, fitly in praise of poetry: "Generations of the imagination piled / In the manner of its stitchings." Because "peace after death" is "vested in a foreign absolute," beyond our images, Stevens' inventive powers are severely tested. He wavers for a moment into the rhetoric of *To the One of Fictive Music* ("The inhuman brother so much like, so near"), but gets past his own pre-Raphaelite hard edgings and inchings of final form to achieve an immensely dignified representation of a more-than-human peace:

> This is that figure stationed at our end,
> Always, in brilliance, fatal, final, formed
> Out of our lives to keep us in our death,

> To watch us in the summer of Cyclops
> Underground, a king as candle by our beds
> In a robe that is our glory as he guards.

On some level, this austere passage reminds us that peace, in its root, means a fastening, or covenanting into an agreement. At our end, peace-after-death stands as watchman for the covenant our lives have made with our deaths, "to keep us," even as memory the mother cried, "Keep you, keep you," in the first canto, with "keep" taking its older meaning of "guard." "As candle by our beds," wearing the robe woven by poets' imaginations in their lives, peace takes the role of all those images of the scholar-poet's single candle that will culminate in *To an Old Philosopher in Rome*, where "the book and candle in your ambered room," near Santayana's death bed, are crucial parts of the "total grandeur of a total edifice, / Chosen by an inquisitor of structures / For himself." Peace is "the godolphin," prized as that Arabian race horse is prized, yet "estranged, estranged" because he is "inhuman." He is stationed "in the summer of Cyclops / Underground" because death is being visualized as the cave where Ulysses and his men were pent up by the Cyclops. Yet summer is Stevens' enlarged season of contentment, when credences are most intense, and so this Hades-vision is at least oxymoronic.

A less dialectical imagery dominates canto v, the vision of memory the mother, identified here with the Stevensian middle way of "discovery," the poet's path between reductionism and Transcendental or Sublime expansiveness. For once, Stevens wholly rejects trope and insists upon what Emerson termed the "great and crescive self," or the Whitmanian "losing in self / The sense of self." The mother "stood tall in self not symbol," but therefore not imaged, "an influence felt instead of seen." She is precisely a Gnosis:

> It was not her look but a knowledge that she had.
> She was a self that knew, an inner thing.
> Subtler than look's declaiming, although she moved
>
> With a sad splendor, beyond artifice,
> Impassioned by the knowledge that she had,
> There on the edges of oblivion.

O exhalation. O fling without a sleeve
And motion outward, reddened and resolved
From sight, in the silence that follows her last word—

Though this is brilliant in its precise nonimaging, it is also obscurantist, like so much of Whitman in his evasiveness. Yet the motive for the ocularism is impressively clear, since this is death the mother, or the final ambiguity of remembrance, as it fades, with life. The earthly mother gives life but no immortality, and is therefore also the mother of the dead. "A self that knew, an inner thing" has some reference to the final identity of death and the growing inner self, an identity necessarily repressed throughout most of life.

Stevens conveys a sense of release and relief as he gives us the majestic coda of canto vi, where the imagelessness of the maternal canto v can slip away, to be replaced by the marvelous image of the mind as "a child that sings itself to sleep," the mind being that of the old poet chanting the *Owl* as the elegy for his friend. We can interpret the repressed aspect of canto v by a backward glance from the child in vi, perhaps by remembering Keats's similar imagistic difficulties when he confronted the maternal countenance of his Moneta. To look so hard upon the mother is to see one's own death, and for one's own death there can be no wholly appropriate image, "reddened and resolved / From sight." But Stevens is following his own self-admonition, from *Three Academic Pieces,* written just before the *Owl:*

What a ghastly situation it would be if the world of the dead was actually different from the world of the living and, if as life ends, instead of passing to a former Victorian sphere, we passed into a land in which none of our problems had been solved, after all, and nothing resembled anything we have ever known and nothing resembled anything else in shape, in color, in sound, in look or otherwise. To say farewell to our generation and to look forward to a continuation in a Jerusalem of pure surrealism would account for the taste for oblivion. [*NA,* 76–77]

"A former Victorian sphere" is an evident irony, yet it is also the home in which Stevens grew up. Whatever the world of the dead is, in the *Owl* it is closer to "a Jerusalem of pure surrealism" than to "a former Victorian sphere." Stevens' taste for oblivion seems gratified by the stance he assigns to the mother: "There on the edges of oblivion." The recoil from oblivion, in the final canto, is wholly free from irony despite the "monsters of elegy" reservation:

> This is the mythology of modern death
> And these, in their mufflings, monsters of elegy,
> Of their own marvel made, of pity made,
>
> Compounded and compounded, life by life,
> These are death's own supremest images,
> The pure perfections of parental space,
>
> The children of a desire that is the will,
> Even of death, the beings of the mind
> In the light-bound space of the mind, the floreate flare . . .
>
> It is a child that sings itself to sleep,
> The mind, among the creatures that it makes,
> The people, those by which it lives and dies.

What are "their mufflings"? "Muffling," for Stevens, is elsewhere an eclipsing or a misting, concealments carried out here by foldings, robings, adornings, stitchings. These images are all precisely anti-apocalyptic; they are coverings rather than takings off of the lid. Stevens ascribes them not to his own making but to what is "compounded and compounded, life by life." Still, no reader who reflects will easily believe that "these are death's *own* supremest images," when clearly such images are regressively pre-Raphaelite, returning us to Stevens' own earliest poetry. Rather than being "pure perfections of parental space," they come in some instances out of the same labyrinthine ambivalences toward the mother that Whitman so powerfully evidenced. When Stevens says of these images that they are "the children of a desire that is the will, / *Even of death*," he associates them with his own entropic drive beyond the pleasure principle, his own ambivalent will to die. It is "the mind," occurring three times in the last five lines, that dominates those lines. Canto VI is explicitly "about" the images in a poet's mind (much as Yeats's *Byzantium* is), when that mind is at its most creative, in "the floreate flare." The poem ends with the Transcendental image proper in Stevens, the child singing itself to death. We can juxtapose several Stevensian passages with the poem's final tercet:

> The form on the pillow humming while one sleeps,
> The aureole above the humming house . . .
>
> It can never be satisfied, the mind, never.
> > —*The Well Dressed Man with a Beard*

> It is a child that sings itself to sleep,
> The mind, among the creatures that it makes,
> The people, those by which it lives and dies.
> > —*The Owl in the Sarcophagus*

> The two worlds are asleep, are sleeping, now.
> A dumb sense possesses them in a kind of solemnity.
>
> The self and the earth—your thoughts, your feelings,
> Your beliefs and disbeliefs, your whole peculiar plot;
>
> The redness of your reddish chestnut trees,
> The river motion, the drowsy motion of the river R.
> > —*An Old Man Asleep*

> Among the old men that you know,
> There is one, unnamed, that broods
> On all the rest, in heavy thought.
>
> They are nothing, except in the universe
> Of that single mind. He regards them
> Outwardly and knows them inwardly,
> The sole emperor of what they are,
> Distant, yet close enough to wake
> The chords above your bed to-night.
> > —*A Child Asleep in Its Own Life*

The mind cannot be satisfied because its activity is ceaseless, because the mind never sleeps until death. But, in the season of

291

elegy, the mind opposes its singing, its making of fictions, to the ceaseless humming that will not let it be. We live and die by making or reimagining people, in the family romance and in the displacements of romance by friends and lovers. But these makings are also of self and of earth, as in *An Old Man Asleep*, and more startlingly the final making is of one's own mind in old age, the mind of the seventy-five-year-old Stevens in *A Child Asleep in Its Own Life*.

Where have we left the meanings of the *Owl?* So Sublime are the *Owl*'s repressions that the poem, unlike the *Auroras*, is not wholly available to even the most prolonged and loving of readings. The clue, I think, is the image of the mother, a clue that can be investigated by a juxtaposition of the Canon's sister in her performance as a mother of everyday and the mother of the dead in the *Owl*. Stevens says of memory the mother that "she spoke with backward gestures of her hand. / She held men closely with discovery," and the Canon says of his sister, "She held / Them closelier to her by rejecting dreams. / . . . And what she felt fought off the barest phrase." Both mothers are beyond language, and so beyond poetry, and both hold their children closer to them by a discovery that rejects fantasia. Both are in the mold of Keats's Moneta, and like her touch a limit of the muse, after which memory turns against poetry, but such turning can only be dialectical, since poetic thinking is always a mode of memory. It is at this impasse that the *Owl*, like *The Fall of Hyperion*, abruptly touches its *aporia* and becomes uninterpretable. But Stevens, like Keats, had taken meaning further than ever he had before in reaching such a limit, and *The Owl in the Sarcophagus* earns all of those difficulties that do render it the least accessible of Stevens' major poems.

The elegiac intensities of the *Owl* are developed into a greater sublimity in the *Auroras*, as we have seen. Perhaps the resolution of the *Auroras* helped make possible *A Primitive Like an Orb*, the strong doctrinal poem that was the first in an affirmative sequence that continued through 1948 and that prepared Stevens for his last major achievement in *An Ordinary Evening in New Haven* (1949), which I shall demonstrate to be one of the largest indulgences of his imagination's Nietzschean passion for yes. *A Primitive Like an Orb* is Stevens' reduced or abstracted version of a poem like Whitman's *By Blue Ontario's Shore*, and the best case to be made against *A Primitive* is that Stevens had already written it, only better, five years before, in *Chocorua to Its Neighbor*. There is nothing of the hushed splendor or poignant eloquence of *Chocorua* in *A Primitive*, which is rather too much like the weaker Whitman in its constant worrying of doctrine about the nature of the poem.

A Primitive seeks to be at one with "the essential poem at the centre of things," on the Emersonian principle that poetry and *materia poetica* are the same thing. But this "difficult apperception" is haunted, from the start, by very Emersonian, very American doubts about poetry: "this gorging good, / Fetched by such slick-eyed nymphs." Even as Emerson distrusted all poetry *already written*, be it Shakespeare's or Homer's, so Stevens celebrates an instant's apprehension (if that) over all written texts:

> It is the huge, high harmony that sounds
> A little and a little, suddenly,
> By means of a separate sense. It is and it
> Is not and, therefore, is. In the instant of speech,
> The breadth of an accelerando moves,
> Captives the being, widens—and was there.

This approximates the mother in the *Owl* who "in the syllable between life / And death cries quickly, in a flash of voice." If a poem is reduced to "a flash of voice" or "instant of speech," it yet remains a trope of *pathos*, since any image of voice ultimately relies upon a logocentric vision of the universe. Hence Stevens' extraordinary third stanza, where a visionary space grows wide within the single breath of the poetic word:

> What milk there is in such captivity,
> What wheaten bread and oaten cake and kind,
> Green guests and table in the woods and songs
> At heart, within an instant's motion, within
> A space grown wide, the inevitable blue
> Of secluded thunder, an illusion, as it was,

> Oh as, always too heavy for the sense
> To seize, the obscurest as, the distant was . . .

This stanza returns, beautifully, to *It Must Give Pleasure*, IX, "The way wine comes at a table in a wood," but suggests even more pungently the precarious and moving satisfactions of *Credences of Summer*. Something of that qualified yet celebratory fervor continues throughout stanzas IV–VII, as "the world" and "the central poem" merge into an identity. From this arises, for Stevens, the inevitable image, a new first idea of the sun on the horizon, a primitive like an orb of the poem's title, "primitive" throughout Stevens' poetry being used in its etymological sense of "first." The "orb" is the Miltonic–Emersonian sphere that is both sun and eye, directly derived by Stevens from Whitman's poetry and associated with Whitman himself as the autumnal sun of the American evening-land. This image appears first in the poem as "a giant, on the horizon, glistening," the final line of stanza VIII. Imposing power, as a trope or form of power, the giant culminates the Transcendental image of "parental magnitude" in Stevens' poetry:

> Here, then, is an abstraction given head,
> A giant on the horizon, given arms,
> A massive body and long legs, stretched out,
> A definition with an illustration, not
> Too exactly labelled, a large among the smalls
> Of it, a close, parental magnitude,
> At the centre on the horizon, concentrum, grave
> And prodigious person, patron of origins.

"Large" and "origins" are the decisive terms, for this stanza is an epitome of the American version of Romantic origins. In stanza IV, Stevens had substituted "believer" for "lunatic" in a Shakespearean triad with "lover" and "poet." Lover, believer, and poet—the Transcendentalist Orphic trinity—return with a triumphant snap of "That's it" as Stevens proclaims his sense of having gotten·it right in his poem's final stanza:

> That's it. The lover writes, the believer hears,
> The poet mumbles and the painter sees,
> Each one, his fated eccentricity,

As a part, but part, but tenacious particle,
Of the skeleton of the ether, the total
Of letters, prophecies, perceptions, clods
Of color, the giant of nothingness, each one
And the giant ever changing, living in change.

"Eccentricity," as elsewhere in Stevens, plays upon the circularity of Emersonian Spheral Man and is employed here to mean a deviation from the form of the orb, recapitulating the American insight of *Like Decorations*, III:

It was when the trees were leafless first in November
And their blackness became apparent, that one first
Knew the eccentric to be the base of design.

The passage in *Like Decorations* had been preceded by the gorgeously Whitmanian line "Shout for me, loudly and loudly, joyful sun, when you rise." Here, the joyful sun has been called "a source of trumpeting seraphs in the eye, / A source of pleasant outbursts on the ear." Seeing himself as another tenacious particle or minute particular of the colossal sun, Stevens returns to the final lines of *Esthétique du Mal*, affirming both change and unity in change. The Whole of *Harmonium* joins in, "the total / Of letters, prophecies, perceptions, clods / Of color." The affirmation, Emersonian and Nietzschean, is finally of the gaiety of language, for it is poetic language itself that is ultimately "the giant of nothingness," and the First Idea of the sun or Whitmanian giant is not nature but language, in the last vision:

And the giant ever changing, living in change.

The giant returns as the *Large Red Man Reading*, a poignant lyric apologia also written in 1948. As an American poet's defense, this finds its ultimate ancestor in Emerson's strongest poem, *Bacchus*, which ends with the poet's Dionysiac prayer:

Refresh the faded tints,
Recut the aged prints,
And write my old adventures with the pen
Which on the first day drew,
Upon the tablets blue,
The dancing Pleiads and eternal men.

This too is an abstraction or reduction to a First Idea, here of the universe. "The tablets blue" in *Large Red Man Reading* appear as "the great blue tabulae" being read to the poor ghosts who have returned "from the wilderness of stars" to hear again the poetry of earth. Before the poem ends the tabulae have turned a Hoonian purple, as Stevens passes beyond irony to a pure celebration of his own poetry.

This Keatsian insistence that the poetry of earth is never dead is severely qualified in *World without Peculiarity*, a great misprision of the Keats of *The Fall of Hyperion* and the Whitman of *A Song of the Rolling Earth*. "Thou art a dreaming thing, / A fever of thyself" is the condemnation spoken to Keats by Moneta, and she adds, "think of the Earth," as though the earth would suffice to heal the fever of self. In much the same spirit, Whitman declaims, "To her children the words of the eloquent dumb great mother never fail, / The true words do not fail." Against which, Stevens speaks a palinode:

> The day is great and strong—
> But his father was strong, that lies now
> In the poverty of dirt.
>
> Nothing could be more hushed than the way
> The moon moves toward the night.
> But what his mother was returns and cries on his breast.
>
> The red ripeness of round leaves is thick
> With the spices of red summer.
> But she that he loved turns cold at his light touch.
>
> What good is it that the earth is justified,
> That it is complete, that it is an end,
> That in itself it is enough?

To ask such a question is to give us the entropic end of *Harmonium* rather than its promised Whole. It must change, and the final change, "the poverty of dirt," is death viewed as meaningless repetition. From this vision, *World without Peculiarity* grants us no release:

It is the earth that is humanity . . .
He is the inhuman son and she,
She is the fateful mother, whom he does not know.

She is the day, the walk of the moon
Among the breathless spices and, sometimes,
He, too, is human and difference disappears

And the poverty of dirt, the thing upon his breast,
The hating woman, the meaningless place,
Become a single being, sure and true.

Yet this illusion of closure does give pleasure, to Stevens and to ourselves. Why? "A single being, sure and true" is hardly a persuasive trope, for we go on wondering how it can subsume all those particulars of death, in this world without particularity, that is, without any defining characteristics. The clue is the disappearance of "difference," here a synonym for "peculiarity." The cost of poetic comfort is exposed as a world of homogeneity, in a critique not only of Keats and of Whitman but of the residue of heroic naturalism in Stevens himself.

This critique is developed in the even stronger lyric with the stark Freudian title *Imago.* The idealized image of a parent here begins as the postwar Europe of 1948 and then is shown as a characteristic Stevensian "It is nothing" or "a gorgeous fortitude." This is the "something" that returns in February's winter world:

Making this heavy rock a place,
Which is not of our lives composed . . .
Lightly and lightly, O my land,
Move lightly through the air again.

Our lives are a poverty of dirt, but a lightness of the anterior image returns from out the winter air. Is Stevens himself persuaded? The "something" that returns is an idealization, and so the italicized final lines belong to the world of desire and are the poet's hopeless prayer or his wish to be deceived again.

The same self-deception, or the power of the mind over the universe of death and sense, is the impressive theme of the most surprising shorter poem in the *Auroras* volume, the crucial dialogue of *Saint John and the Back-Ache*. The Back-Ache is Stevens' own back-ache, at nearly seventy, and so can stand for all human sense of anteriority, for all that European "history" that Emerson so firmly had dismissed. Saint John is the Transcendental element in Stevens himself, the apocalyptic impulse that he has dismissed for so long but that will begin to break in upon his reveries in *An Ordinary Evening in New Haven* and *The Rock* and then will dominate the poems composed from 1952 through 1955.

Saint John and the Back-Ache turns upon the opposition between "force" or the mind's violence-from-within, and "presence" or nature's violence-from-without. Speaking as if to his priest, the Back-Ache states his frightened awe of the mind:

> The mind is the terriblest force in the world, father,
> Because, in chief, it, only can defend
> Against itself. At its mercy, we depend
>   Upon it.

As the Back-Ache speaks for the reductionist in Stevens, we can name the mind's force as its ceaseless quest for a First Idea. Though the Back-Ache knows only the mind's defenses against the mind, Saint John proposes the "deeper" defense that Wordsworth had miscalled "Nature."

>   The world is presence and not force.
> Presence is not mind.

For the poor Back-Ache, whose essence is anteriority, or the fall of the human into history, "Presence is *Kinder-Scenen*," scenes of childhood that presumably no longer mitigate the mind's force. The apocalyptic reply, twenty-five of the most difficult lines in Stevens, gives us a triumph of the American Sublime, a fierce celebration of the metaphysical illusion of presence. The world, as presence, "fills the being before the mind can think," which makes every image subsequently inadequate to so full a presence, even the image of the beloved:

> Presence is not the woman, come upon,
> Not yet accustomed, yet, at sight, humane

To most incredible depths. I speak below
The tension of the lyre.

Below the lyre's tension means that the speech is not in poetic
images but in an implicit argument transcending any possible
poem. Such speech, denying its own status as poetry, is again a
speech of the self that must sustain itself upon speech, upon
particulars or illustrations that truly surpass the mind's defense
against its own force or violence:

> They help us face the dumbfoundering abyss
> Between us and the object, external cause,
> The little ignorance that is everything,
> The possible nest in the invisible tree,
> Which in a composite season, now unknown,
> Denied, dismissed, may hold a serpent, loud
> In our captious hymns, erect and sinuous,
> Whose venom and whose wisdom will be one.

The imagery, hardly below the tension of the lyre, is derived
from the opening canto of *The Auroras of Autumn.* There, the
"possible nest" is posited at a pole that the auroras may attain,
finally, in the midmost midnight, "another nest," not the "this
is" world of the beach tinted by the autumnal lights. In the
"composite season" prevailing in Eden, the redeemed serpent
will give us venom and wisdom at once, not the poison of disbelief given us in canto I of *The Auroras of Autumn.* Properly
apocalyptic, Saint John has a vision of retiring the stoic and
Eastern turtle that bears up our world:

> Then the stale turtle will grow limp from age,
> We shall be heavy with the knowledge of that day.

The heaviness is a ripeness, and it fits Stevens' distrust of his
own dreams of fulfillment that he allows his Back-Ache the last
word, which is necessarily "pain":

> It may be, may be. It is possible.
> Presence lies far too deep, for me to know
> Its irrational reaction, as from pain.

This is the language of Stevens himself in *Notes toward a
Supreme Fiction:* "It is possible, possible, possible" and "the irra-

tional distortion" that is shown to be "the fiction that results from feeling." For Wordsworth, at the close of the *Intimations of Immortality* ode, visible nature, be it the meanest flower that *blows*, showing life, provoked thoughts that often lie too deep for tears. The Back-Ache echoes Wordsworth, but with a distortion that makes of pain the only fiction that results from feeling. What *Saint John and the Back-Ache* shows is a strain in the old Stevens that is closer to affective self-contradiction than to dialectical interplay. Both the apocalyptic seer and the wary pain-of-the-past speak for Stevens, and so large a split could not be healed, which doubtless was all the better for the final phase of his poetry.

This strain is present again in *Puella Parvula*, which seems to me the strongest short lyric in *The Auroras of Autumn* volume, surpassing even *Large Red Man Reading* (Stevens' own favorite). As Marie Borroff has shown, *Puella Parvula* is one of the poems in which Stevens reviews his entire enterprise, with particular reference to his two major poems before *An Ordinary Evening* (to which *Puella Parvula* was an immediate prelude). The noisy elephant and lion of *Notes*, which I think were at the origin of that poem, return in *Puella Parvula*, and even more crucially there is a renewal of two great images of *The Auroras*, the flame of the lights and the affirming master seated by the fire. But there is also a greater return than any of Stevens' own images. Shelley's fiction of the leaves and his trumpet of a prophecy make a Sublime reappearance, and in colors as much those of the *Ode to the West Wind* as of Stevens himself.

The strain of *Puella Parvula* is indeed the native or Whitmanian strain, as the self divides into a paternal "dauntless master" and the little girl of the title, equivalent respectively to Whitman's "myself" and his "real me" or "me myself." This makes the master a poetic crossing or *logos* of meaning and the little girl a trope of *pathos;* but though Stevens seems to identify with the master the little girl is revealed to be a reborn version of the muse or interior paramour, and we will see the ambivalent address to her as constituting the truly poignant moment in the poem.

The lyric opens with the hyperbolic unweaving of summer's

fictive garment, dissolved by the Shelleyan wind of creation and destruction:

> Every thread of summer is at last unwoven.
> By one caterpillar is great Africa devoured
> And Gibraltar is dissolved like spit in the wind.
>
> But over the wind, over the legends of its roaring,
> The elephant on the roof and its elephantine blaring,
> The bloody lion in the yard at night or ready to spring
>
> From the clouds in the midst of trembling trees
> Making a great gnashing, over the water wallows
> Of a vacant sea declaiming with wide throat,
>
> Over all these the mighty imagination triumphs
> Like a trumpet.

The mighty imagination or repressive Sublime is Stevens' own reading/misreading of the Shelleyan Sublime, while the "all these" over which it triumphs is a giant, composite pathetic fallacy or series of impositions of an animal consciousness upon the reality of nature. Of these, the most important for Stevens is the last, for it is Whitman's trope of the bereft mother, fiercely crying out for her castaway, the poet. "Of a vacant sea declaiming with wide throat" Stevens has sung many rhapsodies, but such a sea always has triumphed over his imagination. Divesting the sea of the muse, he now asks us to believe that she is thoroughly internalized within the poet himself:

> Over all these the mighty imagination triumphs
> Like a trumpet and says, in this season of memory,
> When the leaves fall like things mournful of the past,
>
> Keep quiet in the heart, O wild bitch. O mind
> Gone wild, be what he tells you to be: *Puella.*
> Write *pax* across the window pane. And then
>
> Be still. The *summarium in excelsis* begins . . .
> Flame, sound, fury composed . . . Hear what he says,
> The dauntless master, as he starts the human tale.

Can we give credence to this triumph over the muse, over the ocean, and over the now-mastered auroras: "Flame, sound, fury composed"? The bare displacement of a pious authority in *pax* and in the *summarium in excelsis* implies a considerable poetic anxiety, as does the characteristic third-person presentation of the master. "Dauntless" responds to the "And he feels afraid" of *The Auroras*, VI, yet can we forget that this master is identical with "the scholar of one candle"? The most persuasive answer the poem gives to these doubts is in the final trope: "as he starts the human tale," where "starts" takes an even more acute emphasis than "human" does.

The epilogue to *The Auroras of Autumn* is best assigned to the famous *Angel Surrounded by Paysans*, a poem perhaps better in the context of its volume than in isolation. Stevens was sensitive to the weak misreading the poem seemed to encourage, in isolation, as two different letters remark:

The question of how to represent the angel of reality is not an easy question. I suppose that what I had in mind when I said that he had no wear of ore was that he had no crown or other symbol. I was definitely trying to think of an earthly figure, not a heavenly figure. The point of the poem is that there must be in the world about us things that solace us quite as fully as any heavenly visitation could. [*L*, 661]

The angel is the angel of reality. This is clear only if the reader is of the idea that we live in a world of the imagination, in which reality and contact with it are the great blessings. For nine readers out of ten, the necessary angel will appear to be the angel of the imagination and for nine days out of ten that is true, although it is the tenth day that counts. [*L*, 753]

Yet the poem's text is rather more equivocal than these firmly naturalistic comments would allow. The reader is left asking what the countrymen open the poem by asking:

> There is
> A welcome at the door to which no one comes?

We can grant Stevens that his angel is not Elijah but merely a part of that visible that his creator labored always to make a little harder to see. Yet an angel of earth termed "necessary," whose presence clears the earth of "its stiff and stubborn, man-locked set," is clearly neither just human nor natural, and yet it is not enough to say that he is purely fictive, like the angel dreamed by the Canon Aspirin. Such a fictive being is no less human than the bird of hammered gold was still natural in Yeats's *Sailing to Byzantium,* as Sturge Moore told Yeats. There remains only the daemonic or repressed possibility, prophesied by Whitman in a similar vision in his earliest extant notebook, dated 1847:

> I am the poet of reality
> I say the earth is not an echo
> Nor man an apparition;
> But that all the things seen are real,
> The witness and albic dawn of things equally real
> I have split the earth and the hard coal and rocks and the solid
>   bed of the sea
> And went down to reconnoitre there a long time,
> And bring back a report,
> And I understand that those are positive and dense, every one
> And that what they seem to the child they are
> [And the world is no joke,
> Nor any part of it a sham]

Of the two texts, Whitman's is stronger, since to speak thus is to persuade that the speaker is a necessary poet of reality, whereas Stevens' concluding question is more open and less rhetorical than his necessary angel could wish us to believe:

> Am I not,
> Myself, only half of a figure of a sort,
>
> A figure half seen, or seen for a moment, a man
> Of the mind, an apparition apparelled in
>
> Apparels of such lightest look that a turn
> Of my shoulder and quickly, too quickly, I am gone?

This is so qualified that it becomes the wrong sort of strain for the reader, imparting an anxiety unable to achieve an identifiable form. Stevens as dauntless or more severe master had to take the risk of sometimes writing such poems, and unfortunately this one is sentimentally evasive enough to have become fairly popular. But his manner as extemporizer, though it resulted in so weak a poem as late as 1949, gave him in that same year *An Ordinary Evening in New Haven*, a severe poem that compensates by raising "the intricate evasions of as" to a true triumph for the imagination.

12 *An Ordinary Evening*
in New Haven

The poet who writes *An Ordinary Evening in New Haven* is about to turn seventy, but as a poet he is never less desiccated or leafless. Nothing else by Stevens is more exuberant or extravagant than this second longest and most indirect of all his poems. Yet even the indirection is Whitmanian and exhibits a passion for yes that could not be broken.

Stevens sanctioned the shorter, eleven-section original version of *An Ordinary Evening* by including it in his carefully chosen British *Selected Poems*. I will take as text here the definitive, thirty-one-section poem, which scrambles the continuity of the final three sections with poetically happy results, and I will introduce comparisons with the original sequence when I approach the poem's conclusion. But I will note which sections were part of the original as I go, for structural reasons which should become apparent.

I am going to assert more for *An Ordinary Evening* than criticism as yet allows it, and so I will begin by giving something of the contrary case. By this, I do not intend the merely ignorant hostility of many negative critics of the poem, but rather its very best expositor, Helen Vendler, for whom the poem is strong only where she judges it to be a portrayal of desiccation, of an old man's most deliberately minimal visions. The critic, though I judge her to be mistaken here, is formidably eloquent:

In this, the harshest of all his experiments, Stevens deprives his poetry of all that the flesh, the sun, the earth, and the moon can offer, and, himself a skeleton, examines the bare possibilities of a skeletal life. . . . It is, humanly speaking, the saddest of all Stevens' poems. One wants it to have succeeded totally, to have proved that Stevens could find, in life's most minimal offering, something which would suffice. . . . *An Ordinary Evening* is, in short, almost unremittingly minimal, and over and over again threatens to die of its own starvation.

I myself, as I read *An Ordinary Evening*, encounter a very different poem from the one just described. There is much harshness, yes, but a great deal also that is rather more genial than is usual in Stevens. There is some deprivation, and yet the flesh, the sun, the earth, and the moon are all there, and so are a surprising vigor and joy. The poem I read is threatened not by its own starvation but by its own copiousness, its abundance of invention that varies the one theme, which is the problematic Stevensian image that he unhelpfully always called "reality." Critics can diverge absolutely on this poem because the text is almost impossible to read, that is, the text keeps seeking "reality" while continually putting into question its own apotheosis of "reality." Stevens said of the poem: "Here my interest is to try to get as close to the ordinary, the commonplace and the ugly as it is possible for a poet to get. It is not a question of grim reality but of plain reality" (*L*, 636). We can observe that this intention is wholly Whitmanian, and on that basis we might doubt Vendler's judgment that the celebrated title is polemic. "Ordinary" here seems to mean "true" or at least "not false," but true in the root sense of "ordinary," *ar* or "fitted together." New Haven is simply any city that is not home, a city that unsettles the self just enough so that it is startled into meditation, but close enough to home so that the meditation keeps contact always with the commonplace.

Kermode usefully points to the prose first section of *Three Academic Pieces* for a sentence that illuminates Stevens' intentions: "What our eyes behold may well be the text of life but one's meditations on the text and the disclosures of these meditations are no less a part of the structure of reality" (*NA*, 76). But that leaves us with the word "reality" in Stevens, a word I wish Stevens had renounced, since it takes away more meaning than it tends to give. He was addicted to it in prose; he used some form of it well over a hundred times in his poetry, and it appears in thirteen different sections of *An Ordinary Evening*. The best attempt to reduce it to order is made by Frank Doggett in his useful book, *Stevens' Poetry of Thought*:

Reality, in Stevens' use of the word, may be the world supposed to be antecedent in itself or the world created in the specific occurrence of thought, including the thinker himself and his mind forming the thought. Often the term offers the assumption that if the self is the central point of a circle of infinite radius, then reality is the not-self, including all except the abstract subjective center. Sometimes *reality* is used in the context of the nominalist position—then the word denotes that which is actual and stands as a phenomenal identity, the existent as opposed to the merely fancied. Stevens usually means by *reality* an undetermined base on which a mind constructs its personal sense of the world. Occasionally he will use the word *real* as a term of approval, as a substitute for the word *true*, and, therefore, no more than an expression of confidence.

All of these meanings of "reality" occur in *An Ordinary Evening*. The commonest is the Emersonian one in which reality is the not-self, or as Emerson said, Nature or the Not-Me, including one's own body, other selves, the external world, and the anteriority of art. That leaves only one's own mind or imagination to set against a reality that comprehends all otherness, in a dialectical struggle without a victory.

An Ordinary Evening begins, "The eye's plain version is a thing apart" and ends with the premise that reality, rather than being a solid, "may be a shade that traverses / A dust, a force that traverses a shade." The eye's plain version *is* the First Idea as an imagined thing, abstracted, "a thing apart," and like reality this plain version is force, shade, dust, and so a palpable crossing into an impalpable. "Crossing" is of the essence, because "traverses" means "crosses." Force or a trope of Power crosses shade or the residuum of the Freedom of meaning, and shade crosses dust or a trope of Fate. Reality or the eye's plain version thus turns out to be only a crossing between turnings, a continual troping in, through, and with the eye. Haunting *An Ordinary Evening*, as Vendler demonstrates, are three ancestral versions of the eye: Keats's bright star, Milton's universal blank, and Emerson's transparent eyeball. All these return us ultimately to the *res* or thing that is close to the root of reality, that root being *rei,* meaning "possession." "Plain" for Stevens also goes to the root, to flat, clear vision of what is spread out before us, as in the 1952 poem *The Plain Sense of Things:*

> After the leaves have fallen, we return
> To a plain sense of things. It is as if
> We had come to an end of the imagination,
> Inanimate in an inert savoir.
>
> It is difficult even to choose the adjective
> For this blank cold, this sadness without cause.
> The great structure has become a minor house.
> No turban walks across the lessened floors.
>
> The greenhouse never so badly needed paint.
> The chimney is fifty years old and slants to one side.
> A fantastic effort has failed, a repetition
> In a repetitiousness of men and flies.
>
> Yet the absence of the imagination had
> Itself to be imagined. The great pond,
> The plain sense of it, without reflection, leaves,
> Mud, water like dirty glass, expressing silence
>
> Of a sort, silence of a rat come out to see,
> The great pond and its waste of the lilies, all this
> Had to be imagined as an inevitable knowledge,
> Required, as a necessity requires.

A total leaflessness returns us to a plain sense of things, yet at first this plainness is not ordinary. That is, it does not help fit things together. The "blank cold" seems to defy imagination, and yet is shown to be itself an imagining, though not yet a reimagining. That "a fantastic effort has failed" hardly can be an indictment of nature, but refers back to *Blue Guitar,* xi, where repetition is a nightmare: "The fields entrap the children, brick / Is a weed and all the flies are caught."

The difference is in the vision of Ananke, if not quite of a Beautiful Necessity, since Stevens considers his reduction to a

First Idea as an inevitable knowledge: "Yet the absence of the imagination had / Itself to be imagined." What *The Plain Sense of Things* omits is a reimagining; for Stevens in his early seventies, to live with the First Idea alone was no longer wholly dehumanizing.

An Ordinary Evening opens with a five-canto meditation upon just such a plain sense of things, culminating in canto v with an Emersonian vision of the fall of the self. Cantos II through v are all organized as commentaries upon canto I, which suggests the curious, genetic principle of structure in the longer, thirty-one-canto version of *An Ordinary Evening*. All of the twenty cantos added to the later version are in support of, or in apposition to, the eleven cantos of the shorter version. Since the shorter version itself followed the characteristic image patterns of the post-Wordsworthian crisis-poem, the two can be mapped together, with some revealing emphasis. Here are the poem's divisions, in the longer version, with the first canto in each group occupying also its position in the original sequence, except at the end:

1	I–V
2	VI–VIII
3	IX–X
4	XI
5	XII–XV
6	XVI–XXI
7	XXII–XXVII
8	XXVIII
9	XXX
10	XXXI
11	XXIX

In the original eleven-canto poem, cantos v–vII are a unit, and vII–xI are another. Indeed, the same division prevails in the longer version, which thus falls into the familiar patterns of the post-Romantic crisis-poem:

Clinamen	I–V
Tessera	VI–VIII
Kenosis	IX–X

Daemonization XI
Askesis XII–XXVII
Apophrades XXVIII–XXXI

It will be observed that, in the poem's amplification, its movement of metaphoric sublimation, the *askesis* of the original cantos V–VII, was elaborated into cantos XII–XXVII; or sixteen out of thirty-one cantos, more than half the poem. This accounts for that curious impression of "total leaflessness," as Stevens endlessly elaborates, usually by apposition, a brilliant series of images that substitute for his poem's central trope, "the eye's plain version" that begins it, in a swerve initially away from Emerson. The epigraph to *An Ordinary Evening* might well have been from the first paragraph of Emerson's *Circles*, an essay that could have been called *Freedom* or *Wildness:*

The eye is the first circle; the horizon which it forms is the second; and throughout nature this primary figure is repeated without end. . . . Our life is an apprenticeship to the truth that around every circle another can be drawn; that there is no end in nature, but every end is a beginning; that there is always another dawn risen on mid-noon, and under every deep a lower deep opens.

Emerson genially undoes, in that closing trope, the Miltonic, tragic moral of Satan's self-realization on Mt. Niphates. An American Satan merely discovers, "There are no fixtures in nature. The universe is fluid and volatile." Emerson's nature is, as we will see, Stevens' "reality," and the fitting together on an ordinary evening in an ordinary city of the different degrees of reality will expose a volatile interplay of ocular circles. So, at the start, the thing apart or abstracted is again the First Idea as an imagined thing, the perceptual language of experience. "Experience" is as central and as precise a term here as it is in Emerson. The root of "experience," *per*, means "risk," and Stevens like Emerson had used "experience" as a mode opposed to the higher activity of perception. *Poem Written at Morning*, in *Parts of a World*, insists, "The truth must be / That you do not see, you experience, you feel," and *Description without Place* had set description as a revelation by seeing against "the experience of sun / And moon." The late poem *Recitation after Dinner* (*OP*, 86–88) was to venture a final definition of experience:

> Is it experience, say, the final form
> To which all other forms, at last, return,
> The frame of a repeated effect, is it that?

An Ordinary Evening labors to bring experience and seeing together, but inevitably they keep parting, and Stevens will opt for the priority and necessity of seeing even what you cannot hope to feel, whether ever or ever again. But he knows his own preferences from the start, and these are the "an and yet, and yet, and yet" that parodistically start off his poem, genially mocking his own incessant self-qualifications. Where "experience" risks the beginnings of thought as an activity of testing, "description" attempts an image-thinking that cannot be bounded by the otherness of "reality." Freud had remarked that it was an error to apply the standards of "reality" to repressed psychical structures, and we can note that everything Stevens sees in *An Ordinary Evening* inhabits the same universe as such structures. This means that "the never-ending meditation" is not "experience" but rather the process of Stevens' writing, which asks the question that reduces to the First Idea and its thinker, the giant; the question being how to begin perceiving the inconceivable idea of the sun. The second giant that kills the first is once again the reimagining of any single First Idea, and the similitude suggested by that idea invokes a familiar compound ghost in Stevens' poetry:

> Much like a new resemblance of the sun,
> Down-pouring, up-springing and inevitable,
> A larger poem for a larger audience,
>
> As if the crude collops came together as one,
> A mythological form, a festival sphere,
> A great bosom, beard and being, alive with age.

It was Whitman's ambitious dream, in particular, to write "a larger poem for a larger audience," and the "festival sphere" or eye as first circle is Whitman-as-Jehovah, the paternal, affirming, farewell-saying figure throughout Stevens. Yet this is not Whitman or any man, because the collops or crude rolls of flesh are being fitted together as myth, and Stevens' own ambivalence is conveyed by the adjective "festival," though the Transcendental image of spheral man or human globe is scarcely qualified by Stevensian anxiety. Nor are anxieties emphasized in the cantos of commentary that follow the originary text of this canto. In canto II, Stevens internalizes New Haven as a visionary city, impalpable as we are impalpable, because we live in the mind. New Haven too is half sun, half mind, as much poem or trope as it is anything else, if only imagined but imagined well. So dialectical is this canto that the reader can judge no longer whether New Haven is an image of total presence or of total absence, and a curiously complex irony is developed as Stevens exploits a synesthesia of the spirit: "impalpable town," "impalpable bells," "transparencies of sound," "transparent dwellings," "impalpable habitations," "seem to move," "obscure," "uncertain," "indefinite, confused illuminations and sonorities," "cannot tell apart." Presumably, these all are part of "the hum of thoughts evaded in the mind," part of a dilemma that is "so much ourselves." The dilemma is neither philosophic nor psychological, though it can be mistaken for both. Most simply, it is a need for poetry that cannot be satisfied by poetry, whether written or to-be-written. This is Stevensian "poverty" or "misery," too rich in desire to be gratified by fulfillment, too imaginative in need to be redressed by imagination. No attitude toward poetry could be more American or more Emersonian, more hopeful or more frustrating. "The misery of man is to be balked of the sight of essence and stuffed with conjectures," said Emerson cheerfully, as he proceeded to deplore "the coldness and poverty of our view of heaven," while dialectically humming, "Dependence is the only poverty." Stevens put his earlier version of this best in *Poetry Is a Destructive Force:* "That's what misery is, / Nothing to have at heart. / It is to have or nothing." His definitive meditation upon "misery" and "poverty" is *In a Bad Time*, written the year after *The Auroras of Autumn*, and a year before *An Ordinary Eve-*

ning, and constituting a powerful commentary upon both major long poems:

> How mad would he have to be to say, "He beheld
> An order and thereafter he belonged
> To it"? He beheld the order of the northern sky.
>
> But the beggar gazes on calamity
> And thereafter he belongs to it, to bread
> Hard found, and water tasting of misery.
>
> For him cold's glacial beauty is his fate.
> Without understanding, he belongs to it
> And the night, and midnight, and after, where it is.
>
> What has he? What he has he has. But what?
> It is not a question of captious repartee.
> What has he that becomes his heart's strong core?
>
> He has his poverty and nothing more.
> His poverty becomes his heart's strong core—
> A forgetfulness of summer at the pole.
>
> Sordid Melpomene, why strut bare boards,
> Without scenery or lights in the theatre's bricks,
> Dressed high in heliotrope's inconstant hue,
>
> The muse of misery? Speak loftier lines.
> Cry out, "I am the purple muse." Make sure
> The audience beholds you, not your gown.

The order of the northern sky initially was Sublime terror and then was transformed into innocence in *The Auroras of Autumn*, an innocence close to a poverty that "becomes his heart's strong core." Theatre, for Stevens always a negative image, belongs here to a sordid muse of tragedy, akin to Coleridge's wind in *Dejection: An Ode*, which is addressed as an actor rather too close to perfection in all tragic sounds. Stevens ends *In a Bad Time* by advising Melpomene to be more like Hoon, which means that she too must find herself more truly and more strange. This attitude informs the difficult canto III of *An Ordi-*

nary Evening, which returns "desire" to its root meaning of "longing for by shining forth," *sweid*, and so can locate it "deep in the eye, / Behind all actual seeing." This is desire transcending the world of Keats's Grecian Urn, for this emptiness and denial are only potentially a porcelain, being still in the state of the bats or lumps of clay out of which the artifact is to be formed.

A crucial image of voice, the savage cry of a savage assuagement, rises in canto IV, as another commentary upon the plainness of plain things or the achieved abstraction of a First Idea. Like so many fierce cries in Stevens, this goes back to Whitman's ocean crying for its castaways and suggests something of the cost of poetic incarnation. Canto IV begins as ironic comedy, with Stevens himself as the "man who has fought / Against illusion and was." "Illusion" here is the pathetic fallacy, and "was" is time's "it was" against which Nietzsche urged the will's revenge. The cry, as a "mating of surprised accords," undoes the pain of the seasonal cycle, rendering the reduction of cold into a similitude of "a sheen of heat romanticized." Again, we have an argument against illusion conveyed in the *illusio* of irony, as the supposedly plain version of the eye turns out to be a wholly visionary or Transcendental circle. This irony emerges overtly in canto V, to conclude the poem's first movement. Reality or the Not-Me is itself found to be "inescapable romance, inescapable choice / Of dreams." Stevens resumes the self-mockery of *Auroras*, V, when he brings his chant of the inauthentic to its pitch by declaiming, "Everything as unreal as real can be, / In the inexquisite eye," a long fall from having been the nomad exquisite of *Harmonium*. A precisely Emersonian fall of the self is then recorded, albeit with considerable gusto:

> Why, then, inquire
> Who has divided the world, what entrepreneur?
> No man. The self, the chrysalis of all men
>
> Became divided in the leisure of blue day
> And more, in branchings after day. One part
> Held fast tenaciously in common earth

And one from central earth to central sky
And in moonlit extensions of them in the mind
Searched out such majesty as it could find.

There is no better description in Stevens' poetry of his characteristic dualism and of his precise variety of self-consciousness. The poetry of earth is only one part of him; the Transcendental searcher is after all the more dominant part. What has
the eye's plain version to do with this questing after majesty,
with these moonlit extensions? I read Stevens as answering
such a question himself, by the disjunction between cantos I–V
and VI–VIII. Canto VI, the second section of the poem's original,
short version, presents a fable of naked Alpha, the ever-early
candor, and the hierophant Omega, the late plural. When we
pass from "searched out such majesty as it could find" to "Reality is the beginning not the end," we negotiate, with Stevens, a
Crossing of Election, another testing of his poethood. Canto VI
shows a fresh triumph in such a crossing:

> Reality is the beginning not the end,
> Naked Alpha, not the hierophant Omega,
> Of dense investiture, with luminous vassals.
>
> It is the infant A standing on infant legs,
> Not twisted, stooping, polymathic Z,
> He that kneels always on the edge of space
>
> In the pallid perceptions of its distances.
> Alpha fears men or else Omega's men
> Or else his prolongations of the human.
>
> These characters are around us in the scene.
> For one it is enough; for one it is not;
> For neither is it profound absentia,
>
> Since both alike appoint themselves the choice
> Custodians of the glory of the scene,
> The immaculate interpreters of life.
>
> But that's the difference: in the end and the way
> To the end. Alpha continues to begin.
> Omega is refreshed at every end.

So inspired is this synecdochal representation that at first we may miss the sense in which Stevens turns against himself here, though the two cantos VII and VIII, added as commentary, clarify the compensating sorrows that pay for this poetic election. Naked Alpha or the infant A is the reduction of the Not-Me, of reality as an otherness. The aged Z occupies the position that the palm at the end of the mind holds in Stevens' death-poem *Of Mere Being*, at the edge of space, beyond the last thought, and therefore can be called the final reimagining of all First Ideas. We live with both "characters," beginnings and ends of alphabets, and we depend upon both, and though Stevens seems to insist upon the difference between them there now seems less distinction between abstraction or Alpha and reimagining or Omega than ever before. To continue to begin is to be refreshed at every end, which means that reality as Alpha does the same work for us that the finished fiction of the self does as Omega. A variation occurs in canto VII, where the chapels and schools of New Haven, the visible towers of Yale, play the role of Omega, redressing the poverty or imaginative need of their makers but also of Stevens as spectator, the poet as Alpha or representative of reality. New Haven as vision of Omega or the incredible ends by becoming again the credible day of the eye's plain version.

More interesting is the variation of canto VIII, where Stevens descends out of his hotel onto the streets of New Haven, and finds his love of the real leading him to "the syllable / Of recognition, avowal, impassioned cry, / The cry that contains its converse in itself." This cry is a recognition of origins, here "the origin of a mother tongue," and should arouse in the reader a recognition of how prevalent and central in Stevens such a cry is, taking him back to Whitman's fierce old mother, the sea, crying out in the night for her sons, the poets, who have been cast away from her, who have fallen down into the occasions that are the cries of their poems.

A new movement, this time of undoing or emptying out of the poetic self, begins in canto IX and receives its commentary in canto X. In IX, the third canto of the original poem, Stevens returns to the hotel as the real to seek "the poem of pure reality, untouched / By trope or deviation," which is necessarily not a poem at all but rather New Haven as seen through the Emersonian transparent eyeball, "the eye made clear of uncertainty, with the sight / Of simple seeing, without reflection." Where the Emersonian epiphany is invoked, we can expect high vision to follow:

> We seek
> Nothing beyond reality. Within it
>
> Everything, the spirit's alchemicana
> Included, the spirit that goes roundabout
> And through included, not merely the visible,
>
> The solid, but the movable, the moment,
> The coming on of feasts and the habits of saints,
> The pattern of the heavens and high, night air.

Some critics have deplored this vision as not being Stevens' own, or at least as not being the authentic speech of his own self. Yet the passage is the purest Stevens, though this is the central Whitmanian strain in Stevens. It is the poet of *Song of Myself* who keeps going "roundabout / And through," and who is likely to see visions in the high, night air. Stevens qualifies, as elsewhere, by stressing the moment-to-moment, glimpsing nature of his vision, and also by stressing that what he seeks is part of "the coming on" and not part of what already is. But, most of all, this is not poetry, not "of the hymns / That fall upon it out of the wind." By going "straight to the transfixing object," Stevens is destroying the only language in which poems can be written. The commentary on this metonymic rejection of poetry comes in canto x, where the drive "straight . . . to the object / At the exactest point at which it is itself" is severely qualified by the admission "We do not know what is real and what is not." But this is then shown to be a saving ignorance, part of living in change, which is repetition as the fulfillment of expectations, spoken of as "this faithfulness of reality." The rejection of a poetry of language for the poem of pure reality is itself partly undone by Stevens' praise for a mode of being, the joyous acceptance of change, that makes "gay the hallucinations in surfaces." It does not matter if they are hallucinations, particularly since the crossing to the poem's next movement juxtaposes "Make gay the hallucinations in surfaces" with "In the metaphysical streets of the physical town." This is a disjunction that does the work of a Crossing of Solipsism, as Stevens mounts into a very Emersonian version of the American Sublime:

> In the metaphysical streets of the physical town
> We remember the lion of Juda and we save
> The phrase . . . Say of each lion of the spirit
>
> It is a cat of sleek transparency
> That shines with a nocturnal shine alone.
> The great cat must stand potent in the sun.
>
> The phrase grows weak. The fact takes up the strength
> Of the phrase. It contrives the self-same evocations
> And Juda becomes New Haven or else must.
>
> In the metaphysical streets, the profoundest forms
> Go with the walker subtly walking there.
> These he destroys with wafts of wakening,
>
> Free from their majesty and yet in need
> Of majesty, of an invincible clou,
> A minimum of making in the mind,
>
> A verity of the most veracious men,
> The propounding of four seasons and twelve months,
> The brilliancy at the central of the earth.

Except for the poem's final four cantos, this fourth canto of the shorter version is the only one upon which Stevens wrote no commentary in the form of interpolated cantos. No qualification or expansion seemed possible because of the strength of this lyric. The lion, here as elsewhere in Stevens an emblem of the power and menace of poetry, enters as the traditional phrase "the lion of Juda" and is then converted into each or any lion of the spirit, Transcendentalist in its imagery:

Say of each lion of the spirit

It is a cat of a sleek transparency
That shines with a nocturnal shine alone.

Though this is metaphysical, high and bright, it is in the physical town that mere being centers itself: "the great cat must stand potent in the sun." The fact takes up the phrase's strength, or rather the phrase alters itself to "the lion of New Haven," so that the lion of the spirit participates also in the being of fact. Stevens, the subtle walker in New Haven's metaphysical streets, is accompanied by the profoundest forms of lions as he goes. Any waft of wakening can destroy these irrealities, and yet Stevens needs them as evidences of the majesty of poetry. The invincible clou, the peg or point of greatest interest for Stevens, is still a point of brightest origin in a logocentric universe of discourse. Stevens acquires daemonic or Sublime force as he mounts into the hyperboles he insists are for him the given: a Gnostic, Emersonian uncreated element or "minimum of making in the mind" and an attendant truth founded upon the seasonal cycle and the earth's central splendor. The strength of repression in Stevens here is awesome, yet it is the menace of the lions that is being repressed when the poet too easily says that he is free from their majesty.

It is vital to any interpretation of *An Ordinary Evening* that the reader consider how extraordinary an elaboration Stevens made of cantos v–vii of the original version, which in the final text become cantos xii, xv, and xxii. With the cantos written as commentary upon them, these form now the long movement xii through xxvii. This dominant movement is the most protracted and ambitious development, in all of Stevens' poetry, of the revisionary ratio I have called *askesis*. The huge curtailment or limitation of meanings centers upon two Shelleyan metaphors: the fiction of the leaves in cantos xii and xvi, and the image of the evening star in canto xxii. The movement is through three phases of an ascetic reduction of the image-making power, from "leaves . . . resembling the presence of thought" on to "the total leaflessness" and then at last to the internalization of the star so that, like desire, "it shines / From the sleepy bosom of the real."

Stevens begins this movement of self-deconstruction with one of his major triumphs or central poems, another revision of the *Ode to the West Wind*, the eloquent cry of canto XII:

> The poem is the cry of its occasion,
> Part of the res itself and not about it.
> The poet speaks the poem as it is,
>
> Not as it was: part of the reverberation
> Of a windy night as it is, when the marble statues
> Are like newspapers blown by the wind. He speaks
>
> By sight and insight as they are. There is no
> Tomorrow for him. The wind will have passed by,
> The statues will have gone back to be things about.
>
> The mobile and the immobile flickering
> In the area between is and was are leaves,
> Leaves burnished in autumnal burnished trees
>
> And leaves in whirlings in the gutters, whirlings
> Around and away, resembling the presence of thought,
> Resembling the presences of thoughts, as if,
>
> In the end, in the whole psychology, the self,
> The town, the weather, in a casual litter,
> Together, said words of the world are the life of the world.

An occasion is an event or happening, but its etymological meaning is a falling down, and its Indo-European root means falling *or* dying. To be the cry of fallen leaves is to be a cry in the etymological sense of crying out or imploring the aid of one's fellow citizens ("cry" is from the Latin *quiritare*, in turn from *quiris* for a Roman citizen). A poem is a cadence, and so etymologically a dying fall, as when in *Credences of Summer*, VIII, the poem's "resounding cry / Is like ten thousand tumblers tumbling down." In what had been the next canto of the shorter version, now canto XVI, Stevens associates himself as his poem's speaker with the occasion as a falling into or near death:

"The venerable mask, / In this perfection, occasionally speaks / And something of death's poverty is heard." Here, in canto XII, the poem as deathly cry is "part of the res itself and not about it," which means that the thing itself is death or the reality principle. Speaking the poem as it is, not as it was, is to speak the poem as part of the reverberation of a night when the wind, more even than in *The Auroras of Autumn*, is blowing one toward destruction, as indeed it did in Shelley's *Ode*. "Reverberation" is a peculiarly rich word for and in Stevens, meaning not only a re-echoing or resounding (etymologically a relashing, as of a whip) but also a rewording or reverbalization, here of Shelley, but also of earlier Stevens. *Man and Bottle* had featured the realization that "the poem lashes more fiercely than the wind," that is, the poem reverberated more in the fierce mode of the maternal sea than even the Shelleyan wind rebounded against Stevens' precursor. Two cantos on, in XIV, "reverberation" receives Stevens' own commentary when "the point of reverberation" is identified as "not grim / Reality but reality grimly seen / And spoken in paradisal parlance new." Reverberation that is a grim seeing of the reality principle is now precisely the Stevensian *askesis*, but by no means the final resting point of his vision, even in canto XII of this poem.

In the present that is more absence than presence, Stevens locates his poem or fiction of the leaves "in the area between is and was." The trope is exactly Shelley's "my dead thoughts . . . like withered leaves," and the occasion is not wholly dissimilar: "What if my leaves are falling like its own!" Nor are the conclusions fundamentally different, though Shelley even in despair is a prophet, and Stevens merely meditates upon loss and gain. Shelley also "said words of the world are the life of the world," though the Shelleyan hope for "a new birth" was not to be Stevens' until the final phase, when it emerges in *A Discovery of Thought* and some related lyrics.

Cantos XIII–XV scarcely come near the achievement of XII, but they do illuminate it, as is their function. Stevens himself is the solitary ephebe of XIII, defining his enterprise in terms taken from his anti-Eliotic lyric, *The Creations of Sound*. Professor Eucalyptus, the Canon Aspirin of New Haven, makes his first entrance in XIV as a parody of Stevens, not so much mocking the quest for reality as repeating it in a coarser tone. But canto XV raises Eucalyptus to a first glory and implicitly reveals why the Yale Professor of Metaphysics has received the name of so aromatic a tree. The flowering leaf of the eucalyptus is a well-covered flower until it opens, hence the tree's name from the Greek for "covered" or "hidden." One of Stevens' early *Primordia* poems (*OP*, 7–9) thirty years before had spoken of a

> Compilation of the effects
> Of magenta blooming in the Judas-tree
> And of purple blooming in the eucalyptus—
> Map of yesterday's earth
> And of tomorrow's heaven.

Professor Eucalyptus is himself a mapper of yesterday's earth and tomorrow's heaven:

> The instinct for heaven had its counterpart:
> The instinct for earth, for New Haven, for his room,
> The gay tournamonde as of a single world
>
> In which he is and as and is are one.

Either Stevens remembered *Primordia* across thirty years, or else we have yet another instance of the uncanny persistence of his work. "Tournamonde" is his own coinage, of which he said, "For me it creates an image of a world in which things revolve and the word is therefore appropriate in the collocation of is and as" (*L*, 699n.). We can say that "tournamonde" is an economical equivalent of the Nietzschean motive for metaphor: "The desire to be different, to be elsewhere." Professor Eucalyptus merges into Stevens as the meditation attains a majesty of fresh desire, as much a part of this poem as is any vision of a reality principle:

> The hibernal dark that hung
> In primavera, the shadow of bare rock,
>
> Becomes the rock of autumn, glittering,
> Ponderable source of each imponderable,
> The weight we lift with the finger of a dream,

The heaviness we lighten by light will,
By the hand of desire, faint, sensitive, the soft
Touch and trouble of the touch of the actual hand.

This hushed eros, so little credited to Stevens, is wholly characteristic of him. Though the image here is of a world in which things revolve, Stevens subtly sublimates the summer of that revolution, as the passage goes from wintry dark hanging in early spring, or bare rock, to glittering rock of autumn. Summer would be too imponderable a source, as *Credences of Summer* had shown its poet, who nevertheless remained uniquely grateful for that poem and who echoes it again in canto XVII. Too large for the somewhat sublimated desires of this poem, summer by its absence qualifies this final commentary upon the ways in which "words of the world are the life of the world."

Canto XVI, originally VI, begins another submovement of Stevens' triple *askesis*, setting the image of "the total leaflessness" against the fiction of the leaves. Though I will dispute an aspect of Helen Vendler's interpretation of canto XVI, like her I am moved by its expressive power, astonishing even for Stevens:

Among time's images, there is not one
Of this present, the venerable mask above
The dilapidation of dilapidations.

The oldest-newest day is the newest alone.
The oldest-newest night does not creak by,
With lanterns, like a celestial ancientness.

Silently it heaves its youthful sleep from the sea—
The Oklahoman—the Italian blue
Beyond the horizon with its masculine,

Their eyes closed, in a young palaver of lips.
And yet the wind whimpers oldly of old age
In the western night. The venerable mask,

In this perfection, occasionally speaks
And something of death's poverty is heard.
This should be tragedy's most moving face.

> It is a bough in the electric light
> And exhalations in the eaves, so little
> To indicate the total leaflessness.

This, to Vendler, is "desiccation itself," and "the venerable mask" is hieratic, hiding, "with its stiff grandeur, the unimaginable ruin which has befallen the lapidary rock." The issue between interpretations here turns upon tone, so frequently uncanny in the later Stevens. I take "venerable mask" as ironic metaphor, since "venerable" and "mask" both have an ironic anteriority in Stevens' poetry. Stevens had played upon the venery in "veneration" in *Le Monocle de Mon Oncle:* "Most venerable heart, the lustiest conceit / Is not too lusty for your broadening"; and he had ended the paternal canto IV of *The Auroras of Autumn* with the bitter rhetorical question "What company, / In masks, can choir it with the naked wind?" As "the wind whimpers oldly of old age / In the western night," Stevens assumes the mask of the most venerable of hearts, in the double sense of age and of a barren desire, "above / The dilapidation of dilapidations," his decayed body, but more significantly and particularly his sexual power. A "dilapidation" is what has fallen into a state of ruin, but etymologically it means to throw the stones apart, and it is like Stevens to play at so elegant a sexual bitterness. Reality or the Not-Me comprises for him, as it did for Emerson, four sundries: nature, art, other persons, and one's own body. Art here is represented by "time's images," nature by night, day, and the night wind, other persons by the obscure contrast between the Oklahoman and Italian blue skies, evidently standing for feminine and masculine meeting: "Their eyes closed, in a young palaver of lips." Like the decayed body, all this is estrangement for Stevens, an otherness, ironically "this perfection," that he cannot address, because reality seems complete without him. His stance approximates that of Yeats in the first stanza of *Sailing to Byzantium* and recalls also *The Poems of Our Climate*, where "the imperfect is our paradise" because the perfect, being finished or done completely, does not allow for the delight that "lies in flawed words and stubborn sounds." The mask of aged desire, speaking as the cry of its occasion, speaks the poem of death's poverty, which fails to be "tragedy's most moving face," because it is still only a mask that we hear speaking.

But what does it mean that Stevens compares his own poem to "a bough in the electric light" or to "exhalations in the eaves"? Are those analogues of what is "altogether drier and more brittle," as Vendler says? A bough in artificial light makes a very different and doubtless more qualified impression than a bough in sunlight, yet it is a bough. Exhalations in the eaves are spookily out of context, yet remain exhalations. *An Ordinary Evening in New Haven* is an index, a forefinger indicating much by little, and here at the close of canto XVI it does show the total leaflessness of Stevens' still poignant desire. Yet this is only the start of the middle movement of the Stevensian *askesis*, and from the deliberate nadir at his poem's midpoint we will watch Stevens slowly, steadily, and as deliberately rise to "an alteration / Of words that was a change of nature."

Cantos XVII through XXI, the commentary upon XVI, adumbrate the total leaflessness and in every instance mitigate it. In XVII, the Arnoldian high seriousness is saluted, with the effect of dismissing comedy and tragedy alike in the name of commonplace reflection, or a mirroring of reality by that "dominant blank" that Stevens had seen, in *The Auroras of Autumn*, as Emerson saw it, but now sees as the true mode, the eye's plain version. This is severely said, but its rhetoric is uneasy, as when Stevens too insistently deprecates his usual repressed combination of Jehovah and Whitman:

> Like blessed beams from out a blessed bush
>
> Or the wasted figurations of the wastes
> Of night, time and the imagination.

The repetitions of "blessed," and "wasted" and "wastes," are an index of Stevensian anxiety.

More persuasive is the fable of the carpenter in XVIII, where the "clear water in a brilliant bowl, / Pink and white carnations" of *The Poems of Our Climate* are reduced to "a fuchsia in a can." The eye's plain version being a thing apart, not of the

mere present, and life and death being at least as much metaphysical as physical, even so "this carpenter," Stevens, lives
and dies in perceiving the poems, "a carpenter's iridescences,"
of his own climate. New Haven, "slapped up like a chest of
tools," rises in the poet's mind as an iridescence of purged
thought, a sublimation of reality. The sublimating force is personified in the less vital canto XIX as "a figure like Ecclesiast,"
whose chant presumably would be the traditional "all is van-
ity."

Another of Stevens' fierce reductions dominates canto XX,
with a characteristic reimagining coming on as fiercely in XXI.
Both of these cantos again are uncannily Emersonian if we
think of the Emerson of *The Conduct of Life* rather than of *Nature*. Stevens begins canto XX by apprehending the cloudiness
for him, now, of his past poems and his memories of his own
past feelings. New Haven, juxtaposed with such an estrangement, is "a neuter shedding shapes in an absolute," not even an
auroral serpent of a change. Yet it remains "a residuum," reminding us of the positive coloration that word has elsewhere in
Stevens, the sense it conveys of a reduced substance in us that
nevertheless prevails. In canto XIX, thinking back to the nineteenth century and to the celebration of great and central men,
Stevens had invoked the personage who was the axis of vision
for his time, Emerson, as "an image that begot its infantines."
Here in XX, Stevens deliberately becomes a bitter version of the
transparent eyeball, an infant of solipsism:

> In this chamber the pure sphere escapes the impure,

> Because the thinker himself escapes. And yet
> To have evaded clouds and men leaves him
> A naked being with a naked will

> And everything to make. He may evade
> Even his own will and in his nakedness
> Inhabit the hypnosis of that sphere.

But this Emersonian reduction becomes Emerson again, at
the opening of canto XXI, in what could be the epigraph to *The
Conduct of Life:*

> But he may not. He may not evade his will,
> Nor the wills of other men; and he cannot evade
> The will of necessity, the will of wills.

The power of necessity restitutes every ascetic movement of the spirit, though it be a power at last of death's necessity. Cythera, island of Venus, appears as Baudelaire's isle of Cythère, and yet Stevens' "black shepherd's isle" is secondary here in comparison to "another isle," where the senses give without taking, an island of a more sympathetic imagination:

> The opposite of Cythère, an isolation
> At the centre, the object of the will, this place,
> The things around—the alternate romanza
>
> Out of the surfaces, the windows, the walls,
> The bricks grown brittle in time's poverty,
> The clear. A celestial mode is paramount,
>
> If only in the branches sweeping in the rain:
> The two romanzas, the distant and the near,
> Are a single voice in the boo-ha of the wind.

The "romanza out of the black shepherd's isle" joins with Stevens' "alternate romanza" in the single voice of the wind, yet Stevens' kind of poetry is near, "this place, / The things around." Such a finding cannot alter the interpretation of the wind of section XVI; it still "whimpers oldly of old age / In the western night," yet those "branches sweeping in the rain" have more life in them than their status as commentary upon "the total leaflessness" might indicate.

With the re-entrance of Professor Eucalyptus in canto XXII (originally VII), Stevens begins the final phase of his threefold *askesis*, this one comprising six cantos, XXII–XXVII. As before, Eucalyptus parodies Stevens, and the high pomposity scarcely conceals the intensity of Stevens' own quest: "The search / For reality is as momentous as / The search for god." The inside / outside jugglings between philosopher and poet betray the obsessiveness of Stevens' lifelong anxieties concerning the rival authorities of philosophy and poetry. More impressive is

Stevens' conscious palinode in the matter of the First Idea, "the inhalations of original cold / And of original earliness." The First Idea is no longer seen as a reduction, "the predicate of bright origin," but simply as the eye's plain version, the daily sense of cold and earliness. Returning to Crispin, and to Crispin's precursor in the Poet of *Alastor*, Stevens now dismisses the romance of the solitary quester: "Creation is not renewed by images / Of lone wanderers." Reimagining from the eye's plain version is still praised, though Stevens' example of such re-creating is beautifully equivocal:

> Likewise to say of the evening star,
> The most ancient light in the most ancient sky,
>
> That it is wholly an inner light, that it shines
> From the sleepy bosom of the real, re-creates,
> Searches a possible for its possibleness.

This is primarily the evening star of *Adonais* and of many other Shelleyan texts, but "the sleepy bosom of the real" may be an allusion to Keats's sonnet *Bright Star*, where the poet wants to be at once the star "in lone splendour" but also pillowed upon the sleepy bosom of the real, which for him is "my fair love's ripening breast." The evening star is one of time's images, ancient in its anteriority. By saying that it is an inner light and then calling its home the real, Stevens has introjected reality even as he tries to draw the star out of the Not-Me into the me. Re-creating the High Romantic metaphor of the star as the endurance and immortality of poetry involves a troping from metaphor to metalepsis, to the Power or *pathos* of possibleness or *potentia*. The evening star remains, in part, a sublimating metaphor, but rather less so than the fictions of the leaves or of leaflessness.

Canto XXIII, which begins the commentary upon the evening-star canto, is one of my special favorites. Having written of it elsewhere at length, particularly in *Poetry and Repression*, I will note here only the link between its repressed Whitmanian desire for the "cozening and coaxing sound" of the maternal sea of night and the Shelleyan and Keatsian use of the evening star as an emblem of the persistence of desire. After this strength, canto XXIV disappoints in its rhetorical execution, though its importance for Stevens is clear. The "escape from repetition," at the edge between afternoon and evening, hints at the difficult theme of the last of Stevens, after *The Rock*, the topography of a new birth into Transcendental perceptiveness. As New Haven poises at the horizon's dip, Stevens prepares for the visions that will begin for him a year later, in 1950, with *A Discovery of Thought*.

There is a sudden onslaught of Stevens' uncanny power again in canto XXV, with its obsessive imagery of eyes, looks, watched, stared, as the poet confronts man with the blue guitar, earlier form of his own vocation and identity, and so his Whitmanian *daimon*, akin to the figure who mocks Whitman on the beach in *As I Ebb'd*. The demands made upon Stevens by the hidalgo are necessarily too stern, reminding us that "hidalgo" means "son of something" where "something" is substance or property. There may be a memory here of the bitter *Thought Revolved*, IV, published with the *Blue Guitar:*

> Behold the moralist hidalgo
> Whose whore is Morning Star.

Description without Place, VII, spoke of how "the hard hidalgo / Lives in the mountainous character of his speech." The hidalgo of *An Ordinary Evening* is both a moralist and a hard looker, "a hatching that stared and demanded," the egg of the eye never quite hatched. Though "permanent, abstract," the hidalgo is hardly a muse but more nearly a superego, whose scrutiny withers every privileged moment. This withering extends into canto XXVI, which is a kind of late revision of *Sea Surface Full of Clouds*. Stevens would like to indulge in the perspectives of distance and so to see the earth as inamorata. But with the attentive eyes of his own hidalgo-aspect upon him, he regards the earth in a plainer version in canto XXVII:

> Again, "The sibilance of phrases is his
> Or partly his. His voice is audible,
> As the fore-meaning in music is." Again,

"This man abolishes by being himself
That which is not ourselves: the regalia,
The attributions, the plume and helmet-ho."

As so many times, elsewhere, Stevens is at his most tender, even Whitmanian, when he accepts a self-imposed poverty of vision. The whole of this most extensive of all his sublimations ends in this flamboyant canto, the fable of the Ruler of Reality and his spouse, the Queen of Fact. If reality is the otherness beheld by the eye, then the unreal self is the peculiar kingdom ruled by the Queen of Fact. The scholar's Segmenta are Stevens' own notes for an unwritten poem, and they celebrate a major man precisely like the MacCullough of *Notes toward a Supreme Fiction*. Like the MacCullough or like the Whitman of *Sea-Drift*, the Ruler of Reality lies lounging by the sea, doubtless "reading in the sound, / About the thinker of the first idea." Yet the later fable is fuller, because of the presence of the Queen of Fact, or theorist of death, the true muse of Stevens' poetry.

In the transition from "and, with the Queen / Of fact, lies at his ease beside the sea" to the final four cantos, we move with Stevens through the most complex of all his Crossings of Identification, because on the other shore of this disjunction he makes a truly central defense of his own poetry, a defense that turns against his worthiest opponent, himself:

If it should be true that reality exists,
In the mind: the tin plate, the loaf of bread on it,
The long-bladed knife, the little to drink and her

Misericordia, it follows that
Real and unreal are two in one: New Haven
Before and after one arrives or, say,

Bergamo on a postcard, Rome after dark,
Sweden described, Salzburg with shaded eyes
Or Paris in conversation at a café.

This endlessly elaborating poem
Displays the theory of poetry,
As the life of poetry. A more severe,

More harassing master would extemporize
Subtler, more urgent proof that the theory
Of poetry is the theory of life,

As it is, in the intricate evasions of as,
In things seen and unseen, created from nothingness,
The heavens, the hells, the worlds, the longed-for lands.

This, the eighth of the original eleven cantos, is the most famous and I think the best, surpassing even "The poem is the cry of its occasion." The key word is "misericordia," a dispensation from the ordinance of fasting and, in this context, a release from the necessities of reduction and from the anxieties of seeking to determine the divisions between real and unreal. On the premise that reality has been taken up into the mind, that the First Ideas of nature, other persons, art, and one's own body have been reimagined fully, then it follows at last that real and unreal, reduction and expansion, are two in one; both of them are synecdoches for the desire to be elsewhere, the desire to be different, to be anywhere in the world except New Haven, or anywhere out of the world except the poem of *An Ordinary Evening in New Haven*. The rocking cradle that endlessly vexed Yeats's rough beast to nightmare, or that earlier first stirred Whitman to the life of poetry, has become in Stevens his variational appositional stance. Stevens elaborates precisely as the Whitmanian maternal ocean rocks, because he too is calling home his castaway, whose name is reality.

Always precise about language, Stevens does not deprecate his poem by describing it as "endlessly elaborating." To elaborate is to execute with truly painstaking detail, to pay attention so that every part is in place, to work the poem out. Yet Stevens says "elaborating" and not "elaborated," which means not that his is a process-poem but that it demands active reading even as it actively reads. "Theory" etymologically means a "viewing," as at a theatre, and "life" goes back to a root meaning "to adhere or stick," or charmingly enough, "fat." To "display" is to "exhibit" yet goes back through a word meaning "scatter" to a root meaning "plait" or "weave." Endlessly working itself out, *An Ordinary Evening in New Haven* scatters and weaves a vision of poetry as being that which sticks or adheres in poetry, the fat of poetry as it is of life. We have met this viewing throughout the poem's theatre, and we now can name it for what it is, the attempt to see earliest, the Emersonian and American doomed attempt to establish a priority in seeing, as though Europe had seen nothing before us. Stevens knows himself to be a great elaborator of this program, but he cannot extemporize as subtly and as urgently as the greatest of all poetic extemporizers, Whitman.

Whitman's art, far more than Stevens', is to give the effect of an impromptu, to deceive us into the confidence that we listen to an orator who can function without a prepared text. Stevens cannot harass us as Whitman can; his poem is not as severe as *Song of Myself* or *The Sleepers*, because "severe" in its root means "true" and Stevens is too Nietzschean to assert that his poem can give truth. "Life, as it is, in the intricate evasions of as" is the enormous, the truly supreme fiction of Whitman, not of Stevens, who knows that what he believes in cannot be true. Yet Stevens is never more moving than when he affirms the Transcendental nostalgia by negating it. Out of the nothingness of his fictive self, Whitman, no snow man, created "the heavens, the hells, the worlds, the longed-for lands." Stevens is not, cannot be, such a master, but no proclamation of his poverty, and of ours, is more poignant than this great canto that concludes by singing so passionately what Stevens says he cannot sing.

When we reach the final three cantos of *An Ordinary Evening*, we confront the complexity of Stevens' self-revisionism, since cantos IX, X, XI of the shorter version appear in the definitive poem as XXX, XXXI, XXIX. Since I am following here the sequence of the later, longer version, I pass now to canto XXIX, yet it remains important to remember that this had been the original closure of the poem. Canto XXIX is as brilliant a fable as Stevens wrote, yet it may be a fable impossible to interpret, a text too problematic to read fully or at least for the reader to persuade himself or others that he has read severely enough:

> In the land of the lemon trees, yellow and yellow were
> Yellow-blue, yellow-green, pungent with citron-sap,
> Dangling and spangling, the mic-mac of mocking birds.

In the land of the elm trees, wandering mariners
Looked on big women, whose ruddy-ripe images
Wreathed round and round the round wreath of autumn.

They rolled their r's, there, in the land of the citrons.
In the land of big mariners, the words they spoke
Were mere brown clods, mere catching weeds of talk.

When the mariners came to the land of the lemon trees,
At last, in that blond atmosphere, bronzed hard,
They said, "We are back once more in the land of the elm
      trees,

But folded over, turned round." It was the same,
Except for the adjectives, an alteration
Of words that was a change of nature, more

Than the difference that clouds make over a town.
The countrymen were changed and each constant thing.
Their dark-colored words had redescribed the citrons.

There are two lands in this fable, or rather there is only one land, since the real land of the elm trees, New Haven, and the unreal, Goethean paradise or Stevensian Florida of the citrons are two in one. The mariners desire to be elsewhere, to be different, to forsake the fulfillments of reality for an Eden of language or simply to be poets. But they take New Haven with them, and neither they nor Stevens (since they *are* Stevens) can decide whether this means that nothing can change or whether it means that there is nothing except change.

In the *Harmonium* world of "dangling and spangling, the micmac of mocking birds," the yellow of the lemons was both blue and green, pungencies alike of mind and of earth. In New Haven, traditionally the land of the elm trees (Stevens writes just before the major elm blight of the 1950's), wandering, big mariners (or Odysseus assimilated to Stevens) stare at autumnal women, women more of the earth and its ripeness than of the mind's desires. Language also is gaudy, in the *Harmonium* world, but the language of New Haven is again too much of the earth our mother. Presumably, it is in search of a language "to roll / On the expressive tongue, the finding fang" that the mariner Stevens comes to the land of citrons. But his representatives, arriving at last in their Eden, proclaim, "We are back once more in the land of the elm trees, / But folded over, turned round." I know of nothing else in Stevens so problematic in tone; is this a lament, a defiance, or simply a kind of statement as to that which is? Vendler, with a most acute ear, reads the third possibility:

> This possibly depressing recognition is certainly anticlimactic, but Stevens expresses it without tone, as though he wished the moment to be neutral. The repetitiveness of experience is no new theme in Stevens, but here he refuses to speak of it either as pleasurable or as diminishing. Instead, it is factual; and he has it both ways.

The recognition, as I read it, is not depressing or toneless, but positive, even a touch truculent and defiant. An adjective is an addition, something thrown on to something else, so that to say, "It was the same, / Except for the adjectives" is more self-contradictory than dialectical. The mariners have been troped in being "folded over, turned round"; they have been recolored, and so the mariner Stevens is not just a permanently dark-colored self. He is not within the difference, but beyond the difference, in the faith that "an alteration / Of words that was a change of nature" may be an authentic alteration in the fiction of the self.

What was the force of the original close of the poem, when it ended that "Their dark-colored words had redescribed the citrons"? Too hopeful an earliness, is surely part of the answer. After so many sublimations, so ever-early a candor would not have been appropriate. With marvelous judgment, Stevens took the original cantos ix and x and placed them after the fable of the mariners as cantos xxx and xxxi. It is not a total leaflessness that is observed in xxx, but what nevertheless presents itself as a barrenness:

> The last leaf that is going to fall has fallen.
> The robins are là-bas, the squirrels, in tree-caves,
> Huddle together in the knowledge of squirrels.

The wind has blown the silence of summer away.
It buzzes beyond the horizon or in the ground:
In mud under ponds, where the sky used to be reflected.

The barrenness that appears is an exposing.
It is not part of what is absent, a halt
For farewells, a sad hanging on for remembrances.

It is a coming on and a coming forth.
The pines that were fans and fragrances emerge,
Staked solidly in a gusty grappling with rocks.

The glass of the air becomes an element—
It was something imagined that has been washed away.
A clearness has returned. It stands restored.

It is not an empty clearness, a bottomless sight.
It is a visibility of thought,
In which hundreds of eyes, in one mind, see at once.

After so many dominant blanks, so many staring eyes hatching like an egg, so many parodied transparent eyeballs, as well
as eyes' plain versions, inexquisite eyes, and assorted reflections, we experience a profound sense of liberation when we are
told: "A clearness has returned. It stands restored." Truly, the
clarity has its menace; it is the moment poised just before winter. But though those hundreds of eyes may belong to the
animal kingdom, to the huddled squirrels sensing the imminence of winter, they suggest also Shakespeare's play upon a
bottomless dream, and more directly the American Transcendentalist dream of open vision, of seeing as Whitman hoped to
see, with the eyes of a multitude. Something strange begins to
come on and come forth in Stevens, that "visibility of thought"
which will be the discovery of the final phase, when the course
of all the particulars of vision and visionary sound is finally
tracked. Summer was imagined well but has been washed
away, and what remains is no longer an abstraction or reduction to a First Idea. This is revelation without description, tentative and yet definitive, and rhetorically a troping upon all the

earlier undoings and sublimations in the poem. There is no finer example in Stevens of a scheme of transumption or metaleptic reversal, the far-fetching of an antipodal creature, worthy of birth.

Stevens does not end the poem upon this introjection of a fresh earliness that huddles expectantly, waiting for the blasts of winter. He goes back to the central Paterian trope of *Harmonium*, the apprehension of reality as the solipsistic recognition of privileged moments, sudden perfections of sense, flakes of fire, fluttering things having distinct shapes:

> The less legible meanings of sounds, the little reds
> Not often realized, the lighter words
> In the heavy drum of speech, the inner men
>
> Behind the outer shields, the sheets of music
> In the strokes of thunder, dead candles at the window
> When day comes, fire-foams in the motions of the sea,
>
> Flickings from finikin to fine finikin
> And the general fidget from busts of Constantine
> To photographs of the late president, Mr. Blank,
>
> These are the edgings and inchings of final form,
> The swarming activities of the formulae
> Of statement, directly and indirectly getting at,
>
> Like an evening evoking the spectrum of violet,
> A philosopher practicing scales on his piano,
> A woman writing a note and tearing it up.
>
> It is not in the premise that reality
> Is a solid. It may be a shade that traverses
> A dust, a force that traverses a shade.

The first six lines refine *Harmonium*, but the next three genially mock the Hoonian vision. "Flickings from finikin to fine finikin" transumes earlier Stevensian intimations as to the high fastidiousness of poetry and of poetic perception, of which the crucial instance is *Like Decorations*, XXXII:

Poetry is a finikin thing of air
That lives uncertainly and not for long
Yet radiantly beyond much lustier blurs.

The mockery in that early passage is overbalanced by the praise
of poetry, and so it is here in the final canto of *An Ordinary Evening*. Even "the general fidget," the nervous decline of representation "from busts of Constantine" to the aptly named Mr.
Blank, perhaps a departed insurance executive, is redeemed as
one of "the edgings and inchings of final form," of history getting at getting it right. There is no full stop in the canto until
evening evokes, the metaphysician plays, and the woman makes
up and unmakes her mind, presumably upon an issue of erotic
choice. What are all these but variant versions, analogues, of
Stevens' own appositional method in *An Ordinary Evening?*
They share Stevens' achieved premise, that reality, whether it
be nature, art, others, or one's body is a crossing or transition,
a disjunctive versing of force, shade, dust. "Dead candles at the
window" may be only a poignant emblem of ineffectual inchings toward final form, when the sun comes up, yet they are
part of the emblematic reality of poet or scholar, the solitary
outward form of his internalization of the evening star. Stevens
ends his great poem on "shade," but the final emphasis is upon
a force crossing a shade, and so freshly breaking a form, writing
another canto on an ordinary evening in New Haven.

13 *The Rock* and Final Lyrics

Stevens' last phase (1950–55) was his best. No single poem written after he turned seventy has the scope and ambition of his three masterpieces, *Notes, The Auroras, An Ordinary Evening.* But *The Rock*, the elegy *To an Old Philosopher in Rome*, and some twenty-five shorter poems have an uncanny intensity and originality that surpass nearly all his previous work at middle length or shorter.

As at a Theatre (1950) can be taken as the inauguration of the final phase. The images are all familiar denizens of Stevens' theatre of mind: green and blue, the "primitive," "reality," the candle of being. The stance is different, however, and the poet's vision asserts its conscious change. For the sunlight is "another sunlight," and the yearning is for "the artifice of a new reality," a "time to come," though all this is heavily qualified by a customary sequence of "likes." What might be is "the candle of another being," a self-meditating image in a wholly transcendental world, a world without walls. All this is "as at a theatre," yet the azure world-beyond (outre-terre) disclosed is important not for the content of fulfilled desire, or "universe without life's limp and lack, / Philosophers' end," but for the only difference Stevens now seems compelled to recognize. The mind, which could never be satisfied, never, just for once requires a sense of having fulfilled itself. This impatience is so much against the wisdom that Stevens has spent a lifetime acquiring that his reader is warned of another crisis, to which *The Rock* is addressed, together with its triad of related lyrics of 1950: *A Discovery of Thought, The Course of a Particular,* and *Final Soliloquy of the Interior Paramour.*

Of all Stevens' poems, none opens so bleakly as *Seventy Years Later*, the first section of *The Rock*. The poet is seventy years old, and so the "later" in the title evidently means "since birth." Seventy years after our birth, we have touched a moment in consciousness that makes having lived at all, let alone being alive now, seem an illusion. "Illusion" always had been a hurtful word for Stevens and had meant (as it does here) an error in the perception of reality. *Extracts* had identified being "naked of any illusion" with being "in poverty," but *An Ordinary Evening*, IV, mocked its poet's "last plainness of a man who has fought / Against illusion and was," a fight dismissed in the next canto as "inescapable romance, inescapable choice / Of dreams, disillusion as the last illusion." Stevens' challenge to himself now is to call life an illusion without indulging in another romance of disillusion. His precursors, as always when he is in crisis, come out of his American tradition. Emerson's motto to his powerful essay *Illusions* could be the epigraph to *The Rock*:

> Flow, flow the waves hated,
> Accursed, adored,
> The waves of mutation;
> No anchorage is.
> Sleep is not, death is not;
> Who seem to die live.
> House you were born in,
> Friends of your springtime,
> Old man and young maid,
> Day's toil and its guerdon,
> They are all vanishing,
> Fleeing to fables,
> Cannot be moored.

Though there are echoes of *Illusions*, and of other essays in *The Conduct of Life*, throughout Stevens' last phase, the precursor text in Emerson for *The Rock* is the essay *Experience*, as J. Hillis Miller has shown. The sequence of *Experience* is like that of *The Rock*; it begins with a first third that proclaims a series of illusions, so intense that Emerson is driven to the ironic assertion: "Nothing is left us now but death. We look to that with a grim satisfaction, saying, There at least is reality that will not dodge us." Stevens lacks even that grim satisfaction in the opening tercets of *The Rock:*

> It is an illusion that we were ever alive,
> Lived in the houses of mothers, arranged ourselves
> By our own motions in a freedom of air.
>
> Regard the freedom of seventy years ago.
> It is no longer air. The houses still stand,
> Though they are rigid in rigid emptiness.

In his vision of the mother's house in *The Auroras of Autumn,* III, Stevens had been driven to the image of two-dimensionality: "Upstairs / The windows will be lighted, not the rooms," an image made more powerful because the lighting is being done by the aurora borealis. The house reduced from three dimensions to just two has its parallels in the reduced mementoes and memories of the mother: "The necklace is a carving not a kiss. / The soft hands are a motion not a touch. / The house will crumble." In the first of *Three Academic Pieces,* written in 1947 just before *The Auroras of Autumn,* Stevens had a stronger sense of the link between memory and resemblance: "Apparently objects of sentiment most easily prove the existence of this kind of resemblance: something in a locket. . . . One may find intimations of immortality in an object on the mantelpiece; and these intimations are as real in the mind in which they occur as the mantelpiece itself" (*NA,* 75).

One way of understanding the opening of *The Rock* is to see it as the last of three phases in the decay of Stevens' version of the Wordsworthian intimations or visionary gleam, in which the first phase is a reality in the mind as the mind perceives resemblances, and the second is when "the necklace is a carving not a kiss." Regarding (not beholding) his origins, the poet sees his memories as having suffered a loss of air, until

> Even our shadows, their shadows, no longer remain.
> The lives these lived in the mind are at an end.
> They never were . . .

It is not that memory is dying but that memory is no longer *felt.* Precisely what Wordsworth feared most has happened to

Stevens. And if memory has no vitality, then Stevens was not and is not a poet:

> The sounds of the guitar
> Were not and are not. Absurd. The words spoken
> Were not and are not. It is not to be believed.

Stevens' tone was never more uncanny. As I read this, "The sounds of the guitar / Were not and are not" is flat, almost toneless, but the following "Absurd" is a shocked, disbelieving, anguished whisper. Again, "The words spoken / Were not and are not," though a touch harsher, returns to relative tonelessness, but then an even more hushed, bewildered, quasi-protesting urgency is heard in "It is not to be believed." What follows is an even greater anguish, as the one great romantic memory of the poet's life is rehearsed as though it too was not and is not:

> The meeting at noon at the edge of the field seems like
>
> An invention, an embrace between one desperate clod
> And another in a fantastic consciousness,
> In a queer assertion of humanity.

Again Stevens returns to a vision of *The Auroras of Autumn*, but in an ironical substitution for the tenderness of the earlier account:

> The rendezvous, when she came alone,
> By her coming became a freedom of the two,
> An isolation which only the two could share.

Regarding that freedom of forty-six years ago, Stevens again must think: "It is no longer air." Yet his language is more positive in its implications: "invention," "fantastic consciousness," "queer assertion of humanity" all convey the humanizing struggle to imagine love, to speak words of the world that might become the life of the world. It is important to notice that there is no full stop after "it is not to be believed" until Stevens reaches close to the end of *Seventy Years Later* with "In a birth of sight." From "The meeting at noon" until "a birth of sight" is a continuity, in which the meeting at last engenders the birth. Where does the upward movement begin that allows Stevens to begin a sense of "being alive, an incessant being alive"? This upward turn can be located, retrospectively but precisely, when we re-enter the poem just where we left it:

> A theorem proposed between the two—
> Two figures in a nature of the sun,
> In the sun's design of its own happiness,
>
> As if nothingness contained a métier,
> A vital assumption, an impermanence
> In its permanent cold, an illusion so desired.

From clods to mathematical figures is only an abstract upward turn, but "figures" is revealed to mean "tropes" as well as "persons" or "forms," images of the sun's cosmos, but even more of its "design of its own happiness," and with "design" the poem has changed. Where there is design, there can be métier, vital assumptions, and a movement from mere illusion to desired illusion. Stevens' qualifications are, as always, intense, yet they do not withdraw the assertion of the change that desire makes, the effect of an illusion so desired:

> That the green leaves came and covered the high rock
> That the lilacs came and bloomed, like a blindness cleaned,
> Exclaiming bright sight, as it was satisfied,
>
> In a birth of sight. The blooming and the musk
> Were being alive, an incessant being alive,
> A particular of being, that gross universe.

The fictions of the leaves, the rock, and the lilacs are synecdoches or tropes of Power, not ironies or tropes of Fate like the undesired illusions of the first sixteen lines of the poem. When we reach the dash at the end of line sixteen, "A theorem proposed between the two—" we touch the disjunction between the *illusio* of Stevens' opening swerve away from origins and the synecdoche that antithetically restitutes or completes the poet's initial dearth of meaning. Between the proposed theorem and the sun's nature a crossing or crisis of interpretation takes place, very subtly between "two" and "two," that is, between clods and figures, things and words. This is the most rarefied of all

Stevens' Crossings of Election, strongly and affirmatively answering the question "Am I still a poet, or was I truly a poet?"

Of the three synecdochal fictions, that of the leaves is Shelleyan and Whitmanian, the lilacs wholly Whitmanian, and the high rock uniquely Stevens' own, the most original of his major tropes. To catalog the whole course of this particular in Stevens would occupy too much space; I give here only what seem to me the main phases of its development in his work. The sole appearance of the image in *Harmonium* is very tentative, at the close of the odd allegory *The Bird with the Coppery, Keen Claws*, of which the final revision was to be the great death-poem, *Of Mere Being*. The "parakeet of parakeets" ends the early poem by continuing to flare "in the sun-pallor of his rock," which is evidently mere nature or things-as-they-are. Far more remarkable is the sudden emergence of the image of the rock in *How to Live. What to Do* (*CP*, 125) in *Ideas of Order*, where "this rock" is a great height, "beyond all trees," participating in the heroic isolation of the human as beaten upon by a cold wind of solitude. In *The Man with the Blue Guitar*, xi, "time grows upon the rock," which appears to have widened so as to be all of the earth. When the rock returns, in the more positive *Blue Guitar*, xxvi, it is the world as shore, "whether sound or form / Or light, the relic of farewells, / Rock, of valedictory echoings." This is the metaphysical rock that recurs in Stevens' later poetry, at once land, sea, air, and sound, and always a little beyond common experience. In *This as Including That* (*OP*, 88), the rock is wholly internalized, for the first time: "It is true that you live on this rock / And in it. It is wholly you." *Two Versions of the Same Poem*, in *Transport to Summer*, presents the sea as "insolid rock" and the earth as a rock against which "the human ocean beats." We have seen the culmination of the image in *Credences of Summer*, vi, where the rock explicitly is made equal to, but not the same as, the Christian emblem of the truth, and where it is identified with the visible and the audible of summer.

This aspect of the rock is summed up in *The Auroras of Autumn*, vi, where the terrestrial cosmos is seen in one Sublime vision:

> It is a theatre floating through the clouds,
> Itself a cloud, although of misted rock
> And mountains running like water, wave on wave,
>
> Through waves of light.

The painful and eloquent poem *Imago*, also in *The Auroras of Autumn* volume, extends this image into the February expectation of a return of warmth:

> Something returning from a deeper quarter,
> A glacier running through delirium,
>
> Making this heavy rock a place,
> Which is not of our lives composed . . .

This progression toward the poem *The Rock* ends in *An Ordinary Evening*, xv, where "the shadow of bare rock, Becomes the rock of autumn, glittering, / Ponderable source of each imponderable." How are we to interpret the image's anteriority in Stevens, when we encounter it as "the high rock" toward the end of the first section of *The Rock*? Stevens' own interpretation comes in the "Introduction" to *The Necessary Angel* (1951), where he quotes himself as saying, "[Poetry] is an illumination of a surface, the movement of a self in the rock" (viii). Further on in the book (48–49), Stevens quotes Henri Focillon (*The Life of Forms in Art*) as saying of Piranesi's *Prisons:* "Twenty years later, Piranesi returned to these etchings, and on taking them up again, he poured into them shadow after shadow, until one might say that he excavated this astonishing darkness not from the brazen plates, but from the living rock of some subterranean world."

Shall we say of Stevens' rock that at last it is both self *and* other, me *and* not-me, mind *and* sky, imagination *and* reality? That would make it his image-of-images, a composite trope for his repression or internalization of poetic tradition. Of course, that makes it also too large and self-contradictory a trope, which is the particular fault of section III, *Forms of the Rock in a Night-Hymn*. There the rock is alpha and omega, final reduction and final reimagining, the way up and the way down, and too much else besides. As we begin reading section II, *The Poem as Icon*, we can say, provisionally, that the rock is the given, the most barren of all first ideas, life as it is, which has been covered with green leaves and lilacs by the "illusion so desired" of the poet's love for his wife.

Why the poem as *icon?* The word "icon" does not appear anywhere else in Stevens' poetry, so that we have no clues as to what precise shade of meaning it had for him. "The fiction of the leaves is the icon / Of the poem, the figuration of blessedness, / And the icon is the man." Are these two icons the same, so that the poet himself is only a fiction of the leaves? "These leaves are the poem, the icon and the man," the text goes on to say, and section II ends by proclaiming, "His words are both the icon and the man." The Shelleyan fiction of the leaves here is largely displaced by the Whitmanian one, though Whitman's fiction owed much to Shelley's. Yet Whitman's fiction, more than Shelley's, aptly can be called poem, icon, and man. "Icon" does not offer a varied choice of meanings. Essentially there are only three (and these tend to merge rather easily): a representation or image, a symbol or synecdoche, and a sacred picture of a sacred person in the Eastern Orthodox church. Stevens' "icon" seems to be a precise synonym for synecdoche as a trope of Power and restitution, and by calling fiction, poem, figuration, self, man, and word, each and all of them, tropes, Stevens follows Emerson and Whitman; he does not deconstruct or undermine his American precursors. Probably he is remembering the derivation of "icon" from the Greek *eikon*, "likeness," but he wishes also to appropriate for his poem some of the spiritual force of the Christian synecdoche, so as to give a kind of sacredness to the poem, as Whitman triumphantly had done before him.

What does Stevens mean by "cure" in *The Poem as Icon?*

> It is not enough to cover the rock with leaves.
> We must be cured of it by a cure of the ground
> Or a cure of ourselves, that is equal to a cure
>
> Of the ground, a cure beyond forgetfulness.

J. Hillis Miller has written the fullest commentary yet ventured on *The Rock*, and the notion of "cure" is central to his reading:

> The cure of the ground would be a caring for the ground, a securing of it, making it solid, as one cures a fiberglass hull by drying it carefully. At the same time the cure of the ground must be an effacing of it, making it vanish as a medicine cures a man of a disease by taking it away, making him sound again, or as an infatuated man is cured of a dangerous illusion. "Cure" comes from Latin *cura*, care, as in "curate" or "a cure of souls." The word "scour" . . . has the same root. A cure of the ground would scour it clean, revealing the bedrock beneath. . . . The cure of the ground proposed in the poem is the poem itself. The poem is an icon, at once a "copy of the sun" and a figure of the ground, though the relation of sun and ground remains to be established. The icon (image, figure, resemblance) at once creates the ground, names it "properly," reveals it, and covers it over.

Following Derrida, Miller's comments depend upon the assumption that, as he phrases it, "The vocabulary of a poet is not a gathering or a closed system, but a dispersal, a scattering." To which I would both assent and disagree; a poet's vocabulary is not a closed system, but it is not just a dissemination. It is both a breaking apart and a restituting, and Stevens' "cure" is each, a scouring clean of the ground and a healing of it, but not I think a securing of it, which Miller admits as one of his meanings. A cure of the rock is a cure of one's own reductiveness and, with it, freedom to have a larger idea of what it is to be wholly human. But a cure of the rock is not possible, since that means curing either nature, "the ground," or the self, and neither is going to be cured beyond the possibility of perpetual repression:

> And yet the leaves, if they broke into bud,
> If they broke into bloom, if they bore fruit,
>
> And if we ate the incipient colorings
> Of their fresh culls might be a cure of the ground.

"Culls" means having been picked out rather than having been rejected. "Incipient" is a strong word for Stevens. On it he centers the meaning of *July Mountain*, one of his very last poems (*OP*, 114–15):

We live in a constellation
Of patches and of pitches,
Not in a single world,
In things said well in music,
On the piano, and in speech,
As in a page of poetry—
Thinkers without final thoughts
In an always incipient cosmos,
The way, when we climb a mountain,
Vermont throws itself together.

Stevens might have called this *Anecdote of the Jar Retold*, except that he dispensed with the jar and relied instead on the idea of the poem, always freshly beginning, to firm up Vermont even as the perspectivizing jar had firmed up slovenly Tennessee. In *The Rock*, insofar as we are poets or "thinkers without final thoughts," our ingestion of the perpetual fresh possibilities of our own tropes might do for us what Keats did for himself in the induction to *The Fall of Hyperion*. The cure of the ground took him back into Eden and then to the shrine of poetry. Steven hints at as great a transformation:

The fiction of the leaves is the icon

Of the poem, the figuration of blessedness,
And the icon is the man. The pearled chaplet of spring,
The magnum wreath of summer, time's autumn snood,

Its copy of the sun, these cover the rock.
These leaves are the poem, the icon and the man.
These are a cure of the ground and of ourselves,

In the predicate that there is nothing else.

What matters here is the absence of winter, or the uncovered rock, true ground of our being. So much comes together in these lines that, for the reader of Stevens, they are indeed inexhaustible, whether to analysis or to meditation. They are the prelude to a final Crossing of Solipsism that intervenes between their climactic "nothing else" and the subsequent passage of ecstasy that begins "They bud and bloom and bear their fruit without change." The fiction of the leaves is now Stevens' fiction, as well as that of the precursors Shelley and Whitman, and the story it figures is its poet's own blessedness, his new freedom from winter or: "the icon is the man." Spring, summer, and autumn adorn the rock of reality even as a woman is adorned, the principle being the Platonic one of copying the sun as source of all images. "These leaves" finally take on the emphasis the phrase has when Whitman applies it to his own poems, and so "these leaves" means "the whole of *Harmonium*," which lends the peculiarly American *ethos* to this enterprise of the Native Strain: "In the predicate that there is nothing else," a line whose grim dignity is at once Emersonian and Nietzschean.

That predicate, which might be phrased as "all is trope," is a negative moment of freedom, the freedom of crossing into meaningfulness, which is the Romantic predicate proper. When the crossing has been accomplished, Stevens is able to grant himself a chant of the Sublime, of a quiet glory unmatched elsewhere in his work:

> They bud and bloom and bear their fruit without change.
> They are more than leaves that cover the barren rock.
>
> They bud the whitest eye, the pallidest sprout,
> New senses in the engenderings of sense,
> The desire to be at the end of distances,
>
> The body quickened and the mind in root.
> They bloom as a man loves, as he lives in love.
> They bear their fruit so that the year is known,
>
> As if its understanding was brown skin,
> The honey in its pulp, the final found,
> The plenty of the year and of the world.

If they *are* more than leaves, then they are no longer language, and the leaves have ceased to be tropes or poems and have become magic or mysticism, a Will-to-Power over nature rather than over the anteriority of poetic imagery. Stevens literalizes his own images in an overtly fine desperation that itself is another version of the American Sublime. But this belated version, by necessity, fiercely represses not only the history of the fiction of the leaves but Stevens' own psychic history of doubting or denying his own Transcendentalism. For once he seems willing to risk becoming the rabbit masquerading as king of the ghosts, a consciousness asserting that it holds "the plenty of the year and of the world." So thoroughly has he trained us, his readers, that we are made to be both uneasy and exalted by this denial of all reductiveness, this sudden representation of what it might mean "to be at the end of distances." When we reach "so that the year is known, / As if its understanding was brown skin," we are rightly moved, and the erotic force of this trope of *pathos* seems as fully earned as the parallel moments in Whitman's dark sublimities. This "final found" is of touch, or touch taken up into the mind, and contrasts significantly with "the final finding of the ear" in *The Course of a Particular*, a poem composed very soon after *The Rock*.

Perhaps Stevens should have ended *The Poem as Icon* with "The plenty of the year and of the world," but he risked an even more self-assertive exaltation:

> In this plenty, the poem makes meanings of the rock,
> Of such mixed motion and such imagery
> That its barrenness becomes a thousand things
>
> And so exists no more. This is the cure
> Of leaves and of the ground and of ourselves.
> His words are both the icon and the man.

In gesture, in imaginative *stance*, these seem to me the most Whitmanian lines in Stevens, the lines asserting the largest claims for poetry and for the poet. "Mixed motion" is the truly difficult trope here, reminding us how vital the image of motion is for Stevens. Verses, waves, thought, music, women, wind and weather, time, and indeed all things are in rapid, Paterian flux and motion throughout Stevens' poetry, and the word "motion" is for him an honorific term. Perhaps the key line is from the late *Looking Across the Fields and Watching the Birds Fly*: "A moving part of a motion, a discovery"; or else the prayer to the affirming father in *The Auroras of Autumn*, the father who is "of motion the ever-brightening origin." "Mixed motion" is the true cure "of the ground and of ourselves," but what is this motion if it is not the movement, tropological and topological, of substitutions, of crossings that generate meaningfulness in poems?

The Rock's forward motion, as poem, ends there, but Stevens added, as reflective coda, *Forms of the Rock in a Night-Hymn*, which may be the lasting glory of the whole poem and is an authentic rival to the majestic closing strophes of Whitman's *Lilacs* elegy. Stevens hardly could hymn the night without invoking Whitman, whose visions had established the difference of the American night, a night wider, more fragrant, more vivid and promising, and finally more mothering in its erotic deathliness than even the nights of southern European tradition.

Yet Stevens' night-hymn begins most deceptively with a parodistic language of metaphysical description, which modulates from the rock's identity with "the gray particular of man's life" through the rock as "the stern particular of the air" on to the evening redness of decay and "evil dreams." But a different movement begins with "The difficult rightness of half-risen day," as Stevens reminds himself of his love for that daily moment of crossing when "there are no shadows in our sun." By the time Stevens has modulated to a final perspective upon the rock, we come to see that the poet is at a Transcendental degree of a Crossing of Identification, a massive, Whitmanian acceptance or coming to terms with the necessity of his own dying:

> It is the rock where tranquil must adduce
> Its tranquil self, the main of things, the mind,
>
> The starting point of the human and the end,
> That in which space itself is contained, the gate
> To the enclosure, day, the things illumined
>
> By day, night and that which night illumines,
> Night and its midnight-minting fragrances,
> Night's hymn of the rock, as in a vivid sleep.

"I fled forth to the hiding receiving night that talks not," Whitman gratefully sang, after he had learned to walk "as with companions, and as holding the hands of companions," these being the knowledge of death and the thought of death. In *A Clear Midnight* (a short poem that Stevens quoted, as we have seen), midnight is the hour of the soul's full emergence into the theme it loves best: "Night, sleep, death and the stars." What the night (and its equivalents) meant to Whitman, the rock finally now means to Stevens, the refuge that the end creates, the hiding and receiving hypostasis to which one might flee. The self cites its own tranquility as means of proof, at the rock, where by apposition the mind and the external realm are brought together as a dialectical alpha and omega. In the closing lines, Stevens makes a Transcendental lunge beyond, to a larger hypostasis, containing space and day and night, and something more than those, something illumined and minted by fragrances: "Night's hymn of the rock, as in a vivid sleep." A vivid sleep that is also a hymn suggests the world of dream, but here a dream of what is to come, or what Keats might have called a dream of reality. Wherever these last tropes abandon us, what matters is how remarkably far we have come from "It is an illusion that we were ever alive." Perhaps no other single poem by Stevens travels so far, in so brief a compass.

These difficult variations concluding *The Rock* are illuminated by the three clairvoyant lyrics that accompanied the composition of *The Rock* in 1950: *A Discovery of Thought*, *The Course of a Particular*, and *Final Soliloquy of the Interior Paramour*. Each of these poems sums up the course of Stevens' evolution, and each points to a beyond, to what might suffice, though in very different ways and in sharply contrasting tones and modalities. All three stand with the best of Stevens, and all need the closest kind of antithetical readings, in which they are compared both with earlier Stevens and with his inescapable precursors.

"Discovery" is for Stevens one of the strongest of words, a finding that holds the middle ground between imposition or expansion and the perilous attractions of yet another reduction to a First Idea. *A Discovery of Thought* as a title implies that this finding or invention belongs to mind and not to fact, and should remind us of the nuances in Stevens' uses of the word "thought." There is the Canon Aspirin's flight to the point "beyond which thought could not progress as thought." Stevens' discovery is beyond that point and is akin to Henry Church's quest in the *Owl* when he "walked living among the forms of thought," a state reached by Stevens himself when he proclaimed, in *An Ordinary Evening:* "It is a visibility of thought." Yet it stays within the natural powers of the mind, unlike the death-vision in *Of Mere Being* that "beyond the last thought, rises." The meaning of the poem centers upon its title to a degree remarkable even for Stevens, but increasingly characteristic of the apodictic poems written during the final five years of his life. To interpret precisely what "a discovery of thought" or "the course of a particular" or "the world as meditation" means is also to venture a full interpretation of the poem each phrase heads.

What is it that thought discovers in this uncanny lyric? "One thinks," in this poem, not down to the First Idea, but to "the first word," the poet's initial trope, "when the houses of New England catch the first sun," which is a trope of power, possession, and desire: "The desire for speech and meaning gallantly fulfilled." The poem's alternate word for this word is the "susceptible," a new word, never used before in Stevens' poetry, and whose prime meaning is "open to influence." We do not think of Stevens as a "susceptible" man, particularly in his seventies. The poem opens in a mode more to be expected of him:

> At the antipodes of poetry, dark winter,
> When the trees glitter with that which despoils them,
> Daylight evaporates, like a sound one hears in sickness.

The World Is Larger in Summer, a later Stevensian title (for the second part of *Two Illustrations That the World Is What You Make of It*) is an apt commentary upon the first line here. Any New England scene after an ice storm evokes the second line, but the third line of the tercet is properly more mysterious and begins the poem's movement into the domain of the Sublime. The verb "evaporates" begins a series that continues in "dissolved," "trinkling," and "forming":

> One is a child again. The gold beards of waterfalls
> Are dissolved as in an infancy of blue snow.
> It is an arbor against the wind, a pit in the mist,
>
> A trinkling in the parentage of the north,
> The cricket of summer forming itself out of ice.

"The cricket of summer" goes back through *Le Monocle* to Keats's sonnet *On the Grasshopper and Cricket*, and so implies the same affirmation: "The poetry of earth is never dead." But the perspective is more reductive than Keats allows himself to be, and its invocation of the child's vision suggests Wordsworthian primal perceptions, colored here by deliberate Stevensian fancifulness or even phantasmagoria. "It is" opposes the "It is possible" of *Notes* to the grim "This is" of *The Auroras*, and so trinkles away "the parentage of the north." However reduced, Stevens allows himself a susceptibility to an influx of what Emerson called the Newness, a Transcendental second birth:

> One thinks, when the houses of New England catch the first
>   sun,
> The first word would be of the susceptible being arrived,
> The immaculate disclosure of the secret no more obscured.

A discovery of thought, at the end of a particular winter, is the arrival of a new primal word, logos, or meaning that immaculately discloses a secret long obscured. "Immaculate" is another strong word in Stevens, associated with the good and with language and imagery as such, and also with beginnings and ends, so as to remind us again of the motive for questing after the ever-early candor of a stainless First Idea. Stevens is rarely more legitimately difficult than he is in seeking closure for *A Discovery of Thought*:

> The sprawling of winter might suddenly stand erect,
>
> Pronouncing its new life and ours, not autumn's prodigal
>   returned,

> But an antipodal, far-fetched creature, worthy of birth,
> The true tone of the metal of winter in what it says:
>
> The accent of deviation in the living thing
> That is its life preserved, the effort to be born
> Surviving being born, the event of life.

Winter is to become like the serpent of *Saint John and the Back-Ache*, "erect and sinuous, / Whose venom and whose wisdom will be one." Spring, as in *It Must Change*, is not to "be a question of returning or / Of death in memory's dream." But there, the fiction was part of the new start or fresh reimagining. Here we are asked to believe in miracle rather than conscious fiction. We are to give credence to preposterousness, to "an antipodal, far-fetched creature," a new life and newly open vision both in the world and in Stevens. "The accent of deviation" identifies the new first word as trope, recalling *An Ordinary Evening*, IX, where "we seek / The poem of pure reality, untouched / By trope or deviation, straight to the word." That search is over. Life and trope are seen as one, part of the effort or *pathos* that is the Will-to-Power of struggling into birth, a will that continues in the realization or discovery of thought that life itself is an event, a significant incident or coming out, or as *An Ordinary Evening*, XXX, phrased it "a coming on and a coming forth." But there "the barrenness that appears is an exposing," another grand reduction; here we confront invention, "the accent of deviation," the Nietzschean error about life that is necessary for life.

Marvelous as this poem is, it may be overmatched by its even more uncanny companion, *The Course of a Particular*, which packs a volume of meaning, or of the achieved absence of meaning, into just fifteen lines. The "particular" is the fiction of the leaves; its "course" is that it is finished "in the final finding of the ear," a finding that is an invention, the Sublime cry of the leaves that continues despite every Stevensian rejection of it as pathetic fallacy. Stevens is never more cunning than in this poem, as the reader is gradually startled into realizing that all of the poet's negations of the cry count for little compared to the phenomenal truth that "the leaves cry," as the text three times

repeats. The cry goes on, at the close, and even the final negation, that "at last, the cry concerns no one at all," gives the
triumph of endurance to the cry and not to the poet's consciousness, which has become a trope for death.

The Course of a Particular, as a title, refers to the onward
movement in a particular direction, death, of a single aspect of
the fiction of the leaves, the cry. A particular, as opposed to a
universal, is associated with some single thing, and for Stevens
appears to have had some Blakean overtones, as in such minute
particulars as: "the spontaneous particulars of sound" (*The Creations of Sound*), "sprinklings of bright particulars from the sky"
(*Description without Place*), and most crucially "forth the particulars of rapture come" (*Notes*). *The Rock* centered upon "a particular of being," at once "the stern particular of the air" and
"the gray particular of man's life." All of these ran the course,
beyond the pleasure principle, through Freud's "detours to
death." The rose rabbi of *Le Monocle*, pursuing "the origin and
course / Of love," had developed into the beach walker of the
Auroras turning blankly on the sand, observing a whiteness that
was "a consequence / Of an infinite course." As the hearer of
the cry of the leaves, he hears also the reverberation of *An Ordinary Evening*, VII, of which *The Course of a Particular* is a dark
revision. "The poem is the cry of its occasion"—that occasion, a
falling down or detour to death, being a windy night in which
leaves, in whirlings, resembled the presence and presences of
thought, as they did for Shelley. But, in that reverberation, the
leaves had not cried aloud. Wind, the sea, falling soldiers, birds
cry out all through Stevens, but the only prolepsis of the cry of
the leaves (that I can recall) is in the powerful and bitter *No Pos-
sum, No Sop, No Taters* of 1943:

> In this bleak air the broken stalks
> Have arms without hands. They have trunks
>
> Without legs or, for that, without heads.
> They have heads in which a captive cry
>
> Is merely the moving of a tongue.
> Snow sparkles like eyesight falling to earth,

> Like seeing fallen brightly away.
> The leaves hop, scraping on the ground.

From that captive cry to *The Course of a Particular* is less of a step than it seems, because here Stevens does not protest or seek to negate the fantasia or transcendence of his own hearing, whereas the later poem both reveals and negates with every phrase. Fiercely repressing into an American Sublime, Stevens begins as a post-Emersonian must, in the Not-Me of wind and weather that separates what Emerson called the two over-whelming facts, *I and the abyss:*

> Today the leaves cry, hanging on branches swept by wind,
> Yet the nothingness of winter becomes a little less.
> It is still full of icy shades and shapen snow.

Why does Stevens write "yet" rather than "and" to begin the second line, and why does he write the archaic "shapen" for "shaped"? Why "today," as though perhaps they had been si-lent yesterday, and might be silent forever tomorrow? "The leaves cry" as if imploring aid before the wind, Shelleyan destroyer and preserver, sweeps them off the branches where they hang. "Yet" may mean that the cry is out of the depths of winter and that Stevens' eye and self are ahead of the leaves in perceiving an end to winter. "Still," winter remains full of in-fernal imagery, not so much Dante's as Keats's in *The Fall of Hyperion.* The assonance of "shades" and "shapen" suggests an identity between Hades and New England winter, reinforced by the archaic touch in "shapen." Much of the burden of this first tercet is in its subtle implication that the anteriority of win-ter, of many winters, has become a damnation, a cry of tor-ment. But it is a cry that Stevens wills neither to join nor to ac-knowledge, though his denial of concern is itself the largest of involuntary acknowledgments:

> The leaves cry . . . One holds off and merely hears the cry.
> It is a busy cry, concerning someone else.
> And though one says that one is part of everything,
>
> There is a conflict, there is a resistance involved;
> And being part is an exertion that declines:
> One feels the life of that which gives life as it is.

As in *An Ordinary Evening*, XII, the language implies a knowledge of the origin of "cry" in the Latin imploring of aid from a fellow Roman citizen. "Concerning" carries something of the meaning of relating to, or giving anxiety to, but also touches on its Latin origin of sifting and sieving the hearer, who holds off on this occasion. "Concern," like scribble, crisis, and critic, is another word going back finally to the root *skeri*, and it carries here some of the anxiety of crisis, however rejected. Calling the leaves' cry "a busy cry" is a New England dismissal, a way of saying that the leaves will not mind their own business. Stevens is massively strong, and very self-deceived, as he insists that nothing is alien to him but that this synecdochal relation yields with age to an augmenting solipsism. The monosyllabic line "One feels the life of that which gives life as it is" echoes the reductions of *An Ordinary Evening*, XII: "The poet speaks the poem as it is," and even more, *An Ordinary Evening*, XXVIII: "the theory / Of poetry is the theory of life, / As it is." But how is it that "life as it is" should contain also the sound of leaves crying aloud?

> The leaves cry. It is not a cry of divine attention,
> Nor the smoke-drift of puffed-out heroes, nor human cry.
> It is the cry of leaves that do not transcend themselves,
>
> In the absence of fantasia, without meaning more
> Than they are in the final finding of the ear, in the thing
> Itself, until, at last, the cry concerns no one at all.

There is a mounting insistence upon the fact that "the leaves cry," conveyed by the changes in punctuation and sentence structure, from "Today the leaves cry, hanging on branches swept by wind," through "The leaves cry . . . ," on to the complete "The leaves cry." Stevens was a man "to whom things spoke," as they spoke to Wordsworth and to Ruskin, but he emulated Ruskin more than Wordsworth in seeking to evade this speaking. No more involuntary Transcendentalist ever existed than the Stevens of the final phase, but the text under consideration is wildly and indubitably Transcendentalist, and I hesitate now to add "despite itself." Stevens' poem is deceiving not itself but only its unwarier readers. Leaves that do not transcend themselves are not leaves that utter a cry, and such a cry testifies to the presence of fantasia. Two years later, in *A Quiet Normal Life*, Stevens opposed the actual candle of his solitary imagination, blazing with artifice, to "transcendent forms" divested of fury, the opposition being an unconvincing defense against his having made such a form of his own imagination. Later in 1952, in *Looking Across the Fields and Watching the Birds Fly*, written against Emerson as Mr. Homburg of Concord, Stevens, as "a new scholar replacing an older one," reflects upon Transcendentalism as "this fantasia." But the position of the new scholar turns out to be precisely Emersonian, and the notions attributed to Mr. Homburg do not resemble Emerson's at all. Stevens evidently is to be trusted neither on what does or does not transcend itself nor on the presence or absence of fantasia. What then are we to make of *The Course of a Particular?*

The cry means no more than it is, whatever that is, "in the final finding of the ear," which is in apposition to "in the thing / Itself." The poem as cry is also the thing itself and not "about" or on the outside of the thing itself. The ear, soon to go beyond hearing, into the last things, finds finally that the leaves cry and that the poem is the cry of *its* occasion. When there is no one to sift or sieve the cry, of either kind, then the detours will be over. The cries of the Not-Me and of the self end in a trailing off. Still, the reader needs to go on questioning the poem: why the three commas in the last line? How differently would the poem mean if it read, at the end:

> in the thing
> Itself until at last the cry concerns no one at all.

Clearly, the three commas, in "itself, until, at last," make a subtle difference in meaning, a difference ensuing from the slowing down of the reader. The isolation of "the thing / Itself" reminds us that Stevens chose to end his *Collected Poems* with the 1954 lyric *Not Ideas about the Thing but the Thing Itself*, where the thing itself is "a scrawny cry" that may be a bird's cry from outside or may be a sound in the poet's own mind. Isolating the "until" forebodes that the poem's "today" might turn out to be the final day or that it might be any day soon. When "at last" is emphasized, then the entropic necessity of the course of this particular, leaves' cry or poet's cry, is forced upon us. This amazing poem prolongs itself until at last Stevens' reductiveness is exposed as a lifetime's self-deception, and he emerges more clearly as what he was, a true poet, who heard and saw into the life of things, perhaps most acutely when he willed neither to hear nor to see.

The last of the great poems of 1950, the year of *The Rock*, is the popular *Final Soliloquy of the Interior Paramour*, where the title may imply not that the muse is about to perish but that poet and muse are about to be so joined that every remaining poem will be a dialogue of one. As the poem of that "intensest rendezvous," *Final Soliloquy* wraps "tightly round us, since we are poor, a warmth, / A light, a power, the miraculous influence." This pathos evokes Coleridge aging at Highgate, image of weakness and of strength wrapped tightly together. Whitman, saying goodbye to his Fancy, hovers here also:

> Here, now, we forget each other and ourselves.
> We feel the obscurity of an order, a whole,
> A knowledge, that which arranged the rendezvous,
>
> Within its vital boundary, in the mind.
> We say God and the imagination are one . . .
> How high that highest candle lights the dark.

How high does any single candle, even the highest, light the dark? Stevens is not being ironic, but the passage, and the poem, assert less than they seem to assert. But I do not believe that Stevens, like Eliot, is constructing something upon which to rejoice. The same guilty sensibility that appears to relax in *Final Soliloquy* speaks also in *Madame La Fleurie* of the following year and tells us the final finding of the knowledge that arranged the rendezvous:

> Weight him down, O side-stars, with the great weightings of
>   the end.
> Seal him there. He looked in a glass of the earth and thought
>   he lived in it.
> Now, he brings all that he saw into the earth, to the waiting
>   parent.
> His crisp knowledge is devoured by her, beneath a dew.

Weight him, weight, weight him with the sleepiness of the
  moon.
It was only a glass because he looked in it. It was nothing he
  could be told.
It was a language he spoke, because he must, yet did not
  know.
It was a page he had found in the handbook of heartbreak.

The black fugatos are strumming the blacknesses of black . . .
The thick strings stutter the finial gutturals.
He does not lie there remembering the blue-jay, say the jay.
His grief is that his mother should feed on him, himself and
  what he saw,
In that distant chamber, a bearded queen, wicked in her dead
  light.

Better than Lawrence's poem that appropriated the title, this might have been called *Reply to Whitman*, for this is truly the last version of the American muse-as-mother, and so a more authentic final vision of the interior paramour. Stevens turns his allusiveness most cruelly against himself by the intertextual play between the final lines of *Madame La Fleurie* and the too hopeful prophecy that had concluded *The Man with the Blue Guitar:*

Here is the bread of time to come,

Here is its actual stone. The bread
Will be our bread, the stone will be

Our bed and we shall sleep by night.
We shall forget by day, except

The moments when we choose to play
The imagined pine, the imagined jay.

Madame La Fleurie is not characteristic of Stevens' final phase, but rather of the ebb that dialectically keeps crossing the Transcendental influx dominating the phase. Influx of the "beyond" pervades the major poem of 1952, *To an Old Philosopher in Rome*, a celebration of the dying Santayana, "inquisitor of structures," as he stops upon the threshold of heaven. Stevens returns, in this poem, to the mode of *Chocorua to Its Neighbor* and *A Primitive Like an Orb*, a mode that declares rather than discovers the credences of poetry. There are moments in the pre-elegy for Santayana that surpass even the hushed splendors of the *Chocorua* poem, though Stevens is so moved by the poem's dangerous eloquence that in some sense his true subject is his awareness of that eloquence. Santayana becomes a surrogate for Stevens himself, poised upon the threshold of heaven, much as Keats becomes a surrogate for Shelley in the last third of *Adonais*.

In the English Institute essay, *Imagination as Value* (1948), Stevens had written a prose scenario for his poem:

Most men's lives are thrust upon them. The existence of aesthetic value in lives that are forced on those that live them is an improbable sort of thing. There can be lives, nevertheless, which exist by the deliberate choice of those that live them. To use a single illustration: it may be assumed that the life of Professor Santayana is a life in which the function of the imagination has had a function similar to its function in any deliberate work of art or letters. We have only to think of this present phase of it, in which, in his old age, he dwells in the head of the world, in the company of devoted women, in their convent, and in the company of familiar saints, whose presence does so much to make any convent an appropriate refuge for a generous and human philosopher. [*NA*, 147–48]

Santayana's will to await death in the convent, but without believing, is read by Stevens as a trope of *pathos*, a noble synecdoche for Stevens' own poem. The American elegiac mode that Stevens had inherited from Whitman dominates here, as it does in *The Rock*, but the interplay of "small" and "large" is a deliberate swerve away from Whitmanian enlargements. Indeed, the poem chooses to open with images of perspectival diminishment:

> On the threshold of heaven, the figures in the street
> Become the figures of heaven, the majestic movement
> Of men growing small in the distances of space,
> Singing, with smaller and still smaller sound,
> Unintelligible absolution and an end—

> The threshold, Rome, and that more merciful Rome
> Beyond, the two alike in the make of the mind.
> It is as if in a human dignity
> Two parallels become one, a perspective, of which
> Men are part both in the inch and in the mile.

"Beyond," mark of the Transcendental will in Stevens, as in Emerson, defines the perspective:

> How easily the blown banners change to wings . . .
> Things dark on the horizons of perception
> Become accompaniments of fortune, but
> Of the fortune of the spirit, beyond the eye,
> Not of its sphere, and yet not far beyond,
>
> The human end in the spirit's greatest reach,
> The extreme of the known in the presence of the extreme
> Of the unknown.

How are we to read these figurations? This very late version of an American Sublime represses all of Stevens' naturalism and skepticism, but the strain of the repression is audible in every line. The rewards of such repression mount up to a daemonic intensity:

> The bed, the books, the chair, the moving nuns,
> The candle as it evades the sight, these are
> The sources of happiness in the shape of Rome,
> A shape within the ancient circles of shapes,
> And these beneath the shadow of a shape
>
> In a confusion on bed and books, a portent
> On the chair, a moving transparence on the nuns,
> A light on the candle tearing against the wick
> To join a hovering excellence, to escape
> From fire and be part only of that of which
>
> Fire is the symbol: the celestial possible.

This is the final form of Stevens' vision of the man of imagination as scholar of one candle, and it returns to its origin in Emerson's *Society and Solitude*, so that the "moving transparence" and the "celestial possible" scarcely evade their Transcendental references. At the poem's end, the Sublime images return, and with them the sense that the "illumined large" has replaced permanently the "veritable small":

> It is a kind of total grandeur at the end,
> With every visible thing enlarged and yet
> No more than a bed, a chair and moving nuns,
> The immensest theatre, the pillared porch.
> The book and candle in your ambered room,
>
> Total grandeur of a total edifice,
> Chosen by an inquisitor of structures
> For himself. He stops upon this threshold,
> As if the design of all his words takes form
> And frame from thinking and is realized.

What I find most remarkable about these moving stanzas is Stevens' evasion of some of his own characteristic poetic anxieties. No trace of reductionism haunts him here. Santayana, despite the "as if," is allowed an almost unqualified realization of the "total edifice" of his philosophy, since "design" in "the design of all his words" refers both to pattern and to intention, beyond the recalcitrance of the philosopher's language. The link to Stevens himself is through *As at a Theatre* of two years before, for "the immensest theatre" refers us back to that poem's positive transformation of "theatre" from its earlier, pejorative aura in Stevens. There we find "the artifice of a new reality" associated with the candle meditating its own image, and with the notion of a philosophic closure in which "the mind, for once, fulfilled itself." Freed by an identification with Santayana as a liminal figure, Stevens for once allowed himself to repress his strong awareness that the mind could never be satisfied lest it fall into the error of ceasing to remember that ceaselessly it was an activity.

This awareness returns in the greatest of the poems of 1952, *The World as Meditation*, where the never-satisfied mind of Penelope is analogous to the mind of Stevens, hoping to find Ulysses or a new First Idea of the sun rather than merely the returning sun of spring. Penelope is a reimagined Nanzia Nunzio of *It Must Change*, viii, a decade before. Where that mistaken messenger stripped to confront reality, taking off necklace and belt, only to be told that "the spouse, the bride / Is never naked," Penelope "wanted no fetchings. His arms would be her necklace / And her belt." The world, conceived as meditation, becomes "a fictive covering" woven "always glistening from the heart and mind." Penelope ends as Stevens' finest vision of his muse, of the interior paramour subdued to a continuous process edging toward the little beyond of a possible transcendence:

> She would talk a little to herself as she combed her hair,
> Repeating his name with its patient syllables,
> Never forgetting him that kept coming constantly so near.

This curious tone, of a kind of triumphant tenderness, but uncannily so, is replaced by a cooler clairvoyance in the great poems of the final finding of Stevens' ear, from 1953 until his death in 1955. Three poems of 1953 together form another unified meditation, with a thesis in *The Dove in Spring*, an antithesis in *The Planet on the Table*, and a quietly exultant synthesis in the almost preternaturally strong *The River of Rivers in Connecticut*. Stevens' poetry ruefully associates the dove, as bird of Venus, with the frustrations of an aging male's sexuality. The prime text, as we saw, is the fable of the Arabian in *Notes*, but the dove figures less equivocally in two difficult short poems in *Transport to Summer*. *Thinking of a Relation between the Images of Metaphors* ends with a powerful trope suggesting that erotic anxiety can be mastered:

> The fisherman might be the single man
> In whose breast, the dove, alighting, would grow still.

The Dove in the Belly charmingly deprecates the erotic drive by gently mocking the whole of appearance as a toy. In a world of play, repressed sexuality or the "deep dove" can be asked to "placate you in your hiddenness." *The Dove in Spring* tropes upon the two earlier dove poems, comparing the "small howling" of the erotic impulse, reawakened by the advent of spring, to "a thought / That howls in the mind" or, more surprisingly, to "a man / Who keeps seeking out his identity / In that which is," the quest of Stevens himself. The thesis or issue is still the

Whitmanian stance of the poet confronting the sunrise, which would kill the poet-as-poet if he could not "now and always" send sunlight out of himself. That full transcendence is not available to Stevens, yet the poem ends with a recognition that the erotic force within him is still a possible strength free of the sun's gift:

> There is this bubbling before the sun,
> This howling at one's ear, too far
> For daylight and too near for sleep.

The antithetical reply is made in *The Planet on the Table*, the title itself perhaps referring to the manuscript that was to become *The Collected Poems of Wallace Stevens* in 1954. Here the brooding, interior dove or erotic self does not precede but is one with the sun:

> His self and the sun were one
> And his poems, although makings of his self,
> Were no less makings of the sun.

The difficult synthesis, at once associating self and sun and yet asserting the priority of self, is proclaimed in *The Rivers of Rivers in Connecticut*, a paean to vitalism unmatched elsewhere in Stevens. "River" here is a trope for force as opposed to presence, the force or power of mind or self over a sun that nevertheless shares in the Nietzschean gaiety of "the mere flowing." Where *Asides on the Oboe* rejected the "obsolete fiction of the wide river in / An empty land," this definitive poem accepts the myth of Stygia, region of the river Styx, in order to transcend the role of Charon and the oblivion of Hades.

> There is a great river this side of Stygia,
> Before one comes to the first black cataracts
> And trees that lack the intelligence of trees.
>
> In that river, far this side of Stygia,
> The mere flowing of the water is a gayety,
> Flashing and flashing in the sun. On its banks,
>
> No shadow walks. The river is fateful,
> Like the last one. But there is no ferryman.
> He could not bend against its propelling force.

It is not to be seen beneath the appearances
That tell of it. The steeple at Farmington
Stands glistening and Haddam shines and sways.

It is the third commonness with light and air,
A curriculum, a vigor, a local abstraction . . .
Call it, once more, a river, an unnamed flowing,

Space-filled, reflecting the seasons, the folk-lore
Of each of the senses; call it, again and again,
The river that flows nowhere, like a sea.

"The river is fateful" is a trope of power, despite the limitation
of fate. We can remember Emerson, in *Fate*, remarking that
"limitation is power that shall be." The "propelling force" is a
running ("curriculum") and a vigor, as in *The Sail of Ulysses* written soon after:

That which is more than anything else
The right within us and about us,
Joined, the triumphant vigor, felt,
The inner direction on which we depend,
That which keeps us the little that we are,
The aid of greatness to be and the force.

But, most significantly, the river of rivers is "a local abstraction," a saving withdrawal or fresh vision centered at Farmington and at Haddam, in a Connecticut itself a transcendence,
and so "not to be seen beneath the appearances / That tell of
it." The appearance itself, a flowing that is "the third commonness with light and air," is "space-filled, reflecting the seasons, the folk-lore / Of each of the senses." As such, it is "half
sun, / Half thinking" (to cite *Extracts*, VI), which means that the
mind, at last, is satisfied. And that must be why Stevens ends
the poem so emphatically, by telling us to call the river of
rivers, "again and again, / The river that flows nowhere, like a
sea," for this "unnamed flowing" is precisely his late version of
transcendence, of what Freud, in *The Future of an Illusion*,
eloquently deprecated as "the oceanic sense."

Stevens chose to end his *Collected Poems* with a poem written
specifically for a magazine that was devoting a special issue to

him in honor of his seventy-fifth birthday. *Not Ideas about the Thing but the Thing Itself* resumes both *An Ordinary Evening*, XII ("Part of the res itself and not about it"), and *The Course of a Particular* ("in the final finding of the ear, in the thing / Itself"). The thing itself is again a cry, here neither a poem nor leaves uncannily crying out, but a bird's cry, yet ultimately a "part of the colossal sun." Stevens' vision of the sun here, "surrounded by its choral rings," seems to go back to the concluding passage of Blake's prose *Vision of the Last Judgment*, which Stevens had cited in a journal passage of 1904 (*L*, 71). Whether or not there is an allusion to Blake, the poem ends in a comparison of the bird's cry to "a new knowledge of reality," a barely qualified affirmation of "a clearness emerging / From cold," of "a perfection emerging from a new known," as *On the Way to the Bus*, another poem of 1954, phrases this fresh realization.

Perhaps as early as 1947, Stevens had written a poignant poem, which he left unpublished, *First Warmth:*

I wonder, have I lived a skeleton's life,
As a questioner about reality,

A countryman of all the bones of the world?
Now, here, the warmth I had forgotten becomes

Part of the major reality, part of
An appreciation of a reality;

And thus an elevation, as if I lived
With something I could touch, touch every way.

In 1954, he revised this into something closer to a final statement:

As You Leave the Room

You speak. You say: Today's character is not
A skeleton out of its cabinet. Nor am I.

That poem about the pineapple, the one
About the mind as never satisfied,

The one about the credible hero, the one
About summer, are not what skeletons think about.

367

> I wonder, have I lived a skeleton's life,
> As a disbeliever in reality,
>
> A countryman of all the bones in the world?
> Now, here, the snow I had forgotten becomes
>
> Part of a major reality, part of
> An appeciation of a reality
>
> And thus an elevation, as if I left
> With something I could touch, touch every way.
>
> And yet nothing has been changed except what is
> Unreal, as if nothing had been changed at all.

First Warmth is perhaps too simple, or even simplistic, a palinode, a turning against a poetic lifetime's reductions to that imagined thing, a First Idea. As an incessant "questioner about reality," Stevens worries that his life may have been skeletal, equivalent to the martyr's bones upon the mount of contemplation that Mrs. Alfred Uruguay was determined to climb up so laboriously. This worry or wonder is impressive, and Stevens himself evidently could not believe in the "now, here" of *First Warmth*, supposedly when and where a lifetime of repressed warmth suddenly returns. "Part of / An appreciation of a reality; / And thus an elevation" suggests a Paterian epiphany, but the sense of a privileged moment is dispelled by the too-characteristic "as if." Nor is it persuasive when Stevens asks us to conceive of him, of all poets, as if ever he had "lived / With something I could touch, touch every way."

The revisions of *First Warmth* in *As You Leave the Room* are postponed until Stevens first allows himself a unique moment of satisfaction at his own achievement as a poet. Perhaps remembering Blake's declaration, in his last letter, that dying was no more than going out of one room and into another, Stevens addresses himself as though he were dying. Four of his poems stand as synecdoche for all the others: *Someone Puts a Pineapple Together* (1947), *The Well Dressed Man with a Beard* (1941), *Examination of the Hero in a Time of War* (1942), and *Credences of Sum-*

mer (1946). If these "are not what skeletons think about," are we to attribute to Stevens the judgment that these are his most life-affirming poems? Something of an answer emerges as his revisions of *First Warmth* now begin. "A questioner about reality," which is what Stevens truly was, like Santayana, is replaced by "a disbeliever in reality," too harsh a judgment, but Stevens seeks to compensate for his own self-praise as a poet. "The warmth I had forgotten" yields to "the snow I had forgotten," which was a repression never manifested by the poet whose work moved from *The Snow Man* to *The Course of a Particular*. "The major reality" is diminished to "a major reality," preparing for the largest revision, which is the closure of the new final lines:

> And yet nothing has been changed except what is
> Unreal, as if nothing had been changed at all.

What do the four poems cited change that might be considered "unreal"? "That poem about the pineapple" insists that the incredible also has its reality, so that reality is divested "of its propriety," until, at last, "the total artifice reveals itself / As the total reality." What is changed, then, is not less than everything. The poem "about the mind as never satisfied" insists that "a petty phrase" would suffice the never-satisfied mind in its passion for yes. Any one thing believed and affirmed will heighten reality. The poem "about the credible hero" asserts that: "The hero / Acts in reality, adds nothing / To what he does," and ends by affirming summer as the hero's season. The poem about summer, peculiarly Stevens' favorite among all his works, presents a limit of reality, while yearning in vain for a transcendence of all natural limits. *As You Leave the Room*, by its choice of allusions to earlier achievements, attains the conviction best summed up by the title of another transcendental lyric of 1954: *Reality Is an Activity of the Most August Imagination*.

This lyric's contrast between Hartford and Venice had been anticipated more than a decade before in the essay *The Figure of the Youth as Virile Poet:*

By process of the personality of the poet we mean, to select what may seem to be a curious particular, the incidence of the nervous sensitiveness of the poet in the act of creating the poem and, generally speaking, the physical and mental factors that condition him as an individual. If a man's nerves shrink from loud sounds, they are quite likely to shrink from strong colors and he will be found preferring a drizzle in Venice to a hard rain in Hartford. Everything is of a piece. [NA, 48]

The man who preferred the hard rain of Hartford is the visionary of the late *Reality* lyric:

> Last Friday, in the big light of last Friday night,
> We drove home from Cornwall to Hartford, late.
>
> It was not a night blown at a glassworks in Vienna
> Or Venice, motionless, gathering time and dust.

Emersonian cultural nationalism always was a vital element in Stevens. There had been the polemic of *Extracts*, and the *Memorandum* printed in 1947:

> Say this to Pravda, tell the damned rag
> That the peaches are slowly ripening.
> Say that the American moon comes up
> Cleansed clean of lousy Byzantium. [OP, 89]

This seems more an anti-Yeatsian than an anti-Soviet squib, and something of the same spirit of a Native Strain asserting itself is at work in the celebration of what Stevens takes to be a peculiarly American night:

> There was a crush of strength in a grinding going round,
> Under the front of the westward evening star,
>
> The vigor of glory, a glittering in the veins,
> As things emerged and moved and were dissolved.

As in his final vision of the Rock, so Stevens in this lyric asserts an interchange of the elements, a visible reality "in the big light" that enhances rather than affrights as the auroras did. The same clairvoyance informs the serene *Clear Day and No Memories*, where the poet at last asserts, "Today the mind is not part of the weather." The mind, when no longer part of anything, is freed for Stevens' ultimate vision, the mysterious and definitive *Of Mere Being*:

The palm at the end of the mind,
Beyond the last thought, rises
In the bronze decor,

A gold-feathered bird
Sings in the palm, without human meaning,
Without human feeling, a foreign song.

You know then that it is not the reason
That makes us happy or unhappy.
The bird sings. Its feathers shine.

The palm stands on the edge of space.
The wind moves slowly in the branches.
The bird's fire-fangled feathers dangle down.

The "mere" in the title is both a litotes and a play on the archaic meaning, which is "pure," and perhaps even carries a hint of the root, which means "flickering." But "mere" has a special force in very late Stevens anyway. There is the sun of *The World as Meditation* "whose mere savage presence awakens the world in which she dwells," and the joy of *The River of Rivers in Connecticut:* "The mere flowing of the water is a gayety." Perhaps we can say that "mere" is Stevens' final trope for reducing to a First Idea. In that case, the final First Idea is the sight and sound of a gold-feathered bird singing a final song in a palm that rises in a bronze decor at the end of the mind.

Blake, Valéry, and Yeats may be contributing, in very different ways, to Stevens' final finding of the eye and ear. Valéry's *Palme* ends by calling the tree the image of a thinking mind that is augmented by its own gifts of the spirit:

Pareille à celui qui pense
Et dont l'âme se dépense
À s'accroître de ses dons!

Blake is closer to Stevens in that he stations the palm tree "upon the edge of Beulah" in *Jerusalem*, 23, so that the emblem of Christ's entrance into Jerusalem represents also the verge of the abyss, the last barrier before the void where the souls of the dead are caught. But Stevens' palm is finally more a rival to Yeats's vision of a golden bough, upon which a metal bird prophesies in the Byzantium that is a city of the mind. As a rival to Yeats's finalities, Stevens' poem alludes to a lifetime's work upon which the authority of this majestic sense of mere being is founded. *Sunday Morning* had denied the "cloudy palm / Remote on heaven's hill" because it had not endured "as April's green endures." Poor Crispin had been saluted as "the poetic hero without palms / Or jugglery, without regalia," in a parodic fulfillment of Wordsworth's prophecy of poetic maturation: "Another race hath been, and other palms are won." The most memorable image of a palm in *Harmonium* is the vitalistic "big-finned palm / And green vine angering for life" of *Nomad Exquisite*. Closest to the palm in *Of Mere Being* is *Description without Place*, v:

> It is an expectation, a desire,
> A palm that rises up beyond the sea,
>
> A little different from reality.

But the last vision is considerably beyond this sea, beyond thought as well as fact, in the bronze decor of death. "Beyond . . . thought" appears to be directed against the "human meaning" and "human feeling" of the song of Yeats's bird, which sings of what is past, or passing, or to come. Stevens hears a "foreign song," perhaps remembering that "foreign" is derived from the Latin for "out of doors" or "abroad" and that its root means "doorway." The song is a doorway to what is beyond the mind, and so beyond even the later reason or rational irrational with which Stevens has learned to imagine his poems. That the bird *sings*, that its feathers *shine*, that it is the synecdoche of mere being is what makes us happy *or* unhappy, depending presumably upon our own natures. But that it makes Stevens happy, here at the very close of life and of poetry, is made clear by his language:

> The palm stands on the edge of space.
> The wind moves slowly in the branches.
> The bird's fire-fangled feathers dangle down.

There is still weather at the end, as the wind moves slowly and helps create the final Stevensian trope with its curious, slight suggestion of a phoenix, as the fire-fashioned feathers of the bird transumptively repeat the concluding trope of *Sunday Morning:* "Downward to darkness, on extended wings." Yet these feathers of fire dangle down rather than undulate ambiguously. The essential gaudiness of *Harmonium* is more than fulfilled in the gaiety of "dangle," of a last daring in hanging loosely while swinging and swaying to and fro, there at the edge of space, and in the ultimate dandyism of "fire-fangled," with its hint of a supernatural foppery, an audacious sense of having fabricated or tricked out oneself, a sense that is inescapably Whitmanian. In *Our Stars Come from Ireland* (1948), Stevens had enjoyed an American vision of "The Westwardness of Everything":

> The whole habit of the mind is changed by them,
> These Gaeled and fitful-fangled darknesses
> Make suddenly luminous, themselves a change,
> An east in their compelling westwardness,
>
> Themselves an issue as at an end, as if
> There was an end at which in a final change,
> When the whole habit of the mind was changed,
> The ocean breathed out morning in one breath.

"Fire-fangled feathers" are "fitful-fangled darkness / Made suddenly luminous," and Stevens himself, "in a final change," perhaps now sees himself as "an east in their compelling westwardness." Yet even such a vision is more playful than exalted, thanks to "dangle" and to the internal rhyming of "the bird's fire-fangled feathers dangle down." Stevens had been experimenting with this effect, in 1949, in *An Ordinary Evening in New Haven*, XXIX: "Dangling and spangling, the mic-mac of mocking birds," and *The Old Lutheran Bells at Home:* "As they jangle and dangle and kick their feet." The insouciance of the final image was best anticipated in *A Lot of People Bathing in a Stream* (*CP*, 371):

> We bathed in yellow-green and yellow blue
> And in these comic colors dangled down.

That his death image proper should be so innocent a dangling down is wholly appropriate for Wallace Stevens. *A*

Mythology Reflects Its Region, also of 1955, raising the question of the truth of images, asserts, "The image must be of the nature of its creator." There is a Sublime chill in *Of Mere Being*, but there is also an increasing or heightening that is of the nature of the American Sublime. Stevens—like Emerson, Whitman, Dickinson, Frost, Hart Crane—has become a vital part of the American mythology:

> It is he, anew, in a freshened youth
> And it is he in the substance of his region,
> Wood of his forests and stone out of his fields
> Or from under his mountains.

14 Coda: Poetic Crossing

It is easy to find hidden things if their places are pointed out and marked, and, in like fashion, if we wish to track down an argument we should know places.

—Richard McKeon

Not through subtle subterranean channels need friend and fact be drawn to their counterpart, but, rightly considered, these things proceed from the eternal generation of the soul. Cause and effect are two sides of one fact.

—Emerson

A poem begins because there is an absence. An image must be given, for a beginning, and so that absence ironically is called a presence. Or, a poem begins because there is too strong a presence, which needs to be imaged as an absence, if there is to be any imaging at all. So Stevens began *Domination of Black*, suspended between these dialectics and troping for the first time against Shelley's fiction of the leaves:'

At night, by the fire,
The colors of the bushes
And of the fallen leaves,
Repeating themselves,
Turned in the room,
Like the leaves themselves
Turning in the wind.

With just a few other poems written in 1915–16 (including *Blanche McCarthy*, *Sunday Morning*, the unfinished *For an Old*

Woman in a Wig, and *Six Significant Landscapes*), this text was Stevens' true starting point as a poet. He was thirty-seven years old as he wrote, yet the short lines carry the resonances of a master, who knows fully what it means to say that the colors of the fallen leaves are *"repeating* themselves." Thirty times and more in the next forty years Stevens' poetry would repeat, crucially, some form of the word "repeat," until Stevens could write of his Penelope meditating the repetitious but never culminating advent of her Ulysses:

> She would talk a little to herself as she combed her hair,
> Repeating his name with its patient syllables,
> Never forgetting him that kept coming constantly so near.

But that meditation, forty years later, though it turns upon a dialectic of presence and absence, relies less upon images than the image-named *Domination of Black*. In this early lyric we sit at night by the fire and we associate the colors turning in the room, by firelight, with the autumnal and the literary colors of bushes and fallen leaves, in a repetition that is qualified by the closing lines of the first stanza:

> Yes: but the color of the heavy hemlocks
> Came striding.
> And I remembered the cry of the peacocks.

As in Yeats, the cry of Juno's birds presages the end of an era, and the domination of black plays against the multicolored and Shelleyan trope of the leaves. "Colors" are a traditional synonym for "tropes," and to trope is to execute a "turning." Stevens had begun his poem with what the Freudians, in their tropological system, call a "reaction formation," a defensive movement of the spirit that is opposed to a repressed desire and so manifests itself as a reaction against that desire.

In 1940, Lionel Trilling, in his ambivalent and moving essay *Freud and Literature*, remarked that "it was left to Freud to discover how, in a scientific age, we still feel and think in figurative formations, and to create, what psychoanalysis is, a science of tropes, of metaphors and its variants, synecdoche and metonymy." Trilling prophesied many later recognitions, Gallic as well as American, and we can add to his insight now by tracing the derivation of Freud's formulations, from ancient rhetoric through the transitional discipline of associationist psychology. But I wish that Freud had used the ancient names, as well as the old notions, so that we could call a reaction formation what rhetorically it is, an *illusio* or simple irony, irony as a figure of speech. Stevens says that the autumnal colors troped in the room, yet he means mostly that they repeated themselves, with the repetition being a play of substitutions and not of the colors themselves. "Repeated themselves" requires to be read as its opposite, "failed to repeat themselves," which is why Stevens is vulnerable to the black dominant of the hemlocks and the other cry of mortality, that of the peacocks. To get started, his lyric had to say the exact opposite of what it meant.

To explain how and why that observation is accurate is to arrive at a theory of poetic interpretation. This theory depends upon the verifiable pronouncement that the language of British and American poetry, from at least Wordsworth to the present, is overdetermined in its patternings and so necessarily is underdetermined in its meanings. When Stevens turns against his lyric's opening figurations, he must give us a synecdoche for death in the domination of the black color of the heavy hemlocks, and it is equally predictable that the next movement of his little dejection ode should substitute a metonymic reduction as an obsessive undoing of that synecdoche:

> The colors of their tails
> Were like the leaves themselves
> Turning in the wind,
> In the twilight wind.
> They swept over the room,
> Just as they flew from the boughs of the hemlocks
> Down to the ground.

The peacocks, like the leaves, are in the room only as colors or turnings, and these momentarily repeal the sombre figuration of the hemlocks. But these colors too yield next to a hyperbolic figuration, the high dominant of the peacocks, wonderfully caught up in the synesthesia of "the loud fire":

I heard them cry—the peacocks.
Was it a cry against the twilight
Or against the leaves themselves
Turning in the wind,
Turning as the flames
Turned in the fire,
Turning as the tails of the peacocks
Turned in the loud fire,
Loud as the hemlocks
Full of the cry of the peacocks?
Or was it a cry against the hemlocks?

These eleven lines about the cry can be termed one of Stevens' earliest achievements of the Sublime. If the cry is against the turning of the leaves, then it is a lament against mutability. But, as in *Sunday Morning*, the final form of change is death, and so the second question contains the first; the cry is against the trope of the hemlocks, against the color of mortality.

Had Stevens ended the poem there, it would have been little more than the Imagistic exercise some critics have praised it as being, a kind of Shelleyan lament assimilated to the mode of Laforgue or the early Eliot. But the final stanza has two sharply contrasting tropes, moving the entire poem into a very different mode. First, there is a fine transformation of one of Coleridge's best moments, when Stevens sets himself as inside observer against a cosmic outside, in a juxtaposition that prophesies the great confrontation of *The Auroras of Autumn:*

Out of the window,
I saw how the planets gathered
Like the leaves themselves
Turning in the wind.

In *Dejection: An Ode,* Coleridge looks out of the window at the western sky, just before a storm, "and with how blank an eye!" anticipating both Emerson's *Nature:* "The ruin or the blank that we see when we look at nature, is in our own eye," and Stevens' *Auroras:* "The man who is walking turns blankly on the sand." What Coleridge sees, stars and moon, he sees precisely, but without the capacity to rejoice in his own seeing:

> I see them all so excellently fair,
> I see, not feel, how beautiful they are!

Stevens, out of his window, sees his own (and Shelley's) trope; the gathering planets are *like* the leaves turning in the wind. This giant perspectivizing shrinks the cosmos to one autumnal metaphor, but Stevens ends his poem with a very different figuration:

> I saw how the night came,
> Came striding like the color of the heavy hemlocks.
> I felt afraid.
> And I remembered the cry of the peacocks.

This is a prolepsis again of the Stevens of the *Auroras*, who as "the scholar of one candle" gazes upon the flames of the northern lights, "and he feels afraid." Yet, in this early poem, Stevens is content to taste the defeat of belatedness. The length of the oncoming night's steps renders the blackness more vividly, because the tropic "striding" itself undoes an earlier trope in the first stanza, where "the color of the heavy hemlocks / Came striding." So the striding night tropes upon a trope, in a metaleptic reversal, raising the poem's final lines to an almost apocalyptic pitch of rhetoricity, of excessive word-consciousness (a text's equivalent of human self-consciousness).

I have been mapping *Domination of Black* as a tropological pattern, yet to do so is to invoke also a pattern of psychic defenses. Stevens concludes his poem by introjecting the imminence of death and so by projecting the fiction of the leaves, which in Shelley as in Wordsworth intimates an immortality. I want now to develop a technique for the antithetical mapping of poems, one that should bring us closer to the cognitive workings of poetry, from Wordsworth to Stevens and beyond, and that will return to *Domination of Black* as a later example. In order to make this suggestion, I must begin by entering again the problematic of Romantic imagery, by way of the largest inventor of the Romantic image, Wordsworth.

Owen Barfield's theory of Romantic imagery, in his brilliant theosophical study *Saving the Appearances*, depends on the notion he calls "participation," which is our awareness "of an

extra-sensory link between the percipient and the representations." As participation waned, down the centuries, memory-
images were substituted for it, and we fell into an idolatry of
these memory-images. Barfield's high evaluation of Romanticism results from his conviction (in which he follows Rudolf
Steiner) that the Romantic image was an idol-smashing weapon
meant to return men to their original participation in the phenomena. For Barfield, the Romantic image is thus certainly a
figure of will:

> There *is* a close relation between language as it is used by a partici-
> pating consciousness and language as it is used, at a later stage, meta-
> phorically or symbolically. When we use language metaphorically, we
> bring it about of our own free will that an appearance means some-
> thing other than itself. . . . We start with an idol, and we ourselves
> turn the idol into a representation. . . .
> As long as nature herself continued to be apprehended as image, it
> sufficed for the artist to imitate Nature. . . .
> Henceforth, if nature is to be experienced as representation, she
> will be experienced as representation of—Man. . . . It is part of the
> creed of idolatry that, when we speak of Man, we mean only the body
> of this or that man, or at most his finite personality.

Barfield says that the will gives us imagistic representations
of human personality, and he terms these representations
images of nature, or in effect pathetic fallacies, as Ruskin called
them. Romantic iconoclasm, for Barfield as for Ruskin, did not
go far enough. It is curious to find an exact parallel to this judgment in the subtlest and most advanced essay yet ventured on
these matters, Paul de Man's *Intentional Structure of the Romantic
Image*. De Man emphasizes the absolute separation between
consciousness and nature in early Romanticism:

> Poetic language can do nothing but originate anew over and over
> again: it is always constitutive, able to posit regardless of presence
> but, by the same token, unable to give a foundation to what it posits
> except as an intent of consciousness. The word is always a free pres-
> ence to the mind, the means by which the permanence of natural enti-
> ties can be put into question and thus negated, time and again, in the
> endlessly widening spiral of the dialectic.

De Man's Romantic dialectic widens its spiral so endlessly that we will see him concluding his essay by saying that the works of the early Romantics, Rousseau and Wordsworth, give us *no* "actual examples" of Romantic imagery! Indeed, though de Man credits Rousseau and Wordsworth with being "the first modern writers to have put into question, in the language of poetry, the ontological priority of the sensory object," he is still compelled to say that they were "at most, *underway* towards renewed insights." Yet no one knows or asserts better than de Man the continued priority of Rousseau and Wordsworth over all later writers, who compared to those great precursors are scarcely even underway. And no one, in my judgment, has gone beyond de Man's statement about Wordsworth's concept of "imagination":

This "imagination" has little in common with the faculty that produces natural images born "as flowers originate." It marks instead a possibility for consciousness to exist entirely by and for itself, independently of all relationship with the outside world, without being moved by an intent aimed at a part of this world.

What de Man has done is to trace the intentional structure of the Romantic image in Rousseau and Wordsworth and also to assure us, convincingly, that this structure has yet to be interpreted accurately by scholarship, but then finally to assure us also that even Rousseau and Wordsworth actually could not carry out their own structural intentions. The Romantic image, on this account, turns out to be neither hyperbolical nor transumptive but purely visionary, an aspiration beyond the limits of art.

We might credit de Man with considerable irony in this essay, irony being his favorite trope. His formula, "to put into question," equals "to undergo the process of rhetorical substitution" by, as he says, "the word," *logos* in the sense of "meaning." Wordsworth's "word" puts into question "the permanence of natural entities," the *ethos* of nature, by substituting tropes of *pathos*, of passion and suffering, for tropes of *ethos*, of character and incident. I think that we can analyze Wordsworth's originality more fully than has been done if we continue and expand the study of the interplay of *ethos* and *pathos* in his poems, a study begun already by a group of scholars including Klaus Dockhorn, Herbert Lindenberger, Robert Langbaum, and Geoffrey Hartman.

Ethos, the Greek word for "custom," "image," "trait," goes back to a root meaning "self." We use it now to mean the character or attitude of a group, but Aristotle meant by it the character of an individual, as opposed to his emotions, or perhaps he meant what was permanent or ideal in anyone's character. *Pathos*, the Greek for "passion," goes back to a root meaning to "suffer." We use it now to mean a quality in someone that arouses feelings of pity or sympathy in anyone else, but Aristotle meant by it something like any person's transient and emotional frame of mind. Quintilian usefully remarks that *ethos* and *pathos* are different degrees of the same entity, the emotions, with *ethos* meaning the less violent and continuous emotions, such as affection, and *pathos* the more violent and momentary emotions, such as those we now call Romantic love. Quintilian's most useful insight is to associate *ethos* with irony and comedy, and *pathos* with tragedy; and so, by implication, with irony's rival as a master trope, synecdoche.

In more Freudian terms, *ethos* results from the successful translation of the will into an act, verbal or physical, whereas *pathos* ensues when there is a failure to translate will into act. In the terms I employed in *Poetry and Repression*, *ethos* is a reseeing and *pathos* a reaiming, with the middle position between them in the dialectic of revision being taken by *logos* as a re-esteeming or re-estimating. Rhetoric, conceived as a text or system of tropes, is an *ethos*, while rhetoric as persuasion falls under *pathos*, with an *aporia* between them as a *logos*. This formulation is de Man's, and I will use it more fully later in this chapter. But now I want to inquire, what is the value of analyzing Wordsworth's poetry in terms of *ethos*, *logos*, and *pathos*, rather than in terms of the revisionary dialectic I employed in *A Map of Misreading* and *Poetry and Repression*, the Kabbalistic triad of limitation, substitution, and representation?

The Kabbalistic terms themselves were derived, ultimately,

from the Greek terms anyway, and this is certainly part of the answer. But Wordsworth himself uses his own variants of these traditional terms of rhetoric, as Dockhorn and Lindenberger have shown. *Ethos* in Wordsworth is "character" or "incident," or more structurally the spirit of place revealing its character, with or without incident, through images of voice. *Logos* in Wordsworth is what Hartman calls a "re-cognition leading to recognition," with "recognition" being another name for *pathos* as suffering and passion. We can surmise that Wordsworth surmounted his own epistemological confusions about the status of poetic images by making his great images *afterimages of voice*, usually the voice of the dead or of his own dead self. "Images of voice" is a tricky notion, worked out in different ways by Hartman, Angus Fletcher, and John Hollander, and I will consider their formulations in a later book when I explain more fully the concept of *topos* that is involved in my theory of Poetic Crossing.

It is a truism of criticism from Aristotle through Sidney to Northrop Frye that poetry takes place between the concept and the example. In Wordsworth, this old realization becomes dialectical, in that poetic meaning or poetic thinking takes place in the substitution not only of *pathos* (example) for *ethos* (precept) but of *ethos* for *pathos* also. This dialectical movement supports Hartman's contention that Wordsworth was neither a "transcendentalist" nor an "associationist" or "sensationalist." Wordsworth's thinking, Hartman says, "starts with objects not as they *are* but as they *appear* to a mind fruitfully perplexed by their differing modes of appearance, and which does not try to reduce these to a single standard."

We can contrast Hartman's account with an accepted British scholarly analysis of the same problematic in Wordsworth, C. G. Clarke's *Romantic Paradox*. Clarke says that "if, like Wordsworth, we retain a layman's faith in the independent existence of everything—or virtually everything—given to sense, and yet remain covertly convinced that what the senses know is an attribute of *consciousness* . . . then we may well find perceptual experience contradictory." The result, in Clarke's judgment, is the equivocal status of Wordsworth's Romantic image, so that it is an appearance plus a thing. But here is Hartman, subtly tracing Wordsworth's dialectic of *ethos, logos, pathos,* or spirit of place haunted by images of voice, substituted for through a re-cognition of the place and ensuing in a recognition that clarifies the image. I run together in the following some widely separated passages from Hartman's book on Wordsworth, so as to give a cento on the dialectic of Wordsworthian imagery:

The power of nature to retard, or to transmute from action to passion the brief moment of truly individual being, is what raises the largest emotions: pity, perplexity, wonder. . . .

The soul needs the "inscrutable workmanship" of its early association with nature in order to resist the crude interventions and immediate demands of reason. . . .

Cognition is recognition as generation should be regeneration. . . .

[The after-image] expresses the possibility of the renewal (or at least recurrence) of a certain experience by including that possibility in the very structure of the experience. . . .

The after-image could be defined as a re-cognition that leads to recognition.

Hartman is arguing that Wordsworth refused to yield up a residue of associationism because that would have meant starting the poetic process at a point beyond object-consciousness, as Blake did. Wordsworth raises himself to a transcendence of object-consciousness through his faith that, as he remarked against Ossian, "in nature everything is distinct, yet nothing defined into absolute independent singleness." Or, as Wordsworth phrased this elsewhere, in a letter to Landor, a truly imaginative passage will follow such natural vision until, in a heightening, "things are lost in each other, and limits vanish, and aspirations are raised." We can sum this in a formula: The authentic temporal moment is thwarted *by nature,* which reveals to the poet that immediacy or presence is indeed an *illusio* or ironical dialectic, a here and now always self-negating.

But this natural thwarting educates the poet's mind, by reading the *ethos* of nature, its "action," without an immediately full significance. *Ethos* has become limitation, a contraction or withdrawal of meaning, that opens the way for a rethinking that is necessarily a remeaning. This is very much akin, as we will see, to the delayed signification that Freud calls *Nachträglichkeit*, or "aftering." *Ethos* or character or natural action is converted into a poet's fate, and the re-cognition becomes the path of imaginative freedom, until the power of self-recognition intervenes, completing the dialectic with a passage into the ultimate *pathos* of wonder.

Hartman, in his own later work, the essays on psychoesthetics in *The Fate of Reading*, uses this Wordsworthian dialectic of afterimaging as an excess-and-defect model that might replace I. A. Richards' stimulus-and-response psychic model for poetry. The topical image-of-voice becomes an excess of demand, the poem's redundancy of pressure upon both language and the self. *Ethos* thus is what language cannot sustain, or rather *ethos* works to limit unsustainable demands upon language. *Pathos* or recognition becomes a defect of response, or the survival of a will-to-representation after representation has been attained. I want now to translate these Hartmanian ideas into a stricter language of psychologized trope, but here I verge upon the barrier of what I take to be the most clarifying mode of criticism currently available to us, the "deconstruction" of Paul de Man and Jacques Derrida.

I have encountered no clear definitions of deconstruction as a criticism of poetry and so offer the following. Marie-Rose Logan sees Derridian philosophical deconstruction as a process aiming "at unveiling the implicit or uncritically accepted memory of any given concept," and she cites *Positions*, where Derrida says: "To deconstruct philosophy would thus mean to think the structured genealogy of the philosophical concepts in the closest and most intimate way and yet to determine, at the same time, from a certain outside unwarrantable, unnamable by philosophy itself, what this history might have dissimulated or forbidden."

Let us transpose this from philosophy to poetry. To deconstruct a poem would mean to uncover whatever its rhetoricity conveyed, even if the poem, the poet, and the tradition of its interpretation showed no overt awareness of what implicitly was revealed by such word-consciousness. Rhetoricity, in this sense, is a questioning on the poem's part of its place in literary language, that is, the poem's *own* subversion of its own closure, its illusory status as independent poem. Again, this sense of rhetoricity (which is de Man's) would include both major aspects of word-consciousness, rhetoric as persuasion and rhetoric as a system of tropes. Between these aspects, in de Man's interpretation of Nietzsche's theories of rhetoric and of identity, there falls always an *aporia*, a figuration of doubt, which may be the prin‚le of rhetorical substitution itself. To deconstruct a poem is to indicate the precise location of its figuration of doubt, its uncertain notice of that limit where persuasion yields to a dance or interplay of tropes.

Hartman keeps hinting that this process of deconstruction is not "reading," but necessarily Hartman's "reading" is itself a figuration for his own kind of interpretation, his own Will-to-Power over texts. *Contra* Hartman, it would not be unfair to say that the Derrida–de Man "deconstruction" is simply the most advanced form of a purely rhetorical criticism now available to us. "Deconstruction" *is* reading, but this is Over-Reading, or the reading of an Over-Man, who knows simultaneously how to fulfill and to transcend the text, or rather how to make the text expose the *aporia* between its self-fulfillment and its self-transcendence. For Over-Reader we could substitute "analytical or conceptual rhetorician" or simply "philosopher of rhetoric."

The limits of a purely rhetorical criticism, however advanced, are established by its inevitable reductiveness, its necessary attempt to see poetry as being a conceptual rhetoric, *and nothing more*. Rhetoric, considered as a system of tropes, yields much more readily to analysis than does rhetoric considered as persuasion, for persuasion, in poetry, takes us into a realm that also includes the lie. Poems lie primarily against three adversaries:

There is a hidden relation between the "end" of classical rhetoric and the rise of the eighteenth-century psychology founded upon the association of ideas, and indeed an even more complex hidden relation between four modes that assert more diversity than they possess: Classical and Renaissance rhetoric; seventeenth-century and eighteenth-century association-of-ideas psychology; Romantic poetry, from Wordsworth to this moment; Freudian psychoanalysis. When the associationists— Locke, Hume, Gay, Hartley, Tucker being the progression of founders—developed their psychology, they founded it (perhaps unconsciously) upon the topics or commonplaces of rhetoric, precisely because they wished to usurp the place and function of rhetoric. But Wordsworth, Coleridge, and their followers, by translating the commonplaces to their own purposes, brought back a powerful, implicit psychologized rhetoric in which topics regenerated tropes, and these tropes in turn elaborated themselves as defensive structures of consciousness. Happily unaware of this return of repressed rhetoric, the main associationist tradition passed on to Bentham and the Mills. Freud, translating the younger Mill, took over from him the Lockean notion of object-representation, which thus became the common ancestor both of Freud's system of defenses and of the tropological patterns of Romantic imagery.

Here I want to open again the large question of what rhetoric is: What is a trope? What is a topic or commonplace? What is the large relation of meaning to rhetoric, in poetry? Aristotle distinguished sophistic, as a mode of logic, from both analytical demonstration and dialectic. Sophistic relies upon premises that are not commonly held or even relevant, though they *appear* to be both. Aristotle says of the wielders of sophistic that they are those who argue as competitors and as rivals unto the death, which I believe to be one of the stigmata that necessarily afflict belated poets. This leads Aristotle to his crucial definition of rhetoric: it stems from dialectic or *logos* and from morals or *ethos* and *pathos*, yet it is only a faculty, or way of choosing, the best means of persuading an audience. Aristotle locates in the audience the *logos* or reason that needs to be satisfied, and also in that audience the *pathos* that needs to be moved, whereas the speaker is the locus of the *ethos* involved, since he must persuade his auditors of his own reliability or virtue.

That is the traditional vision of rhetoric, and we can say of it that it followed Plato's lead in "correcting" Gorgias, with his despised "relativism." Untersteiner, in his book *The Sophists*, illuminatingly defends Gorgias from the misrepresentations of Plato and of Aristotle. Gorgias exalted the orator as a *psychagogos*, a poet leading souls through incantation to the relativity of all truth, and doing this through an antithetical style, one which offered contrasts and alternatives for every definition ventured, in contrast to the Socratic mode of arriving at supposedly absolute truth. This ensues, in Gorgias, in the splendidly poetic notion he called *to kairon*, "the opportune," prophesying the opportunism that is the quick of every poetic invention. Since two antithetical statements can be made on anything, any subject involves a choice between or mixture of two antitheses, so that consideration of *kairos* (time, place, circumstance, or as Stevens or a modern Greek would say, the weather) must solve the *aporia* and lead first to a choice of a relative truth, and subsequently to action. *Kairos* then for orator or poet determines choice of organization, mode of proof, and stance and style. This, as Untersteiner says, is "the adaptation of the speech to the manifold variety of life, to the psychology of speaker and hearer: variegated, not absolute unity of tone." We can apply here, as a powerful ally for Untersteiner's defense of Gorgias, the insistence of Nietzsche that the Sophists were truly Hellenic, and the Socratic polemic against the Sophists a symptom of decadence. I now give a cento of Nietzsche's critique of Greek philosophy in aphorisms 427–30 of *The Will to Power:*

Good and evil of differing origin are mingled: the boundary between good and evil is blurred— This is the "Sophist"— . . .

It is a very remarkable moment: the Sophists verge upon the first *critique of morality*, the first *insight* into morality:—they juxtapose the multiplicity (the geographical relativity) of the moral value judgments. . . .

What, then, is the significance of the reaction of Socrates, who recommended dialectics as the road to virtue . . . ?

. . . *In praxi*, this means that moral judgments are torn from their conditionality, in which they have grown and alone possess any meaning, from their Greek and Greek-political ground and soil, to be denaturalized under the pretense of sublimation. The great concepts "good" and "just" are severed from the presuppositions to which they belong and, as liberated "ideas," become objects of dialectic. One looks for truth in them, takes them for entities or signs of entities: one *invents* a world where they are at home, where they originate—

I follow de Man when I observe that the "tearing" and "severing," of which Nietzsche speaks here, are linguistic events. These late Nietzschean aphorisms juxtapose illuminatingly with an early Nietzschean reflection on the process of rhetorical substitution that de Man has cited as basic to Nietzsche's theory of rhetoric:

The abstract nouns are properties within and outside ourselves that are being torn away from their supports and considered to be autonomous entities. . . . Such concepts, which owe their existence only to our feelings, are posited as if they were the inner essence of things: we attribute to events a cause which in truth is only an effect. The abstractions create the illusion as if *they* were the entity that causes the properties, whereas they receive their objective, iconic existence only from us as a consequence of these very properties.

One of de Man's great contributions lies in his having shown us how Nietzsche links a theory of rhetoric with a theory of action and identity. The best commentary on both the Nietzschean passages I've quoted is de Man's vision of Nietzsche dismissing the reductive meaning of rhetoric as eloquence and concentrating instead upon the epistemology of the tropes:

Nietzsche's final insight may well concern rhetoric itself, the discovery that what is called "rhetoric" is precisely the gap that becomes apparent in the pedagogical and philosophical history of the term. Considered as persuasion, rhetoric is performative but when considered as a system of tropes, it deconstructs its own performance. Rhetoric is a *text* in that it allows for two incompatible, mutually self-destructive points of view and therefore puts an insurmountable obstacle in the way of any reading or understanding. The *aporia* between performative and constative language is merely a version of the *aporia* between trope and persuasion that both generates and paralyzes rhetoric and thus gives it the appearance of a history.

De Man's achievement is to have defined, following Nietzsche, the *aporia* or figuration of doubt that the principle of rhetorical substitution always constitutes in any poetic text. He locates this *between* rhetoric as the *art* of persuasion and rhetoric as *persuasion*. De Man does not attempt to name this mental dilemma or *topos* of liminality, yet he implies that such an *aporia* participates in the problematics of Derrida's "différance," the postponement or swerving repetition that is manifested in the dance and interplay of tropes within a poetic text. The de Manian *aporia*, despite its Nietzschean origins, is indistinguishable from a Gnostic formulation such as the Valentinian or Lurianic Breaking of the Vessels. Like a vision of the Gnosis, this *aporia* is a transgression that leads from taboo to transcendence, or in the imagery of Romance it serves as the threshold between temple and labyrinth. Because he is a conceptual rhetorician, defending poetry against the grammarian on one side and against the semiologist on the other, de Man valorizes the *aporia* between system of tropes and persuasion as the *logos*, a valorization that audaciously redefines poetic thinking *as* the process of rhetorical *substitution* rather than as a thinking by particular trope. In de Man's view, poetry cannot be reduced to the interplay between metonymic and metaphorical thinking, which is the Jakobsonian reduction, nor to ironic thinking (though this is a temptation for de Man), nor to the various forms of representational thinking—synecdochal, hyperbolic, even metaleptic—that have characterized Romantic and psychoanalytical conceptualizings. If the *aporia* is the only *logos* that modern poetry possesses, then the negative moment in any poem, the moment that locates the *aporia*, is necessarily an epistemological moment, with the authority to deconstruct its own text, that is, to indicate the text's cognitive awareness of its own limit as text, its own status as rhetoricity, its own demystification of the fiction of closure.

For de Man, then, criticism *begins* with the Nietzschean act of locating the *aporia* and continues by relocating it anew with each reading of each text. But here, up to now, de Man appears to me to limit himself by the asceticism of his own concept of trope, which isolates too purifyingly the trope from the *topos* or commonplace that generates it. With reverence for this advanced critical consciousness, the most rigorous and scrupulous in the field today, I now part from him to what I consider a larger and deeper concept of trope, a misprision of trope undoubtedly. Yet I believe that every critic necessarily tropes the concept of trope, for *there are no tropes*, but only concepts of tropes or figures of figures.

What is a trope? It is one of two possibilities only—either the will translating itself into a verbal act or figure of *ethos*, or else the will failing to translate itself and so abiding as a verbal desire or figure of *pathos*. But, either way, the trope *is* a figure of will rather than a figure of knowledge. The trope is a cut or gap made in or into the anteriority of language, itself an anteriority in which "language" acts as a figurative substitution for time. Just here, though it is rather late to be attempting fundamental definitions, I am compelled to explain the vision of rhetoric that my enterprise has taken as starting point. This vision is Gnostic and Kabbalistic in its ultimate origins.

Kabbalistic rhetorical theory, as formulated particularly by Cordovero in the figurations he called *behinot*, leads one to consider texts not as linguistic structures but as instances of *the will to utter within a tradition of uttering*. The *behinot*, as composite tropes, are magical devices for gaining the power that lies *beyond* the literal or proper truth. Such devices, as orthodox Talmudists said against Kabbalah, are dangerously close to wishes, equivocations, or lies told to the self by the self. John Hollander is knowingly within Talmudic tradition when he sums up the Lurianic dialectic of creation as "concepts of withdrawing from linguistic signification (or indeed from truth), filling it with meaning (as an effusion of will, of intending to utter) to overflowing, and a final restitution of meaning in a transformed significance." Hollander's summary is brilliantly apt, and yet its perspective is anything but Kabbalistic. Such a summary, in the tradition of the Gaon of Vilna, while it does not assume that proper or literal meaning necessarily exists *in* language, still implies that truth can be expressed *through* the interplay of proper and figurative meaning. Kabbalah, as a Gnosis, starts with the rival assumption, which is that all distinction between proper and figurative meaning in language has been totally lost since the catastrophe of creation. Another way of saying this is that a Kabbalistic or Gnostic theory of rhetoric must deny that there can be any *particular* semantic tension in language, because in the Kabbalistic vision all language is nothing but semantic tension raised to apocalyptic pitch.

The contemporary French rhetorician Gérard Genette says that a trope is nothing but a reader's awareness of a trope, an awareness that comes into existence only when the reader either recognizes or half recognizes that a text is problematic or ambiguous in its evasions of, or schematic deviations from, proper meaning. I would say rather that a trope is a reader's awareness of a poet's willed error and results only from a reader's *will to be lied to*, or to be repersuaded of persuasions already implicitly formulated that are crucial for the survival of the reader's own internal discourse, the hum of thoughts evaded in the reader's own mind. But I verge here upon the true outrageousness of Kabbalistic theory of rhetoric. Kabbalah misreads all language that is not Kabbalah, and I assert now that belated strong poetry misreads all language that is not poetry. Another way of saying this, in terms currently fashionable, is that all rhetoric as a system of tropes is a synchronic rhetoric, but all rhetoric as persuasion is diachronic, so that the *aporia* between the two indeed is beyond resolution. Poems misread earlier poems, yet they also misread every use of language that is not poetic, which means that the history of any language is an endless process of misprision. If a condition of poetic strength is a cunning in evading and distorting tradition, as I think it is, then what can persist and become tradition in any language must be a strength of misprision also.

Here I am compelled to clarify or perhaps even revise my own notion of misprision, to make a misprision of misprision, as it were. Misprision is the process by which the meanings of intentionality trope down to the mere significances of language, or conversely the process by which the significations of language can be transformed or troped upward into the meaningful world of our Will-to-Power over time and its henchman, language. Here I will cite Hollander again, and at length:

Tropes, or turns that occur between the meanings of intention and the significances of linguistic utterances, are twisted through the plane of truth while yet all the more strongly connecting the will and the text which it flies like a flag "as it fitfully gleams, half-conceals, half-discloses" the impulses which raise it. Whereas formalist criticisms have concerned themselves with the trope in the text alone, Bloom's sees this kind of study as two-dimensional and paradigmatic at best. For him, a trope is a twisted strand of transformational process, anchored deep in a rock of expressive need, and stretched upward, taut, to a connection at the surface with a flat sheet of text. Formalist and structuralist readings would be like more or less detailed plans of the textual surface, affording a view of the end-section only of the tropical rope. Bloom is concerned with the length of the rope, the layers of whatever it is through which it passes, the ways in which, at any particular level, the strands may seem in their twisting to be pointing away from the determined direction upward, the relative degrees of tension and slackness and so forth. His is the most recent manifestation in a strange history of troping the concept of trope itself.

If I may trope Hollander's troping of me, tropes have nothing to do with not being literal, since ordinarily nothing is literal anyway, or to quote again a line of Hollander's: "All is trope save in games." A trope is a stance or a ratio of revision; it defends against other tropes. But what, in language, is a stance? Ancient rhetoricians derived their notion of stance from boxers and wrestlers; modern rhetoric ought to derive its notion from batters and pitchers in baseball. Stevens' apparent ironies remind us of a batter swinging several bats together in the batter's circle before stepping up to the plate with a single bat, which will feel surprisingly light in his hands. The several bats do the work of "the final no" after which "there comes a yes / And on that yes the future world depends." The major Hellenistic *rhetor* Hermagoras, who taught misprision circa 150 B.C., said that *heuresis* or invention included *staseis* or stances, which were modes by which problems could be assaulted. Hermagoras perfected four stances: 1) the question, "Did my client do it?" 2) the end, "Was it a crime, anyway?" 3) the quality, "Was it an act of honor, or of expediency?" 4) the metalepsis, "It was all the victim's fault, anyway." I am delighted to find a precursor in Hermagoras and quote Hollander again to establish that I am a properly unscrupulous ephebe of Hermagoras:

> Bloom . . . , in his concern for the schematic and deep connections between stances toward a predecessor, stances taken by utterance itself against what one means to say, stances taken by what one means to say against what the unconscious means for one to mean, and so forth, has undertaken to deal with a concept of trope far more general than that of the rhetorician. Operating in the realm in which the relation between realities and superstructures (Freudian, Marxian), between source and manifestation, usually seeks to reduce the latter to the former, he has propounded a kind of opening unscientific preface to a quest in these dialectical regions. [He sees] the war for authenticity and finality between surface (text) and depths (intentions variously clear and dark) as a true struggle of contraries.

To trope Hollander again, the conceptual rhetorician's notion of trope, whether de Man's or Genette's, does not interpret this war between text and intentions but fights instead on the side of text. Even de Man is thus part of the problem and not of the solution, for the pure rhetorician who regards the psyche as merely another text himself therefore argues on only one side of an authentic and ancient battle: with Socrates, Plato, and Aristotle against the sophists; with Plotinus against the Gnostics; with the Talmudists against the Kabbalists. Every notion of the will that we have is itself a trope, even when it tropes against the will, by asserting that the will is a linguistic fiction. Consciousness and writing alike take us back to the will and what it intends, and however such intentions are viewed they are being troped, for this history too has been adopted by both parties. But poets, at least belated strong poets or the ones we have who matter during the last two centuries, are less conceptual rhetoricians than they are masters of misprision, and to study them more truly and more strange we need a wilder definition of trope than de Man or Genette affords us. We need, I think, to revivify the ancient identity between rhetoric and psychology that is still being partly obscured by that endless clearing or curing of the ground now being called "deconstruction." Such an identity, though itself figurative, momentarily takes us away from the tropological to the topological, to the commonplaces or places of invention, but only for a brief time, after which we can return not with one *aporia* or negative moment or crossing, but with three, thus going de Man two better in our quest after images for the act of reading poems.

Walter J. Ong regards the *topoi* as modes of information storage and of conceptualization characteristic of oral culture, which were preserved in the age of writing, and then in the age of print, as the *loci communes*, associated also with the history of Latin as a subject of academic rhetoric. Richard McKeon sees them as "arts of places." The oldest authorities describe them as a means of amplification, since they are "topics of invention." Cicero lists sixteen as being intrinsic to any subject: definition, division, genus, species, contraries, contradictories, comparison, similarity, dissimilarity, adjuncts, cause, effect, antecedent, consequences, notation, and conjugates. I will discuss these not in that traditional order but rather in the order that I believe they assumed in the tropological patterns of the Romantic and post-Romantic crisis-poem. Yet, to account for their reappearance in that patterning, I turn at last to the curious link between the "disappearance" of classical rhetoric in the seventeenth century and the rise of associationist psychology. W. J. Bate's formula for the complex movement I am trying to sketch envisions a five-stage process: from rhetoric to the Johnsonian universality of general nature to the growth of individualism first on the premise of associationism, and then of feeling or sensibility, until the Romanticism of Coleridge and Wordsworth arrived as a culmination. Associationism can be defined most simply as the psychological implications of the empirical tradition of Locke and Hume. It implies that ideas similar to one another, or ideas that have tended to recur in series or simultaneously, automatically call one another up. Locke, who invented the phrase "association of ideas," founded the notion on habit and memory as modes of repetition that fixed ideas through the accompaniment of pleasure and pain. Later associationists, culminating in Hartley, went from this process to the formation of habits of thought and feeling that resulted in principles, incentives, and actions. Hartley confected a visionary physiology of vibrations and tremblings that the more rational Scottish associationists graded down to a subtler intuitionism.

I will venture the speculation, not altogether playfully, that associationism was the "structuralism" of the eighteenth and nineteenth centuries and is not all that different from the "structuralism" of the twentieth century. Indeed, we can try a formula: associationism plus differential linguistics equals structuralism. Locke fathered Condillac, and can be called Lévi-Strauss's great-grandfather, so that structuralism can be regarded as belated Lockeanism flowering strangely upon alien soil. Hartley even invented the synchronic/diachronic distinction, which he called the synchronous and the successive. This is Part I, Proposition 10, of his *Observations of Man:* "Sensations may be said to be associated together, when their impressions are either made precisely at the same instant of time, or in the contiguous successive instants. We may therefore distinguish association into two sorts, the synchronous, and the successive."

The leading ideas of associationism, both synchronous and successive, were resemblance, contiguity, cause and effect, and contrariety, with occasional excursions into comparison and into division and definition. Essentially, associationism put the emphasis upon what we might call the topics of *ethos*, leading to reductive tropes of *ethos*, and rather less upon topics and figures of *pathos*. It could even be said that the advance beyond associationism taken by Wordsworth and Coleridge was to attempt to reconcile or balance a Romantic rhetoric of *pathos* with the associationist rhetoric of *ethos*. It is a mystery to me why neither the associationists nor their modern scholars have traced the clear displacement, by the associationists, of the places of invention into the psychological notions governing the formation of ideas. I suspect that the cause is inherent in an ambiguity in the topics of invention, which I will explore now en route to a theory as to how the imagistic and tropological patterns of the High Romantic crisis-poem were generated by associationist ideas and by the earlier forms of those ideas in the topics of classical rhetoric.

I take it that the shuttle or dialectic between topic and trope is a form of a larger struggle between speech and writing, or between wandering utterance and wandering signification. A *topos* truly is not so much a commonplace or a memory place as more nearly *the place of a voice*, the place from which the voice of the dead breaks through. Hence, a *topos* is an image of voice or of speech, or the place where such an image is stored. The movement from *topos* to *topos*, the crossing, is always a crisis because it is a kind of judgment or criticism between images of voice and between the different kinds of figurative thinking that opposed topics generate. Working from personally modified associationist premises, Coleridge and Wordsworth wrote crisis-poems like *Frost at Midnight* and *Tintern Abbey* by drawing their subjects through the topics of invention, in an alteration of the Classical or Ciceronian pattern. They opened with the topics of contraries and contradictories, producing tropes of simple irony that by naming one contrary intended another, so as to appear in images of presence and absence. From this trope of *ethos* they then moved to definition and division, the most fundamental of artificial or poetic arguments, allied to the lesser topics of genus and species, all of which tended to result in synecdochal figures. The rhythm of invention then took them back to problems of spatial cause and effect, with the allied topics of associationist contiguity—characteristics, adjuncts, notations—all of which tended to produce metonymic figurations, with attendant imagery of a prior fullness emptying itself out as spatial effects were seen reducing to spatial causes. The next step of this process of invention tended to be that of comparison—greater, equal, less—with its conveying trope of hyperbole, imagistically presented in the Sublime visions of height and depth. I recall here two observations of Martin Price, the first being that associationism had a way of dissolving itself into a Platonism: "The recognition of a transcendental self that lies behind its empirical experience is one of the most intense expressions of the self-consciousness of the age. It absorbs and transforms much of the interest in association of ideas." We can combine this with another remark by Price concerning the reliance of the Sublime poem upon hyperbole: "We are moving from image to figure, from the picture to the dislocation of words that indicates the inadequacy of any picture." This movement, I would say, attains its climax in the Wordsworthian transformation of the associationist topic of comparison into the hyperbole of the Romantic Sublime.

But the curious rhythm of Romantic figuration then led Wordsworth and Coleridge back to the topics of similarity and dissimilarity, with their inevitable production of dualizing or High Romantic metaphors or "nature imagery," and subsequently into a final group of topics that commenced with reversible-cause-and-effect, or rather temporal effect-and-cause, which together with antecedents, consequences, and conjugates resulted in metaleptic or transumptive figurations, final reversals of temporal belatedness. I am aware that this is heavy going, but I press on now to those "crossings" or crisis-points, the three negative moments or *aporias*, whose function seems to me crucial in post-Romantic poetry and particularly in Wallace Stevens, as the great inheritor of that poetry.

A crisis is a crucial point or turning point, going back to the Greek *krisis*, which derived from *krinein*, "to separate" or "to decide," from which came also the Greek *kritos*, "separated" or "chosen," and so *kritikos*, "able to discern," and so to be a critic. The Indo-European root is *skeri*, "to cut, separate, sift," from which stem such allied words as scribble, script, and hypocrisy, as well as crisis and critic. "Crossing" comes from a different root, a hypothetical one, *ger*, for "curving" or "crooked," but the accidents of linguistic history make it natural for us to associate "crossing" with the group that includes crisis, criticism, and script. I use "crossing" arbitrarily but precisely for the negative moments that collect meaning in the post-Romantic crisis-poem, insofar as meaning ever is present within a single text rather than wandering about between texts. But meaning also wanders about within a text, and its location by crossings ought to provide a perspective for interpretation that we haven't had before, a more certain link between rhetoric and psychology than my own ventures into identifying tropes and defenses have thus far been able to establish.

Let us say (following de Man) that rhetoric *is* a text, and that its opposed aspects (system of tropes versus persuasion) make it an impossible text to read and understand, thus amassing all of rhetoric into One Enormous Poem (like Kabbalah, or like the Gnosis, or like Neoplatonism, or like Christianity, for that matter!). Between theology (system of tropes) and belief (persuasion) there comes always the *aporia* (figuration of doubt, uncertain notice, mental dilemma, the necessity of misreading). Theology and a system of tropes are an *ethos;* belief and persuasion are a *pathos.* The *logos* of meaning is generated either by the repressive passage (representation) from *ethos* to *pathos* or by the sublimating passage (limitation) from *pathos* to *ethos.* The dynamism of the substituting process is the *logos,* which tells us that meaning in a poem is itself liminal, transgressive, a breaking as much as a making. But these violations of threshold are necessarily tropological *and* topological. A tropological deconstruction locates images of writing and then is forced to reduce to such images. Yet, the *places* of poetry are images of voice, even as the *figures* of poetry are images of writing. Poetry is a debate between voicing and writing, an endless crossing between topics *or* tropes, but also an endless shuttling between topics *and* tropes.

Of what use is my curious mixed discourse or Gnosis? How can we find the crossings in a poem, and what use can we make of them once they are found? I return to my map of misprision, with its three pairs of dialectical ratios, for I am going to complete it now by saying that a crossing is what intervenes at the crisis-point in each of the three pairs, that is, at the point where a figuration of *ethos* or Limitation yields to a figuration of *pathos* or Representation. I think that there are only two fundamental tropes, tropes of action and tropes of desire. Tropes of *ethos* are the language of what Emerson and Stevens call "poverty," of imaginative need, of powerlessness and necessity, *but also* of action, incident, and character. Tropes of *pathos* are the language of desire, possession, and power. In poetry, a trope of action is always an irony, until it is further reduced to metonymy and metaphor; whereas a trope of imaginative desire always begins as a synecdoche, until it is further expanded to hyperbole and metalepsis, the trope that reverses temporality.

I follow the rhetoric of Kabbalah by calling the three degrees of *ethos* or verbal action three phases of limitation, since all of them, as Hartman says, point to a lack in language or a lack in the self, to a dearth of meaning, a withdrawal or contraction of the image (presence to absence, fullness to emptiness, insideness to outsideness). Yet all are instances of figures of will successfully translated into verbal act, a translation that leaves the will baffled at the inadequacy of language to its desires. The three degrees of *pathos*, as images of restitution or representation, strengthen or intend to strengthen both language and the self, but do so only through repression, or the failure to translate will into act, which leaves will or desire rampant with *pathos*. These three degrees of *pathos* or representation point to a greater capacity to respond in language and in the self, and so to a willed excess in meaning, a restitution or expansion of the image (part to whole, low to high, late to early).

I go back now to the relation of associationism to the topics of rhetoric, so as to advance into the Wordsworthian crisis-poem and its crossings, and then to complete my circle by returning to Stevens' *Domination of Black*. Because of their distaste for the Neoclassical or Popean–Johnsonian universal or general truth, the associationists did not much use definition and division or synecdochal thinking, and also avoided comparison or hyperbolical thinking and the transumptive thinking that could reverse the temporal aspect of cause and effect. The major associationist faculties are contrariety, contiguity, cause and effect, and resemblance. There is thus very little *pathos* or representation in their system. They emphasize Lockean views of the object, and when Wordsworth reacts against them he emphasizes the category he calls "passion" or "excitement." Wordsworth got beyond his confusions on the image by making his greatest tropes *afterimages of voice*.

In the Wordsworthian crisis-poem, three crossings come together, even as they did in that place where Oedipus killed a stranger over the right to cross first. Let me name these crossings, though I will illustrate them here not from Wordsworth but from Stevens' *Domination of Black*, with which I began this discourse. Also, I will describe them primarily not in terms of trope but in those of psychoanalytical defense, following the schemes I set forth in *A Map of Misreading*.

Crossings, translated out of the abstract into the world of a poem's imaginings, address the mental dilemmas of confronting death, or the death of love, or the death of the creative gift, but in just the reverse order. The first crossing, which I have called the Crossing of Election, faces the death of the creative gift and seeks an answer to the question Am I still a poet, or, perhaps, am I truly a poet? This is the crossing between irony and synecdoche, or psychologically between reaction formation, where one defends against one's own instincts by manifesting the opposite of what one both wants and fears, and turning against the self, which is usually an exercise in sadomasochism.

The second crossing, which I have called the Crossing of Solipsism, struggles with the death of love, and tries to answer the fearful query Am I capable of loving another besides myself? This is the crossing between metonymy and hyperbole, or defensively between regressive and isolating movements of one's own psyche, and the massive repression of instinct that sublimely augments one's unconscious or inwardness at the expense of all the gregarious affects.

The third and final crossing, which I have called the Crossing of Identification, takes place between metaphor and metalepsis, or psychoanalytically between sublimation and introjection, that is between substituting some labor for one's own prohibited instincts and the psychic act of so identifying oneself with something or someone outside the self that time seems to stand still or to roll back or forward. The dilemma here is the confrontation with mortality, with total death, and the prohibited instinct is the drive toward death, the self-destructiveness that Freud hypothesized "beyond the pleasure principle."

I will add that each of these crossings seems to me to have

three characteristic marks in nearly every poem in which they occur. These are:

1) A dialectical movement of the senses, usually between sight and hearing, though sometimes between different degrees of clarity in sight.

2) A movement of oscillation between mimetic and expressive theories of poetic representation, between mirror and lamp, to employ the terms that M. H. Abrams derived from Yeats.

3) A movement toward an even greater degree of internalization of the self, no matter how inward the starting point was.

I conclude by taking Stevens' *Domination of Black* as my text again, so as to trace its three crossings, the three negative moments or places where its rhetoric is most disjunctive and where paradoxically its meaning is therefore strongest, that is to say, where poetic or disjunctive thinking is going on most intensely. The Crossing of Election in *Domination of Black* takes place in the first stanza, between "Like the leaves themselves / Turning in the wind" and "Yes: but the color of the heavy hemlocks / Came striding," for this is the poem's first crisis or turning point, where Stevens meets the fear that he may not be able to become a poet or to maintain his own poethood. In the dialectic of the senses, he is moving from sight to sound, preluding the menace of hearing the cry of the peacocks. In the struggles of the growing inner self, he is threatened with loss of self through the loss of voice. As poet he is moving from the mimesis of the fallen leaves to the expressive cry of the peacocks, a cry to which the cry of his own poem is joined. Having seen that this is a Crossing of Election, successfully made, we can explain the puzzling and disjunctive "Yes," which thus becomes an affirmation of strength, an evidence of poetic election. In the midst of the longer second stanza, Stevens negotiates the Crossing of Solipsism, finding his way past his constant temptation to know both the externality of nature and the existence of other selves only as an irreality. The disjunction occurs between "They swept over the room, / Just as they flew from the boughs of the hemlocks / Down to the ground" and "I heard them cry—the peacocks." The movement is again from sight to sound (each more urgent than before) and again also from mimesis to expressiveness, but the internalizing movement is reversed, as the shadow of an external world comes near again. The surprise of meaning is clearest in the remarkable trope "loud fire," where the synesthesia hints at a lost eros, as it frequently does in Stevens, but here an eros directed toward the world that *Harmonium* calls "Florida."

The Crossing of Identification comes in the third stanza, between "I saw how the planets gathered / Like the leaves themselves / Turning in the wind" and "I saw how the night came," with its introjection of mortality. I cited earlier the prolepsis of *The Auroras of Autumn* in "I felt afraid." The special quality of the fear, in *Domination of Black*, is that it comes from a particular kind of seeing, again akin to the seeing of *The Auroras of Autumn*. It is a seeing that hears, because it hears a remembered cry, and so is disjunctive with the seeing of "I saw how the planets gathered." Adding to the fear are a sense of lost mimesis and the further sense that the final internalization is the internalization of death. A Crossing of Identification defensively tropes against death, and also tropes toward it, confirming the ambivalence of Freud's hypothetical yet Romantically based "death instinct."

I find that as poetry becomes more afflicted by a sense of its belatedness the rhetoric of poetry becomes more and more disjunctive. The formal history of rhetoric tells us very little about disjunctiveness, since whether it has been analyzed as system of tropes or as persuasion it has been treated as though it were always primarily conjunctive, as though one figuration joined itself to another without rugged transitions taking place between, say, ironic and synecdochal (or allegorical and symbolic) thinking.

I have described, in earlier works, the paradigm of the post-Enlightenment crisis-poem as being a definite progression of six tropes, which themselves might be troped as each strong poet's version of the Six Days of Creation. Obviously, I am *not* saying that every strong poem in English during the last two hundred years follows a prescribed dance of tropes. Variations are profuse, permutations abound, and yet there is a pattern to the

405

dance. But that pattern is conjunctive, and it is oddly enlightening to remember that the words "join" and "junction" have the same Indo-European root as *yoga*, a root meaning "union." Against the unifying interplay of the steps that tropes constitute in the dance of meaning, there is always a disjunctive or intertropical movement, which is a missing element in our understanding of the reading process. Stevens' grammar is as disjunctive as his syntax tends to be conjunctive. His syntax affirms; his grammar is heavily conditional and reductive; his rhetoric is complexly balanced but becomes more and more disjunctive as his poetry advances. I hope to have demonstrated, in this book, that a theory of crossings can aid us in finding his poetry more truly and more strange than it has yet been found.

◇ Index of Stevens' Works

Index of Stevens' Works

Index of Authors

WALLACE STEVENS

Designed by R. E. Rosenbaum.
Composed by Vail-Ballou Press, Inc.,
in 11 point VIP Janson, 2 points leaded,
with display lines in VIP Janson.
Printed offset by Vail-Ballou Press
Warren's No. 66 text, 50 pound basis.
Bound by Vail-Ballou Press
in Joanna book cloth
and stamped in All Purpose foil.